GLOBALIZED ISLAM

OLIVIER ROY

Globalized Islam

The Search for a New Ummah

Columbia University Press
New York
*in association with the Centre d'Etudes et de
Recherches Internationales, Paris*

Columbia University Press
Publishers Since 1893
New York
Copyright © 2004 Olivier Roy

Library of Congress Cataloging-in-Publication Data

Roy, Olivier, 1949–
    Globalized Islam : the search for a new ummah / by Olivier Roy.
        p.   cm. – (The CERI series in comparative politics and international
    studies)
    Includes bibliographical references and index.
    ISBN 0-231-13498-3 (alk. paper)
    1. Globalization--Religious aspects--Islam. 2. Islam and politics--Islamic
    countries. 3. Islamic countries--Politics and government. 4. Ummah
    (Islam)--Islamic countries. I. Title.
II. Series.

BP163.R693 2004
297.2'72--dc22

2004050161

Printed in England

CONTENTS

PREFACE

Globalised Islam refers to the way in which the relationship of
Muslims to Islam is reshaped by globalisation, westernisation and
the impact of living as a minority. The issue is not the theological
content of the Islamic religion, but the way believers refer to this
corpus to adapt and explain their behaviours in a context where
religion has lost its social authority. We do not consider it to be
a different Islam. The corpus, the basic tenets and rituals, the pillars of the faith are absolutely consistent with the learned tradition of theological and legal knowledge. Moreover, certain forms
of globalisation of Islam are explicitly fundamentalist by stressing
the need to return to a 'pure' Islam, that of the Salaf, the pious
ancestors. By global Muslims we mean either Muslims who settled permanently in non-Muslim countries (mainly in the West),
or Muslims who try to distance themselves from a given Muslim
culture and to stress their belonging to a universal *ummah*, whether in a purely quietist way or through political action. As far as
sources are concerned, we work by definition on a contemporary
supranational corpus (what they read, preach, write in the perspective of reaching outside pristine cultures and societies). The corpus
we work on is thus very often in Western languages, because it is
aimed at reaching the Muslim in the Western street. We have neither the competence nor the intention to refer this corpus to the
learned tradition; for instance, we use the term 'Salafi' the way it is
used among the people who use that name for themselves. When
Bin Laden says that jihad is *fard 'ayn* (a personal religious duty),
we have no intention to look at what the Koran (or Ibn Hanbal)
says on that issue: it suffices to look at the present debate among
Muslims to assess the meaning of such a statement (and its political

consequences). We try to look at the way this corpus is produced, circulated and used by actors and 'customers' (that is, people who passively buy and read such literature, but who are not militant). This corpus consists of booklets, audiotapes and videotapes, but also extensively of internet websites. The overwhelming importance of the internet is consistent with our study of global Islam, as exemplified in the texts, ideas and speeches that are circulating worldwide in an accessible form.

The use of internet as a source creates many methodological problems: it is difficult to check the impact of websites, and to make a sociological study of their promoters as well as of their users. Given that the survival of many websites is uncertain (especially after 9/11), it is difficult to provide the reader with a way to check our quotations (although I keep a printed version). But experience shows that the most important texts are circulating on a number of websites and could be retrieved even if the site I have given as a reference has disappeared or changed its address. Usually it is sufficient to enter in a search engine the title of the article quoted to find it on another site.

Another problem is that of transcription. It is impossible to adopt a uniform transcription of proper names and counterproductive to adopt an academic transcription, because it will make the checking of our sources almost impossible. For example Shaykh, Sheykh or Sheikh Othaymeen, Othaimeen, Uthaymeen, Othaymin, Otheymine or Uthaimin is the same man. When I quote his name from a number of websites I use the various transcriptions of those sites to allow the reader to check. Apart of the quotations, however, I have tried to use an identical transcription throughout the book. Book reviewers will have the simple pleasure of pointing out the discrepancies, mistakes and incoherencies. I promise that by the tenth edition these usages will finally appear coherent.

Interestingly, when transcribing Arabic names into Western languages, most Islamic preachers and Muslim translators use non-academic transcriptions; in French they even stick to old-fashioned, purely French method of transcription, ignoring the simpler English spellings that are now familiar to the French readership. For example, they write Eldjazaïri for al-Jazairi.[1]

1.　Aboubaker Djaber Eldjazairi, *La Voie du Musulman* (transl. by Mokhtar Chakroun), Paris: Maison d'Ennour, 2001.

This book is not an exact translation of my book in French *L'Islam mondialisé* (Editions du Seuil, 2002). I rewrote this whole book directly in English, updating, adapting for a wider audience, expanding upon some ideas and remarks, and sometimes shortening (the chapter on the internet, for instance). But the poor quality of my English has necessitated a significant amount of editing by David Barrett and Michael Dwyer. Let me thank them here.

In the writing of this book I benefited from a fellowship from the Institute for the Transregional Study of the Contemporary Middle East, North Africa, and Central Asia, at Princeton University.

Dreux   OLIVIER ROY
July 2004

1

INTRODUCTION

ISLAM: A PASSAGE TO THE WEST

THE FAILURE OF POLITICAL ISLAM: AND WHAT?

This book is the sequel to my *Failure of Political Islam* (first published in French in 1992 and in English in 1994),[1] in which I argued that the conceptual framework of Islamist parties was unable to provide an effective blueprint for an Islamic state. I concluded that Islamist movements were running out of steam as a revolutionary force and had reached a crossroads: they could either opt for political normalisation within the framework of the modern nation-state, or evolve towards what I termed neofundamentalism, a closed, scripturalist and conservative view of Islam that rejects the national and statist dimension in favour of the *ummah*, the universal community of all Muslims, based on *sharia* (Islamic law).

At first glance neofundamentalism is less politically minded than Islamist movements – being more concerned with implementing *sharia* than with defining what a true Islamic state should be. The past decade seems to have confirmed these views. Ten years after the overwhelming victory of the Islamic Salvation Front (Front islamique du Salut, or FIS) in Algeria's elections, a new popular uprising in the spring of 2001 sent hundreds of thousands of young demonstrators into the streets of Algiers and the Berber-speaking towns of the Kabylie region. Slogans calling for an Islamic state were noticeable by their absence; instead the crowds demanded 'freedom' and 'democracy'. Moreover, since the second Palestinian intifada began in the autumn of 2000 it has been increasingly difficult to distinguish between a Hamas Islamist militant and a

---

1. Olivier Roy, *The Failure of Political Islam*, Cambridge, MA: Harvard University Press, 1995.

1

supposedly secular member of Arafat's Fatah. The evolution of Algeria's FIS, Turkey's Refah Partisi (Welfare Party), Tunisia's Nahda party and the liberals in Iran towards if not democratic, then at least parliamentarian movements – advocating elections, political coalitions, democracy and the defence of 'civil society' in the face of authoritarian secular states or conservative religious leaders – is evidence enough that many Islamist groups have become 'normal' national parties, and that the principal obstacle to democracy is not the Islamists *per se*, but the Muslim world's more or less secular authoritarian states, supported by the West.

Notwithstanding its internal dynamic, Islamism (the building of an Islamic state) has little appeal for many Muslims who have no desire to be involved in such a project because they are uprooted, migrants and/or living in a minority. These Muslims experience the deterritorialisation of Islam. When they turn to religious revivalism, other paths, including neofundamentalism, appeal most strongly to them.

Neofundamentalism has gained ground among rootless Muslim youth, particularly among second- and third-generation migrants in the West. Even if only a small minority is involved, the phenomenon feeds new forms of radicalisation, among them support for Al Qaeda, but also a new sectarian communitarian discourse, advocating multiculturalism as a means of rejecting integration into Western society. These Muslims do not identify with any given nation-state, and are more concerned with imposing Islamic norms among Muslim societies and minorities and fighting to reconstruct a universal Muslim community, or *ummah*. Thus they occasionally resort to the sort of internationalist and jihadist militancy directed against the Western world that was previously the Islamist trademark. The recent political radicalisation of conservative Islam (embodied by the Taliban) is blurring the lines between moderate conservatives and radicals. The spread of a radical and militant neofundamentalism has developed in parallel with two growing trends: the burgeoning throughout the Muslim world of networks of more or less private *madrasas* (religious schools), with curricula based on a Salafi or Wahhabi doctrine; and the deterritorialisation through migration of a huge proportion of the Muslim population. The strategic partnership of Mullah Omar and Osama Bin Laden is a good example of this realignment and of the blurring of the divide between modern educated Islamists and traditional *ulama*.

The two main issues I address in this book are post-Islamism and globalised Islam, both revolving around the concept of de-territorialisation. A post-Islamist society is one in which the Islamist parenthesis (in the sense of a temporary experiment) has profoundly altered relationships between Islam and politics by giving the political precedence over the religious in the name of religion itself. The paradoxical result of the overpoliticisation of religion by Islamism is that Muslim religious sentiment is seeking, beyond or beneath politics, autonomous spaces and means of expression, feeding contradictory and burgeoning forms of religiosity, from a call for wider implementation of *sharia* to the revival of Sufism. In this sense neofundamentalism is just one of many forms of religious revival, albeit one at the core of our analysis.

The contemporary religious revival in Islam is targeting society more than the state and calling to the individual's spiritual needs. This leads to multiform expressions of religious practice and discourse, which are linked with social movements as well as group or individual strategies. The Islamist myth was that of the unification of the religious and the political; post-Islamism means that both spheres are autonomous, despite the wishes of the actors concerned (the fundamentalists and the secularists).[2] Post-Islamism does not go hand in hand with a decline of religion; rather it expresses the crisis of the relationship between religion and politics and between religion and the state, as well as a trend towards a fragmentation of religious identity and authority, a blossoming of new and different forms of religiosity that might be antagonistic towards each other, and paradoxically a blurring of the lines between Christian and Muslim religiosity (not dogmas, of course). This is coupled with a reinforcement of 'imagined identities', from religious communities to invented neo-ethnic, or even racial, denominations. An Asian is

2. In the West secularisation is seen as a prerequisite for democratisation, but in the Middle East it is mostly associated with dictatorship, from the former Shah of Iran to President Ben Ali in Tunisia. The contradiction of secularists in many Muslim countries is that they favour state control of religion and often ignore or even suppress traditional and popular expressions of it (for instance, Kemal Atatürk banned Sufi brotherhoods, while establishing the Diyanet İşleri Başkanliği, or Directorate for Religious Affairs); such a policy maintains a link between state and religion. More generally, in most Muslim countries secularisation has run counter to democratisation, the best example being the cancellation of the Algerian parliamentary elections of 1992 under the pretence that they would have been won by the Islamists.

a South Asian, often a Muslim, in Britain, whereas in the United States he or she is somebody with slanted eyes; a Caucasian has dark skin in Moscow but white skin in Washington; a *beur* (North African) in France is an Arab under thirty from a poor neighbour-hood, while a Saudi prince of the same age living in Paris is simply a Saudi prince.

Post-Islamism does not imply the emergence of a secular society as such. It is primarily the reaffirmation of the autonomy of the political, of the struggle for power, of the logic of national or ethnic interests, of the precedence of politics over religion. It means that even in an 'Islamic' state like Iran the role and status of religion are decided by the political. (Ali Khamenei is referred to as a grand ayatollah – the supreme religious authority, the Guide of the Is-lamic Republic – because he is an appointee of a political body, the country's highest political authority, and not the reverse.) It thus sets the conditions for secularisation, albeit in this case through the endeavour to build an autonomous sphere for religion, ahead of a pervasive politicisation of the religious sphere. Even more self-evidently 'fundamentalist' movements can be understood in politi-cal terms: the Taliban was essentially an ethnic Pashtun movement, while the conservatives in Iran are a post-revolutionary élite who mobilise nationalism to retain the perks of office.

Contrary to the situation in Europe, where secularisation sprang from the rejection of the overwhelming ideological domination of religion, what we are witnessing in the Muslim world is the process by which a religion, which almost everybody considers to be pre-dominant, is trying to live up to its *de facto* political marginalisation. The fact that any politician has to pay lip-service to Islam does not make it a dominant political factor. The cliché which states that in Islam there is no difference between politics (or state, *dawlat*) and religion (*din*) is used to justify the claim that the difficulty of sepa-rating state from religion in Islam militates in favour of the preva-lence of religion in the social and political realms. On the contrary, I argue that the exact reverse is true: it works in favour of the politi-cal, in the broad sense. The contemporary wave of re-Islamisation is, even unconsciously, a quest for the autonomy of the religious in an already secularised society. We wonder why Islam missed out on the Enlightenment that shaped the new relationship between politics and religion in eighteenth-century Europe, but we are overlooking the way in which Islam is adapting to contemporary forms of Western religiosity. It makes no sense to hope that Muslim societies might undergo the same process of secularisation as did the Christian societies of the West, because the everyday relationship between religion and politics is different. The difference is not the overwhelming influence of religion on politics in Muslim countries, but rather the predominance of political (and sociological) factors and actors (not necessarily the state) that, because they have instrumentalised religion, are at ease with a conservative, inward-looking and ossified religion. State secularism, from Algeria to Turkey and Tunisia, promotes not a critical and reformist religion, but a conservative and subservient one. In this sense secular states differ little from Saudi Arabia: criticism from the *minbar* (pulpit) is forbidden. Democratisation goes along with religious freedom, not with a curb on theological debate and various expressions of religiosity.

The multiple forms of religious revivalism and expression in Muslim societies bypass or ignore the state. This also occurs when there is no state to be fought for, and where Muslims are in a minority that is, moreover, divided and lacks cohesion. Islamisation in this case accompanies the privatisation of faith, the formation of closed religious communities, the construction of pseudo-ethnic or cultural minorities, and identification with Western forms of religiosity or with the choice of a new kind of radical violence, as embodied by Al Qaeda. There is definitely a link between the growing deterritorialisation of Islam (namely the growing number of Muslims living in Western non-Muslim countries) and the spread of specific forms of religiosity, from radical neofundamentalism to a renewal of spirituality or an insistence on Islam as a system of values and ethics.

However, my intention is not to produce a scholarly survey of new forms of religiosity among Muslims. Nor is this book a work of religious anthropology. Put simply, my aim is to open up some new lines of intellectual inquiry. What we understand by 'new forms of religiosity' does not imply, without excluding it, the 're-formation' of Islam in the sense of the Protestant Reformation of the sixteenth century, because 're-Islamisation' does not entail a re-examination of basic religious dogmas. The new forms of religiosity under scrutiny have more to do with the transformation of religiosity that has been observed in Christianity during the late twentieth century, or more precisely the predominance of religiosity (self-formulation and self-expression of a personal faith) over religion (a coherent corpus of beliefs and dogmas collectively managed by a body of legitimate holders of knowledge). The stress in religiosity is upon dogmas (as in the Christian charismatic movements), the importance of self-achievement, attempts to reconstruct a religious community based on the individual commitment of the believer in a secular environment (hence the blossoming of sects), a personal quest for an immediately accessible knowledge in defiance of the established religious authority, the juxtaposition of a fundamentalist approach to the law (to obey God in every facet of one's daily life) with syncretism and spiritual nomadism, the success of gurus and self-appointed religious leaders, and so on.[3] Islam cannot escape the New Age of religions or choose the form of its own modernity.

As we shall see below, neofundamentalism and radical violence are more linked with westernisation than with a return to the Koran. In short, we are following a transversal approach to Islam, by means of a comparison with the Western world, rather than a diachronic approach, looking to history to understand the roots of 'Muslim anger'.

This approach presents us with a methodological problem: which Muslims and which Islam are we discussing? We use in this book many terms, such as Islamism, neofundamentalism, Salafism, humanist Islam, spiritualism, secularism, globalisation and westernisation. How do we begin to isolate and categorise the complex and multilevel practices of more than 1 billion Muslims living in so many different social, cultural and geographical conditions? How are we to designate a specific attitude as 'Muslim' or 'Islamic'? Are there any sociological bases and data to support our classifications and, more profoundly, the ways in which we ascribe them to certain groups of people? As long as we remain in the field of political science, we can head off these critics: Islamist movements are organised; they have an official ideology and program, and official publications; they participate in political life; their leaders (who write and speak) are known public figures. There are (sometimes) elections, opinion polls, demonstrations, arrests (more often) and trials. We can use statistical data, biographies, texts and interviews.

3.   I rely heavily on the works of Danièle Hervieu-Léger on Christianity, such as *La religion pour mémoire* (Paris: Éditions du Cerf, 1993; *Religion as a Chain of Memory*, Rutgers University Press, 2000).

In other words, we have facts and data. The same applies to tightly knit radical movements, even clandestine ones, like Al Qaeda or the Pakistani religious movements. We know the biographies of the 9/11 attackers, and Bin Laden has made enough public pronouncements for us to know about his world view. By the same token, Islamic radicalism in Western Europe can be studied by examining the life paths of the hundreds of militants who have been prosecuted and gaoled (and sometimes killed) – the only caveat here being that we must take great care in using the term 'terrorist' or 'radical' as it is used by the media and/or the authorities.[4]

When we begin to discuss attitudes and beliefs, the issue becomes less clear. Yes we have data: books, articles, sermons, interviews, and the vast amounts of material to be found on the internet, including private sites, chat rooms, and random postings. But it is difficult to ascribe to those who generate such material specific social categories and strategies, and to fathom the impact they have on their fellow Muslims. To what extent do these floating discourses give way to social and political movements or even shape the behaviour and thinking of a significant number of believers? The individuals behind such conventional and electronic publications are usually drawn from a narrow range of 'floating' social categories: students, self-taught *imams*, and cadres of Islamic movements, usually comprising individuals whose claim to have influence is difficult to assess accurately. In *Globalised Islam* we have chosen instead to focus on several different empirically relevant sources. The publications of the Salafi sheikhs of Saudi Arabia are so often quoted, discussed and circulated that they have to have some relevance to the task at hand. Similarly a book that is a bestseller in many Muslim bookshops in Paris is obviously of some importance, even if there is no indication of who buys and reads it. A website to which there are links in hundreds of other sites or emails, or which is nominated as a favourite by search engines, is also worthy of study. But what about the religiosity of a Tunisian shopkeeper who sells wine, groceries and vegetables late in the evening on a Parisian street corner? He does not write on Islam, has no website, attends a mosque where he can find people with whom he has affinities, and may

4.   An accidental explosion at a chemical plant in France was hastily attributed to Islamic suicide bombers by Daniel Pipes ('Terror & Denial [at LAX]', *New York Post*, 9 July 2002; <http://www.danielpipes.org/article/431>).

donate money to a 'fundamentalist' organisation, because he is 'for Islam', even when selling wine. Yet he also may vote for a rightist French party because he is upset by crime, while conversing in a friendly manner with a gay activist who is his best customer and neighbour. As I have said, there is a glaring need for this sort of religious anthropology, but it is not my field of expertise and there are many scholars far better equipped than I to carry it out.[5]

Beyond the scholarly references given in this book, much of my thinking on these issues draws on my personal experience and even intuition when investigating various phenomena related to my field of research. In addition to the research I conducted on French Muslims and on Islamist movements more generally, I have some informal familiarity with 'Western' Muslims because I live in France in a small town where a third of the population is of Muslim origin. Teaching philosophy for eight years in a secondary school with a large number of 'Muslim' pupils helped sharpen my observations, while spending several years with the Afghan *mujahedin* was also not a bad way of grasping the differences between religiosity and religion. I have also twice lectured in Iran's holy city of Qom on my book *The Failure of Political Islam*, itself a good way of stirring up interesting discussions with *ulama*.

Another debatable methodological issue is the way in which, in this book, I jump from discussing neofundamentalism and the Taliban to liberal spiritualist preachers as if they were part of the same intellectual family. I shall most of the time refer to what I call 'neofundamentalists', because by definition they are at the core of the tensions between Islam and the West, but I shall also frequently turn to more liberal or spiritual expressions of Islam, which may seem confusing to some readers. There are two reasons for this. First, I consider that at the roots of neofundamentalism, spiritualism and liberal Islam are many points they have in common. The

5. See the classic book by Clifford Geertz, *Islam Observed: Religious Development in Morocco and Indonesia*, University of Chicago Press, 1968. More recent works include those by John Bowen (*Muslims through Discourse: Religion and Ritual in Gayo Society*, Cambridge, MA: Princeton University Press, 1993; and *Entangled Commands: Islam, Law, and Equality in Indonesian Public Reasoning*, Cambridge University Press, 2002). We must not overlook the vast number of sociological studies of immigrants, although I consider that it is becoming increasingly irrelevant to study Islam in the West through the prism of immigration.

primary parallel is the shift of emphasis from religion to religiosity – that is, the individualisation of religiosity and the crisis of the social authority of religion – leading to the reconstruction of a purely religious community. Second, the many different Islams (liberal, fundamentalist, conservative) with which we are familiar are more a construction than a reality, especially if one looks not at ideas but at the life path of an individual: he may live in a very secular manner, then experience a mystical crisis, may later join a fundamentalist group before turning more 'bourgeois' as he grows old and perhaps becoming a community leader in some European neighbourhood. We speak about trends, poles, and not about given and structured schools of thought. People change and adapt.

Perhaps this book (which has already been a decade in the writing) is being published prematurely and should have been postponed while I collected more data and did more research in the field. But since 9/11 the debate on Islam has become more confused than ever and, if anything, sometimes more nasty. I do not intend to take a stance over every polemic, but one element of the debate seems as widely known and accepted as it is irrelevant, while striking a chord among a public that is rather too fond of ready-made analyses. I am referring to the culturalist approach, which states: Islam is the issue.

It is striking how the debate on Muslims turns around one question: what is Islam? Most events involving Muslims are related to Islam as such: what does Islam say about *jihad*, suicide bombers, violence, Judaism, Christianity, democracy, secularisation, and so on? Islam is seen as a discrete entity, a coherent and closed set of beliefs, values and anthropological patterns embodied in a common society, history and territory, which allows us to use the term as an explanatory concept for almost everything involving Muslims. Samuel Huntington is regularly accused of having introduced the concept of the 'clash of civilisations', but he is more a symptom than a cause. The culturalist approach is pervasive among traditional orientalists like Bernard Lewis (who does not need Huntington to explain what Islam means), social scientists (like Huntington), politicians, newspaper leader-writers, strongly pro-Israel right-wing academics (such as Daniel Pipes), and the person in the street. But this approach is also shared by fundamentalists and conservative Muslims, for whom everything pertaining to Islam is or should be related to something in the Koran. It is also very evident among opponents of Islamophobia and among moderate Muslims. Nevertheless, to say that the Koran never promoted *jihad* as a military campaign or to stress the tolerance of the Ottoman Empire is irrelevant in explaining current events. Like many of my colleagues, I have been dismayed by the short-cutting innuendoes and ready-made statements (often used by Islamic fundamentalists themselves, such as 'In Islam there is no separation between religion and politics'), and by apologetic and boring conferences on Islam ('Islam: A Message of Peace', 'Human Rights in Islam') that preach only to the converted (and not even to all of them). Critics and 'defenders' of Islam remain locked in a culturalist approach. This mirror effect ossifies the debate and misses what is happening under our own eyes but lies outside our mental framework.

There is constant confusion between Islam as a religion and 'Muslim culture' (if the expression makes sense, which I doubt). Islam as a religion comprises the Koran, the Sunnah and the commentaries of the *ulama*; Muslim or Islamic culture includes literature, traditions, sciences, social relationships, cuisine, historical and political paradigms, urban life, and so on. Such a culture is difficult to spot outside cultures based in certain historical eras or geographical regions. We tend to explain all the problems of the contemporary Muslim world in terms of Islam. The status of women, terrorism and the absence of democracy are analysed in terms of 'Islamic culture or religion'. After 9/11 the Koran became a bestseller in the West. What does Islam say about this and that? I do not intend to enter into a sterile debate. A sacred book is not Napoleon's Civil Code or an insurance policy, where everything is put in unequivocal terms. By definition it has various meanings and is subject to argument and interpretation. If there is still a debate about what the Koran really says, it means that nobody really knows, or at least that the people who think they know disagree among themselves – thus we find ourselves back at square one. The key question is not what the Koran actually says, but what Muslims say the Koran says. Not surprisingly they disagree, while all stressing that the Koran is unambiguous and clear-cut. The issue here is not Islam as a theological corpus, but the discourses and practices of Muslims. The same is true of Islam as 'a culture'.

The idea that a perennial, religion-based culture is a relevant factor in explaining most of the characteristics (and specifically most of the drawbacks, failures, dead ends, hopelessness, disillusion and illusions) of Muslims is a cliché in many fields including politics, economics, civil society and the law. What is striking is that many learned scholars (I shall ignore non-academic jumpers on the bandwagon) are repeating the same clichés, without any research to substantiate their arguments. Culturalism is in fact a philosophical approach, which goes back to Montesquieu but was elaborated in the nineteenth century when Max Weber made a convincing case for the influence of religion on economics. But most of Weber's intellectual heirs, as is so often the case, took the worst and not the best of his legacy. The culturalist approach is based on one principle: culture does exist in itself, is transmitted from generation to generation, and is the ultimate explanatory model of any society. This reminds me of one of my closest Russian colleagues, who told me in 1990: 'Marx was mistaken: it is not the economy which determines culture, but culture which determines economy.' Maybe, but we are still following the same lines of holistic, causalist, immanentist and mechanical dogmatic thought given us by culturalism.[6] No wonder many former Marxists became culturalists.

Part of the debate is blurred by a constant confusion between religion and culture. A religion is usually embedded in one or more cultures, but cannot be reduced to a single culture. Common to all fundamentalist or reformist movements is a quest to define a 'pure' religion beyond time and space. One can of course outline some correlations between a religion and a set of social practices (the Weberian relationship between Protestantism and capitalism), but it is difficult to establish a causal relationship between them. If Protestantism has provided a fertile ground for capitalism, why did it make a breakthrough in northern Europe? Is there a pre-existing factor that could explain both Protestantism and capitalism, such as the Teutonic character and customs, oat cultivation and a taste for beer? If the anthropological prevalence of 'group feeling' (*asabiyya*) in loyalty to the state is linked with Islam, why does this model prevail in Sicily and not in southern Spain, which was under Muslim control for much longer? If this model is linked with Arab culture, why does one systematically confuse Islam and Arab culture under

6. David Landes is himself an interesting case of an economist who supports free market and individualism, but recycles the Marxist historical conception of development (capitalism is born from feudalism) by simply replacing modes of production with cultures. David Landes, *The Wealth and Poverty of Nations: Why Are Some So Rich and Others So Poor?*, New York: W.W. Norton, 1998.

the absurd concept of 'Arabo-Muslim' societies? Arab societies
include Arabic-speaking Christians and Jews, while most of the
world's Muslims are not Arabs. Why did Muslim Turkey develop
a modern state system? Is it simply because its people are Turks
and not Arabs? In that case, is not Arab culture the main reason
for the political backwardness of the Arab world, instead of Islam?
But how does one dissociate Arab culture from Islam? Just bring
the two words together and you have the explanation! To explain
a society by a religion leads full circle. Interestingly, an argument
used by many non-Arab Islamic reformists (for example, the liberal Iranian cleric Mohsen Saidzadeh) consists of blaming the Arab
social milieu of the time of the Prophet for the conservative and
rigid implementation of the Koranic message.

The culturalist approach is reinforced by the confusion between
Middle East and Islam. In particular the Israeli-Palestinian conflict
tends to shape in the United States the debate on Islam. There is a
constant confusion between Muslims and Arabs. Most of the examples used to show that Islam has a problem with modernity deal
with the Arab Middle East, but not with Malaysia or Turkey. Books
such as Bernard Lewis's *What Went Wrong?*, supposedly written to
explain why there is a problem with Islam, deal exclusively with
the Middle East.[7]

The discourse of nostalgia among Arab Muslims is certainly important to our understanding of the sense of demotion experienced
by many Muslims. Why is the 'best religion' embedded in nations
that have been colonised and feel humiliated by the military superiority of their enemies, and by the incompetence and corruption
of their own authoritarian regimes? Why is Islam in Europe the
dominant religion in impoverished neighbourhoods? But nostalgia
for the Golden Age of Islam does not offer any solution. It does
not explain the failure of Islam (except in terms of conspiracy).
The Golden Age is also a historical artefact (Andalusia as the model
of religious coexistence), while few contemporary Muslims dream
of the return of the Ottoman Empire. By systematically referring
to history and Islamic civilisation, one misses what is going on now

7.   For a pertinent critique, see Juan Cole, 'Review of Bernard Lewis' "What
     Went Wrong: Western Impact and Middle Eastern Response"', *Global Dia-
     logue*, 4, 4 (2002). This can also be found at <http://www.juancole.com/
     essays/revlew.htm>.

among the vanguard of Islamic militants. They do not work for the return of a Golden Age. On the contrary, they play on globalisation to build what they see as the future Golden Age: a new universal community that can bypass and transcend the failure of past models. The historical and culturalist view, whatever its erudition and insights, is also running out of steam to explain what is new.

One cannot understand the current process of Islamic radicalisation by focusing almost exclusively on the Middle East crisis and the Arab world. Of course, both the Israeli–Palestinian conflict and the invasion of Iraq have led to a crystallisation of anti-US and anti-Western feeling among a section of Muslim youth. But this connection remains symbolic. The new generations of radicalised Western Muslims do not go to Palestine to fight the infidels: they went to Afghanistan, Chechnya, Bosnia, Kashmir and, of late, Iraq; they go to New York, Paris and London. The time and space of modern Islamic radicalism is emancipated from the Middle East. It is a global space. To avoid such pitfalls as equating Islam with the Middle East, we should more than ever separate Islamic studies from Middle Eastern studies.[8]

But of course Islam cannot be discarded as a relevant ideological or sociological factor. Nevertheless, to avoid the self-fulfilling affirmations of the culturalist approach, comparison should be made with comparable objects: the economic backwardness often linked with Islam vanishes if we compare Muslim countries with a non-Muslim neighbour (for example, Indonesia with Philippines, or Kosovo and Macedonia) and not with the West.[9] Muslim Malaysia has a *per capita* income slightly higher than that of Buddhist Thailand, while the *per capita* incomes of Senegal and Côte d'Ivoire are almost the same. In 2000 Muslim Indonesia had a fertility index of 2.6, while that of the Catholic Philippines was still at 3.6. In sociological terms, Muslim societies tend to align, in the middle term, on Western societies. The fecundity index has dropped dramatically over the past twenty years (1980–2000: 6.36 to 2.67 for

8.   This was also the approach of Edward Said in his critique of Western orientalism, but the issue then became how to deal with Islam. Why does Islam (still) matter?

9.   See Daniel Cohen, 'Y-a-t-il une malédiction économique Islamique' in *Chronique d'un krach annoncé*, Paris: l'Aube, 2003. See also Marcus Noland, 'Religion, Culture, and Economic Performance', Institute for International Economics, <http://www.iie.com/publications/wp/2003/03-8.pdf>.

Algeria; 5.06 to 3.03 for Egypt; 4.90 to 2.10 for Tunisia, which is
nearing the French level). Everywhere women are more educated
and marry later, while the age difference with their husbands is also
decreasing.[10] It is interesting to see that this sociological modernisation has nothing to do with state legislation. The Islamic Republic of Iran has lowered the legal age of marriage for women to 9,
but the real average age of marriage for women rose to 22 in 1996
(while a man's average age at marriage has remained around 24.4
over the past twenty years, which means greater educational equality between spouses). The Islamisation of family law in Iran did
not even lead to an increase in the number of polygamous families
(around 2 per cent of permanent marriages during the past forty
years) or in the divorce rate (which has decreased slightly since the
1970s).[11] Literacy rates among Iranian women rose from 28 per
cent to 80 per cent between 1976 and 1996.

What does this mean? It means that the role of Islam in shaping
contemporary societies has been overemphasised. Westernisation
(or globalisation or modernisation) is happening, whatever the official ideology of certain countries says to the contrary. The obvious manifestations of re-Islamisation in terms of personal behaviour
(*hijab*, or veil; beards) and a growth in religious practices and even
state legislation (from Algeria to Iran) did not prompt a reversion
to traditional patterns of family life (such as polygamy and the extended family with numerous children); on the contrary, it accompanied a process of westernisation. We tend to overemphasise the
Islamic factor in the very process of Islamisation, and miss all the
others. Relationships between Islamisation and globalisation must
be scrutinised more closely, therefore.

But the process of westernisation is not confined to purely
sociological factors. It also includes ethics and religiosity (with the
stress on values, professional success and personal achievement).
The perception of the opposition between the West and Islam in
terms of a debate on 'values' (are they Western or universal?) is

10. For the Arab countries, see Philippe Fargues, *Générations arabes. L'alchimie du
     nombre*, Paris: Fayard, 2000. In Iran the husband–wife age difference fell be-
     tween 1980 and 2000 from around 7 to 2.1 years; see Marie Ladier-Fouladi,
     Population et politique en Iran, Paris: Institut national d'études démographiques,
     2003.
11. Marie Ladier-Fouladi, cited in Azadeh Kian-Thiébaut, *Femmes iraniennes entre
     islam, État, famille*, Paris: Maisonneuve et Larose, 2000, pp. 128, 149.

biased because Western values are seen in the West as being con-
sensual, which is nonsense. Dialogue between pro-lifers and pro-
choicers, patriots and human-rightists, statists and free-marketeers,
Christian rightists (from Saint Louis to the Vatican) and liberation
theologians, conservatives and liberals, and so on, shows that in
the West there is a debate on values, which could cross-cut the
same debate in Muslim countries. Most culturalist approaches fail
because they see a culture as a fairly homogeneous set of values,
downplaying a centuries-old history of civil wars, *Kulturkampf* and
ideological conflicts. The dominant and final consensus in the West
is about institutions, not values. Once again, the real explanation is
at the political level, not that of cultural factors, which are elusive
and difficult to prove.

Historical and cultural paradigms are misleading to the extent
that they do not help us to understand what is new. There is a
definite crisis of orientalism – that is, the study of Islam *sub specie
aeternitatis* – which does not mean that I subscribe to the anti-
orientalist view, which tends to ignore what pertains to religion. I
suggest not that we have to look beyond Islam, but that we should
take Islamisation as a contemporary phenomenon that expresses
the globalisation and westernisation of the Muslim world.

A critical approach to the orientalist view is nothing new. But
the drawback of the 'secularisation' of Middle Eastern studies is
that it misses the permanence of the religious dimension, and, as a
reverse effect, it reinforces identification of Islam with the Middle
East by reducing the religious dimension of a sociopolitical approach to Middle Eastern societies. The idea that there are 'different' Islams is also an old one, but it usually sees an Arab-centred Islamology, as opposed to other geocultural identities: African Islam,
Indonesian Islam, and why not European Islam? The culturalist
approach has also been given new life by immigration: the presence of religious minorities in the West has usually been dealt with
under the concept of 'multiculturalism', which contributes to the
restoration of the idea of distinctive 'cultures'. In fact the multiculturalist approach works both on the side of the conservative Western Right and among progressive intellectuals and social workers.
For the former there is a Western civilisation based on Christianity,
whose identity is revitalised because the 'other' belongs to a symmetrical religion, which helped in history to build a mirror identity between Islam and Christendom. For the latter the assumption

of different cultures in the West is a way to demote Christianity
from its dominant position. But for me both approaches tend to
subsume the diversity and creativity of the individual approaches
inside each of the 'cultures', and to ignore the transversal patterns
common to these 'cultures'.

Finally, the culturalist approach has been reinforced by recent
tragic events, and more precisely by the way in which observers, politicians and public opinion are trying to cast these events
into an intelligible conceptual framework that might explain the
incomprehensible. The need to devise a policy of 'countering' the
threats also contributes some reality to hitherto elusive notions:
targeting the *madrasa* system and pushing openly for a moderate
Islam[12] means that religion is the issue. Strategic and political events
contribute to the shaping of cultural paradigms.

Since the Iranian revolution of 1979, the collapse of the USSR
and the 9/11 attacks, Islam has been seen by many observers as
the main threat confronting the West (including Russia). Many, if
not most, of the conflicts where Western interests are concerned
involve Muslim countries. The most active radical organisations of
the past twenty years have been Islamic. Moreover, an important
Muslim population has recently been established in the West, mainly in Western Europe, while the Muslim question has resurfaced in
Eastern Europe with the creation of two new 'Muslim' countries,
Bosnia and Kosovo, even if the latter is nominally part of Serbia.
The reluctance shown by European public opinion to envisage the
entry of Turkey into the European Union is largely linked to it being a Muslim country. Even Russia, which is no longer an empire,
has a sizeable Muslim population (of around 12 million). In Europe
the issue of immigration is also largely linked with the issue of
Islam (which is not the case in the United States).

There is, in Europe, a conjunction between Islam, colonial history, a territorial frontier with the south, immigration, and the
contemporary spaces of social exclusion. This conjunction, which
shapes the European perception of Islam, makes no sense to Americans, whose short-lived colonial history never involved a Muslim

12. See the numerous speeches of Paul Wolfowitz, in which he openly advo-
    cates support for moderate Islam (for instance, a September 2002 lecture
    on 'US Relations with the Muslim World after 9/11', at the Brookings In-
    stitution, Washington, DC, <http://www.brook.edu/dybdocroot/comm/
    events/20020905.pdf>).

country. The 'south', for the United States, is Latino, as are most recent immigrants. Muslims in the United States, if we exclude Black
Muslims, are usually better off than Latinos and Blacks. Ostensible
religiosity is part of US social and political life, while it always
comes under some suspicion in Europe. The debate on Muslim
public religious expression is rather different. European Christian
churchgoers share the same reluctance as secularists towards the in-
scription of Muslim religious practices in the public sphere; in fact
they would like to have more secular Muslims, while in the United
States the debate is not about public expression of religiosity but
about sharing common values, in religious and ethical terms. And
last but not least, US policy towards fundamentalist groups and
regimes (Taliban, FIS, Pakistan, and so on) has always been less dogmatic and more flexible than the European equivalent. Under such
circumstances, one might have expected a more flexible approach
from the United States on the 'Muslim issue'. But this is not the
case. Since 9/11 the same clichés regarding Islam have been at work
in the intellectual debate on both sides of the Atlantic. In this sense,
despite the differences in the historical backgrounds of the United
States and Western Europe, and in the sociological composition of
the Muslim population in those regions, now we can speak of a
common Western approach to Islam.

ISLAM AS A MINORITY

Islam is a Western religion, not through military conquest or mass
conversions, but as a consequence of the rapid and voluntary displacement of millions of people looking for jobs in Europe or a
better life in the United States, and who have settled there (even
if the first generation going to Europe was supposed to return
home after several years of working there).[13] The second and third

13. Patterns of immigration differ between the United States and Western Eu-
     rope. Migrants *en route* to the United States are going there to stay and belong
     to all strata of society. But most migration to Western Europe in the 1960s and
     1970s comprised workers who conceived of their sojourn as temporary and
     who, for the most part, left behind their families in their country of origin.
     It was only in 1974, when Europe closed its borders to labour migration but
     extended facilities for the reunion of families, that settlement became per-
     manent, even though the durability of the settlement was unintended. The
     migration of the 1990s is closer to the US model. its participants are more

generations have definitely taken root in the West. The result has been the emergence of huge Muslim minorities in non-Muslim countries. The phenomenon of Muslims living as a minority is not new, but historically it has been a consequence of conquests or reconquests (in, for example, the Russian Empire or the Balkans), trade and conversions (for example, China, Africa), or loss of political power (as in Mughal India, where Muslims were demographically in a minority but held power till 1857). What is new is the choice made by individual Muslims to migrate to a country knowing that they will live there as a minority.

The blurring of the borders between Islam and the West is not just a consequence of immigration. It is linked with a more general phenomenon: deterritorialisation. Islam is less and less ascribed to a specific territory and civilisational area. This is visible also in the slow integration of Eastern Europe into Western Europe, and in Turkey's candidacy for EU membership. The evolution of Eastern Europe has, of course, more to do with the collapse of the communist empire than with the expansion of Islam, but one consequence is that Europe has rediscovered that there are European Muslim countries (Albania, Bosnia and, tomorrow, Kosovo). Contrary to what has been more or less openly advocated by many conservative Europeans, Europe, after some hesitation, chose not to side with 'Christians' against 'Muslims', whatever the real motivations for the strategic choice of supporting the Bosnians and the Kosovars.

The deterritorialisation of Islam is also a result of globalisation and has nothing to do with Islam as such, even if it concerns millions of Muslims. But through the increase in migratory and population flows, more and more Muslims are living in societies that are not Muslim: a third of the world's Muslims now live as members of a minority. While old minorities had time to build their own culture or to share the dominant culture (Tatars, Indian Muslims, China's Hui), Muslims in recently settled minorities have to reinvent what makes them Muslim, in the sense that the common defining factor of this population as Muslim is the mere reference to Islam, with no common cultural or linguistic heritage.

---

socially mixed and have no intention of returning to their countries of origin (for example, Kurds and Algerians). As we shall see, the permanent aspect of immigration has consequences for the expression of Muslim identity.

Moreover, a Muslim might experience this deterritorialisation without leaving his own country. The sense of belonging to a minority has been exacerbated by the 'westernisation', or at least globalisation, of the traditional Muslim world, to the extent that many practising Muslims consider Islam to have been 'minoritised' in the Muslim world too (in Turkey, for example). While many Muslims live in a demographic minority, many others (including, of course, the more conservative or radical Muslims) feel themselves to be a minority in their own Muslim country. The Muslim *ummah* (or community) no longer has anything to do with a territorial entity. It has to be thought of in abstract or imaginary terms.

The frontier between Islam and the West is no longer geographical, and is less and less civilisational. The process of westernisation of Muslim societies over two centuries has had obvious and permanent effects, even if it has entailed a backlash in the past thirty years, taking the form of 'Islamic revival' at different levels (political with the Iranian revolution, societal with the re-Islamisation of daily life, the increase in the number of veiled women or of references to *sharia* in the law, and so on). This backlash does not mean a return to a 'premodern' society nor to an authenticity that is supposed to have been destroyed by acculturation. It is more an attempt to 'Islamise modernity', as Sheikh Yassin wrote.[14] Academic literature on the 'modernity' of Islamisation is abundant, even if it opposes a popular view among Western media and public opinion. Modernisation and re-Islamisation are, of course, rather problematic concepts. Islamisation might be both a reaction against and a factor of modernisation (which is the case with the Islamic revolution in Iran), in the sense that the dominant perception of what modernisation meant in the 1960s and 1970s was rather ethnocentric and linear (from religious tradition to secular modernity). But the issue of cultural and social change no longer rests on a dichotomy between tradition and modernity, religion and secularisation, or even between liberalism and fundamentalism.[15] We shall see, for example, how neofundamentalism is an agent of acculturation and

14. Sheikh Abdessalam Yassin, *Islamiser la modernité*, Rabat: al-Ofok Impressions, 1998. Sheikh Yassin is from Morocco.
15. The modernity of the Islamist movements has long been recognised (see the works of Gilles Kepel and of the author of this volume). On the modernity of non-political Islamisation, see works by Fariba Adelkhah, Nilüfer Göle, Olivier Roy and Patrick Haenni.

not a return to a lost authenticity. In short, the confrontation between Islam and the West is cast in Western categories. The illusion
held by the Islamic radicals is that they represent tradition, when in
fact they express a negative form of westernisation.

At a time when the territorial borders between the great civilisations are fading away, mental borders are being reinvented to give
a second life to the ghosts of lost civilisations: multiculturalism, minority groups, clash or dialogue of civilisations, *communautarisation*
(communitarisation),[16] and so on. Ethnicity and religion are being
marshalled to draw new borders between groups whose identity
relies on a performative definition: we are what we say we are, or
what others say we are. These new ethnic and religious borders do
not correspond to any geographical territory or area. They work
in minds, attitudes and discourses. They are more vocal than territorial, but all the more eagerly endorsed and defended because they
have to be invented, and because they remain fragile and transitory.
Deterritorialisation of Islam leads to a quest for definition, because
Islam is no longer embedded in territorial cultures, whatever their
diversity – which, incidentally, is always experienced from outside. For example, an Afghan Muslim living in Afghanistan does
not understand his religion as being 'Afghan', at least so long he
is not challenged by an Arab Wahhabi who blames him for having
blended Islam with Afghan traditions. Diversity is not an argument
for tolerance whenever it is not experienced as a value.

Such westernisation is not necessarily perceived as a trauma by
the 'Muslim in the street'. The challenge of westernisation is clearly
understood, but is experienced in practical terms without drama
and trauma by the majority of Muslims, either in Muslim countries or in the West. Although there is a long tradition of exegesis
and *fatwa* on what a Muslim should or should not do when confronted with a non-Muslim environment and practices (and we
shall deal with some of them in this book), most Muslims find a
way to deal with that without contacting fatwa-online.com. We
must return to the discourses and practices of the actual actors,
without lingering over the theological issues of such cohabitation.

16. This term is widely used in France to describe the trend in which people
    want to be recognised first as a group (usually ethnocultural) and only second
    as individual citizens, which means ethnocultural identity stands between the
    state and the individual. It is a negative term for multiculturalism.

Makeshift compromises, personal construction of attitudes, casual use of various levels of self-identity, *ad hoc* quotations from Hadith or the Koran, dogmatic or liberal *post hoc* rationalisation to answer unsolicited inquiries from the non-Muslim colleague or sociologist doing fieldwork – the range of attitudes is very wide and flexible. To be a Muslim in the West is not a schizophrenic experience. Clear-cut categories (like Islamist or neofundamentalist) are useful but cannot pretend to subsume the real life of millions of people, even if these terms are heuristically relevant. The same individual may employ various levels of conceptual references, jumping from the letter to the spirit of the scriptures and back again. Nonetheless, if we study the available literature (in books or on the internet), our categorisations make more sense but do not exhaust the complexity of individual religious experience.

ACCULTURATION AND 'OBJECTIFICATION'[17] OF ISLAM

Whom do we call a Muslim? A mosque-goer, the child of Muslim parents, somebody with a specific ethnic background (an Arab, a Pakistani) or who shares with another a specific culture? What is Islam? A set of beliefs based on a revealed book, a culture linked to a historical civilisation? A set of norms and values that can be adapted to different cultures? An inherited legacy based on a common origin?

Most of the debate about Islam either jumps from one to another definition or persists with one alone, disregarding the relevance of the different levels, while anthropological research deals with the multilevel dimensions of religious identity. However, it is noteworthy that the question 'What is Islam?' is no longer discussed only among outsiders. It is nowadays a cornerstone of all revivalist Islamic movements.

The common point between all fundamentalist and Islamist movements is that they draw a line inside the Muslim world between what is Islamic and what is not. A 'Muslim' society, in the cultural and sociological sense, is not for them an 'Islamic' society *per se* (that is, it is not a society based on the principles of Islam). And the need to formulate what it means to be a Muslim, to define

---

17. The term 'objectification' comes from Dale Eickelman; see Dale Eickelman and James Piscatori, *Muslim Politics*, Princeton University Press, 1996, p. 38.

objectively what Islam is – in short, to 'objectify' Islam – is a logical consequence of the end of the social authority of religion, due to westernisation and globalisation.

Re-Islamisation is part of a process of deculturation (that is, of a crisis of pristine cultures giving way to westernisation and re-constructed identities). Of course, I do not believe that such 'pristine' cultures were static and immune from global influence. When speaking of pristine culture, we refer more to what is reconstructed by first-generation immigrants as their own past, and to what is called 'traditional' by most Western actors dealing with immigration, including social workers and anthropologists, but also lawyers when they have to explain specific sociological practices (like arranged marriages) or defend certain customs (like female circumcision or honour crimes) in courts. References to 'tradition' by community leaders in the West or politicians from the country of origin serve as a means of maintaining a link between immigrants and the 'home' country, which could function as a political lever in the host country, as a channel for funds in both directions, or as a basis for business relationships. Youngsters who argue with their parents (or grandparents) about speaking English, wearing Western-style clothes, dating and dancing are confronted with an image of a pristine culture, even if anthropologists know well that such an encapsulated culture never existed (and is actually transformed by the debate). Reference to tradition also has a performative function: tradition is what I call (or, more exactly, what my grandfather calls) tradition.

The relationship between Western Muslims and Muslim countries is no longer diasporic. Syrians or Yemenis in the United States feel above all that they are Arab-Americans. The link is no longer one between a diaspora and a host country, but between immigrants and new sets of identities, most of them being provided by the host country. *Maghrébin* and *beur* in France do not correspond to pristine identities (in North Africa, or the Maghreb, one is first an Algerian or a Tunisian, second an Arab, but never a *maghrébin*). Of course some groups retain longer than others a diasporic dimension, enhanced by arranged and often endogamous marriages with a spouse from the village of origin (for example, Anatolian Turks in Europe, or Sylheti Bengalis in Britain). But among Islamic activists in Europe a trend favours a new sort of Muslim identity detached from pristine cultural links. As we shall see below, a good example of this phenomenon is the growing gap between the Turkish heirs of the Refah Partisi and the Milli Görüs movement, which was initially the European section of the Refah party but has over time become an autonomous religious movement in a purely European context. The quest for authenticity is no longer a quest to maintain a pristine identity, but to go back to and beyond this pristine identity through an ahistorical model of Islam. It is not a matter of nostalgia for a given country, for one's youth or for one's family roots. In this sense westernisation means something other than becoming Western, hence the ambivalent attitude towards it.

How do we reconcile manifesting hatred for the West with the queues for visas outside Western consulates? It is not a contradiction, even if it is often the same people who do both. And we would be mistaken to take the aspiration of Iranian youths for democracy as an invitation for a US military intervention to topple the conservative regime in Tehran. The confrontation with the Western model is a call for another kind of globalisation, expressed in Western terms such as culture, minority rights, Third World and South (developing world). The quest for authenticity is expressed against the culture of origin and Western culture, but by referring indifferently to traditional (*ummah*) or Western (anti-imperialist) categories. There is a constant struggle among many Islamic intellectuals and Third Worldist authors to historicise Western culture in order to debunk its claim to be universal, specifically of course in the field of human rights. But the critique of Western cultural hegemony is not necessarily sustained by a valorisation of existing traditional cultures, but more often by modern reconstructions of new identities, even if they resort to historical themes (for example, Confucian values in China and Singapore). Westernisation, migration and uprooting go hand in hand with the quest for another universality.

Re-Islamisation is part of this process of acculturation, rather than being a reaction against it. It is a way of appropriating this process, of experiencing it in terms of self-affirmation, but also of instrumentalising it to 'purify' Islam. Re-Islamisation means that Muslim identity, self-evident so long as it belonged to an inherited cultural legacy, has to express itself explicitly in a non–Muslim or Western context. The construction of a 'deculturalised' Islam is a means of experiencing a religious identity that is not linked to a given culture and can therefore fit with every culture, or, more precisely, could be defined beyond the very notion of culture. The issue is one not only of recasting an Islamic identity, but also of formulating it in explicit terms. Resorting to an explicit formulation is important, because it obliges one to make choices and to disentangle the different and often contradictory levels of practices and discourses where a religion is embedded in a given culture. Especially in times of political crisis (such as 9/11), ordinary Muslims feel compelled (or are explicitly asked) to explain what it means to be a Muslim (by an opinion poll, a neighbour, a news anchorman or spontaneously, because Muslims anticipate the question). The Western press publishes many opinion pieces and other articles, written by 'moderate' or 'liberal' Muslims, stating what Islam is or is not (usually what it is not: radical, violent, fanatical, and so on). This task falls on the shoulders of every Muslim, rather than on legitimate religious authorities, simply because, as we shall see, there are so few or no established Muslim authorities in the West. Each Muslim is accountable for being a Muslim, which offers researchers an interesting opportunity. Instead of trying to penetrate a closed and intimate milieu in order to understand what people think, they are deluged with declarations and statements. To publicly state self-identity has become almost a civic duty for Muslims.

But this objectification of Islam is not only a result of political pressure and events: it is also a mechanical consequence of the de-linking of religion and culture. Globalisation has blurred the connection between a religion, a pristine culture, a specific society and a territory. The social authority of religion has disappeared, specifically but not solely, through the experience of being a Muslim in the West. What is nowadays perceived as a pervasive movement of re-Islamisation or Islamic revivalism has been explained in terms of identity protest[18] or as a way to reconcile modernity, self-affirmation and authenticity (as has been said, for example, of the return of the *hijab* among Western-educated women). True enough, but it is also a consequence of the need explicitly to formulate what Islam means for the individual (rather than what it is) when meaning is no longer sustained by social authority. Explicit elaboration also entails a projection into the future, a wish to realise the *ummah* beyond the heterogeneity of societies and cultures.

18. See François Burgat, *Face to Face with Political Islam*, London: I.B. Tauris, 2003.

This leads to the endeavour to define a 'universal' Islam, valid in any cultural context. Of course, by definition Islam is universal, but after the time of the Prophet and his companions (the Salaf) it has always been embedded in given cultures. These cultures seem now a mere product of history and the results of many influences and idiosyncrasies. For fundamentalists (and also for some liberals) there is nothing in these cultures to be proud of, because they have altered the pristine message of Islam. Globalisation is a good opportunity to dissociate Islam from any given culture and to provide a model that could work beyond any culture.

This is coherent with the centuries-old struggles of true fundamentalists (the Wahhabis, for instance) to delink Islam from ethnic cultures. Everywhere they not only contested 'local' Islams (for example, Sufism in South Asia, marabouts in North Africa, specific music and rituals everywhere), but also fought against the historical schools of law (such as Shafism and Hanafism) that became embedded in local cultures. (One cannot understand Yemen without Shafism and Zaydism, or Afghanistan without Hanafism.) The Saudis tried very hard to reintegrate African-American Muslims (through Waris Mohammed, the son and heir of Elijah Mohammed) into mainstream Islam, with no ethnic or racial connotations. The new generation of educated, Western born-again Muslims do not want to be Pakistanis or Turks; they want to be Muslims first. Fundamentalism is both a product and an agent of globalisation, because it acknowledges without nostalgia the loss of pristine cultures, and sees as positive the opportunity to build a universal religious identity, delinked from any specific culture, including the Western one perceived as corrupt and decadent – a constant topic of fundamentalist literature. But maybe this last twist is the real victory of westernisation.

This quest for a 'pure' Islam entails also an impoverishment of its content, which has to be thoroughly explicit and not linked with inherited cultural habitus or collateral knowledge (literature, oral traditions, customs). Islam has to be thought of as a 'mere' religion (which is, incidentally, also a prerequisite for secularisation). Here a choice has to be made between 'liberals', who finally accept a secular space, outside the realm of religion, and fundamentalists, for whom religion is still an all-encompassing system. But due to the minority status of Islam in the West, the 'external' space could be redeemed only by an individual 'sacralisation' of everyday life (as found in certain Jewish practices), or by the establishment of Islamised spaces (such as neighbourhoods or local mosques) or by an activist, radical and, ultimately, suicidal rejection of Western society, which goes along with secularisation. In any case, both the liberal and the fundamentalist view are based on the individual, not the collective.

This has two primary consequences. First, globalisation can be accommodated through a liberal reformist view of Islam, a charismatic and spiritual approach (like the Christian evangelical movements), or a neofundamentalist stress on *sharia* (laws) and *ibadat* (rituals). All of these approaches are based on individual reformulation of personal religiosity (even if it leads to a reaffirmation of the role of the community). What the last two approaches share in common is that they reject any theological or philosophical dimension in favour of devotion (*ibadat*). Fundamentalism is synonymous with westernisation, and above all is also (but not exclusively) a tool of westernisation. Moreover, it is presently more successful than liberalism or spiritualism in terms of visibility (not in terms its number of adherents among the 'Muslims in the street'), for reasons we shall analyse below.

Second, if we want to understand change in contemporary Islam, in terms of religiosity and of violence, we need a transversal approach, which means looking at other Western religions (namely Christianity, but also New Age forms of religiosity, or the Lubavitch communities of retraditionalised Jews) and at contemporary forms of political radicalisation among Western youth, at least since the 1960s. This is more useful in understanding new trends among Muslim youth than trying to reread the Koran.

RECASTING IDENTITIES, WESTERNISING RELIGIOSITY

As we have seen, there is a tendency to overemphasise the role of Islam in problems pertaining to Muslim migrants and societies, while disregarding the impact of westernisation and the transversal influence of Christian or leftist patterns of religiosity or political radicalisation.

We cannot understand 'Islamic fundamentalism' outside a transversal study of how established religions see themselves in the globalisation era. This transversality involves not a comparative study of the Koran, the Bible and the Torah, but a quest to define what a religion is. Common features of religiosity among born-again or 'true' believers include the crisis of the social authority of religion, the delinking of religious and cultural patterns, the constitution of religious communities on the basis of an individual self-definition of 'me as a believer', the explicit criticism of 'non-religious elements', and the will to return to the true tenets of the religion. More important, however, the experience of living as a minority in a secular or even pagan world is a common topic of discussion among such believers, whether Christian, Jewish or Muslim.

There are thus many commonalities between Christianity and Islam in responding to secularisation.[19] Of course the reality of secularisation is debatable.[20] Critics of the concept refute the notion that religion is waning and consider secularisation more an ideology than a sociological reality. It is true that secularisation is manifested differently in Western Europe and the United States. In both cases the role of religion in public life has nothing to do with the legal status of the church. In the United States, where there is constitutional separation between church and state, the expression of religiosity in political life is nevertheless mandatory (especially for politicians running for election). In Britain, which has a state church, the number of churchgoers has drastically decreased, as it has everywhere in Europe. In fact Europeans share a cultural perception of religion, and especially Christianity, as part of European identity and history, but do not care about faith and religiosity. They may object to siding with Muslims in the Balkans against Christians, they may object to Turkey's entry into the European Union, but they will vote for avowedly atheistic politicians. In the United States the situation is reversed. There has been no religious objection (although, of course, there have been other kinds of opposition) to supporting Muslims in the Balkans, but an openly atheistic President could never be elected. Religiosity is more important than religion, while in Europe it is the reverse. Hence there is a difference in approach towards the ostensible religiosity of Muslims. There is an interesting conjunction in Europe between Christian churches and secularist movements when dealing with

19. For the Catholic Church, see Danièle Hervieu-Léger, *Catholicisme, la fin d'un monde*, Paris: Bayard, 2003.
20. For a critique of the very idea that religion is on the decline, see Peter Berger, 'Secularism in Retreat' in John L. Esposito and Azzam Tamimi (eds), *Islam and Secularism in the Middle East*, London: Hurst, 2000.

Muslim migrants: Europeans want Muslims to be more secular-
minded, but do not challenge Islam as a 'true' religion. For example, in France, during the 'headscarf affair' (a debate leading to a
legal ban on the wearing of headscarfs by schoolgirls), the Catholic
Church, the Protestant synod and the Chief Rabbinate maintained
a balanced stand supporting the 1905 law that formally separated
church and state, but opposing a ban on religious symbols at school.
In the United States the Christian Right is either openly hostile
to Islam as a religion, in the name of the Bible (and will try to
convert Muslims to Christianity, something that would seem very
odd in Europe), or sides with Muslims in the defence of religion in
the public sphere (for example, prayers at school) and conservative
values (against feminists or homosexuals, for instance).[21] Europeans
want secular Muslims, Americans want Protestant Muslims.

But whatever the transatlantic differences, it is clear that the
'return of the religious' takes some common forms in Christianity and Islam. Religiosity is in both cases more important than
religion: intellectual and theological debates give way to the expression of a personal relationship to faith, deity and knowledge.
The self, and hence the individual, is at the core of the contemporary religiosity. This has been the main basis of the evangelical
and charismatic movements. Religion is experienced through an
inward-looking community of believers, often local, not an established church or academic institution. Knowledge of the truth is
achieved through personal faith, not through years of theological
learning, nor through obedience to religious scholars and clerics.
Leaders are charismatic, from Pope John Paul II to Fethullah Gülen.
But all revivalist movements acknowledge the irreligiosity of society; here the differences between Europe and the United States
disappear. Preachers in the United States speak of good Christians

---

21. See the speech of Reverend Jerry Vines at the Southern Baptist convention
    (*Saint Louis Post*, 12 June 2002), in which he said 'Allah is not Jehovah', and
    went on to call the Prophet a paedophile. Yet both religions can join to-
    gether to fight against sexual freedom. For instance, most Catholic bishops in
    Africa, as well as many Islamic leaders, oppose 'prevention campaigns that pay
    special attention to those at highest risk of HIV infection, including homo-
    sexuals, prostitutes and people who inject drugs, saying that such recogni-
    tion would imply approval of immoral acts' (Karen de Young, 'The Catholic
    Church: AIDS, Condoms and the Roman Catholic Church', *Washington Post*,
    13 August 2001).

as a minority in a society obsessed by sex and drugs (Europeans add money to this list of modern evils). This is exactly the same view held by Catholics in France, still a Catholic society, or by fundamentalist Muslims in Turkey: true believers are in a minority. (The Taliban said nothing different in Afghanistan.)

Religiosity is a personal experience, not a legacy. A born-again believer is by definition sceptical of the religion of his family and forefathers. (As I have said, we overemphasise the role of Islam in re-Islamisation.) The approach of Pope John Paul II is the same as that of Fethullah Gülen or Khomeini (or Mao in his time) – bypassing institutional and generational hierarchy to appeal to the 'youth'. The generational dimension is emphasised and used as leverage; but to prioritise youth against older generations means to acknowledge and bolster the crisis of authority and academic knowledge. The consequence – less dramatic in some cases than in others – is the delegitimation of the hierarchy and even the discipline of acquiring knowledge normatively. A personal and emotional experience leads directly to the truth. Discursiveness is rejected in favour of feeling. The Pope's World Youth Day also plays on bypassing differences in culture and language by using stereotypical formulas presented in many different languages, with a sideshow made of folkloric, equally stereotypical cultural representations, such as songs with the same lyrics, national cuisine and flags.

WHERE ARE THE MUSLIM REFORMERS?

Patterns of belief and authority are changing, even if the theological content remains the same. Globalised Islam is not a new Islam. On the contrary, most of the actors concerned are keen to adhere to the basic tenets of their religion. What is changing is their relationship to religion, what I call religiosity, not the religion itself.

Here we encounter a common misunderstanding: the idea that westernisation of Islam necessarily means reform and liberalisation, while all sorts of conservatism and fundamentalism are a return to the past or an importation by Muslim migrants to the West of Middle Eastern culture and politics. In fact westernisation is not only perfectly compatible with a new fundamentalist discourse, but may favour it.

For many neofundamentalists, globalisation is an opportunity, not a loss. It may also provide an antidote against cultural westernisation, because when Muslims are cut off from pristine cultures that were for them largely influenced by non-Islamic customs and traditions, an opportunity presents itself to reconstruct a Muslim community based solely on Islamic tenets. This community is not the product of a given culture or civilisation, but of the will of individuals who experience a process of individualisation through deculturation and who, explicitly and voluntarily, decide to join a new community based solely on the explicit tenets of religion. The quest for explicit formulation is part of individualisation. Neofundamentalists transmute their weakness (a by-product of globalisation) into a strategy of rebuilding the *ummah* on the ruins of vanishing cultures, including Western ones. The failure lies in the project itself, as it did in the myth of an Islamic state, because it has no concrete basis (territorial, cultural, ethnic or economic) on which to build such a community. This leads to an imaginary escape from a political deadlock, and even to the bloody nightmare of Al Qaeda. But the struggle to achieve some of these goals impacts on politics and society: shunning integration into Western societies by playing on the set of religious and sociological tools available on the Western market.

The fundamentalist discourse can be recast in terms of values, self-assertion and multiculturalism, while focusing on modern social issues (the defence of family values, for instance, instead of the strict implementation of *sharia*). Westernisation has nothing to do with dogma. What is changing is not religion but religiosity – that is, the personal relationship between the believer and his faith and creed, the way he formulates and performs it. The contemporary history of Christianity and Judaism is the best proof that modernisation does not automatically entail more liberal views regarding what believers should think and how they should behave.

A puzzling problem remains to be answered, however, namely the apparent dearth of reformist thinkers in the Muslim world. If westernisation is such a tremendous challenge, and no matter what the practical adaptations to it of the average Muslim, what accounts for the seeming lack of theological debate? In fact there are many modern Muslim thinkers (such as Mohammed Arkoun, Khaled Abou El Fadl, Abdolkarim Soroush, Muhammad Shahrur and Mohsen Kadivar). The issue is not about writers but about readers. Why are reformists so little read? Do literacy or censorship or wealth explain this paradox? Censorship exists in most Middle Eastern countries, but not in the West, where Muslims have at least the same level of literacy as the people who avidly read Martin Luther in the sixteenth century. The reason for the lack of readership is simple: the new theologians wish to challenge the conservative theology with an interpretation of their own (*kalam-e no* in Iran). Whatever their academic background, they consider themselves scholars, modern *ulama* or philosophers, and wish to propound their academic theological learning. They therefore do not appeal to born-again Muslims, who prefer gurus to teachers, consider that too much intellectualism spoils the faith, and seek a ready-made and easily accessible set of norms and values that might order their daily lives and define a practical and visible identity. Liberal thinkers do not meet the demands of the religious market.

There is among all religious revivalist movements of the late twentieth century a widespread anti-intellectualism that favours a more emotional religiosity, linked with individualism and with the crisis of intellectual authority. Charismatic Christian movements, as well as the Jewish Lubavitch, explicitly propose an alternative to an intellectualised faith. They play on emotion through rituals and collective expressions of faith, using symbolic and ostensible markers of belonging to a community (such as candle-lighting for the Lubavitch). The Catholic Church's World Youth Day plays on a direct emotional encounter between the Pope and 'youth', while bypassing the religious establishment. Many of the youngsters do not know and do not care about the specific teachings of the church. They simply 'enjoy' meeting the Pope. At the same time Pope John Paul II has systematically displaced, banned or sidelined those theologians who were pushing for a more liberal, human-centred theology. The youngsters who attend World Youth Day are not interested in liberal theology, but in an emotional celebration. Many of them acknowledge that they neither know nor care what exactly the Catholic credo is. They are there for a spiritual experience.

Born-again believers have an obvious contempt for intellectualism. Feelings are more important than knowledge. An enjoyment of faith, a pleasure in belief, in being in touch with God are clearly manifested. Religious meetings are like festivals in that this religiosity is modern, based on the idea that the self is at the centre of religion. The self and hence the individual is at the core of religiosity. Faith is personal, faith is the truth. Faith is not religion.

Islam in the West is Western not to the extent it changes its theological framework, but because it expresses that framework

Introduction

more in terms of values than of legal norms, whatever the content
of those values. Even when the mainstream Muslim approach in
the West is very conservative (towards homosexuality or abortion,
for example), it is usually expressed in line with the position of
the Catholic Church or Christian Right, not in reference to the
orthodox debate of *sharia* in terms of *hudud* (except among the
most conservative Salafi groups or radical movements like al-
Muhajiroun, which explicitly refuse to make any concession to
the West, even in terms of formulation of their laws). Abortion is a
typical case. It has never been central in the *fiqh* debate in history,
where it is usually condemned except under certain circumstances,
but never becomes a central issue. (The Taliban never ruled on
abortion, for example.) But many Muslim preachers in the West
will side with conservative Christians, who see abortion as a sign
of moral decline. The sudden legal prosecution of homosexuals in
Egypt in 2000 was paradoxically a sign of the westernisation of
Muslim religious conservatism. Homosexuality was forbidden, of
course, by Islam, but Egyptian society and the *ulama* used to turn
a blind eye to it, so long as there was no scandal, and people were
left to their private sexual lives. (Sexual tourism to Muslim countries by wealthy westerners looking for a more permissive homosexual life is a cliché of travel writing.) Suddenly the issue became
one of 'cultural authenticity' against the West (and Israel), but the
confrontation utilised the language of the West: moral values and a
formal categorisation (almost medical) of sexual life.

The language in which opposition to the West is expressed is
often Western. It is interesting to witness the borrowing of 'Western' themes and ideas by mainstream Islamists. 'Civil society' is
positively referred to by the Refah Partisi (*sivil toplum*), Ayatollah Khatami of Iran (*jame'yé madani*) and Rachid Ghannouchi,[22]
as are for example democracy, pluralism and human rights. But
Muslim conservatives are also compelled to use Western concepts,
as evidenced by the *Universal Islamic Declaration of Human Rights*
(1981), issued by a Saudi-sponsored, British-based body.[23] Debates

---

22. Rachid Ghannouchi, 'Secularism in the Arab Maghreb' in John Esposito
    and Azzam Tamimi (eds), *Islam and Secularization in the Middle East*, London:
    Hurst, 2000, p. 114.
23. Ann Elizabeth Mayer, *Islam and Human Rights*, 2nd edn, Boulder, CO: West-
    view Press, 1995, p. 22.

on *sharia*, women and legal punishments are regularly expressed in terms that fit modern Western concerns or even pretend to show how Western concepts are better implemented in Islam. (A favourite theme is to show how *sharia* ensures women's rights better than the women's liberation movement in the West – a perspective rather different from that of the classical *fiqh* literature.)

As we shall see, Muslim activists in the West call upon modern cultural or legal concepts, such as minority group rights and anti-racism, in order to be recognised as a minority. Islamic revival is often recast in terms of multiculturalism, authenticity and identity, discourses that are an obvious product of the West. Terms such as 'Islamic culture' or 'Islamic identity' are by definition modern. It makes no sense for a traditional *alim* to speak about Muslim culture. To ask to be recognised as a minority group with its own values is also to admit the pluralism of values and creeds. Nor is it only a matter of convenience and tactics: these Western categories are deeply entrenched even among fundamentalists. The constant use of concepts and categories does not transform people into demo-crats, but pushes them to internalise a common grammar of social relationships, even if they stick to their own values. One can use a Western syntax with an Islamic morphology.

Such a perspective entails some contradiction: it is the secu-lar and permissive Left that is more inclined to see Muslims as a minority group (like gays and lesbians), and the conservative and Christian Right, which shares many of the same values (on family, drugs, sexuality, and so on), that is more reluctant to recognise Muslims as a legitimate minority.

CRISIS OF AUTHORITY AND SELF–ENUNCIATION

As we have seen, the passage to the West entails a delinking of Islam as a religion from a given culture – from any given culture. In this sense westernisation is not the embedding of Islam in a Western culture, but goes against the very concept of a given cul-ture. This leads the actors themselves to reformulate the tenets of a religion that no longer has social authority. Collective manifesta-tions of social authority (parents, social environment, *ulama*, state law, customs and habits) do not provide any pressure or incentive to behave in a Muslim way (even in a purely conventional way); to find halal meat is not an issue in Afghanistan, although it may

be one in Moab, Utah. (This example may not be so pertinent
for alcohol, which is equally difficult to find in both places.) The
crisis of 'religious authority' is not confined to Islam in the West. In
Europe Christianity is no longer a self-evident part of our cultural
and social landscape. Public forms of devotion are seen as eccentric
or denoting membership of some extreme movement. But even
in a 'religious' country like the United States there is a growing
discrepancy between established churches and the burgeoning of
charismatic communities, part of a kind of 'takeaway' attitude, a religious consumerism applied to the supermarkets of Faith. The way
in which many Latinos convert to Protestantism is a good example
of the same process of combining deculturation and religiosity (the
same is true, of course, of conversion to Islam). Examining the path
of converts is interesting. They often choose Islam after having experienced other religions. (It is a theme of the apologetic literature
about conversion to Islam: he or she was born a Protestant or a Jew,
became a Buddhist, but finally, after comparing them all, 'reverted'
to the true religion.) Established religions are often deserted in favour of a personal reconstruction that always has to be 'proven' by
the believer's own behaviour and attitudes, because it does not rely
on something that is socially obvious.

We are also witnessing a general crisis of learned clerical bodies. In Iran this has become obvious since the failure of the Islamic
revolution. In Sunni Islam, classical teaching institutions (such as
Al-Azhar University in Cairo) are less and less influential or, more
precisely, are watered down into new forms of re-Islamisation.[24]
The crisis of the Catholic clergy is obvious everywhere: fewer and
fewer men take up the vocation of priesthood, there is a crisis of
confidence, resistance to a female priesthood, and so on.

The crisis of authority (which goes along with the emphasis
on charisma quite logically because charisma means direct access
to transcendence) is plain to see in the Catholic Church. A phenomenon like World Youth Day combines a charismatic religiosity
with a contempt for any form of established church and with a
low level of religious knowledge. (All the polls conducted during
these meetings show that few among those attending know the
basic principles of the Catholic faith or are regular members of a

24. Malika Zeghal, *Gardiens de L'Islam. Les oulemas d'Al Azhar dans l'Egypte contemporaine*, Paris: Presse de Sciences Po, 1996.

congregation.)[25] Charismatic leaders help to bypass institutions and academic authorities. Everybody can speak about the truth because they are experiencing it. Emotional relationships with religion at the expense of an intellectual and scholarly approach are a feature common to Christianity and Islam. The way in which a conservative establishment in both cases has devalued philosophical research (for example, the dismissal of the most famous progressive Catholic theologians, like Hans Küng, by Pope John Paul II in 1979; conformism in the teaching at Al-Azhar University) did not push youths to support the 'liberals' (except in Iran), but led to a more fideist and less critical approach to dogma. Anti-intellectualism is a common thread of all revivalist movements of the beginning of the twenty-first century. The shared anti-intellectualism of the born-again believers and a conservative establishment did not bring about greater institutionalisation, but led, on the contrary, to a more segmented, elusive and individualised community. In this sense the conservative endeavour to reintroduce youth into the fold of the established institutions has failed. The success of conservative values is not the success of religious institutions.

RELIGION AS IDENTITY

Another common feature of Christianity and Islam in the West is that the religious community is increasingly seen as an identity group, emphasising the 'us and them' approach. Universality of religion, or the idea that the born-again hard core is just the vanguard of a larger community of lukewarm or sociological casual believers, who consider themselves followers of a religion without practising it, is less and less accepted by the 'true believers'. A common expression is 'proud to be … [a Christian, a Jew or a Muslim]'. Beside

25. As a Catholic journalist working for a Vatican website wrote: 'During the early years of the World Youth Day phenomenon, the bishops of France were not really convinced of their necessity. "France always had a very organised pastoral ministry for the youth," said Father Joseph Vandrisse, *Le Figaro*'s Vatican correspondent. "This did not fit into their old structures." This factor, coupled with the French Church's traditional independence from Rome and a sometimes inward-looking culture, led to an unintended indifference.' Sabrina Arena Ferrisi, 'World Youth Day 1997 Bears Fruit for France in Rome', <http://www.catholic.net/rcc/Periodicals/Igpress/2000-10/youth97.html>.

36 *Introduction*

religiosity, religion becomes an identity group. Showing the flag, being unashamed to be a Christian or a Muslim, denotes a situation in which the believer thinks of himself as being in a minority identity group. The process of re-Islamisation or re-Christianisation, especially in its preaching dimension (usually towards those coreligionists who are not born-again), is a process of drawing lines between true believers and the rest of the world.

Muslims and Catholics tend to see themselves increasingly as members of a specific insecure and inward-looking community, obsessed by its own frontiers, rather than as members of universal religions well-entrenched in given societies and cultures. Modern culture (perceived by many Catholics as a negation of culture) is seen as perverting religion and not as enhancing it by being a source of inspiration. The feeling of being part of a minority is an issue not of demography but of alienation from a dominant culture that is totally secular or that refers to religion in a neurotic way (the code of censorship in the US film industry, for example: the utmost violence accompanied by tepid prudishness and political correctness – no longer Marlboro land but land of the 'non-smoking killer'). Hence there is a sense of belonging to a community encapsulated in an indifferent or hostile society. This triggers a defensive attitude: pervasive critiquing of coeducation, films and television. The pride in being a Christian is a new motto: it addresses the issue of personal identity through a community and not through one's own faith. (One is proud to belong to something when one feels that one belongs to a minority.)[26]

The shift from self-evident universal religions embedded in given cultures, to religious communities surrounded by secularised societies is obvious in the approach to conversions. One is no

26. '"This is an opportunity for them to affirm how they are proud of being Christians and Catholic," said Bishop Jacques Berthelet, of the St-Jean-Longueuil parish on Montreal's south shore ... "Very often they don't have an opportunity to express they are Catholic because they are isolated," Berthelet said. "With the hundreds of the thousands of people, it will help them to feel a new pride and a new courage in affirming their faith," he added.' Sarah Green, '"New Pride" in the Faith', *CNEWS*, 28 March 2002 <http://cnews.canoe.ca/CNEWSWorldYouth/0328_faith-sun.html>. '"In France, Catholic people were hidden," said Matthieu Grimpret, twenty-three, author of a book on Catholicism among French youth. "This is because of a certain complex regarding religion. World Youth Day allowed French Catholics to show themselves."' Ferrisi, 'World Youth Day 1997 Bears Fruit'.

longer a true member of a community simply by birth. One has to prove one's faith and commitment. The community is not a given fact but a reconstruction. The distinction between practising and not practising tends to deepen. The neofundamentalist writings are full of critiques of Muslims who behave like non-Muslims. Even if orthodox Islam and Catholicism state that everybody who is born as a believer (either through baptism for the latter, or because the father is Muslim for the former) remains a member of the community, individuals are increasingly asked about their credentials. While everybody (circumcised or baptised) was supposed to be a member of a community, however virtual that membership, there is a trend now among religious activists (including priests and *mullahs*) to ask believers to show, even to exhibit, their faith.

Two generations ago, it was not very difficult to undergo a formal conversion in order to marry somebody from another faith (social prejudices apart). To recite the *shahada* or to have been baptised was enough. But today in all the three monotheist religions it is increasingly difficult. The Catholic Church asks the applicant to go through a process of catechism and join a local community to show a genuine personal commitment. Even in a secular Muslim country like Tunisia, the *ulama* request the would-be Muslim to undertake a number of courses. In France the chief rabbinate is nowadays strongly opposed to conversion of convenience for a marriage; it was far more flexible in the 1950s. Increasing numbers of believers think of themselves as belonging to a faith community, and not to society in which religion is more a cultural marker than an actual practice. The end of social conformism in religion in favour of a personal commitment redefines any church, even a dominant one, from an inseparable component of a given society to a distinct community, if not a minority, where the fact of being a believer supersedes all other identities. Catholics in France tend, since the 1970s, to perceive themselves no longer as a central component of French society and culture – 'France, fille aînée de l'Église' ('France, older daughter of the Church') – but as a minority group surviving in an indifferent and sometimes hostile secular environment.[27] This feeling of belonging to a minority,

27. Lawsuits against films that are seen as anti-Catholic are brought for defamation against a community and not for *atteinte aux bonnes mœurs et à la moralité* (infringement of public morality), which means that in the first case the

even if the religion is linked with the history of the country and is still formally the dominant one, is even present in some Muslim countries, such as Turkey, where Ali Bulaç went so far as to ask for recognition of Muslims as a *millet* (an ethnoreligious community with its own law) following *sharia*, not *vis-à-vis* other religious communities (Christians and Jews, as during the Ottoman Empire), but ahead of the 'secularist' (that is, Kemalist) Turks, who would follow the Western legal system. We shall see how this sense of 'minoritisation' of Islam is reflected in the sudden concern for Christian proselytising in such countries as Afghanistan.

THE TRIUMPH OF THE SELF

Religion and culture no longer have a relationship with a territory or given society, which is what we call *deterritorialisation*. It means that religion has to define itself solely in terms of religion: there is no longer any social authority or social pressure to conform (by praying, observing Ramadan, wearing the *hijab*, and so on). It has to define itself in comparison with all 'others' – other religions, other values, other environments. Hence the recurrent question: What is Islam? The answer has to be individual, not so much in terms of elaborating new theoretical answers (there are still many ready-made corporate discourses from political parties, movements, schools of thinkers, institutions) but in terms of self-appropriation of the answer. In short, through the weakening of prior social ties, identities are recast by reference to codes of comportment, values and beliefs, and not on a 'substantial', even reconstructed new identity. Such a move supposes a personal choice, even if it is the result not of a rational and abstract decision but of a personal itinerary. Community is based on individuals and not on the translation of pristine groups into a new world. The self is the truth; faith, not religion, is the truth. It is surprising to find so many writings (in booklets or on the Web) reduced to simple statements – 'Islam says …' – and the author could be Mr Anybody. Religion is everybody's business. There is no institutionalised intercessor, which fits with a general pattern in Sunni Islam.

---

values are specific to a given community, while in the second they were supposed to be shared by the whole society.

This importance of self-enunciation is also confirmed by the addressee of the statement or of the preaching: it is an individual, a self. What is offered to the believer, through all born-again forms of religiosity (Islamic and Protestant, but not so much Catholic) is the realisation of the self: to be happy in this earthly life by strictly focusing on religious precepts, identifying health with faith (rationalisation of the halal rules and of fasting, or of sexual abstinence for Protestants, and so on). Religion heals current evils and diseases: drugs, AIDS, and so forth. Love for God, acting for God's pleasure without caring for success, insistence on repentance (*tawba*),[28] salvation as the ultimate issue[29] – all these show a congruence between contemporary Islam and Christianity, even if as they come closer they become more antagonistic, precisely because they are no longer separated by linguistic or territorial borders. Once again I am not suggesting that contemporary Muslims borrowed these themes from Christianity: all of them are in the Koran. I am referring to changing stresses and priorities, not to theological innovation. This call to values could be 'positive' (love and responsibility) or negative (to be killed for the sake of Allah). It underlines once again that globalisation does not necessarily imply moderation.

Muslim identity is recast according to what are seen as purely religious behavioural patterns, and not on the basis of a given culture. Even if the term *culture* is used, it is more the meaning of a set of values than the expression of a given literary or anthropological culture. (Usually the term *values* is preferred because it emphasises belief and ethics in culture.) The definition of a religious community as a voluntary gathering of believers who intend to live according to the definite patterns of their faith – either in harmony with the external society or in opposition to it, but with no possibility of translating it into organisational political terms – is a Western (or more precisely US) view of religion in society.

But trends we can identify in the West also apply to Muslim countries. The stress on certain forms of religiosity is also congruent

28. Repentance is a recurrent theme of the Egyptian popular television preacher Amr Khaled. In Baku, Azerbaijan, an Islamic movement dedicated to curing drug addicts is named Tawba.
29. Salvation is a classical theme of Islam (many miniatures figure the bridge where the righteous and the damned passed the final test), but I am quite convinced that there might be an increasing stress on salvation in contemporary sermons.

with modern forms of economic liberalism based on individual practices, on ethics and not on culture. The Islamist organisation MÜSIAD (Independent Industrialists' and Businessmen's Association) in Turkey explicitly extols the 'work ethic' in Islam and is more Weberian in deed than many Western culturalists are in their writing. In this sense changing patterns of religiosity are in line with the entrenching of modern models of economic liberalism, entrepreneurial individualism and compassionate conservatism.

SECULARISATION THROUGH RELIGION?

The failure of political Islam means that politics prevail over religion, as is obvious in Iran. The utopian Islamic state has faded away in favour either of practical politics or of another utopia, the *ummah*. Daily politics, political management of issues linked to religion (*sharia*), concrete economic and social challenges, strategic constraints, personal rivalries and corruption, not to mention senseless violence (for example, in Algeria) led to the desacralisation of politics, however Islamic. On the other hand, Islamisation of society led to the Islamisation of secular activities and motivations, which remain secular in essence: business, strategies of social advancement, and entertainment (like the five-star Islamic resorts in Turkey, where the real issue is fun and entertainment, not Islam). When everything has to be Islamic, nothing is.

A final paradox is that the reformulation of Islam as a mere religion is carried out not only by believers who want to secularise their religion (that is, moderate or liberal Muslims), but also by the very ones who deny any delinking of religion, state and society. To be provocative, I would say that the in-depth secularisation of Islam is being achieved by people who are denying the very concept of secularism. 'Secular' Muslims are not the actors of secularisation, because they are not involved in the process of formulating religiosity or shaping the community. The real secularist are the Islamists and neofundamentalists, because they want to bridge the gap between religion and a secularised society by exacerbating the religious dimension, overstretching it to the extent that it cannot become a habitus by being embedded in a real culture. This overstretching of religion, after a period of paroxysmal parousia (for example, the Islamic revolution of Iran, or any given *jihad*), necessarily leads to a new schism: politics is the ultimate dimension of any

religious state, and the death of any *jihad* waged out of a concrete
strategy, nation or social fabric. What resurfaces is politics, as in the
case of Iran, but also religion as a multifaceted practice, hence the
heterogeneous dimension of Islamic revivalism. Redefining Islam
as a 'pure' religion turns it into a mere religion and leaves politics
to work alone.

Islam is experiencing secularisation, but in the name of fundamentalism. It is a bit confusing for everybody, which is quite logical
so far as a religion is concerned and so long as God will let humans
speak on His behalf. Secularisation is the unexpected but logical
destiny of any mediator of a religious fundamentalism that happens
to be taken seriously by a whole nation and society, from Martin
Luther to Ruhollah Khomeini.

IS *JIHAD* CLOSER TO MARX THAN TO THE KORAN?

Where does the violence of Al Qaeda come from? Islamic radicals
as well as many Western observers and experts try to root this violence in an Islamic tradition, or even in the Koran. As we have stated, the debate on what the Koran says is sterile and helps only to
support prejudice. The reverse attitude (to explain that the Koran
does not define *jihad* as an armed struggle, and so on) is equally
sterile. That the terrorists claim their violence is religiously motivated and legitimate is in itself important, but does not preclude
what Islam really says on violence or from where the terrorists are
really coming. We speak about people, acts and motivations, not
theology. Interestingly, however, the terrorists in their endeavour to
root their wrath in the Koran are introducing some obvious religious innovations. The most important is the status of *jihad*. Whatever the complexity of the debate among scholars since the time of
the Prophet, two points are clear: *jihad* is not one the five pillars of
Islam (profession of faith, prayer, fasting, alms-giving and pilgrimage) and it is therefore a collective duty (*fard kifaya*), under given
circumstances. But the radicals, since Sayyid Qutb and Mohammed
Farrag, explicitly consider *jihad* a permanent and individual duty
(*fard 'ayn*).[30] This is probably the best criterion with which to draw

30. See Gilles Kepel, *Muslim Extremism in Egypt: The Prophet and Pharaoh* (transl.
by Jon Rothschild from the French *Le prophète et pharaon*, 1984), Berkeley:
University of California Press, 1993.

a line between conservative neofundamentalists and radical ones: the latter are rightly called 'jihadist' by the Pakistani press. Among the few writings of Osama Bin Laden, the definition of *jihad* as a permanent and personal duty holds a central place.[31] His concept of suicide attack is not found in Islam.[32]

It is paradoxical that the very people who claim to follow the path of the ancestors (the Salaf), and declare *kafir* (infidel) anybody who seems to stray from the imitation of their forefathers, graft their political activism onto an obvious innovation (*bid'a*), *jihad* as a *fard 'ayn*. From that example it is clear that, far from being a collective answer from the 'Muslim community' to Western encroachment, the new *jihad* is an individual and personal decision. As we shall see, most radical militants are engaged in action as individuals, cutting links with their 'natural' community (family, ethnic group and nation) to fight beyond the sphere of any real collective identity. This overemphasis on personal *jihad* complements the lonely situation of the militants, who do not follow their natural community, but join an imagined one.

There has almost never been an example in Muslim history to parallel today's terrorist acts. When Bernard Lewis tried to link present-day terrorism to the Ismaili–Hashshashin paradigm, he proved precisely the opposite: the extraordinary Hashshashin (Assassin) saga is an exception in Muslim history, an isolated and weird episode born out of a marginal heresy.[33] Conversely, connections between Osama Bin Laden's violence and recent leftist and Third Worldist movements have more grounding in fact.

31. See Bin Laden's *fatwa* (published by the London newspaper *Al-Quds al-'Arabi* on 23 February 1998) stating that 'to kill Americans is a personal duty for all Muslims'. The text can be found at <http://www.ict.org.il/articles/fatwah. htm> ('Text of Fatwah Urging Jihad against Americans').

32. Many sheikhs have condemned the World Trade Centre attacks, while often supporting the Palestinian suicide bombers. See, for example, Sheikh Al Al-bani's *fatwa* 'Suicide Bombing in the Scales of Islamic Law', which condemns any suicide attacks ('These suicide missions are not Islamic - period!'; <http://www.muslimtents.com/aminahsworld/Suicide_bombing2.html>); and the *fatwa* of Sheikh al-Qaradawi, which forbade attacks on civilians, except in Palestine (Doha, Qatar, 13 September 2001; <http://www.islam-online.net/English/News/2001-09/13/article25.shtml>. See also the *fatwa* of Qaradawi and others at <http://www.unc.edu/~kurzman/Qaradawi_et_al.htm>.

33. Bernard Lewis, 'The Revolt of Islam', *New Yorker*, 19 November 2001. Lewis argues that terrorism is consistent with mainstream Islam, while including Ismailis in this history.

If one looks to modern times, Al Qaeda is not an isolated phenomenon. Suicide attacks became a standard of guerrilla warfare in the 1980s through the Liberation Tigers of Tamil Eelam (or Tamil Tigers), who supposedly practise Hinduism, the religion of Mahatma Gandhi. Simultaneous aeroplane hijacking was invented by the Palestinians (then secular) with the help of the ultra-leftist and Western Red Army Faction. The first suicide attack on Israeli soil was perpetrated, in 1972, by the Japanese Red Army (supposedly the product of the Confucian civilisational region). It is rather difficult to link suicide attacks to specific religious or cultural areas. The figure of the lonely metaphysical terrorist who blew himself up with his bomb appeared in Russia at the end of the nineteenth century and was treated as a literary topic by André Malraux in *La condition humaine* (1933). (Cheng, the terrorist, commits a suicide attack because he feels that his ideal of purity and justice will fail if he wins, to the benefit of an earthly and disappointing compromise with human mediocrity.) The real genesis of Al Qaeda violence has more to do with a Western tradition of individual and pessimistic revolt for an elusive ideal world than with the Koranic conception of martyrdom. The delusional overemphasis on Islam is particularly striking in the clichéd reference to the seventy-two *houris*, or perpetual virgins, who are expecting the martyr. I doubt that the two Palestinian women who committed suicide attacks in 2002 were interested in the prospect of *houris*.

Some have suggested that most present-day conflicts involve Muslims. Maybe so, maybe not. (One should probably elaborate: most conflicts that are of interest to the West involve Muslims.) But clearly few of these conflicts involve Islam as such, even if the reference to Islam contributes in the aftermath to reshaping these conflicts in ideological terms. Serbs promoted the religious factor when they attacked the Bosnians, but did not refer to religion when attacking the Croats. In both cases the conflict was ethnonational and the actors alternately stressed or downplayed the religious factor to attract support. The Bosnians were defined not by their supposed Muslim faith but by the administrative decision made by Tito to use the term Muslim as an ethnic one, with political consequences (the right to administrative autonomy). By contrast, Serbian Muslims (that is, Serb–speaking Muslims living in Serbia) were uninvolved in the war, because they have never been defined as an ethnic group.[34] In Kosovo the divide was ethnic from the start. Christian Albanians sided with their Muslim fellows, while Slavic Muslims (the Gorani) and Muslim gypsies joined the Serbs. In Indonesia all conflicts are ethnic, but the fight between the Moluccans and Muslim immigrants is labelled a 'war of religion'. It is, however, the same sort of ethnic conflict as in the separatist movement in the emirate of Aceh (where everybody is a Muslim).

The Chechen and Palestinian movements are classic modern liberation struggles. The Chechens gained no support from their fellow northern Caucasian Muslims. And if one can dispute the existence of a Palestinian people before the emergence of the Israelis, it is clear now at least that there exists such a people, which came into the limelight when the other Arabs were unable to defeat Israel. Incidentally, both Zionism and the Palestinian liberation movement were secular historically. If the Israelis were Protestant and the Palestinians Catholic, the issue would have been the same, as obvious as if it were in some part of north-western Europe. What makes the difference is that it is possible for Muslim national liberation movements to call for Muslim solidarity and, conversely, for their opponents to call for 'Western' support. In Palestine, Christians and secularists (from the Popular Front for the Liberation of Palestine, or PFLP, founded by a Christian, George Habash) are as involved in the nationalist struggle as the Islamists. As we shall see in the next chapter, the key to understanding the contemporary 'territorial' struggle is nationalism and ethnicity, not religion. Two factors give Islam a *post hoc* importance: the reciprocal rationalisation of some conflicts in religious or civilisational terms, and the growing deterritorialisation of Islam, which leads to the political reformulation of an imaginary *ummah*.

Another dimension of the so-called clash between the West and Islam is that, at least for Europe, the fault-line between the North and the South (or developed and developing worlds) goes through Muslim countries (while, for the United States it goes through the linguistic frontier between English and Spanish). This 'frontier' is also a legacy of centuries of confrontation between Christendom and Islam (for example, the Crusades, the *Reconquista* in Spain, and

---

34. Xavier Bougarel and Nathalie Clayer (eds), *Le nouvel islam balkanique. Les musulmans, acteurs du post-communisme 1990–2000*, Paris: Maisonneuve et Larose, 2001.

Habsburg and Russian conquests of Ottoman territories) and of
colonialism (North Africa for France, Egypt for Britain, followed
by the division of the Middle East between those two powers after
1918). This historical frontier has been paradoxically re-enacted by
the labour immigration of the 1960s and 1970s; the space of social
exclusion in Western Europe has been largely (but not exclusively)
filled with immigrants from the former colonies. But the frontier
is also being *de facto* revivified by the European edifice. The extension of the European Union is reaching a historical border: that of
the Muslim world. (The integration of Turkey into Europe will
explode this mythical frontier, hence the resistance to it.) Thus different (and heterogeneous) layers of memories dating back to the
Muslim conquest of Spain and to the Crusades are mutually rein-
forcing each other to construct the present complex and emotional
relationship between Europe and Islam.

A second and third generation born of Muslim migrants may
recast their feeling of being excluded by importing a psychological
frontier to their spaces of social exclusion in suburbs or inner cities.
Islam is cast as the 'otherness' of Europe and thus may be recast as
an alternative identity for youngsters in search of a reactive identity.
The Gulf war or the Israeli-Palestinian conflict may be re-enacted
by local actors playing on a local scene for a local audience, a sort
of cowboys-and-Indians game having little or no connection with
the real world. In France an informal survey of young *beurs* who
claimed to protest Israeli policy by targeting French Jews showed
that none of them was able to name a Palestinian town or even to
map Palestine; and none of them was linked to any Islamic organisation or even to a mosque.[35]

One tends to forget that violence from these spaces of social
exclusion exists even when there is no religious dimension (in the
US inner cities, for example). On the other hand, as we shall see, we
cannot understand the violence coming from second-generation
Muslims in Europe if we miss the European history of these spaces;
there have always been thugs and social protest. As we shall see,
the slang (*verlan*) of the young Muslims of the French suburbs was
forged by their white Gallic predecessors in the nineteenth century.
But protest against the established order, which was rather virulent
in France during the 1970s, was then carried out beneath the red

35. Catherine Bernard, 'L'aveu des trois incendiaires', *Libération*, 6 April 2002.

flag of radical leftist organisations. By the 1990s these movements
had disappeared from the suburbs. The only networks of radical
protest are Islamic, but they recruit from among the same social
categories (outcasts from the educated middle class and dropouts
from the working class), carry the same hatred for 'bourgeois' values and attitudes, have the same targets (imperialists) and often the
same pet guerrillas (Palestine), claim to be internationalist (*ummah* instead of the international working class), and are built on
the same generation gap (rationalised in terms of returning to the
fundamentals to oppose the cultural and political alienation of the
preceding generation).

As in the 1960s and 1970s this malaise of an alienated generation
is expressed in global terms: fighting imperialism (this time by the
United States). Parallels between both mobilisations are striking
but are blurred by the culturalist and orientalist discourse, which
explains nothing but strikes the lazy culturalist chord.

Al Qaeda did not attack Saint Peter's Basilica in Rome, but the
World Trade Center and the Pentagon. It targeted modern imperialism, as the ultra-leftists of the late 1960s and 1970s did with less
success. It did so on a far greater scale, but indiscriminate killings
by secular anti-imperialist or nationalist militants is nothing new.
(Carlos the Jackal threw grenades into the Drugstore Saint-Ger-
main in Paris, Armenian ASALA terrorists gunned down people
queuing at a Turkish Airlines counter in Paris, and Abu Nidal attacked Jewish schools in Antwerp.)

The jihadist discourses and targets often overlap those of the
leftist antiglobalisation movement. A Saudi sheikh who supported
Osama Bin Laden, al-Hilali, called for attacks on major symbols of
US interests – McDonald's, a favourite target of antiglobalisation
militants.[36] Of course the means are totally different, but the present
Islamic radicals cannot be understood if we do not see that its
origins and those of modern Western current of anti-imperialism
are similar. It is common to find among Islamic radicals a mix
of Koranic injunctions and pseudo-Marxist explanations.[37] It has

36. Reuven Paz, *Qai'idat al Jihad*, Herzliya: International Policy Institute for
    Counter-Terrorism, 2002. As we shall see, most fundamentalists prefer halal
    McDonald's food to no McDonald's at all. (Reuven Paz is an Israeli analyst
    of terrorism.)
37. Mohammed Zarif, a former Taliban envoy in Pakistan who was taken as a
    prisoner to Guantanamo Bay, wrote for the *Frontier Post* an article ('America's

been regularly mentioned that after the 9/11 attacks opinion polls in Muslim countries showed some sympathy for the bombing of the World Trade Center or at least the Pentagon, but nobody conducted such polls in Mexico City or Buenos Aires. A pro-independence Basque weekly, *Ekaitza*, was fined in France (February 2002) for publishing a cartoon in the week after 9/11, showing the two collapsed towers with the caption 'We all dreamt of it, Hamas did it'. (The publisher, who confused Hamas and Al Qaeda, did apologise afterwards.) And there is no doubt that large elements of the antiglobalisation Left, while condemning the killing of innocents, refused to support the United States and its war on terrorism, instead opting to stress the need to understand the roots of the radicalism on display.[38]

Of course I am not saying that Al Qaeda is nothing more than an offspring of radical Third Worldist and Marxist movements. It is at a crossroads between such a tradition and Islamic radicalisation. By claiming to be the vanguard of the Muslim *ummah*, it attracts the more radical elements among uprooted Muslims who are in search of an internationalist, anti-imperialist structure but cannot find any leftist radical organisations, or are disappointed by existing ones. But the other consequence also has far-reaching consequences: to join Al Qaeda one must be a Muslim or convert. The movement is thus self-limiting, unless there are massive conversions in the West, which is unlikely because of, among many other things, 9/11.

People do convert (such as Jose Padilla, Richard Reid and Lionel Dumont), but mainly as a form of protest, as a way to recast and make sense of a previous exclusion (the first two were converted in gaol, and Dumont ended up in gaol). But radical Islamic militants have a problem finding allies among other non-Muslim anti-US movements. In particular, no alliance could be made between

---

Military Campaign in the Region', 8 November 2001) that begins: 'It is common knowledge that American imperialism is the custodian of global capitalism ... the capitalist world selected the Americans as their watchdog on the basis of their savageness in WWII' (meaning against the Germans and the Japanese).

38. In the October 2001 issue of *Le Monde Diplomatique*, Ignacio Ramonet wrote an editorial ('Guerre totale contre un péril diffus: L'adversaire') that was typical of such an attitude (roughly saying 'We unanimously condemned the killings of thousands of innocents, but the roots of violence are to be found in US policy').

radical Islam and the antiglobalisation movement, such as that of
Jose Bové, Labour or the Greens. Bové is more at ease with the Pal-
estinian movement as a secular nationalist one. More profoundly, if
Islamic militants and the antiglobalisation movement both oppose
US hegemony, they of course share no common view on the ulti-
mate form of the new society they wish to create.[39]

If one looks at Islamic radicalisation among young Muslims (and
converts) in the West, their background has nothing to do with
Middle East conflicts or traditional religious education (I exclude
the Saudis). On the contrary, they are Western-educated and have
little religious education, and many have a scientific background.
The radicals are often a mix of educated middle-class leaders and
working-class dropouts, a pattern reminiscent of most West European radicals of the 1970s and 1980s (Red Army Faction in Germany, Red Brigades in Italy, Action Directe in France). Many became born-again or converted Muslims in gaol, sharing a common
marginal culture. The converts (whose existence was a well-known
phenomenon in Europe but was suddenly discovered with disbelief by the US public with the case of John Walker Lindh – he was
not a Black) fit the same patterns. A few are from the middle class,
usually the leaders (like Christophe Cazé in France, a doctor who
was killed 'in action' against the police in Roubaix in 1996), and
many are dropouts from working class: Jose Padilla, Richard Reid
and the Frenchman Lionel Dumont (already mentioned), who
joined Islam because 'the Muslims are the only ones to fight the
system' (he fought in Bosnia). Twenty years ago these men would
have joined a radical leftist movement, but such movements have
disappeared from the spaces of social exclusion or have become
more 'bourgeois' (like the Revolutionary Communist League, or

39. While McDonald's might be assailed as a symbol of the United States, the
diffusion of halal fast foods is more a part of neofundamentalism than is
the return to a traditional cuisine. For instance, Muslim (as well as Hindu and Jewish) organisations in the United States filed a suit against Mc-
Donald's, whom they alleged had falsely claimed since the early 1990s that
its French fries and hash browns were fit for vegetarian consumption (see
<http://www.soundvision.com/info/mcdonalds/appeal.asp>). A settlement
was reached in May 2003 between the firm and some religious organisations.
The point here is that, contrary to European antiglobalisation movements
that want to ban McDonald's, many fundamentalist Muslims want to enjoy
eating such food without going against their religious beliefs. They like the
concept, but they have some reservation with the ingredients.

Is jihad closer to Marx than to the Koran?

LCR, in France, whose candidate Olivier Besancenot attracted some 4 per cent of the vote in the 2002 presidential elections). To sum up, there are now in the West only two movements of radical protest that claim to be 'internationalist': the antiglobalisation movement and radical Islam. For a rebel, to convert is to find a cause.

Even the anti-Semitic nature of many Islamic radical movements has more to do with a Western and secular anti-Semitism than with the theological anti-Judaism of Islam. (The Koran sometimes uses harsh terms when referring to the Jews, but historically Jews have been better treated under Muslim power than in Europe.) Radical Muslims (and many moderate conservatives or even left-wing Arab secularists) quote the *Protocols of the Elders of Zion* or Holocaust-denial European authors such as Irving and Garaudy more than medieval Muslim theologians. Roger Garaudy (a former Protestant, then communist, then Catholic and finally Muslim), a famous negationist, is a favourite lecturer in the Middle East, including among secularists. In fact modern (and Western) anti-Semitism is as strong among many secular or leftist Middle Eastern intellectuals as among Islamic radicals, who just add some verses from the Koran. During their trial Action Directe members put forward harsh anti-Semitic statements, while a former lawyer of the Red Army Faction joined the extreme anti-Semitic Right in a strong anti-Semitic stance. Carlos converted to Islam in his French prison. Thus we are again confronted with a 'modern' coalition of 'negative' and radical forces whose roots are not in the Koran but in a Western tradition of a 'red–brown' confusion, which has recently been given some green brushstrokes by Islamic radicals.

Given these conjunctions (more than connections), could the ultra-left and Islamic radicals join together? There is a structural contradiction between these groups, well expressed by a well-known British Islamic activist, Iqbal Siddiqui, who posted on the Web an article ('The Potential and Pitfalls of Working with Non-Muslim Critics of America and the West') in which he commented on a meeting at the School of Oriental and African Studies (SOAS), University of London, on 23 October 2001, protesting against the US campaign in Afghanistan ('A War against Terrorism or a Crusade on Islam'). In this article he summed up the issue:

While many non-Muslims are extremely critical of the US, they have little else in common with Muslims. The anti-US trend is strongest among those who are also the most anti-religious and – in particular – anti-Muslim ... The harsh truth is that there are precious few non-Muslims – if any – who understand that we need either unconditional help or simply to be left alone to solve our own problem.[40]

Radical Islam is part of and heir to the modern Third Worldist anti-US movement, but has been unable to create a grand alliance. But, as we shall see in Chapter 8, times are changing and some links and joint ventures between a new ultra-left and Islamic jihadists may be appearing. Converts are the harbingers of such a possible development.

The conjunction between a modern anti-imperialism and the Islamic radical discourse of *jihad* is nevertheless no surprise, for the reasons we indicated above: the fault-line between Europe and the Third World goes through Muslim countries, and former spaces of social exclusion in Western Europe are partly inhabited by Muslims at a time when the radical Marxist Left has disappeared from them. But a closer look shows that these antagonistic identities are less entrenched in the actors than 'played' by them. The Islamisation of the French suburbs is largely a myth: youngsters are fascinated by Western urban youth subculture (baseball caps, hamburgers, rap or hip hop, fashionable dress, consumerism) and they speak an old French slang (*verlan*); Islamisation works at a very parochial, often ghettoised level, around one mosque and one *imam*. Rivalries, competition for leadership, ethnic origin and political divergences contribute to the division of the re-Islamisation movement. Islamic radical groups have never succeeded (and probably never will) in achieving an organisational level comparable to that, for example, of the French Communist Party in the 1950s and 1960s (or by the Kurdistan Workers' Party (PKK) among the Kurdish diaspora in Europe): a centralised party with front organisations, unions, a women's association, cultural clubs, fellow-travellers, intellectuals and press. Islamic radical movements are always structured as a sect, with a tight-knit core and a looser network of sympathisers. They recruit secretly, remain largely clandestine and tend to ask their

40. Iqbal Siddiqui, 'The Potential and Pitfalls of Working with Non-Muslim Critics of America and the West', <http://www.muslimedia.com/archives/movement01/critics.htm>, 2 November 2001.

members to sever their ties with their environment. Such an attitude makes them difficult to infiltrate but is self-limiting.

Such a policy works better among an uprooted population than in countries where there are clear political issues. Popular mobilisation in the Middle East centres around nationalism, even in the form of an emotional pan-Arabism (as evidenced by the solidarity for the Palestinians), but not around Islam. As we shall see, Islam in the Middle East is now simply part of a broader identity: being an Arab. The blurring of the divide between secularists and Islamists, leftists and clerics is obvious in the Arab Middle East (but not in Turkey or Iran), even in its worst manifestation (anti-Semitism).

What characterises the second generation of Al Qaeda militants (recruited after 1992) is the breaking of their ties with the 'real' Muslim world that they pretend to represent. All (except the Saudis) left their country of origin to fight or study abroad, usually in the West. All broke with their families. The contrast between the Palestinian and Al Qaeda suicide bombers indicates that there is no one category that could be called 'Islamic suicide bombers'. The Palestinian bombers were all socially well-integrated; they were living with their family (often married with children), left in the morning of the bombing on the pretext of going shopping, died in the afternoon and were mourned by a proud family whose neighbours came to congratulate them. By contrast, the families of the World Trade Center suicide bombers met the news with disbelief (even claiming a mistaken identity or an abduction), said that they had had no news for many months, and were more ashamed than proud. The World Trade Center attackers lived as students, with no bonds other than with their comrades (and occasionally a girlfriend, but no family). They did not belong to a neighbourhood or community, even a religious one. They were cultural outcasts, living at the margins of society, either in their country of origin or their host country. But they were all (except the Saudis) westernised in some way: none came from a religious *madrasa*, all were students in technical or scientific fields, and all spoke a Western language. If we include the logistical networks, some had a Western citizenship (Zacarias Moussaoui was born in France). More interestingly, all of them (except, once again, the Saudis), after a 'normal life' in their countries of origin, became born-again Muslims in Europe. In short, they were more a product of the westernisation of Islam than of traditional Middle Eastern politics.

No Al Qaeda members (or radical Islamic activists) left Europe or the United States to fight for Islam in his (or his family's)
country of origin, except for some Pakistanis. All of the Algerians
involved came from Europe, and none was to be found in the Algerian strongholds of the Armed Islamic Group of Algeria (GIA).
Omar Saeed Sheikh, sentenced in Pakistan for the kidnapping of
Daniel Pearl, is a British citizen born in the UK. Two young French
Muslims sentenced in Morocco for firing on tourists in a Marrakech hotel in 1994 were from Algerian families. Sometimes Islamic
violence in the Middle East seems to be a Western importation.

Far from representing a traditional religious community or culture, on the margins of which they lived, and even rejecting traditional Islam, most of these militants broke with their own past
and experienced an individual re-Islamisation in a small cell of
uprooted fellows. Here they forged their own Islam, as shown by
Muhammad Atta's will. They are not disciples of anybody in Islam,
and paradoxically often live according to non-Muslim standards.[41]

This peripheral nature of Al Qaeda militants is reflected in the
geography of the battlefields. There is a paradox. Most Al Qaeda
fighters are ethnic Arabs, while three countries provided the bulk
of the militants (Saudi Arabia, Egypt and Algeria), although there
are many Palestinians with other Arab citizenships (mostly Jordanian). But Al Qaeda has been conspicuously absent from the Middle East. Bin Laden has been ambivalent about his responsibility
in the Khobar truck bombing in 1996,[42] but at the same time US
authorities were constantly blaming Iran for the action. That Saudi
authorities concealed any evidence from US authorities would indicate Saudi rather than Iranian culpability. And 1997 was the year
of the rapprochement between Riyadh and Tehran, which would
have been rather implausible if Iran had had a hand in the attack.[43]

41. *Taqya*, or hiding one's own ideas, was a common explanation for such behaviour, but I do not see how drinking before boarding a plane or trying to hire
prostitutes the night before (as some of the 9/11 hijackers did) would be a
good way to deceive the 'enemy'. All secret agents on duty know that one
should never attract attention. Furthermore, *taqya* is an innovation for the
Sunni world.

42. See David Pallister, Paul Kelso and Brian Whitaker, 'Caught in Bin Laden's
Wave of Terror: Evidence That Shows Attacks on Expats Could Be Work of
al-Qaida Supporters Has Been Suppressed', *Guardian*, 31 January 2002.

43. Of course one can speculate about a joint venture between Al Qaeda and the
Iranians. However, although one cannot exclude some links between Iranian

In fact Osama Bin Laden only paid lip-service to Palestine till the end of 2001.[44] Training to bomb the World Trade Center was initiated before the second Palestinian intifada (most of the actors in the attacks of 11 September 2001 had arrived in the United States in the spring of 2000). The decision to attack had finally been made in January 2000.[45] Al Qaeda and its like have been fighting in the West (New York, Washington, Paris, London), and in Bosnia, Kosovo, Chechnya, Afghanistan, Central Asia, Pakistan, Kashmir, the Philippines and East Africa, but never in the Middle East (Egypt, Palestine, Lebanon, Syria or Algeria), except in Saudi Arabia. They are fighting at the frontiers of their imaginary *ummah*. All the literature and websites linked with Al Qaeda stressed the 'peripheral' *jihad* from Bosnia to the Philippines. Such a focus has been constantly criticised by Arab militants.[46] Most of the *jihadi* websites are based in the West or in Malaysia.[47] This is not simply a matter of censorship, but because the people who are behind such sites are in the West. While Al Qaeda's campaign against US interests has constantly increased and hundreds of Islamic militants have been

---

intelligence operatives and Al Qaeda's people (everything is possible in the world of intelligence), a joint venture is unlikely due to the open hostility of Bin Laden towards the Shiites, and to the tensions between the Taliban and the Iranians.

44. Palestine was regularly mentioned in Bin Laden's statements, but usually after Saudi Arabia and even Iraq. See Paz, *Qai'idat al Jihad*. While stressing links between Palestinians and international terrorist organisations, Paz writes that the 'interest of Al Qa'idah in the Palestinian issue started in December 2001'.

45. See 'Annotated Timeline of the 9/11 Hijackers for Researchers' (<http://www.freerepublic.com/focus/news/683026/posts>), according to which the decision to attack was made on 5 January 2000. In any case it seems that the decision could not have been made later than this date. This clearly indicates that 9/11 had nothing to do with supporting the second Palestinian intifada, which began only in the autumn of 2000.

46. Abu Ayman al-Hilali (quoted in Paz, *Qai'idat al Jihad*), a Saudi cleric close to Bin Laden, took great pains to explain how Bin Laden's *jihad* fits with the fight against Israel. But it is clear that for Bin Laden the heart of the plot against the *ummah* is more Washington, DC, than Israel, which is systematically represented as a US tool (a view close to that of Marxist radical groups), while most Islamic Arab radicals in the Middle East consider, on the contrary, that the United States is ruled by the Israelis/Jews.

47. I came to this conclusion by browsing the internet, although scientific data are not easy to provide. I do not have the technical means to check the origin of the websites that do not give indications of their country of origin.

arrested or tracked down in Europe, Islamist-related violence in the Middle East has steadily decreased since 1997 (the year of the Luxor massacre, in which more than sixty people, mostly tourists, were killed).

As we have seen, the Islamic factor is not important in Palestine and is no longer a key issue in Algeria. It has disappeared in Lebanon in favour of communal identities. It has declined in importance in Egypt. If Ayman al-Zawahiri is supposed to be the head of the Egyptian Islamic Jihad, how do we explain the lack of Islamist-related violence in Egypt between 1998 and 2003, and that hundreds of prisoners related to Egyptian Islamic Jihad have been freed by the Egyptian government?[48] The answer lies in a January 2002 declaration made by Jihad members, explicitly stating that the movement has split from al-Zawahiri.[49] The suicide bombings in Saudi Arabia in 2003 targeted mainly foreigners – including Arabs – but no government buildings or institutions.

Of course it is clearly in the interests of Al Qaeda to play on the Palestinian issue so as to send down deeper roots in the Middle East and to take swift advantage of the next crisis. Al Qaeda is playing on the aggravation of the conflict in Palestine, but by doing so acknowledges that this conflict was not at the core of its strategic concerns. Interestingly, Bin Laden does not attack the United States for its support of Israel. The Israeli state is seen as a tool of the United States (as is the Saudi royal family), not as the main target. Even if Al Qaeda tactically emphasises different battlefields, its aim is clearly to fight the world superpower so as to achieve 'the restoration of the Muslim glory and power, when the banner of Tawhid is raised to control the world and direct it, with no resistance'.[50]

48. Violence certainly did not subside, as such. On 10 August 2002 an unnoticed Associated Press dispatch, which made no headlines in the West, said that twenty-two members of a family had been killed in an ambush related to a family feud. The journalist appropriately ended the dispatch by writing, 'Family disputes and violence are not uncommon in rural and tradition-bound Upper Egypt.' (But no Western tourist was killed.)
49. Declaration by Usama Rushdie (an interesting name), spokesman of Jihad Islamiyya in the Netherlands, quoted in the London pan-Arab daily *Asharq al-Awsat*, 25 January 2002. As we shall see in the next chapter, this declaration expressed a real shift in the organisation's agenda.
50. Call by Al Qaeda, published on 9 April 2002 on the Web page 'The Platform of Tawhid and Jihad' (*Manbar al-Tawhid wal-Jihad*), run by the Palestinian Sheikh Abu Muhammad al-Maqdisi; quoted in Paz, *Qa'idat al-Jihad*. The

WHAT IS BIN LADEN'S STRATEGY?

Osama Bin Laden has no strategy in the true sense of the word. Nothing was organised for the day after 9/11: no other attacks or assassinations, no upheavals in Egypt, Saudi Arabia or Algeria. Some elements suggest coherence in Osama Bin Laden's long-term outlook. The assassination of Commander Ahmed Shah Massoud, an anti–Taliban Afghan leader, on 9 September 2001 was planned months before (the two killers had been waiting for weeks to meet him). Taliban and Al Qaeda troops had been massed on the northern front since June 2001; for the first time fighters from the Islamic Movement of Uzbekistan (IMU) joined an anti-Massoud mobilisation, a sign that this was seen as the final battle. But no real battle happened, as if the troops had been waiting for something: the collapse of the United Front of Afghanistan in the wake of its leader's death. Massoud's assassination nevertheless came too late – just days before the first US military officers entered the Panjshir Valley. Obviously, however, Osama Bin Laden had wanted to clean up Afghanistan before an unavoidable US attack. He knew the United States would retaliate on Afghan territory and he was expecting the offensive. For Bin Laden the references were Vietnam, the Soviet defeat in Afghanistan, and the US withdrawals from Lebanon in 1984 and Somalia ten years later. He was convinced that the United States would not stand a long war and that in any case a protracted war would stir up plenty of turmoil and even uprisings in Pakistan, Saudi Arabia and Egypt – with no need to organise them. The US position would be unsustainable. In short, he was banking on a war of attrition that would destabilise the power of the United States and its allies in the region (the Saudis first, although I do not think that the Saudi regime was the primary target). In this sense, his aim has been inadvertently achieved in Iraq.

Bin Laden made two critical mistakes. First, he did not realise that the Afghan population was fed up with the Taliban and that the Pashtun tribesmen who have been supporting the Taliban (principally over issues of law and order, conservative Islam and Pashtun supremacy) were not willing to lose their lives and

Web page (<http://www.almaqdese.com/afghanistan/fatwa/resalah.html>) has since disappeared, but the site <http://www.almaqdese.com> was still functioning in July 2004 in Arabic.

property for an uncertain worldwide *jihad* against the US hyper-power. The international agenda of Osama Bin Laden simply had no appeal in Afghanistan. He probably did not expect the sudden collapse of his Taliban allies or the thirst for revenge of the non-Pashtuns (ethnic issues were always logically downplayed by Bin Laden, who renounced his ethnic and national backgrounds to fight for a universal cause). Second, he overestimated the reaction of the 'Arab in the street'. Osama Bin Laden did not grasp that the genuine anti-Americanism of the 'average' Arab had never led to a sustainable political mobilisation, and that if such mobilisation ever did happen it would be over Palestine and Iraq – that is, over Arab and not Islamic issues.

In this sense Al Qaeda terrorism is totally different from that of the 'usual' terrorists in the Middle East and elsewhere. Iran-sponsored terrorism in the 1980s, as well as attacks by the Irish Republican Army (IRA) or Tamil Tigers, fitted into a political strategy: Iran wanted to bring about the end of Western support for Iraq and the departure of Western forces from Lebanon, while the IRA and Tamil Tigers wanted to achieve independence (which was also the aim of the Jewish underground movement Irgun Zvai Leumi in Palestine in the 1940s). Palestinian suicide bombers want an end to the Israeli occupation of Gaza and the West Bank (although some would also like to see the end of Israel, which is another issue). Whatever the means, there is room for negotiation. The IRA, the PLO, the Tamil Tigers and even the Basque separatist group ETA are seen as legitimate political actors to the extent they will potentially cease terrorist actions. But with Bin Laden there is no room for negotiation. His aim is simply to destroy Babylon.

In this sense the historical continuity of which Osama Bin Laden is part has nothing to do with the Islamic tradition of *jihad*. Notwithstanding the debate on what the word really means, it is clear that *jihad*, as an armed struggle, has always been instrumentalised for political and strategic purposes, by state actors or would-be state actors. Bin Laden's *jihad* has more to do with the ethos of a modern Western terrorist, as we have seen above. For the sake and pleasure of Allah (*reza*), for the sake of self-achievement (in death), for escaping a corrupt world … There is a strange mix of deep personal pessimism and collective millenarianist optimism among this type of terrorists: they do not trust the people they are fighting for (they are also indifferent to killing Muslims), they are sure to die, and as political scientist Farhad Khosrokhavar pointed out in the case of the Iranian martyrs of the Iran–Iraq War, they know that, even if they succeed, in the future society will not match the ideals for which they are fighting.[51] It is reminiscent of the Russian socialist revolutionaries of the end of the nineteenth century, and the idea that a spectacular attack at the heart of the power will suddenly show the alienated masses that their time has come and they will rise up. As Lenin put it, this is a childish view. Osama Bin Laden has lived in a pre-Leninist world.

But what are the repercussions of these facts? First, there is no basis for negotiation with Osama Bin Laden: his fight, as we have seen, is not directly linked to the various conflicts in the Middle East. These conflicts will certainly provide Al Qaeda with new volunteers, and solving them will not necessarily dry up the pool from which Al Qaeda recruits, because this pool has more to do with the West than with the Middle East. The second consequence is that Al Qaeda is not a strategic threat but a security problem. The war on terrorism is a metaphor, not a real policy.

51. Farhad Khosrokhavar, *L'islamisme et la mort. Le martyre révolutionnaire en Iran*, Paris: Harmattan, 1995.

2

POST-ISLAMISM

THE FAILURE OF POLITICAL ISLAM REVISITED

If neofundamentalist movements, conservative or radical, have spread among a part of the Muslim population, it is partly because the Islamist parties of the 1980s have subsided as an international and revolutionary force. They largely abandoned transnational militant solidarity and are centred on national politics, with an agenda based on three main points: a call to replace corrupt ruling élites, a conservative sociocultural agenda, and robust nationalism.

What I call 'Islamism' is the brand of modern political Islamic fundamentalism that claims to re-create a true Islamic society, not simply by imposing *sharia*, but by establishing first an Islamic state through political action. Islamists see Islam not as a mere religion, but as a political ideology that should reshape all aspects of society (politics, law, economy, social justice, foreign policy, and so on). The traditional idea of Islam as an all-encompassing religion is extended to the complexity of modern society and recast in terms of modern social sciences. Islamists acknowledge the modernity of the society in terms of education, technology, economy, changes in family structure, and so forth. This ideologisation of Islam is explicit among Islamist actors. They use concepts common in 'Western' social sciences: state, ideology,[1] sovereignty (*hakimiyyat*, a neologism borrowed from Maududi's Urdu and taken into modern Arabic)

---

1.   The term is common in the writings of Khomeini and Maududi, among others. For a comment by Rachid Ghannouchi, a Tunisian Islamist leader, on the use of the terms *Islamist* and *ideology*, see Dale Eickelman and James Piscatori, *Muslim Politics*, Princeton University Press, 1996, p. 45, and n. 11, p. 167. For the Bosnian SDA, see Chapter 1 of Xavier Bougarel and Nathalie Clayer (eds), *Le nouvel islam balkanique. Les musulmans, acteurs du post-communisme 1990-2000*, Paris: Maisonneuve et Larose, 2001.

and, more recently, civil society.[2] There is a leftist dimension (often concealed by conservative references to *sharia*) that should not be underestimated and was particularly striking in the Iranian revolution from the outset. If God's sovereignty is congruent with the very idea of a 'religious revolution', one should never forget the populist and revolutionary, even Marxist, origin of the revolution. As Ervand Abrahamian noted, this revolution is the last of the leftist, Third Worldist and anti-imperialist revolutions, although it was carried out under an Islamic cloak.[3] One of the reasons for its success was the combination of this leftist and populist trend with a recurrent traditional search for an Islamic (Shia) order, which attracted a large part of the clergy and of traditional circles (the bazaar, for example). In the process of politicisation, traditional Shia Islam has been recast into a modern revolutionary millenarianist terminology such as 'revolution' or *enqelâb*, 'ideology' or *ideolozhi*, 'classless society' or *jâme'e-yi towhidi*, and the 'party line' turned into *khatt-i Imâm* or '*imam*'s line'. Many Islamist militants elsewhere have a leftist and secular background (for example, Adel Hussein and Abdul Wahhab al Mesiri in Egypt).

The Islamist project also goes so far as to 'unify' the religious field by calling for an end to the differences and divisions between religious schools of law (*mazhab*) and sectarian affiliations (Shiism or Sunnism), as well as criticising the brotherhoods (*tariqat*), as much for their allegedly non-orthodox view of Islam as for their organisational autonomy. Homogenisation of the religious sphere is to be achieved under the auspices of political authority, as is obvious in the case of Iran.

The Islamist movement's intellectual founding fathers were Hassan al-Banna (1906–49), Syed Abul Ala Maududi (died in 1979) and, among the Shias, Baqer al-Sadr (executed in 1980), Ali Shariati and Ruhollah Khomeini. They had a great impact among educated youths with a secular background, including women. They had less success among traditional *ulama*. To Islamists the Islamic state should unite the *ummah* as much as possible, and not be restricted to a specific nation. Such a state attempts to re-create

2. Rachid Al Ghannouchi, 'Traditional Muslim Society is a Model of Civil Society' in John Esposito and Azzam Tamimi, *Islam and Secularism in the West*, London: Hurst, 2000, p. 107.
3. Ervand Abrahamian, *Khomeinism*, London: I.B. Tauris, 1993.

the Golden Age of the first decades of Islam and supersede tribal, ethnic and national divides, the resilience of which is attributed to the believers' abandonment of the true tenets of Islam or to colonial policy.

These movements are not necessarily violent, even if by definition they are not democratic: the Pakistani Jamaat-i-Islami and the Turkish Refah Partisi (Welfare Party), as well as most Muslim Brotherhood groups, have remained inside a legal framework, except where they were prevented from taking political action, as in Syria.[4] We count among the Islamist movements the Pakistani Jamaat-i-Islami, the Turkish Refah Partisi and its successors, the Iranian Islamic revolution, the Lebanese Hezbollah, the Tunisian Nahda, the Islamic Salvation Front (FIS) in Algeria, the National Islamic Front in Sudan, the Islamic Renaissance Party in Tajikistan, Islah in Yemen, the Palestinian Hamas, and the Muslim Brotherhood in Egypt, Syria, Kuwait, Jordan and the Gulf states. Of course, there are many differences between them, but they share a common ideology. Some of them were simply political parties, like the Refah Partisi; others added a social and spiritual dimension, which is manifested in the choice of the name 'Brotherhood' (Jamaat al-Ikhwan) by the Muslim Brotherhood, for example. Al-Banna and even Khomeini were not merely political activists.

The followers of Sayyid Qutb (whose radical activism was blended with mysticism) became so pessimistic about politics that they cared little about building an Islamic state and instead aimed to destroy the very symbols of what they perceived as the rule of *jahiliyya*, or pre-Islamic ignorance (for example, the assassination of President Anwar Sadat in October 1981). Nevertheless, one should not forget that personal trajectories may in the course of time cross a whole spectrum of contradictory attitudes, from reformism to radicalism or the reverse. Ayman al-Zawahiri, grandson of an Al-Azhar sheikh and former Muslim Brother, became the leader of Egyptian Islamic Jihad, and finally became the deputy of Osama Bin Laden, while Alija Ali Izetbegovic, a former Bosnian Islamist, ended up being a well-respected President of Bosnia-Herzegovina,

4. The academic literature on the Islamist movements is abundant. See, for example, John Esposito (ed.), *Voices of Resurgent Islam*, Oxford University Press, 1983; Olivier Roy, *The Failure of Political Islam*, Cambridge, MA: Harvard University Press, 1995; Gilles Kepel, *Jihad: The Trail of Islamism*, Cambridge, MA: Harvard University Press, 2002.

and was even called a *munafiq* (hypocrite; that is, traitor) by the remnants of the internationalist El Mujahid brigade.[5] The history of these Islamic movements spanned some seventy years, and was frequently altered by harsh repression or tactical political choices. But all shared a common goal: to be the first to establish an Islamic state in any given country.

The Islamists have not established a true 'Islamic state', and nor will they, due not only to the inaccuracy of their conceptual framework, but also to the way their own political praxis and experiences have changed their perception of politics.[6] This does not mean that the Islamist movements did little to shape the political and strategic landscape of the Middle East, or that they are out of the game. They played a very important role, albeit not one congruent with their ideology. They contributed to the rooting of the concept of the modern nation-state in Muslim countries, and to enlarging the political scene, by proposing a model of a political party whose members are united by a common perception of the public good and not by *asabiyya*, or clan links.[7] They run counter to a basic tenet of accepted notions about the political anthropology of Middle Eastern societies: the prevalence of personal ties over intellectual loyalties. In this sense the August 2001 decision of the European Court to approve the Turkish government ban on the Refah Partisi was complete nonsense. In terms of political modernity Refah might have been the only modern political party in Turkey (that is, one not based on patron–client relations). The emergence of the AK party as the successor of Refah, and its electoral victory in 2002, marked the culmination of the process of 'normalisation' and democratisation of an Islamist party. Beyond their conceptual failure, the main reason for the retreat of the Islamist movements is that they have been secularised by the very process of politicisation. Political logic won over the religious, instead of promoting it.

5. Jerôme Bellion-Jourdan, 'Les réseaux transnationaux islamiques en Bosnie-Herzégovine' in Bougarel and Clayer (eds), *Le nouvel islam balkanique*, p. 468.
6. I dealt with this point in my *Failure of Political Islam*.
7. Martin Walzer, *The Revolution of the Saints: A Study of the Origins of Radical Politics*, Cambridge, MA: Harvard University Press, 1965. Walzer looks at how 'fundamentalist' Protestants created the concept of modern political parties. The comparison between contemporary Islam and Protestantism will be recurrent in this book.

FROM ISLAMISM TO NATIONALISM

The state Islamist parties are challenging is not an abstract one, but rather one that is more or less rooted in history and part of a strategic landscape. Islamist parties themselves are the product of a given political culture and society. Despite their claim to be supra-national, most Islamist movements have been shaped by national particularities. Sooner or later they tend to express national inter-ests, even under the pretext of Islamist ideology. Empowerment by definition reinforces identification with a given state and nation, as happened with the communist parties of the 1950s and 1960s. The mainstream Islamist movements in the 1990s have failed to pro-duce anything resembling an 'Islamist International' along the lines of the Communist International (or Comintern). As early as the end of 1980 (Iraqi invasion), the Iranian revolution played on pa-triotic sentiment to enlarge its domestic support. At least since the death of Ayatollah Khomeini in 1989, Iranian foreign policy has been shaped by Iranian national interests rather than by ideology: keeping a low profile regarding the Soviet presence in Afghani-stan; support for Christian Armenia against a fellow Shia country (Azerbaijan); joining a strategic axis with an independent Rus-sia against Turkish and Western encroachments in the Caspian Sea and Central Asia (at least until 1998, when Vladimir Putin became President of Russia); rapprochement with conservative Arab states (1997) in order to defuse tensions in the Persian Gulf in the hope of seeing a decrease in the US military presence; and the instru-mentalisation of Shia minorities abroad in the name of the Muslim *ummah* and then letting them down as soon as it suited Iranian national interests (Iraq in 1991, Bahrain in 1996, and Afghanistan after the Taliban offensive of August 1998). Tehran discreetly sup-ported the US operation Enduring Freedom to topple the Taliban regime in October 2001 and did not oppose the occupation of Iraq in 2003. The Iranian revolution never established links with mainstream Sunni Arab Islamist movements (such as the Muslim Brotherhood) because the latter are too close to Arab nationalism (as demonstrated by their support for Iraq during the first Gulf war). But nationalism can also foster certain aggressive positions: maintaining a nuclear program (even if officially peaceful), which had been initiated by the late Shah; keeping a foothold in northern Iraq through some local Islamic-minded radical Kurdish groups (in

Halabja);[8] and supporting Hezbollah in Lebanon as a way to maintain leverage in an all-Arab Near East. Iranian conservatives are still using a radical rhetoric when dealing with the Israeli–Palestinian conflict, which is enough to trigger the wrath of Washington.

This 'nationalisation' of Islamism is apparent in most Middle Eastern countries. In Palestine, Hamas and Islamic Jihad have challenged Arafat's Palestine Liberation Organisation (PLO) not on points relating to Islam, but for 'betraying' the national interests of the Palestinian people, which means that they become reconciled every time the PLO's officers join the fight against Israel. Hasan al-Turabi used Islam as a tool for unifying Sudan, by Islamising the southern Christians and pagans. The Yemenite Islah movement has been active in the reunification of Yemen, against the wishes of its Saudi godfather. The Lebanese Hezbollah, during the Israeli occupation of southern Lebanon, stressed the defence of the 'Lebanese nation' and has established a working relationship with many Christian circles. It has, incidentally, given up the idea of an Islamic state in Lebanon, due to consideration of the role of Christians in defining the nation. The Refah Partisi in Turkey, by stressing its Ottoman heritage, has been trying to affirm a kind of neo-Ottoman Turkish model in the Middle East, as an alternative to the 'Europe or nothing' official policy. By the same token, the radical Shia parties of Iraq, such as Dawa and the Supreme Council for Islamic Revolution in Iraq (both of which support the Governing Council established by the US administration in Iraq in July 2003), are stressing the need for national unity and are working closely with non-Islamic national parties. The FIS in Algeria claims to be the heir to the National Liberation Front (FLN) of the anti-French independence war, and has failed to put down roots in Morocco or Tunisia. During the Gulf war of 1991, each branch of the Muslim Brotherhood took a stand in accordance with the perceived national interests of its own country (for example, the Kuwaiti branch approved the US military intervention during the war, while the Jordanian branch vehemently opposed it). In Bosnia, the Party of Democratic Action (SDA) of Ali Izetbegovic, although stressing the religious dimension of being a Muslim in Bosnia, has achieved nothing other than to embody the national dimension of

8. But pragmatism always prevails over ideological commitment. In September 2002 Iran expelled the Islamist Kurdish leader Mullah Krekar to Norway.

what was no more than a vague ethnoreligious identity (Muslim with a capital M, created by decree in 1971). Once its strategic goal was achieved (the creation of an independent Bosnia), it first expelled most of the 'international' volunteers (the El Mujahid brigade) who had settled in Zenica and, when defeated in elections, relinquished power in favour of more secular forces. The smooth re-Islamisation of Bosnia produced something far closer to westernised Turkey than to Egypt. The Bosnian case shows once again that political integration of Islamists not only is feasible, but also remains the best option with which to defuse radicalism.

The failure of the peace process and the second Palestinian intifada (autumn 2000) have contributed to the blurring of the divide between nationalists and Islamists everywhere in the Arab Middle East, and has favoured a renewal of Arab nationalism. It is often difficult, in the public opinion of Arabs in Palestine and the front-line countries, to detect a difference between secularists and Islamists; all express a strong anti-Israeli and anti-US nationalist resentment, even Christians. (The patriarch of the Egyptian Coptic Church, Pope Shenouda III, has issued a *'fatwa'* of excommunication against Christians travelling to Jerusalem.) Government criticisms of Saad Eddin Ibrahim, director of a US-founded democratisation project in Egypt, were shared by people across the entire political spectrum and often expressed in the same terms by Islamists and secular nationalists.[9] In Palestine, Hamas and Fatah cadres often cooperate, while the Popular Front for the Liberation of Palestine (PFLP) has carried out its share of suicide bombings.

In Afghanistan, following the collapse of the communist regime in April 1992, many former communist military officers joined either the Taliban or the United National and Islamic Front for the Salvation of Afghanistan (Unifsa, commonly known as the Northern Alliance) of Commander Massoud, according to their ethnic affiliation (in this case ethnicity plays the role of nationalism). The success of Operation Enduring Freedom in October and November 2001 can partly be explained by the failure of Islamic radicalisation promoted by the Taliban leadership. The tribal and conservative Pashtun population, which welcomed the Taliban's power and

9.   See Mona El-Ghobashy, 'Antinomies of the Saad Eddin Ibrahim Case', MERIP Press Information Note 106, 15 August 2002 (<http://www.merip. org/mero/mero081502.html>).

implementation of *sharia*, was upset by Mullah Omar's decision to put transnational Islamic solidarity before national interests.

STATES WITHOUT NATION, BROTHERS WITHOUT STATE

There are three apparent exceptions to the above theses: Pakistan and Saudi Arabia (in terms of states) and the Muslim Brotherhood (in terms of an organisation). In the cases of Pakistan and Saudi Arabia, Islamo-nationalism seems to have been superseded by radical Islamic transnationalism. This weakness of Islamo-nationalism is linked with the weakness of the concept of the nation-state in both countries. Pakistan was created recently (1947), not as a territory but as a concept: a nation for the Muslims of the Indian subcontinent. In this sense it could pretend to represent Islam as such in South Asia, by supporting every regional *jihad* (such as those of Afghanistan and Kashmir). It is probably the only country in the world whose official language (Urdu) is not that of the dominant ethnic group, but that of its non-colonial 'immigrants' (the Mohajirs). As an artificial creation, Pakistan should have either rooted its new identity in a land and a nation-state, becoming a Muslim nation (the official stand from 1947 to 1977), or gone back to the description on its birth certificate: an Islamic state (the position of Maududi and then of the army, from Zia ul-Haq's takeover in 1977 to the coup by General Pervez Musharraf in 1999 – until 9/11). With the exception of the Jamaat-i-Islami, all the domestic Islamic militant movements are strongly internationalist and actively supported the Taliban, even by fighting US troops. The killing in Karachi of eleven French engineers and technicians working for the Pakistan navy in May 2002 shows that the radicals do not care about state and nation. The navy could by definition have been involved only against India and should thus have been spared by Islamic radicals whose main objective was to 'liberate' Kashmir. To attack the Pakistan navy was a clear rejection of the concept of patriotism in favour of ideological *jihad*. In fact Pakistani radical Islamic militants are nationalist in their own way: for them Pakistan is the nation of all the Muslims of South Asia, and not a specific territory. They remain aligned with the previously mentioned policy of the ruling military, who have always considered Afghanistan and Kashmir national issues in strategic terms and who used the radical '*jihadis*' as a tool of their regional policy. Until 9/11 there was a joint venture between the Pakistani ruling élites and the Islamic radicals, a rather unusual case in Muslim countries.[10] In this sense they are integrated into a national policy, which imploded because of the contradiction inherent in the events of September 2001: how could Pakistan support Islamic radicalism yet maintain a close alliance with the United States?

Saudi Arabia is both a tribal patrimonial estate (the only country in the world to be named after the ruling family) and the centre of an official transnational religious movement (Wahhabism), which not only claims to represent the only 'true' Islam (Salafism), but also deems irrelevant any tribal, ethnic or national identities. To sum up, a 'Wahhabi Saudi Arabia' is a contradiction in terms, which until recently has been hidden behind a veil of petrodollars and hypocrisies. There is no true 'Saudi' Islamist party, because there is no true Saudi state. The opposition is either within the Wahhabi clergy, or among Islamists with an obvious internationalist agenda. The latter include Doctor Muhammad al-Massari, based in London, who is moving rather closer to the position of the Hizb ut-Tahrir (Liberation Party; see page 309, Chapter 7), advocating that there be no compromise with any non-Islamic government (a typical Salafi position).

The scarcity of Islamo-nationalists in Pakistan and Saudi Arabia is a consequence of the difficulty of defining these two countries as nation-states. Both try to bypass a lack of national identity and roots by pretending to herald a transnational Muslim identity (the king of Saudi Arabia took the title Khadim al-Haramayn, Guardian of the Holy Places, and promoted the Muslim League). In a word, the 'national' project, beyond the narrow political basis of the rulers, is really a transnational one, which explains why most of the Islamic opposition (such as the religious networks in Pakistan, and Muhammad al-Massari in Saudi Arabia) are working at this level to delegitimise the ruling regime. But this does not mean that there is no other opposition. The real opposition to the ruling family in Saudi Arabia will probably emanate from the rising middle class, via a combination of Arab nationalism and Islamic puritanism, than from the Wahhabi clergy.

The case of the Muslim Brotherhood is more complex because it was from the beginning a transnational organisation, although

10. Mariam Abou Zahab and Olivier Roy, *Islamic Networks: The Afghan-Pakistan Connection*, London: Hurst, 2004.

the leadership has always remained in the hands of Egyptians. They also maintained a 'brotherhood' approach, stressing the devotional dimension of membership. Would-be members must undergo a lengthy process of gradual candidacy and provide religious credentials in terms of knowledge and behaviour. The transformation into a purely political party has been thwarted alternately by repression (in Egypt) and by the destructive attitude of an ageing, religious-minded leadership. The movement has always been ambivalent by nature. At regular intervals members have left to build purely political parties (for example, the initial incarnation of Hizb ut-Tahrir, in the 1950s; the Islamic National Front; and the Wasat Party). Outside Egypt the branches, which had been more or less integrated into domestic politics, gave up their reformist and modern nature to become mere rightist conservative parties. In Kuwait they opposed the right of women to vote.

But a specific trait of the Muslim Brothers is that many became 'deterritorialised' through an academic career or in search of a job, specifically when they were barred from government jobs in Egypt, Syria and Iraq. They staff many international Islamic institutions put in place by the Saudis, like the Rabita al-Alam al-Islami (Muslim League), or hold teaching positions in Islamic universities from countries with a dearth of locally trained *ulama* (from Qatar to Britain). In Europe, where they have more 'modern' attitudes, they also play a major role in European Muslim organisations like the Union of Islamic Organisations in France (UOIF). They provide many intellectual experts on Islamic banking, sociology, law, and so on. The Muslim Brotherhood has a great capacity to adapt to different political contexts and a flexible view of what it means to be a Muslim in a modern world, although many of the brothers are increasingly moving closer to the Salafi position, for two reasons: the lure of Saudi money and the intellectual consequences of deterritorialisation, as we shall see in Chapter 6.

THE CRISIS OF DIASPORAS

A logical consequence of this nationalisation of Islamism is that the mainstream Islamist movements, while consolidating a stable constituency inside their own country, are losing their appeal beyond their borders. We have seen how Iran has lost most of its allure among non-Iranian Shias. Two cases illustrate how this appeal has declined: the house arrest in Qom in 1995 of the two sons of Grand Ayatollah Shirazi, spiritual leader of the Bahraini Shia; and the close cooperation between the Afghan Shia party Wahdat and the US army during and, more noticeably, after Operation Enduring Freedom (which began in November 2001). The exception is the Lebanese Hezbollah, which plays a subtle game of equilibrium between Tehran and Damascus. The Refah Partisi (which was to become the Fazilet Partisi, or Virtue Party) between 1983 and 1985 established among Turkish migrants in Europe a subsidiary, Milli Görüs (National Vision – it had existed before under another name), which is less and less aligned with the purely political and nationalist approach of the mother party. The 2001 split of Refah-Fazilet, which gave birth to the AK Party, partly dissociated Milli Görüs (which no longer has active links with the AK party) from domestic Turkish politics. The movement has tended to become increasingly 'European', often associating with Europe-based Arab Muslim Brothers. (One of the founders of Milli Görüs, Zayn al-Abidin, was born in Iraq to an Arab father and a Turkish mother.) Internal debates concentrate on what it means to be a Muslim in Europe and pit a dominant conservative body, often close to the Salafi line, against a liberal wing, represented by the Dutch section (headed by Haci Karacaer).

Similarly, the Algerian FIS failed to make inroads in France among re-Islamised youth of Algerian origin. Instead, as such youth became more radical, they briefly joined the Armed Islamic Group of Algeria (GIA) in France from 1994 to 1996, but never returned to Algeria. When they left Europe for the sake of *jihad* they went to Afghanistan, Yemen, Kashmir or even Los Angeles (for example, Ahmed Ressam, who was convicted in a US court in April 2001 of plotting to bomb Los Angeles International Airport). Interestingly, except for Pakistanis, almost no born-again Muslim radicals from Europe joined a *jihad* in their countries of origin. For them, the concept of 'home country' makes no sense; they are no longer aligned with their family's society of origin. In this regard it seems better to join an 'imaginary' *ummah* than a real country, where they might have met the 'real word'.[11] In some instances, the 'diaspora'

11. It may be not a very good comparison, but Che Guevara never returned to Argentina.

appeared more fundamentalist than the home movements. The protest against Salman Rushdie's *Satanic Verses*, for example, was initiated in Britain by the Bradford Council of Mosques, which organised the burning of the book on 14 January 1989.

The same phenomenon of dissociation is at work among Palestinians, of whom those who joined internationalist organisations including Al Qaeda are all refugees of 1948 and 1967. Many, like Abdullah Azzam, Mohamed Saddiq Odeh and Omar Ibn al-Khattab (known simply as Khattab), were born in Jordan or Saudi Arabia. This internationalisation of Palestinian refugees is quite logical. They know that even if there is an agreement between the Palestinian Authority and the Israelis there will never be a massive right of return; nor will they settle in the overcrowded West Bank or Gaza. Except in Jordan, they are denied citizenship in their country of residence. The militants among them thus tend to adopt an internationalist Islamic identity, as is obvious in the refugee camp Ain al-Hilweh in Lebanon.[12] Many Muslim Brothers who migrated or found work outside their country of origin were confronted with the same choice between an elusive nation and an elusive *ummah*. In France one of the main national Islamic organisations, UOIF, in which the influence of the Muslim Brotherhood is pervasive, seeks to find a balance between an avowed internationalist position and integration into the institutional French landscape through participation in the Conseil Français du Culte Musulman, created by the Interior Ministry in 2003.

The link between territory and nationalism (for example, Bosnia, Palestine), and therefore between deterritorialisation and radical Islamisation, is quite constant.

ISLAM IS NEVER A STRATEGIC FACTOR AS SUCH

The 'nationalisation' of Islamist movements is also largely upheld by strategic factors. In other words, strategic constraints push Islamists to adopt a nationalist position because it allows them to benefit from external support. Willing or not, Bosnia's only possible means of achieving independence was to align with the West and not with a 'virtual' Islamic axis. This dependence provided safeguards that

---

12. Bernard Rougier, 'Le destin mêlé des Palestiniens', *Maghreb Machrek*, 169 (2000).

allowed the country to pass through the troubled waters of war and radicalisation and emerge as an almost 'normal' state, whose existence relies as much on the political and strategic environment as on its domestic strength.[13] In Turkey the Refah Partisi has not found a strategic alternative to the pro-Europe, pro-US and pro-Israeli policy of the Kemalist state, simply because such an alternative does not exist. Moreover, the successor of the Refah, the Adalet ve Kalkinma (AK) Partisi (Justice and Development Party), has everything to gain from the extension of democracy and withdrawal of the army from politics, under pressure from the European Union. Brussels is, incidentally, rightly seen as an ally by many moderate Muslims in Turkey and Western Europe, because the European bureaucracy is more immune from historical and religious prejudices than many elected European governments.

The Taif (1989) and Oslo (1993) accords have respectively enhanced the nationalist dimension of Hezbollah and Hamas, by restoring a Lebanese state (with full recognition of Hezbollah's role in the south) and bestowing recognition upon the Palestinian people. This has contributed to the opening of a national political space, at the expense of transnational solidarities.

The 'nationalisation' of Islamist movements is, incidentally, congruent with a general phenomenon: Islam as such is never a dominant strategic factor. The religious dimension always contributes to more basic ethnic or national factors, even if it provides afterwards a discourse of legitimisation and mobilisation. In the Balkans, as we have seen, political alignments have to do with ethnicity, not religion. In Bosnia the term Muslims was used as an ethnic concept, and not to refer to believers (called muslims with a lower-case initial). It applies to Bosnians, but not to Muslims outside Bosnia (in Serbia's Sanjak and Banat), who were not involved in repression or civil war. In Bulgaria Pomaks, Turks and Romany people (or Gypsies), who are all Muslims but belong to different ethnic and linguistic groups, do not constitute a Muslim community and choose different ways to deal with the dominant state and society (or have been dealt with differently by the same state).

13. Iranian support for Bosnia was certainly helpful but did not result in the laying down of a radical springboard in the area; US support was the decisive factor in the defeat of the Serbs.

In Kosovo alignments during the brief war of 1999 were not based on religion. The Muslim 'Slavs' (Gorani) and Romany people joined the Serbs, while Catholic Albanians remained united with their fellow Muslim ethnics. As Nathalie Clayer said in reference to the Balkans, 'Over about three decades national identities have begun to coalesce and in certain cases to prevail over other types of identification'.[14] In the northern Caucasus, in August 1999, the Chechen commander Shamil Basayev, with the help of the Arab commander Khattab, launched an offensive against the autonomous republic of Dagestan, in the hope of extending the *jihad* against the Russians by joining forces with the Dagestani Wahhabi groups based in certain villages. The offensive was a complete failure. The Dagestanis fought on the Russian side to repulse what they saw as a foreign encroachment, and were happier with distant and benign Russian sovereignty than with Islamic solidarity.

One should note that these ethnonational identities in former communist territories were often a consequence of the 'nation-alities' policies (ethnicisation) pursued by the communist re-gimes in the Soviet Union and Yugoslavia.[15] But ethnicisation also worked elsewhere. In Afghanistan more than twenty years of war (1979–2001) led to an ethnic polarisation between Pashtuns and non-Pashtuns. Although neither the Taliban movement nor the Northern Alliance has an ethnic agenda, they have a definite ethnic constituency. In Pakistan's North-West Frontier Province, Taliban-style neofundamentalism has taken root among Pashtun tribes as a way of expressing new forms of tribal autonomy while traditional leadership (the *khan*) is in crisis.

Islam is recast as a strategic factor only *post hoc*, when there is a coincidence between ethnic and religion affiliations; for example, Muslim Chechens versus orthodox Russians, or Christian Moluc-cans against Muslim immigrants from Borneo. But the separatist movement in the Indonesian province of Aceh is not seen as Mus-lim because both 'sides' (the central government and the secession-ists) are made up of Muslims. The Islamic identity of the Uighurs in China's Xinjiang province is systematically stressed by the media

---

14. Nathalie Clayer, 'L'Islam facteur des recompositions internes en Macédoine et au Kosovo' in Bougarel and Clayer (eds), *Le nouvel Islam balkanique*, p. 207.
15. On the Balkans, see Bougarel and Clayer (eds), *Le Nouvel Islam balkanique*, and in particular Clayer's chapter 'L'Islam facteur', p. 207. On Central Asia, see Olivier Roy, *The New Central Asia*, London: I.B. Tauris, 2000.

(for example, 'Muslim separatists in Sin-Kiang'),[16] while few reports will write 'Buddhist Tibetans are fighting neo-Confucian Chinese' (for Huntington Tibetans are part of the Confucian civilisation). Some see in the Armenia–Azerbaijan conflict a struggle between Islam and Christianity, forgetting that the Armenians are supported by the very anti-Western Muslim Iranians and the Azeris by NATO member and European Union candidate Turkey.

As usual, however, Huntington's culturalist strategy is upheld by Muslim fundamentalists themselves, who also try to explain every conflict in terms of Crusade versus *jihad* (and who are at loss to explain why the United States supported Bosnians, Kosovars and Afghan *mujahedin*, except by referring to very elaborate conspiracy theories).[17] But what proves that Islam is not a strategic factor as such are the constant complaints by internationalist Islamic militants about the lack of interest in contemporary *jihads* from among the *ummah*. They resent this inability of Muslim solidarity to transform itself into a strategic factor. Islamic non-governmental organisations (NGOs) have been created to compensate for the dearth of political commitment and to channel private or semi-official funds. They have been instrumental in Afghanistan and Bosnia, but their overall achievements have been disappointing despite the fuss made about financial support networks for terrorists.[18] Indeed, in terms of international solidarity there is an obvious discrepancy between the global Muslim population and number of countries and the amount of money, volunteers and support effectively marshalled for the current *jihad*.

THE POLITICAL INTEGRATION OF ISLAMISTS

Violence related to Islam has been decreasing in the Middle East since 1996 (not in Pakistan, which is not a Middle Eastern country).

16. See, for example, Bay Fang, 'Troubles in the Neighbourhood: Cracking Down on its Muslim Separatists, China has Reasons for Backing U.S. Actions', *US News and World Report*, 17 October 2001.
17. Such conspiracy theories are not the monopoly of Middle Easterners. For example, Alexandre Del Valle, in his book *Islamisme-Etats-Unis, un complot contre l'Europe* (Lausanne: L'Age d'Homme, 1997), tried to explain how radical Islam was supported by the United States to destroy the Old Europe.
18. See Jonathan Benthall and Jerôme Bellion-Jourdan, *The Charitable Crescent: Politics of Aid in the Muslim World,* New York: Palgrave Macmillan, 2003.

Such violence has migrated outside the Middle East (even if the role of Middle Easterners is dominant), which is what we call the globalisation of Islam. Of course I do not content that Palestinian violence is related to religion. As we have said, if the Israelis were Protestants and the Palestinians Catholics, the antagonism would be the same. Both Zionism and the PLO have historically been secular-minded, but there is a process of recasting in religious terms a conflict that is above all nationalistic.

A specific and interesting case is Egyptian Islamic Jihad. Its supposed leader is Ayman al-Zawahiri, Bin Laden's deputy. If Islamic Jihad was integrated into Al Qaeda through the dual position of its leader, something should have happened in Egypt in the wake of the US campaign in Afghanistan. Not only did nothing happen, but two prominent leaders of Islamic Jihad, Usama Rushdie and Montasser al-Zayat, explicitly denied any link between the movement and al-Zawahiri.[19] Hundreds of Islamic Jihad members were freed between 1999 and 2002, after the organisation's leadership in gaol called for a ceasefire. One of the most violent Islamist organisations has joined a political process, or has been so weakened as to become quite ineffective.

The Algerian FIS became involved with a peace process under the aegis of the Catholic Italian Community of Sant'Egidio in 1993, which tried to find common ground between Algeria's various factions. The FIS gave up the armed struggle in 1997. By accepting the Sant'Egidio process, aimed at a coalition government between parties with different political agendas, the FIS explicitly relinquished the concept of an Islamic state. The process was aborted in the same year because the Algerian ruling regime refused to participate. The ongoing violence in Algeria seems to have as much to do with local vendettas and manipulation by the army as with the fragmentation and radicalisation of the GIA (a radical splinter faction, from as early as 1992, of the FIS). The FIS abroad is typically an 'Islamo–nationalist' movement, but has lost most of its roots inside Algeria. The revolts and demonstrations that took place in 2001 had nothing to do with Islam, although the actors were

19. *Asharq al-Awsat*, 25 January and 5 July 2002. The Web page has disappeared but a summary can be found on the website of Professor Juan Cole, <http://www.juancole.com/archives/2002_12_01_juancole_archive.html>. For al-Zayat, see Marc Epstein, 'Ayman Al-Zawahiri: Le cerveau d'Al Qaeda', *L'Express*, 11 September 2003.

the same as in 1991 (disfranchised youths), as were the targets (the military regime) and the motivation (to protest against corruption). This shows that the social frustrations, poverty and repression that fuelled Islamism may well persist without necessarily refuelling it in the future. The same causes do not always produce the same effects. In fact FIS has been excluded from the political arena by the mutual radicalisation of the army and of the GIA. The political approach of FIS was of no interest to the army, whose strategy has been to use the Islamic threat in order to freeze the political landscape in Algeria, and thus to be granted a free hand by the international community.

In Sudan Hassan Turabi was arrested in February 2001 by his former ally General Bashir, who in 2002 launched peace talks with the country's southern rebels. In Tajikistan the Islamic Renaissance Party (IRP) chose in June 1997 to sign an agreement with the neocommunist faction, under the dual auspices of Russia and Iran. Since then Islam-related violence has ceased and the shaky coalition government headed by President Rahmanov has been able to end the civil war. The IRP is now running in elections. In Afghanistan the Northern Alliance, which took power in the wake of the US campaign of October 2001, has long dropped any Islamist reference.[20] In Tajikistan and Afghanistan, ethnic alignments supersede ideological and religion affiliations. The Tajik IRP sided with Massoud and the neocommunists against the Taliban (Pashtuns), who were supported by the Islamic Movement of Uzbekistan, although many IMU cadres had a long history of supporting the Tajik IRP during the civil war in Tajikistan (1992–7).

Most Islamist movements have become involved in processes of political integration, which have been triggered by a complex mix of failure, repression, isolation, empowerment, war-weariness, self-criticism and political praxis. It was their political practice and experience, not ideology, that pushed them to negotiate and to enter a multiparty political space. This strategy proved successful in Jordan, Turkey, Kuwait, Tajikistan, Yemen and Bahrain, and to a lesser extent (with ups and downs) in Egypt, Morocco and Malaysia.

20. The *Afghan News*, a Jamaat-i-Islami newspaper headed by Engineer Ishaq, a close adviser to Commander Massoud, published an editorial as early as 15 August 1987 claiming that there was no such a thing as an 'Islamic state'.

In Turkey the Refah Partisi has been a coalition partner twice (in 1974 and in 1996–7, when the army forced it to step down). When Refah was dissolved, it took its case to the European Court of Human Rights rather than to the street. The Fazilet Partisi (created in 1997 to succeed Refah, which was on the verge of dissolution) was banned too, in 2001, but that year its heirs split into two new parties: the AK Partisi, headed by the former mayor of Istanbul, Recep Tayyip Erdogan; and the Saadet Partisi (Felicity Party), headed by Recai Kutan of the pro-Erbakan old guard. The AK Partisi no longer has any official commitment to religion. Its cadres, often technocrats, have solid experience in urban management through their tenures as elected mayors and city councillors. They offer a credible alternative to the obsolete and often corrupt political establishment, but their political ascendancy is regularly thwarted by the army.

The Kuwaiti and Jordanian Muslim Brotherhood are running for parliamentary elections whenever they are authorised to do so. In Egypt the split of the Wasat Party from the Muslim Brotherhood clearly shows how a new generation of members are unhappy with the ambivalence of the old guard. The Wasat Party is explicitly a purely political organisation. We shall see how, nevertheless, many Muslim Brothers, for different reasons (such as repression, ideology and internationalisation), joined neofundamentalist organisations. In Iran the liberal Mohammad Khatami won the 1997 and 2001 presidential elections; he and all his political fellows are former actors in the Islamic revolution. In Yemen Sheikh Abdullah al-Ahmar, leader of the Islah party, although defeated in the 2003 elections by the ruling party of President Saleh, was elected chairman of parliament with the support of the ruling party, which shows that the political game is more important than ideology.

The paradox is that in Algeria, Turkey and Tunisia the so-called secular forces are thwarting democracy under the pretext of halting Islamic radicalism. But in all the cases the 'Islamist' parties have proved more politically open than the authoritarian secularists.

FROM UTOPIA TO CONSERVATISM

By entering the political game, Islamist movements also brought in social groups that felt excluded from politics. These included the *mostazafin* in Iran (the urban underclass), even if they were not the

main beneficiaries of the revolution.[21] Khatami's presidential campaign also brought dissatisfied youths back into play, at least during his first mandate (1997–2001). Amal and Hezbollah brought
the Lebanese Shias into mainstream politics, as the Refah Partisi
did (albeit briefly) in Turkey for new urban migrants and Kurds.[22]
Urban youth in Algeria, shocked by the bloody repression of October 1988, joined the FIS. Northern tribes in Yemen found a way to
re-enter the political game, after the proclamation of the republic,
in a more modern way. And so it goes on. Islamist movements have
helped to give root to nation-states and to create a domestic political scene, which was the only real basis for future democratisation,
even if these movements were not promoting democracy.

The Islamist wave has accompanied societal changes, which also
contributed to the modernising of society, even if, once again, they
did not deliberately trigger such changes. The Iranian Islamic revolution heralded, sometimes unwittingly, a modernisation of the
country (even if such trends were already at work under the Shah):
erosion of the differences between countryside and cities, gener-
alisation of education (which contributed to the extension of the
Persian language), greater female participation in the universities,
and urbanisation (even if one of the first mottoes of the regime was
'Back to the village', *Bazgasht be rustâ*). Today there are no Islamists
in Iran. The former revolutionaries have turned into either liberals
or conservatives.[23] In this sense Islamist parties, while they are not

21. See Assef Bayat, *Street Politics: Poor People's Movements in Iran*, New York: Co-
    lumbia University Press, 1997. Bayat calls into question the common wisdom
    according to which the underclass and disfranchised youth were key actors in
    the Iranian revolution.
22. In the 1994 municipal elections, Refah Partisi won in many Kurdish towns;
    in the 1999 contest, it lost some of them (Dyarbakir, Agri, Bingöl, Siirt and
    Van) to Hadep, a pro-Kurd party. This shift of a part of the Kurdish electorate
    was motivated by two facts. First, Hadep was not present in 1994, and Refah
    Partisi at that time appeared to be an opposition party more flexible towards
    the cultural demands of the Kurds (Muslim identity was supposed to bypass
    a perception of Turkish identity that was too narrow). Second, in 1999, when
    Hadep entered the arena, Refah Partisi had cabinet experience, which made
    it seem to the Kurds as nationalist as the other parties. The concessions un-
    willingly made by Refah Partisi to the Kemalist state antagonised its Kurdish
    constituency, but this shows two things: it is not Islam that motivates the
    electors, and Refah Partisi is seen as a nationalist party.
23. See Farhad Khosrokhavar and Olivier Roy, *Iran. Comment sortir d'une révolu-
    tion religieuse*, Paris: Editions du Seuil, 1999.

democratic, foster the necessary conditions for an endogenous democracy, as is clearly the case in Iran. Khatami's election expressed a call for democracy that is possible only because the entire population has been incorporated into a common political space by a popular and deep-rooted revolution.

But whether in power (Iran) or in opposition (Egypt), Islamists have been unable to cope with the social and economic changes of which they are part. The revolutionary social message (or at least the revolutionary terminology) of the Islamists has faded away in favour of a conservative agenda: insistence on the 'shariatisation' of state law, opposition in parliament to women's political participation (Kuwait), and expression of the desiderata of the new middle classes more than those of society's disfranchised. The concept of 'social justice' advocated by Sayyid Qutb or Baqer al Sadr has disappeared. Even the Turkish Refah–Fazilet, the most political-minded of Islamist parties, has forgone its social dimension and been pushing for joint ventures between business and the unions. The union it created (Hakkish) kept a low profile during the tenure of the Refah-led coalition (1996–7) and did not condemn the privatisation campaign led by Refah and the AK party (which has been leading a campaign for privatisation and a free-market economy since its electoral victory in 2002). In Iran the debate on privatisation does not coincide with the divide between liberals and conservatives. It is in Egypt that the rightist approach to the economy by radical Islamic groups is most striking. The agrarian reform law passed by President Mubarak in 1998, which cancels price controls on farm leases and thus allows landowners to regain direct control of their lands, was approved by Gama'at Islamiya because the *sharia* supports full property rights.

What is left of utopia? The Islamists-turned-conservatives cast their call for a moral order in terms of the defence of authenticity and identity, embodied in a set of Islamic values, against the encroachments of Western culture. They joined here the 'clash of civilisations' chorus, which claims that democracy and human rights are tools of Western imperialism, which applies double standards and is more eager to 'culturally' westernise than genuinely to 'democratise' Third World nations. They joined here non-Muslim voices, like Lee Kuan Yew from Singapore or Chinese leaders. But they also joined the Vatican chorus denouncing pro-choice campaigns or rights for homosexuals. By striking a conservative chord in public opinion, they appear still to champion a national identity against forms of neocolonialism. Terms like *values, culture* and *civilisation* superseded *sharia* and Islam. Many Islamists, like the Tunisian Sheikh Ghannouchi and the Refah Partisi, stress the concept of 'civil society', trying to reconcile the ghost of a 'traditional' society and the definition of a modern polity based on personal commitment of the citizens by elaborating the concept of a Muslim community based on a voluntary commitment to fulfil religious precepts, as was the case for the Puritans.[24] In fact, the specificity of 'Islamic societies' is expressed in Western terms: multiculturalism, values, identity, communities.

THE ELUSIVE 'MUSLIM VOTE'

The failure of political Islam is most striking when Islamist parties enter the electoral arena. They claim to have the monopoly of the political representation of Islam. As we shall see, the Iranian constitution recognised two sources of legitimacy: God and the people's will. That these could part company did not occur to the authors of the constitution. By the same token, the Refah Partisi and the FIS based their entire electoral campaigns on the theme that true believers should vote for the party of Islam. They did not accept the idea that true believers could make different and even opposing political choices. Unification of the religious field goes along with that of the political field, which was split between right (*haqq*) and wrong (*batel*). But except for a few paroxysmal events, always linked to a general upheaval against dictatorship, nowhere in the world did Islamist parties attract more than around 20 per cent of the electoral vote, and they frequently polled even lower.[25] This electoral disillusionment led to two different views: elections are

24. See Nazif Shahrani, 'Re-building Communities of Trust in Muslim Central Asia: Past Legacies and Future Prospects', paper presented at the 'Workshop for Home-grown Models of Civil Society in the Muslim World', Watson Institute for International Studies, Brown University, Providence, RI, 12–13 March 1999. See also Mohammed Khatami, 'Jâme'e-ye madani az negâh-ye Islâm' [Civil society from the point of view of Islam] in *Nesbat din va jâme'e-ye madani* [About Religion and Civil Society], 2nd edn, Tehran: Moa-sese-ye neshar va tahqiqâti zekr, 2000.
25. The AK party in Turkey polled more than 30 per cent of the vote in 2002 precisely because it did not present itself as an Islamist party.

wrong, as is democracy (the motto of the present neofundamental-ists, as well as of the Iranian conservatives), or political pluralism is legitimate. Islamists learned about democracy through practice.

An important lesson learned by the Islamist parties was that there is no 'Muslim vote' anywhere, either in Middle Eastern or Western countries. The support of the 'pious bourgeoisie' and of the religious establishment can never be taken for granted. The Khomeinists met discreet but stubborn opposition from very high-ranking ayatollahs (Taleghani, Shariat-Madari, Khu'y, and recently Montazeri). In Turkey, after Erbakan's split with the Naqshbandi order in 1983, the huge reservoir of votes provided by the *tariqat*, or Sufi brotherhoods, went not to his party but to centre-right secular parties (Dogru Yol Partisi, or DYP; Anavatan Partisi). When the FIS was outlawed in Algeria, the regime had no problem with promot-ing a rival Islamist organisation (Nahda). The SDA in Bosnia did not succeed in controlling the clergy. In Uzbekistan the IMU has also been unable to federate the diverse trends of Islamic radical-ism, and is now challenged by the Hizb ut-Tahrir.

When there are elections, and outside the rare cases of paroxys-mal identification with an Islamic revolution (for example, Iran in 1979 and Algeria in 1991, when elections were something new), Islamist parties attract around 20 per cent or less of the vote. In Turkey the Refah Partisi polled around 21 per cent in 1994, and in Yemen (May 1997) Islah polled 18.5 per cent. The Pakistani Jamaat-i-Islami has never received more than 5 per cent of the vote. This means that most believers (mosque-going Muslims) simply do not vote for Islamist parties. This lies at the core of our reassessment of the ideology of these parties. As many Turkish and Iranian militants explained to me, every true believer, once freed from the alienat-ing propaganda of the state, should vote for the Islamic party. But it does not happen. In Turkey Muslims vote more according to local considerations or, more disturbingly, according to the suggestions of the 'brotherhood' to which they belong. In the 1997 presidential elections the people chose Khatami over the candidate put forward by the Guide (Khamenei).

The majority of US Muslims may have voted for George W. Bush in November 2000, but this does not mean they vote as Muslims. Nor in France is there a significant 'Muslim party' or lobby. Any candidate in the West knows that he might be wise to court the ethnic vote, but that the concept of a 'Muslim vote' makes no sense, except in some city council elections in Britain. Muslim activists recognise this and regularly berate their community for its lack of political mobilisation. Many dream of building the equivalent of the 'Jewish lobby'. But this failure is due not to a lack of mobilisation, but to the inability of Islam to supersede other identity patterns, social strategies, economic interests, and so on. Political Islam is a dream or a nightmare, but not a sociological reality.

Moreover, Islamist movements, except to some extent the Muslim Brotherhood, do not control the burgeoning Islamic teaching institutions, specifically the recent private *madrasas*. In Pakistan most *madrasas* are in the hands of the Deobandi school and of the Ahl-i Hadith militants, not of the Jamaat-i-Islami. In Turkey the Refah Partisi has never controlled teaching institutions, which is why the Fethullah Gülen brotherhood has taken advantage of the liberal reforms of former Prime Minister Turgut Özal by establishing private secondary schools.

In sociological terms many believers belonging to social categories that blossomed through the extension of free markets (such as businessmen, lawyers and traders) would prefer a soft re-Islamisation of their society, avoiding revolution, violence and political protest; they especially reject the social dimension of any Islamic revolution, and support the free market and privatisation.[26] The success of the neo-brotherhoods (such as Gülen, Kaftaro and Ahbash) and the popularity of older ones (for example, in Egypt, Sudan and Morocco) shows how large segments of the population are seeking some kind of non-political re-Islamisation.

DEMOCRACY WITHOUT DEMOCRATS[27]

By contributing to the opening up of the political field, by their more or less sincere references to 'democracy' and 'civil society', by their criticisms of authoritarian and corrupt regimes, and by their alliance with non-Islamic forces, the Islamists did contribute to laying the basis of greater democracy and secularisation. Islamism

26. Patrick Haenni, 'Ils n'en ont pas fini avec l'Orient. De quelques islamisations non islamistes', *Revue du monde musulman et de la Méditerranée*, 85–6 (1999), pp. 121–48.
27. Ghassan Salamé (ed.), *Democracy without Democrats? The Renewal of Politics in the Muslim World*, London: I.B. Tauris, 1994.

was a 'failure' only if one took the Islamists at their own words. But they helped to change the political landscape.

First, they opposed the oligarchic systems that dominate in the Middle East, whatever their ideological cloak. They broke the mirror-image relationships between an authoritarian and closed regime on the one hand and, on the other, a civil society that organises itself around traditional networks of family, clans and patronage, knowing that such a dualist system denies any possibility of an open political space. They addressed individuals (particularly youths) rather than traditional solidarity groups; they bypassed the organic hierarchies that were used by authoritarian states, even in the pretence of being modern.[28] Any religious revolution entails the triumph of politics over religion, as shown by Michael Walzer in his study of sixteenth-century Puritan movements, in which he detected the forerunners of modern ideological parties, even if this was not by definition on their agenda, which stressed salvation and not good governance.[29]

Islamist parties thus contribute, contrary to their avowed goals, to the 'secularisation' of politicals. This means not necessarily secularisation of society, but rather the redefinition of the relationships between religion and politics as two quite autonomous spheres. The 'return to religion' that we are witnessing now is largely a reaction against the hyperpoliticisation entailed by the Islamist wave. The issue is not whether democracy and human rights are Western or universal values. It concerns the reappropriation and self-rooting of democracy by a given society. We must address the debate on Islam and democracy in terms not of importation, but of endorsement and appropriation by a society through its own experience and practice, which necessarily implies time, ups and downs, tensions and conflicts. Democratisation should be based on 'real' societies, not on abstract visions of what a society should be. In this sense, the different actors must themselves appropriate the concepts, internalise them, and transform them into a genuine praxis, and not merely

---

28. Republican secular authoritarian states do not hesitate to bypass their own ideology and to play on tribalism. On the retraditionalisation of Iraq by Saddam Hussein, see Baram Amazia, 'Neo-tribalism in Iraq: Saddam Hussein's Tribal Policies 1991–1996', *International Journal of Middle East Studies*, 29 (1997). See also Hosham Dawod and Hamit Bozarslan (eds), *La société irakienne*, Paris: Karthala, 2003.

29. Michael Walzer, *Revolution of the Saints*.

rhetorical terms or administrative definitions. Washington is learning in Iraq and Afghanistan that democratisation is a process, not a philosophy or simply a matter of constitutional law.

The central issue is about the real actors of democratisation. One should be careful not to read too much into what is said by some progressive intellectuals who have the same good ideas as Western political commentators, but are either cut off from their own society or, more often, are themselves (without acknowledging it) part of traditional networks, and combine rhetorical democracy with social patronage. We would do better to address the real actors in the process, even if they are motivated by different ideas. Such an approach would help us to move beyond the usual predicament of the reference to 'civil society'. The term is generally used to refer either to the voluntary grouping of individuals into associations (NGOs) and political parties, combined with a free press and free market, or to the self-organisation of a traditional society, through solidarity networks, endeavouring to challenge and resist an authoritarian and closed state. In this sense calls for westernisation contradict references to authenticity and traditions. Resistance to democratisation is often recast in terms of the defence of identity and tradition, a stand that is adopted by all neofundamentalists, as well as former Islamists turned conservatives. Rather than referring to a clash of values, one would be better served to address the real political actors. Democracy is not an ideology, but merely recognition of the rules of the game: political alternation through elections.

A side-effect of this state crackdown on Islamists is the dissociation of secularism and democracy. Many militant Muslims and even moderate Muslims became convinced that the West was applying double standards, invoking the human-rights argument against Islam but not, for example, against the secularist authoritarian regimes of Algeria and Tunisia. More interestingly, it also pushed the mainstream Islamist movements to protest repression in the name of democracy and to address the issue of human rights and tolerance. Thus democratic values are propounded by non-democratic groups. This is not mere rhetoric, for it pushes such groups to abandon their hegemonist rhetoric and to seek genuine political alliances with non-Islamist forces. This 'social democratisation' of Islamist parties has had tremendous consequences: it makes the ruling regimes appear more authoritarian and more detached from so-called Western values; but it also reveals changes in mentality and attitudes – the Islamists are now pondering political alliances and exploring ways to promote human rights (even if they be 'Islamic' human rights). They tend also to accept political participation wherever it is possible (for example, Jordan, Turkey and Kuwait) and thus become more aware of what governance means.

Thus by the late 1990s most of the Islamist movements had become more nationalist than Islamist. Their field of action is now largely limited to their own country. This nationalisation goes along with a very important element: Islamists have had to abandon the claim that they were the only legitimate movement to represent Islam in the political sphere. They have been forced to recognise the diversity of both the religious and the political fields. The latter may have been forced on to them by repression, failure and pragmatism, but is also a consequence of the former: religious diversity has been exacerbated by years of Islamism, yet one explicit objective of Islamism (as well as present-day Salafism) has been to unify the religious field (erasing the borders between Shiism and Sunnism and between the different schools of law, reducing the incidence of Sufism and popular Islam, and so on).

THE IRANIAN ISLAMIC REVOLUTION: HOW POLITICS DEFINES RELIGION

As we have seen, Islamists, whether in power or in opposition, have been unable to unify the religious field under their political leadership, thus making obvious the dissociation between politics and religion. The discrepancy remains the more obvious because most Islamists were neither clerics nor *ulama*. They systematically tried to reinstate the conjunction between religion and state (*din wa dawlat*) by political means. The most radical way was simply to declare 'non-Muslim' every Muslim who did not follow the path of the vanguard: *takfir* (excommunication) is the watershed between the extreme radical Islamists, or Qutbists (those who follow Sayyid Qutb), and mainstream Islamists. Nevertheless, there is a constant trend among Islamists and neofundamentalists to reject contradicting views from other Muslims as being a consequence of ignorance or bad faith. But the closer they are to power, the more Islamists tend to use political tools to bring religion under their control. The most striking example is the Iranian revolution.

Although there is such an obvious specificity in the Iranian revolution that many Sunni Islamists would deny the validity of any lesson drawn from it, I still consider there to be a symmetry between it and the general perception of an Islamic state, although the solutions chosen by Khomeini and his followers were rather original. Islamic Iran has successfully built institutions.[30] The Velayat-i Faqih is the Shia version of the *emir* or of the caliph. What happened in Iran is a good illustration of the conflicting relations between religion and politics in an Islamist system.

There has been (since around the eighteenth century) a clerical hierarchy in Iran, headed by a handful of grand ayatollahs who were *marja' al-taqlid*, a 'source of imitation'. Interestingly, the Iranian Islamic revolution did not bring this clerical structure into power, but instead built a specific institutional framework, staffing it with either laymen (for example, Raja'y, Habibi and Mussavi) or middle-ranking clerics, the Hojjat ol-Islam (such as Rafsanjani, Khamenei and Khoeyniha), plus some middle-ranking ayatollahs, who were not considered *marja' al-taqlid* (such as Beheshti, Madavi-Kâni and Jannati). The grand ayatollahs were kept aside (like Khu'y, Golpayegani, Araki and Tabataba'y-Qomi) or even repressed (like Kazem Shariat-Madari).

In the Iranian Islamic revolution the status and role of religion are obviously defined by political institutions, not religious ones. Politics rules over religion. The revolution was from its inception explicitly based on the conjunction of two legitimacies, religious and political, through the concept of *velayat-e faqih*, 'rule of the jurist', meaning that the highest authority of the Islamic revolution, the Guide of the Islamic Republic (*rahbar*, hereafter referred to as 'the Guide') should be both one of the highest religious authorities (*marja' al-taqlid*) and the political leader, who 'understands his time' (*agah be zaman*) and therefore can lead a mass movement.[31]

---

30. In December 1995 I visited Mufid University in Qom. I was met by a small group of professors, many of them *mullahs*. The debate was on the title of my book, *The Failure of Political Islam*. I was asked to defend my thesis, which was considered silly by the highest-ranked professor ('How could you speak of "failure"? We won!'). But after twenty minutes of explanations, he interrupted me and declared: 'I agree with you, but your title is simply still wrong. You should have written *The Failure of* Sunni *Political Islam*.'

31. Chapter 1, article 1, of the constitution states that the form of the government, an Islamic republic, has been endorsed by 'the people of Iran …

Chapter 5 of the Iranian constitution stipulates that, in the absence of the Hidden Imam, the leadership of the *ummah* should be entrusted to a 'just and pious jurist [*faqih*] aware of the circumstances of his time [*agah be zaman*]' (which means the leader should have something like 'political consciousness'), who should assume the responsibility of his office in accordance with chapter 107 of the constitution. The 1980s constitution stated that the *faqih* should be chosen from among the *marja' al-taqlid*, using one of two possible modalities: an immediate and direct recognition by the people, both as a 'source of imitation' (*marja' al-taqlid*) and a guide (*rahbar*); or the selection of one outstanding figure or of a collective leadership (three or five *faqih*) through an Assembly of Experts (*majlis-e khobregan*) comprising clerics elected by the Iranian people.

Most of the provisions of the 1980s constitution and all the amendments brought into effect in 1989 show that the requirements for the *faqih* shifted from religious to political qualifications, even if the Guide must always be a cleric. Chapter 107 was amended in 1989, and no longer stipulates that the *faqih* should be among the highest-ranking clerics (*marja' al-taqlid*), although it states that this was the case for Khomeini. The amended constitution of 1989 also dropped the possibility of a direct election of the Guide by the people, as if only Imam Khomeini could have been directly recognised by the people as *marja'* and *rahbar*. The disappearance of any reference to the *marja' al-taqlid* in the constitution of 1989 shows clearly that the Guide, who is the supreme authority in the Islamic Republic of Iran, is not necessarily the leading authority in religion. These dispositions underline the discrepancy between the traditional clerical establishment and the new revolutionary order. According to the Shia tradition, a *marja' al-taqlid*, or grand ayatollah (*ayatolla 'ozma*), is usually selected by his clerical peers through a long process in which *vox populi* has little to say, except that it is

---

through the affirmative vote of a majority of 98.27 percent of eligible voters', implicitly making the people's will one of the sources of legitimacy. Then the absolute sovereignty of God is expressed (article 2/1), while article 5 states that 'the just and pious *faqih*' should exercise '*vilayât*' (guardianship) during the concealment of the Hidden Imam, and article 6 says that 'the affairs of the country should be administered on the basis of public opinion expressed by the means of elections'. Analysing the conceptual origin of the Iranian constitution, Chibli Mallat speaks of a 'dual emanation of sovereignty' (Mallat, *The Renewal of Islamic Law*, Cambridge University Press, 1993, p. 72).

understood that there should be a broad consensus.[32] There is no precise and institutionalised process of appointing a grand ayatollah and there is rarely just one at a time. On the contrary, according to the constitution there should preferably be only one Guide, and he is appointed not by his peers (because he has none), but by an elected body. Of course, the Assembly of Experts that elects him is made up of clerics, but they are elected by ordinary Iranian citizens. Candidacies to the assembly are screened by the Council of Guardians, itself appointed (in part) by the Guide. Thus the council is not the expression of the leading clerical élite. It is a political appointment, not a religious one; it is also a national choice, because the electorate is exclusively Iranian.

It is interesting to note that all the modalities for choosing a Guide from among the *faqih* are by political means (elections) and that only the personality of Khomeini embodied idealistically both legitimacies, religious and political. In the contradiction between the two legitimacies, politics explicitly prevails over religion.

Khomeini's demise meant the end of the double legitimacy. His successor as Guide, Ali Khamenei, was not a leading religious authority. This led to two questions: Should the Guide be predominantly a leading religious authority or a political one? And how could an Islamic state bypass, through a political appointment, the highest religious authorities of its time and even turn its back on certain requirements of the *sharia*? The contradiction unravelled when, in May 1997, President Khatami was elected against the avowed wishes of the Guide, bringing the religious and political legitimacies into contradiction, even if, of course, the new President officially recognised the supremacy of the Guide.

In fact, after Khomeini's death and the appointment of Khamenei as the new Guide, some clerical circles tried to promote either Grand Ayatollah Golpayegani or Grand Ayatollah Araki as the new *marja' al-taqlid*. That would have reinstated a double order and separated the religious legitimacy from the political. But nothing was set up in official terms, even if Araki had supported the appointment of Khamenei as Guide and had issued a number of *fatwas* in support of the regime (including one banning television satellite dishes). The reason is abundantly clear: an official endorsement of a new *marja' al-taqlid* would have acknowledged the dissociation

32. See Mallat, *Renewal of Islamic Law*, p. 44.

between religious authority and political function, which would negate the concept of an Islamic revolution. But the consequence is that the political order is raised above the religious one.

Every time Khomeini had to clarify the complex relations between religious law and revolutionary legitimacy, he opted to put the latter first. Politics prevailed over religion not only in the choice of leader. It also touched the realm of the religious law, or *sharia*, the cornerstone of any 'Islamic state'. Here also the dominance of the state is written into the constitution, even if lip-service is paid to the *sharia* (as to the sovereignty of God). Article 36 of Chapter 3 states that 'the passing of a sentence must be only by a competent court and in accordance with law', meaning that a *qazi*,[33] or judge, cannot use *sharia* in opposition to the state law and may use it only when state law is not explicit. Nobody can take the law into his own hands in the name of the *sharia* (except for a clerical court set up to try clerics on religious matters). Moreover many provisions of the constitution are not in accordance with the *sharia* (definition of citizenship, equality of men and women, and the presence of attorneys in court proceedings).[34]

Khomeini was very keen to clarify the question explicitly. In his famous letter to President Khamenei (6 January 1988), he stated that 'the government can unilaterally abrogate legal [*shari'*] agreements ...'.[35] *Legal* here means conformity to the *sharia*; it does not simply mean that the government might decide upon matters that are not in the *sharia* (like customs duties), which has always been the case even for very fundamentalist regimes. However, he explicitly states that it might ignore or alter some *sharia* requirements. Khomeini explains, for example, that the government might cancel pilgrimage if it is in the interests of the Islamic state to do so. The official reason to permit state law authority over *sharia* is that this allows the achievement of the higher interest of the Islamic state and hence of Islam. But here again it is political considerations

33. This is the Persian spelling of *qadi*.
34. For a study on the discrepancies between the avowed goal of 'shariatisation' and the real practices, see Ziba Mir-Hosseini, *Marriage on Trial: A Study of Islamic Family Law*, London: I.B. Tauris, 1993.
35. For quotations and discussions of this letter and of other declarations of Khomeini, see Mallat, *Renewal of Islamic Law*, p. 90; and Shahrough Akhavi, 'Contending Discourses on Shi'i Law on the Doctrine of Wilâyat al Faqih', *Iranian Studies*, 29, 3–4 (1996), pp. 262–5.

that decide what is essentially Islamic, as opposed to the rules pre-scribed by religion. This assertive policy of binding *sharia* to the state law explains how Ayatollah Khomeini resolved the conflict between the parliament and Council of Guardians, whose duty, according to the constitution, is to check the conformity with the *sharia* of laws passed in parliament. The council was so adamant about its prerogatives that the issue became deadlocked. Many laws were suspended in absence of arbitration, which could come only from the Guide himself. So in 1987 Khomeini created the Expedi-ency Discernment Council of the System (Majma-e-Tashkhis-e Maslahat-e Nezam) as a way to deprive the Council of Guardians, in which religious lawyers had the upper hand, of the preroga-tive of having the last word on the conformity with Islam of laws passed in parliament. Appointments to the Expediency Council were political and the goal was, as stated in its title, *maslahat* ('the common interest'), a very political notion.

The discrepancy between the political and the clerical order has logically been coupled with a slow *de facto* declericalisation of political institutions. For instance, after the reform of the Expedi-ency Council in March 1997, the six religious lawyers from the Council of Guardians lost their right to vote on matters not related to constitutional issues. Most members are nowadays laymen, ap-pointed by the Guide; even those who are clerics are appointed because they are members of the ruling circles and not because of their religious qualifications. It is a mini Central Committee that includes most of the regime's élite. At the same time, the number of clerics elected to parliament dropped from 125 in the first Islamic Consultative Assembly to 50 in the 1996 legislature.[36]

ISLAMISATION AS A FACTOR OF SECULARISATION

Iran is a specific case, but the history of other Islamist movements shows that they are never immune from worldly politics, for exam-ple, from ethnic feuds (Afghanistan), tribal background (Yemen), personal rivalries, political rifts or corruption. The pervasive im-portance of politics has undermined the pristine ideals and values of Islamic ideology. The means may have jeopardised the end, as

36. Jean-Pierre Digard, Bernard Hourcade and Yann Richard, *L'Iran au XXe siè-cle*, Paris: Fayard, 1996, p. 208.

Ayatollah Hossein-Ali Montazeri and the Syrian Sheikh Buti have stressed.[37] The danger according to clerics and true believers is that ordinary Muslims might see Islam as a religion identified with empowered Islamism, which could lead to a sudden crisis of confidence in religion: 'Is that what we wanted?' Not only is the price to be paid for establishing an Islamic regime too high in terms of blood and repression, but the despairing gap between ideals and reality remains. Was the fight worth it?[38] The new Islamist order is simply removing Islamic values. That was the message of Ayatollah Montazeri to Khomeini before the former was dismissed as official heir to the latter in 1988. (The issue was the decision made by Khomeini in July to rid Iran of political prisoners, by either freeing them or killing them; thousands were killed in mass executions in Iranian gaols.) To sum up, politicisation entails desacralisation.

Empowered Islamism provides neither new kinds of social or economic justice. Hypocrisy is dominant: under the veil of moral conservatism, corruption is pervasive. Islamism in power has been unable to deal with westernisation. It has adopted technology, technocracy and political institutional models, but has been unable to give root to another culture or value system. Young people in Iran still prefer Western music and clothing, and seek fun and entertainment. The issue of entertainment and mores, as much as social justice, is probably the major stumbling block of Islamism in power. It has no model of culture other than the neofundamentalist view, based on interdiction and censorship. The proliferation of

37. Muhammad Sa'id Ramadan al-Buti, *Jihad in Islam: How to Understand and Practise It* (transl. by Munzer Adel Absi), Damascus: Dar al-Fikr, 1996. In July 1988, Ayatollah Montazeri sent a letter to Khomeini protesting his order to execute prisoners, claiming that it was against Islam. He was subsequently dismissed as Khomeini's heir. In a speech in 1997 he declared: 'As for the Faqih's role, he must only oversee the implementation of the people's will. He does not have the right to veto it. This is what we meant when we first introduced the notion of Velayate Faqih. Even in the time of the Prophet, the people ran their own affairs. We never thought that this would someday lead to creation of a royal system with multi-million dollar expenses, pompous protocol and luxurious travel.' 'Montazeri Throws down the Gauntlet', *Al-Moujez-an-Iran (Iran Briefings)*, 7, 4 (1997) (<http://www.caisuk.com/alm1297.htm>).
38. Farhad Khosrokhavar (*L'islamisme et la mort. Le martyre révolutionnaire en Iran*, Paris: L'Harmattan, 1995) shows how disillusionment with daily politics has been a factor in the quest for martyrdom among young Iranian volunteers of the Iran–Iraq War.

fatwas aims to ensure the supremacy of politics. Most of the present *fatwas* are not answers to questions asked by individuals, but 'orders' (*hokm*) – that is, political statements.[39]

The overemphasis on state power by Islamists has resulted in the devaluation of religion. Empowerment leads to corruption, compromise and the loss of utopia. (This is also true of Western democracy, although it contains no vision of utopia.) The imposition of Islamic norms through religious police (Basiji in Iran, Mutawa in Saudi Arabia) cannot hide the hypocrisy, which encompasses a vast array of worldly and non-Islamic practices. It is no irony that the young men and strictly veiled women, walking in separate groups but trying to make contact in the streets of Tehran or of Jordan, or in Jeddah's Tahliyya street, are using the same subterfuge: letting fall a piece of paper on which a telephone number is written, while dodging the religious police.[40] The only difference is that the Iranian girls drive themselves to the rendezvous, while Saudi ladies must call their chauffeurs. Was such a tiny difference worth a revolution?

Former militants may adapt to the new situation by sharing the pie and the perks, as did many clerics and Pasdaran (Revolutionary Guards) in Iran, like the former head of the corps, Mohsen Rafighdoust, under either the easygoing Rafsanjani regime or tougher conservative governance. Business and ideology are doing well together, especially when ideology is a means of ridding oneself of competitors. Disillusionment may also lead to political liberalism,

39. In an otherwise very informative book, Mehdi Mozaffari (*Fatwa: Violence and Discourtesy,* Aarhus University Press, 1998) explains that Khomeini never issued a *fatwa* against Rushdie, 'just' a '*hokm*', which is an interesting point. But Mozaffari went so far as to write that it is 'Olivier Roy who coined the term fatwa, and was therefore followed by his colleagues, the media and … the Iranian ayatollahs' (p. 48). Professor Mozaffari surely overestimates my possible influence on Iranian religious thinking. I anticipated the use of the term *fatwa* by the Iranian authorities (which used it) just because, for Islamists in power, *fatwa* is a political issue. The traditional distinctions between *hukm* (or *hukum*) and *fatwa* do not make any sense for empowered clerics. Politics does shape religious legal thinking, which leads to an endeavour by traditional conservative religious leaders to escape politics and to rescind the concept of an Islamic revolution and even of an Islamic state.

40. For information about this practice in Jeddah, see Lisa Wynn, 'The Romance of Tahliiyya Street', *MERIP Report,* 204 (1997), p. 30. The information on Tehran is from my (non-participative) personal observation.

as illustrated by the example of President Khatami. But it may also lead to hopelessness. Farhad Khosrokhavar studied the Iranian martyrs of the war against Iraq and showed how their readiness to die was linked with their conviction that the actual 'Islamic' society they were fighting for would not match their ideals.[41]

De facto secularisation is brought about not only by the hegemony of politics but also by the endeavours of conservative religious milieus to 'save' religion from encroachments by political authority, even if such authority is Islamic. This means that there is a growing tendency, among not only democrats and liberals but also traditional clerics, to separate religion and politics, in this case to save Islam from politics, and not, as during much of the process of secularisation in Western Europe, to save politics from religion. Many high-ranking Iranian ayatollahs have protested at the way in which Imam Khomeini dealt with clerical opponents (like Shariat-Madari and Montazeri) or introduced innovations. In Egypt, Al-Azhar University, however deeply penetrated by the state and by the Muslim Brotherhood, tries to retain some autonomy regarding political influence. In Algeria a leading figure like Sheikh Abdelbaki Sahraoui, although a sympathiser of the FIS, never relinquished his religious authority in favour of political constraints, and hence he was assassinated by young radicals in Paris in 1995.

A secular space, that of politics, does structure the religious space, but it then causes a religious revival that tries to bypass politicisation and address individuals. It is not secularism (or laicism; *laiklik* in Turkish), but it is a form of secularisation, which 'religious intellectuals' like Soroush tried to express in terms of 'religious civil society', where the shaping of social values under a religious paradigm and the adherence to religious norms come from individual citizens and not from the state. The use of the concept of civil society by Islamists (such as Soroush, Khatami, Ghannouchi and the Refah Partisi) leads to the delinking of religion and state politics.

The failure of Islamism does not necessarily mean a decrease in religious observance (even if Iranian youths are shunning mosque attendance) or a surge of reformist Islam versus an Islamism turned conservative. It could, as is evident in Iran with thinkers

---

41. See Chapter 2 of Farhad Khosrokhavar, *Les nouveaux martyrs d'Allah*, Paris: Flammarion, 2002.

like Soroush and Shabestari, lead to theological reformation. But it could also work in favour of some sort of neofundamentalism. The main trend, at least in the short term, is more a 'privatisation' of re-Islamisation combined with more rigid state control of religious institutions. This combination led to the expansion of what I have called neofundamentalism.

CONSERVATIVE RE-ISLAMISATION

Parallel to the growing Islamist political contest of the 1970s and 1980s, a process of conservative Islamisation has been pervasive among Muslim societies, which means, among other things, more veiled women in the streets and more *sharia* in state law. As well as being a social phenomenon, this Islamisation is a consequence of deliberate state policy. Confronted with the Islamist opposition during the 1980s, many Muslim states, even when officially secular, endeavoured to promote a brand of conservative Islam and to organise an 'official Islam'. The first part of the program was quite successful, but state control has never been effective, and the consequence has been a political radicalisation of conservative clerics in, for instance, Saudi Arabia and Pakistan.

In Pakistan a *sharia* bill was introduced into parliament on several occasions after General Zia's coup in 1977, with the ultimate aim of making *sharia* the sole law of the state. The bill was never passed, and only in 1993 did the government of Nawaz Sharif finally enact a *sharia* bill into law. In Algeria the family law of 1984 reintroduced some *sharia* elements; the policy of Arabisation accompanied a *de facto* Islamisation of education (many teachers were Egyptian Muslim Brothers). In Turkey religious teaching in schools was made compulsory in 1983. This last example is notable for its influence on Islamisation. To train teachers the government extended the number of Imam Hatip secondary schools, where religious teaching was added to the normal curriculum. Prime Minister Özal gave graduates of these schools the right of access to the universities; they were also allowed to apply for any civil service positions (the armed forces being excluded). Thus a segment of the Turkish civil service became more religious-minded. Another unexpected consequence was that the Alevis (a minority from an esoteric Shia creed), who used to identify themselves with secularism, were suddenly obliged, when bringing their children to school, either to declare themselves

Sunni Muslims or to stress a specific Alevi identity (whether it be religious or ethnic is a different matter).

In Egypt the number of teaching institutes dependent on Al-Azhar University increased from 1,855 in 1986–7 to 4,314 in 1995–6.[42] In Pakistan official figures from the Ministry of Interior show that the number of registered *madrasas* in Punjab Province doubled in ten years (1985–95).The total number of registered *madrasas* in Pakistan went from 137 in 1947 to 3,906 in 1995.[43] Private networks of Islamic schools compensated for a deficient state educational system, and were also helped by Saudi or Gulf money. In Mali *madrasas* account for approximately one quarter of the children in primary school.[44]

These networks of *madrasas* created generations of 'fellows' who retain close links, irrespective of their nationalities – this is one of the bases of Taliban power in Afghanistan. In Algeria 'Arabisation' has sent to the labour market tens of thousands of young people with lower qualifications than the French-speaking graduates but with as many expectations. In Morocco, at the end of the 1990s, more doctorates were written in religious sciences than in social sciences and literature; in Saudi Arabia the absolute majority of doctorates were in religious sciences. Religious diplomas tend to be shaped along the lines of modern diplomas in form, but not in content (master's degrees and doctorates).

In all these countries the impact of the growth of a network of religious schools is the same. Graduates holding a degree in religious science are now entering the labour market and tend, of course, to advocate the Islamisation of education and law in order to improve their job prospects.

The scope of employment for graduates of religious *madrasas* has increased if we compare it with the dominant trend since the

42. *Al-Ahram Hebdo* (English–language Cairo weekly), 3–9 April 1996. On the development of religious schools in Egypt, see Linda Herrera, 'Song without Music: Islamism and Education: A Case from Egypt', *Revue des mondes musulmans et de la Méditerranée*, 85–6 (1999), pp. 149–59.
43. International Crisis Group, *Pakistan: Madrasas, Extremism and the Military*, Asia Report 36, 29 July 2002 (<http://www.crisisweb.org/home/index.cfm?id=1627&l=1>).
44. Louis Brenner (ed.), *Muslim Identity and Social Change in Sub-Saharan Africa*, London: Hurst, 1993, p. 67. For other examples in Nigeria and Ivory Coast, see pp. 102, 179 and 198 in the same volume.

second half of the nineteenth century. In the classical period (before the nineteenth century), graduating from a religious school
amounted to being recognised as 'learned' and entitled to positions
in the state bureaucracy, as in the Ottoman Empire. This possibility
almost disappeared in the course of modernisation, with the creation of secular government schools (*dar ol olum, dar ol fonun*) and
then secondary schools and universities. At a lower level *madrasa*
graduates were hired as local *mullahs* or *qadis* (judges), and usually
received their subsidies from local communities or, more precisely, local landlords, rich men, notables and aristocrats, thus making
them subservient to the 'secular' local élite. But at the end of the
twentieth century there was a renewed increased in the numbers of
professional *mullahs* with more autonomy from traditional notables,
because they relied on the state, controlled the state, or were able to
raise funds in an independent manner. Many Gulf and Saudi businessmen, and sometimes ordinary shopkeepers, directly subsidise
religious teaching networks, without even knowing exactly where
the money goes.

In Iran a category of state *mullahs* appeared after the Islamic
revolution. The state reduced the financial autonomy of the clergy,
but also empowered a section of it. Before the Taliban local *mullahs* in Afghanistan were dependent on the local community and
notables; they were often paid, as was the barber, a set amount of
wheat, oil and sugar every year in exchanges of 'religious commodities'.[45] But the Taliban movement, even before seizing power
in 1996, was directly able to collect the *zakat* (religious taxes). In
Turkey during the administration of Turgut Özal and in Pakistan,
graduates from religious schools could qualify as civil servants by
joining a university.

Islamisation does provide jobs: in teaching and as *zakat* collec-
tors and religious police ('prohibiting evil, encouraging good'). The
struggle for Islamisation in countries like Pakistan, Iran, Algeria and
Egypt is also competition within the labour market.

Of course the states pushed (and are pushing) for more control
over the religious establishment. In Turkey the Diyanet İşleri
Başkanlığı (Directorate of Religious Affairs, which is directly sub-
ordinate to the Prime Minister) monopolised the appointments of

45. Personal observation during my fieldwork in Afghanistan (1980–5), with a
    specific trip to the *madrasa* of Anardarrah, Farah province, in October 1982.

imams to mosques. In 1998 it was given the exclusive right to pen the sermons to be delivered from the *minbars*. In Kuwait a High Council for Islamic Affairs was established in 1996. In the same year the Egyptian government tried to add an extra 5,000 mosques to the 25,000 already controlled by the state. Almost everywhere (except in Pakistan) there exists either an official *mufti* or a state council of religious affairs in order to place the highest religious authority of the country under political control. In Iran the Guide appoints the 'Friday *imams*' in charge of delivering sermons. The newly independent Muslim states of Central Asia and the Caucasus have all confirmed or appointed a '*mufti* of the republic'. Even in Europe states push for some sort of 'official Islam' (for example, the Conseil Français du Culte Musulman).

Pakistan is certainly the country where the state has least control over religious schools and institutions, and where there has been the greatest increase in the number of *madrasas*. Nevertheless, President Musharraf on 19 August 2001 promulgated an ordinance for the establishment of model Deeni Madaris (religious seminaries) through integration of the Islamic education system with the general public education system. The government decided, under the new legislation – the Madrasah Education (Establishment and Affiliation of Model Deeni Madaris) Board Ordinance, 2001 – to establish an educational board and academic council to affiliate the Deeni Madaris and Darul Uloom (also a type of religious seminaries) to the existing educational boards. But given the balance of power between the state and religious militants, such a move is unlikely to impose any curb on the autonomy of the *madrasas*.

Nevertheless, it has been impossible to build an 'official Islam' from scratch. All the states endeavoured to coopt traditional *ulama*, who would bargain political support (or at least neutrality) in exchange for conservative Islamisation (more *sharia* in the law, and religious censorship). In a short time this Islamisation process went beyond state control. Until 1997 in Egypt, for example, the government had to accept decisions taken by Al-Azhar University or by courts judging solely along the lines of the *sharia*. In Pakistan, local *madrasas* encouraged their students to enlist in the Afghan Taliban army. In Egypt and in Pakistan individual plaintiffs went to court to sue *sharia* offenders, even if they were not personally involved in the case. A man named Semeida Abdul Samad won such a suit in an Egyptian civil court in 1996 to cancel the marriage of a university professor, Nasr Abu Zaid, arguing that the professor's writings showed that he was no longer a Muslim and therefore he should not be married to a Muslim woman. This Islamisation of social life also reached the Egyptian business milieu, with the establishment of Islamic banking institutions in Egypt. One of the more conspicuous developments is the comeback of the *hijab* among modern and educated women. Everywhere from Tehran to Cairo fashion boutiques now offer a wide selection of stylish *hijabs* and Islamic garments, called *tessetür* in Turkey.

Interestingly, this shift towards a conservative, moralist and legalist view of Islam has a dual effect on Islamist parties. On the one hand, it enlarges their electoral constituency to encompass more traditional milieus, bolstering, for example, the Refah Partisi from 13 to 21 per cent in the 1995 Turkish parliamentary elections. On the other hand, the shift deprives the parties of their monopoly on the political use of Islam. In some places mainstream movements have been outflanked by more radical splinter groups – Gama'at Islamiya alongside the Muslim Brotherhood in Egypt, the GIA against the FIS in Algeria. Violent outbursts by such groups accompany state repression and conservative re-Islamisation. Although they advocate *jihad* and armed struggle against all existing regimes and even against their own society, which they accuse of having forgotten Islam, these groups have only one agenda: the *sharia*. They have given up the complex and more modern program of the Islamists. In countries where they are not opposed by the state, they turn their violence against what they see as un-Islamic people, like Shias in Pakistan (and, to a lesser extent, Christians).

Some governments realised quickly that Islamisation was spinning out of control. The electoral success of the Refah Partisi was, among other things, a consequence of the rehabilitation of Islam in public life, promoted by the then Prime Minister Turgut Özal. The sudden appearance of the FIS in Algeria was also a consequence of the policies of Arabisation and Islamisation implemented by the FLN State. If all governments encouraged re-Islamisation in the 1980s, the next decade saw a contrast between states that returned to authoritarian secularism (such as Turkey, Algeria and Tunisia) and others that tried to 'ride the tiger' (such as Pakistan and Saudi Arabia). Meanwhile, Iran grew increasingly divided between liberals and conservatives. The backlash of conservative Islamisation led to a renewal of authoritarian state secularism. In Turkey the army ousted Necmettin Erbakan from his position as Prime Minister in 1997 and banned his Refah Partisi six months later; many Imam Hatip schools were closed, and the ban on *hijab*s and beards in schools and universities was enforced. In Egypt a more liberal dean of Al-Azhar University, Mohammed Sayed Tantawi, was appointed after the death of the very conservative al Gad al Haq in 1996; private legal suits in the name of *hisba* (that is, in the name of *sharia* by persons not personally concerned) were forbidden. In Algeria and Tunisia the Islamists were not only banned, but also gaoled and often tortured.

POST–ISLAMISM: THE PRIVATISATION OF RELIGION

Post-Islamism means the privatisation of re-Islamisation. Many conservative Muslims (in Egypt or in Pakistan, for instance) challenge the prerogative of the state to make laws and to prosecute. They go directly to the (state) courts in the name of the *sharia* (an act called *hisba*). Taking the opportunity presented by economic liberalisation (launched in Egypt under the name *infitah*, and by Turgut Özal in Turkey), many Muslim businessmen invested in the Islamo-business market (*tessetür* fashion clothing in Turkey, Islamic banking and saving institutions, charities, NGOs, private schooling system). In Turkey a dynamic union of small private enterprises, MÜSIAD (M stood for 'Muslim' but was changed to *Müstakil*, 'independent', to avoid prosecution) challenged the TÜSIAD, which represents secular and pro-European big business. Renouncing the statist and vaguely leftist approach of the Islamists where the welfare state and nationalisation are concerned, the new 'Islamic' businessmen openly advocate the free market, and see personal wealth as a blessing from God, to the extent that the money has been made along halal lines or has been purified through *zakat* and alimony. In this sense the growing development of Islamic NGOs and charities has more to do with the development of religious-minded middle-class entrepreneurs than with the call for *jihad*. As we shall see, present forms of re-Islamisation are often linked with the westernisation of Islam.

Conservative in faith and beliefs, but modern in terms of business, a middle class of Islamic puritans with a Weberian work ethic can be seen to be emerging. Many made money by working in the Gulf or abroad, and are eager to invest in order to benefit from the opening of domestic markets (in Egypt, Turkey, Tunisia, Iran and Morocco) or are expecting such an opening (in Syria and Algeria). They push for the abolition of state monopoly. This neo-bourgeoisie adheres to traditional values and is eager to perpetuate them in a modern environment – hence their obsession with education (opposing coeducation) and moral censorship (because of the omnipresence of television, films and advertising). They listen to preachers who insist on spiritual reformation, but do not challenge the present political order.[46]

In a very different context the Taliban embodied just such a neofundamentalist approach to the state and economy. They did not endeavour to build a strong central state, but engaged on the contrary in a policy of deconstructing the state. They fired half of the civil servants (and not only women). The most subsidised ministry, after defence, was that of religious police. The Taliban did not even bother to build a network of *madrasas*. Mullah Omar attended not one cabinet meeting, nor did he receive a non-Muslim ambassador. The Taliban let the free market work and interfered hardly at all with the economy except by collecting *zakat*. They did not oppose smuggling, thus losing the state taxes and customs revenues. Nor did they care about social or economic issues. This could explain why they were seen by many Muslim businessmen as a good compromise between *sharia* and modernity. (Osama Bin Laden's background is linked with this milieu.) Imposing *sharia* also meant giving up state legislation, except through occasional *fatwas* from Mullah Omar. The Taliban banned opium cultivation for religious reasons, but did not encourage crop substitution. Their main field of action (other than fighting against the Northern Alliance) was to ban women from any sort of public appearance and to fight against any form of entertainment that could allow people to stray from strict religious practices.

Neofundamentalism goes along with a belittling and deliberate diminution of the state: it is not the source of legislation, it does not frame the social fabric or the economic strategy, and it should work only as a censorship institution, through religious police. Neofundamentalists want to impose the supremacy of *sharia* (for example, by writing it into the constitution). They want to be entitled to bring a suit to court for any *sharia*-related matters, without

46. Preachers like Amr Khalid in Egypt and Fethullah Gülen in Turkey.

going through state prosecutors, and to take justice into their own hands in cases of transgression. This means depriving the state of its traditional prerogative: making law and having the monopoly on legitimate violence.

Post-Islamist Islamisation is vested in multiple practices and strategies that have nothing to do with the project of reconstructing society from the state and through an all-encompassing Islamic ideology. Contemporary re-Islamisation is a cluster of individual practices that are used as means of finding jobs, money, respect and self-esteem, and bargaining with a marginalised state that has played on conservative re-Islamisation but been unable to control it. The reference to Islam is everywhere and nowhere; it is diluted, pragmatically put forward for any purpose, ostensibly expressed in dress and speech, and instrumentalised in courts. In this sense neo-fundamentalist re-Islamisation has nothing to do with state power and could not be labelled 'totalitarian'. It is, of course, not a factor of democratisation, but contributes to the weakening of the state. The aim is to reconstruct a true Muslim community by starting from the individual. It is based on an individual reappropriation of Islamic symbols, arguments, rhetoric and norms.

Islamism is squeezed into this strange *pas de deux* between individuals and always authoritarian, often secular states, where each hopes to instrumentalise the other, as shown in the cases of Pakistan, Saudi Arabia and even Egypt, where the repression of militant Islam went along with complacency towards the offensive led by some lay Islamic militants against secular thinkers. In this odd association, the winner is not yet known, but the case of Pakistan and the pressure on Saudi Arabia show that this policy cannot continue in the long term. Nowadays radicalisation and re-Islamisation are waged under the banner of neofundamentalism, which is a consequence of the crisis of the state in Muslim countries, but also of the deterritorialisation of Islam, largely under the impact of its passage to the West.

3

MUSLIMS IN THE WEST

The vast majority of the Muslim population in the West consists of recent migrants. Patterns of migration nevertheless differ quite widely between the United States and Western Europe. In Europe Muslims predominate among economic migrants, but in the United States they are outnumbered by Hispanics and Asians. The first generation of European Muslims were mostly working class, while those in the United States were more often from the educated middle class. US Muslims have higher than average incomes. They tend to live in more or less 'ethnic' neighbourhoods in Europe, but in the United States are more scattered. In Europe most Muslims come from specific areas with historical ties to the host country (for example, North Africa for France), while the United States has no colonial past with any Muslim country.

Mass migration to Western Europe began in the late 1950s, reached its peak around 1970, and never ceased, despite more restrictive legislation introduced after 1973 and regularly tightened since then. For historical and geographical reasons most immigrants were Muslims: North and sub-Sahelian Africans for France and Belgium, South Asians for Britain, and Turks for Germany, the Netherlands and German-speaking Switzerland, even if the real picture was more complex. For example, Turks also went to eastern France and Flemish Belgium, and Moroccans to Belgium and the Netherlands. Spain and Italy were not principal migrant destinations before the mid-1990s. At first immigration involved mainly male industrial workers who intended to, and were supposed to, return to their homelands before retiring. No plans were put in place to deal with a long-term Muslim presence in Europe. Around 1973, as a result of the oil crisis and the subsequent economic slowdown, most European countries decided to put an end to such immigration. Fearing they would be permanently banned from Europe if they returned to their countries of origin, most workers decided to stay and bring their families, benefiting from a policy of 'family reunion' that was initiated to smooth the human consequences of the immigration ban.

Millions of second-generation Muslims have since been born in Europe. In some countries (such as France) they were entitled to almost automatic citizenship at their majority (eighteen years of age), while in others (Germany, Denmark and Switzerland) they had to go through a specific and complex process of naturalisation. From the 1990s onwards, however, there was a growing convergence within the European Union to grant the second generation citizenship on the basis of the principle of *jus soli* (through place of birth), including in Germany (where the stumbling block is dual citizenship and not *jus sanguinis*, the principle that a person's nationality at birth is the same as that of his or her parents). Whatever the status of these immigrants, a clear generation gap divides the second generation, born and educated in Europe, from the first, in terms not only of culture and language but also of social expectations.

There are no precise figures for the number of Muslims living in the United States or in Europe, for two reasons: first, the difficulty of defining who should be considered a Muslim, and second, the reluctance of European legal systems to register race and religion in census and identity papers.[1] The criterion of country of origin is no longer relevant as a means of determining the number of Muslims because most of them, at least in France and Britain, have a European citizenship. The statistics usually quoted in Europe vary from 8 million to 12 million,[2] which is about 2.5 per cent of the European Union population; but the visibility of the Muslim population is higher than the figures may indicate, because Muslims are concentrated in urban areas (10 per cent of the population of Berlin and Bradford, for example). Muslim populations will increase inexorably because the present generation of Muslims is younger than that of non-Muslims, even if its fertility rate is beginning to

1. In 2002 Greece, at the request of the European Union, had to give up mentioning religion on identity cards, while any mention of race and religion is forbidden in the French census.
2. See Felice Dassetto, *La construction de l'Islam européen. Approche socio-anthropologique*, Paris: L'Harmattan, 1996.

decline towards the average. France has the highest Muslim population in Europe as a percentage of population and as an absolute
number. As we shall see, the introduction of religious or ethnic
identities in censuses will not necessarily help very much because
of the transient and uncertain nature of these identities. Should
we register a French citizen born of Algerian parents as 'Algerian'
(a political denomination), '*Maghrébin*' (a geographical reference),
'Arab' (an ethnic classification) or 'Muslim' (a member of a religious
community)? Should the term Muslim refer only to a self-declared
believer or to anybody with a familial background linked with a
Muslim society? What about children born of mixed marriages
(which are rather numerous in France)? Are there atheist Muslims?
Symmetry with other faiths does not help: one can countenance
the thought of an atheist Jew, but scarcely the idea of an atheist
Southern Baptist. As the practise of religion declines in Europe,
traditional symmetries cease to work (Christianity versus Islam)
and new ones are built (entailing a mirror ethnicisation of French
or English identity, by referring to '*Gaulois*' or 'Englishness').

Muslims are no longer foreigners. But this integration was
achieved neither through assimilation, as was often hoped by the
host countries, nor through the making of a multicultural society,
as it is often described (that is, the juxtaposition of different corporate cultures). It was achieved through the recasting of pristine
identities into new variable sets of identity patterns, which evade
any attempt to 'substantialise' them. Identities are less a given fact
than an individual choice, and can change over time or in relation
to social circumstances, and overlap with other identities.[3] In the
past twenty years the Western public and authorities realised that
Islam had become a permanent feature of their societies, and this
prompted a reassessment of European national identities, already

3.   US laws changed during the twentieth century from an 'objective' definition
     of ethnicity (skin colour) to a personal choice, which through the famous
     'hyphenation' can combine many sort of different identities. In France, for
     example, the term 'French Muslim' (*français musulman*) referred, from 1962
     until the 1980s, exclusively to the *harkis* (Muslim auxiliaries with the French
     army in Algeria, who were taken 'back' to France after the independence of
     Algeria). In the 1990s, without any official change of terminology, it sim-
     ply came to mean a Muslim French citizen, thus including children of Al-
     gerian *mujahedin*. On US legislation and Muslims, see Kathleen M. Moore,
     *Al-Mughtaribun: American Law and the Transformation of Muslim Life in the Unit-
     ed States*, Albany: State University of New York Press, 1995.

shaken by the development of the European Union. Conversely US identity has always taken immigration into account. But the space, status and definition to be bestowed upon the Muslim population are defined according to national traditions and legal systems: easy access to political citizenship in France, combined with a refusal to take into account ethnic or religious identities; quasi-equivalence in Germany, Denmark and Austria between ethnicity and citizenship (*jus sanguinis*); official multiculturalism in Britain and the Netherlands; and so on. There is a mirror effect in the reciprocal reshaping of different pristine cultures (the Western host culture and the Oriental immigrant culture) according to the dominant paradigms of the Western host country. But while there is no coordination within the European Union concerning citizenship, integration, status of religion, and ethnicity, there is a *de facto* convergence to a 'middle way'. The Netherlands has given up its most salient regulations on legally enforced multiculturalism (like the compulsory teaching of the language of origin for the children of migrants), Germany is slowly easing its laws on citizenship, and *laïque* (secular) France has officially recognised a French Council of Muslim Faith (CFCM).

Although concentrations of Muslims in Europe are based on a mutual relationship between a specific European country and corresponding geographical area (France–North Africa, Germany–Turkey, Britain–Indian subcontinent), the transnational nature of the Muslim population in Europe plays a role in the process of European integration. Many Muslim organisations see in the construction of the European Union an opportunity to bypass their own ethnic and national cleavages and to create something closer to what an *ummah* should be.[4] Immigration has been the demographic cradle of Western Islam, but is less and less relevant to an explanation of the interaction between the West and Islam.

Islam in the West has been systematically researched through the lenses of sociology of immigration and ethnic studies. Such an approach was legitimate in terms of history, but ignores the growing discrepancy between the forms taken by Islam in the West and in the cultures of origin. It tends to underestimate conversions and

4. For instance, a central Muslim organisation at the European level – the Muslim Coordination Council in Europe – has been formed, located in Strasbourg, with Dr Abdellah Boussouf as coordinator.

westernisation of religiosity, and to ignore the growing delinking of faith and pristine cultures, as well as the changing nature of
immigration or, more exactly, migrations. Besides economic immigration, where a given population migrates permanently from
one country to another, new forms of migration and mobility are
emerging that can be described quite simply using the now familiar term globalisation. Apart from resettled migrants, a floating and
mobile population, usually educated, has become globalised and
plays a growing role in the affirmation of a deterritorialised Muslim community. This phenomenon is, of course, not limited to
Muslims.[5] Highly qualified professionals (such as computer experts
and doctors) and scholars are going from position to position according to market opportunities and political circumstances: an
Egyptian-born Muslim Brother may teach in Kuala Lumpur, then
in Tampa or Berlin. Many Middle Eastern students who graduate
in the West never return home. The same happens with political
refugees. An uprooted, deterritorialised and cosmopolitan intelligentsia, sharing a common language (English or, less often, modern literary Arabic), plays a role in producing values, teachings and
world views adapted to globalisation. Even if they differ in their
religious or political commitments, and in their assessment of or
compliance with 'Western values', they circulate in a deterritorialised academic space, shaped by a common curriculum (masters,
doctorates), whatever the country and their specialities. Even if
there is still a 'national' academic production (local authors writing
for a local audience in a national language), it refers to global issues,
topics and discussions: Samuel Huntington is debated everywhere.

This homogenisation of the academic space (usually within the
US and British educational systems, which are far more flexible
than Continental European ones where tenure is bestowed more
systematically to junior faculty) also touches the Islamic educational system. As we shall see, 'local' Islams are giving way to global
Salafism in many Islamic teaching institutions. Countries like Malaysia and Saudi Arabia play an important role in providing temporary positions to non-citizen Muslim scholars. Academe is no
longer related to citizenship. This transnational dimension should
not be thought of in terms of diaspora, because there is less and less

5.   *Intellectuels en diaspora et théories nomades*, special issue of *L'Homme* (edited by
     Jackie Assayag and Véronique Bénéï), 156 (2000).

reference to a country of origin, while patterns of integration do not follow the older patterns of integration or assimilation. New identities are cast in either hyphenated expressions or reconstructed identities ('Arab', 'Arab-American', 'Middle Easterner', 'Asian', and so on). Regional, ethnic or religious identities take precedence over citizenship and pristine nationalities, according to choices made by the individual (an Iraqi Kurd in exile can decide whether he is first an Iraqi, a Kurd or a Muslim). Deterritorialisation also has an impact on the production of the Muslim discourse. First, resettled or uprooted Muslims are more prone to reassess what Islam means for them, either to reconstruct a Muslim identity or to answer questions (and pressures) from the non-Muslim environment. Second, Muslims in the West often enjoy a greater freedom of speech than in Muslim countries, where authoritarian regimes and the religious establishment strive to deter intellectual dissent.

The emergence of transnational identities is also a paradoxical consequence of legal restrictions on citizenship in most Middle Eastern countries, in contrast with the West. At the time of their transformation into modern nation-states, most Middle Eastern countries considered all Ottoman subjects as citizens. (In Egypt, Christians had to give up the protection bestowed by Western powers.) But nowadays in Iran, Egypt, Saudi Arabia and Kuwait citizenship is bestowed only through patrilineal descent. This contributes to an increase in the number of stateless and uprooted persons among refugees displaced by war (for example, Palestinians who fled in 1948 and 1967, or Afghans), unrecognised minorities (in Syria and Kuwait, hundreds of thousands of permanent inhabitants are deliberately deprived of identity cards by the state: the *Makhtumi*, or 'unregistered', who are Kurds in Syria, and the *Bidun*, or 'without [papers]', who are Arabs in Kuwait), or migrant workers, who sometimes outnumber nationals in the Gulf states. Children born to a female citizen and a male foreigner cannot request citizenship of the country in which they have been born and brought up. In Iran the marriage of an Iranian woman and an Afghan man, even if both are Persian-speaking Shias, is considered illegal unless it has been authorised by a special decision from the Cabinet of Ministers. A child born in Kuwait to a Palestinian father and a Kuwaiti mother has no citizenship. Given that millions of Muslim immigrants or refugees are living and working in the Gulf states, Lebanon, Iran and Syria, the floating population is increasing. As we shall see in Chapter 7, many Al Qaeda members fit this pattern, such as Ramzi Ahmad Yousef, one of those implicated in the 1993 bombing of the World Trade Center, who was born in Kuwait to a Pakistani Baluchi father and a Palestinian mother.

Transnationalism is also a characteristic of many networks, like neo-Sufi brotherhoods, the Muslim Brotherhood and Al Qaeda, which cannot be understood in purely Middle Eastern terms. As we have seen, many Muslim Brothers, whatever their citizenship, staff international Islamic organisations and NGOs (such as the Muslim League, or Rabita al-Alam al-Islami) or play a role in establishing Islamic organisations in the West, as did Faysal Mawlawi, the present leader of the Lebanese Jamaat al-Islamiyya, with the Union of Islamic Organisations in France (UOIF). Tablighi Jama'at, based in India and Pakistan, is sending teams of preachers, deliberately chosen from different nationalities, to countries whose language they sometimes even ignore. Muslim communities in Europe enrol professional *imams* from all over the Muslim world, due to a dearth of locally trained preachers. Finally, the openness of Britain's legal system towards political asylum and freedom of speech has turned London (nicknamed Londonistan by French antiterrorist police officers, who resented the lack of cooperation from Britain in the extradition of Rashid Ramdan, a key figure in the 1995 terrorist bombings in Paris) into a sort of international hub for Islamic activists, who live in a fully transnational milieu, united by reference to the *ummah* and the use of English and Arabic.[6] National origin does not matter, even if it is sometimes reflected in the nicknames, or *laqab* (for example, Sheikh Abu Hamza 'al-Masri', or 'the Egyptian', the former head of the Finsbury Park mosque in north London).

The sociological and economic dimensions of many of these networks have been studied closely.[7] What interests us is the sort of imaginary space created by deterritorialisation and transnationalism.

6.   See Dominique Thomas, *Le Londonistan. La voix du djihad*, Paris: Michalon, 2002.
7.   Ariel Colonomos, *Sociologie des réseaux transnationaux*, Paris: L'Harmattan, 1995; Alain Tarrius (with Lamia Missaoui), *Arabes de France dans l'économie mondiale souterraine*, Paris: L'Aube, 1995; Dale Eickelman and James Piscatori, *Muslim Travellers: Pilgrimage, Migration and the Religious Imagination*, Berkeley: University of California Press, 1990; Susanne Hoeber Rudolph and James Piscatori, *Transnational Religion and Fading States*, Boulder, CO: Westview Press, 1997.

What does this imply in terms of personal religiosity, a sense of belonging to a community, its impact on the surrounding society, or more precisely the mutual recasting of identity between the non-Muslim dominant society and a Muslim faith community that no longer lives in a pervasively Muslim cultural environment? What is the 'reality effect' of imaginary constructions? What role, if any, does the imaginary space play in the formulation of Islam as a mere religion, as a set of cultural patterns defining a neo-ethnic identity, or as an all-encompassing ideology seeking an imaginary space beyond a lost territory?

HOW TO LIVE AS A STATELESS MUSLIM MINORITY

When studying a 'new' phenomenon, one often has to subject its 'newness' to careful analysis. There have been Muslim minorities in the past, and a kind of globalisation might have characterised certain other historical periods. The presence of huge Muslim minorities living under non-Muslim rule has been an established fact for centuries. The first case was probably that of Muslims in Sicily in the twelfth century, who were allowed to remain under Christian rule by a *fatwa* of Sheikh al Mazari. Then came the Mudejares in Spain after the *Reconquista* (fifteenth to sixteenth centuries), the Russian Tatars after the fall of Kazan (1552), followed by the Ottoman Muslims, conquered by Russians and Austrians (seventeenth to nineteenth centuries). For instance, Rashid Rida issued a *fatwa* in 1909 allowing the Muslims of Bosnia-Herzegovina to remain there after the Austro-Hungarian conquest.[8] They all accepted Christian rule, although this did not prevent them from being occasionally forcibly converted or expelled, as were the Moriscos from Spain in 1610. Conversely Islam has been officially recognised by Russia since 1784, and by the then Austro-Hungarian empire through the 1874 and 1912 laws, which remain valid in present-day Austria.[9] But the minority status of these Muslims resulted from forced military conquest and was not a voluntary decision.

8.   Khaled Abou El Fadl, 'Striking a Balance: Islamic Legal Discourse on Muslim Minorities' in Yvonne Yazbeck Haddad and John Esposito (eds), *Muslims on the Americanization Path?* Atlanta, GA: Scholars Press, 1998, p. 64.
9.   In 1997 the Russian parliament approved a law stating that Orthodoxy, Judaism, Islam and Buddhism are 'national', recognised religions, implicitly meaning that Protestantism and Catholicism are defined as foreign religions.

Nevertheless there are also many cases of Muslims living from the outset as minorities, due to conversions and trade relations, as in Black Africa or China (the Hui). Finally, the bulk of Indian Muslims remained in India after the 1947 Partition and have always been loyal to the secular Indian republic. This example alone shows how Islam can be compatible with a minority status.

The novelty of Muslim minority status is therefore not on account of that status *per se*, but of the relationships between religion and culture. Many of the minorities mentioned here could be associated with a given culture and language, and sometimes with a territory (for example, the Tatars in Russia), even if they share language and culture with their non-Muslims neighbours (as the Bosnians do, of course, but also Indian Muslims – if Urdu can be considered the 'Muslim' form of Hindi, most Muslims in the Indian subcontinent speak the same vernacular as their non-Muslim neighbours). In this sense Muslims have already experienced a disconnection between religion and culture: the marker of their identity can be a purely religious one within a centuries-old shared cultural and linguistic environment. In any case Islam was rooted in a given culture, whether specific to Muslims (such as Tatars) or shared with others (such as the Hui, or Indian, Yugoslav and African Muslims). What is new in the current wave of globalisation is that the making of Muslim minorities is carried out through a process of deculturation, in which none of the previous cultural markers is retained.[10] The disembodiment of religion from culture may run counter to centuries of practical experience, yet Muslim theologians have been adamant that Islam as a religion should not be identified with a specific culture (the language of the uncreated Koran[11] is thus seen as not being the language of a specific Arab

10. Tatars and Kazakhs in Russia were submitted to a heavy process of Russianisation, but if the bulk of the Kazakhs shifted to speaking the Russian language, they retained the idea of belonging to a specific 'ethnic' group, and the revival of language and literature remained a not-so-utopian ideal. By contrast, Muslims in the West are increasingly 'de-ethnicised' through either voluntary shifts of identity, or mixing with other Muslims with whom they share the language of their non-Muslim common milieu.
11. There is a school of thought in Islam according to which the Koran was not created during the Revelation, but was kept as it was from the creation of the world, the consequence being that its language (Arabic) is not related to a specific land and culture.

society). But this stance was more a methodological approach than a real social experience.

Muslims throughout history have experienced forms of globalisation, through travel, pilgrimage or the widespread role of Arabic and of a common teaching curriculum. A 'community of the learned' existed transcending all linguistic and ethnic divides, using Arabic as its lingua franca, and travelling from Morocco to India to learn and teach in a network of comparable and homogeneous institutions (akin to medieval European clerks, using Latin and travelling from universities to monasteries). This premodern globalisation was effectively connected with the attempt to revive, through the medium of Arabic, a common Muslim culture, although it was an élite phenomenon. The Muslim 'community of the learned' no longer circulates in a purely Arabo–Muslim context, and English is as important as Arabic, if not more so, outside the Arabic-speaking world, which comprises only 20 per cent of all Muslims. In short, the earlier form of globalisation did not borrow its linguistic and technical tools from another culture, as is the case nowadays. Contemporary globalisation is not an élite phenomenon but a mass one, and it has a backlash at the core of the countries of origin, while traditional society was left unchanged by medieval globalisation. Contemporary Muslim minorities have to undergo a process of deculturation that has no precedent in history and is not imposed but is the consequence of voluntary displacement and shifts from pristine cultures to a common, uprooted Muslim identity.

The growing 'deterritorialisation' of Islam nevertheless entails a reflection on what it means to be a Muslim living in a minority. It is often argued that because Islam is an all-encompassing religion that addresses all aspects of individual and social life – from law to politics, from diet to socialisation – it is impossible for true believers to live permanently under non-Muslim rule: they should leave or, more precisely, migrate (*hijra*) to a Muslim land, the Dar-ul-Islam. This premise fuels the debate on the compatibility of Islam with Western values and on its ability to accommodate democracy and secularisation. Such a debate raises two issues. Is there a dominant theoretical paradigm that applies to the case? And even there is, can the practices and choices of today's Muslims really be shaped by a theological paradigm? In a word, to what extent is the question 'What does Islam or the *ulama* say about …?' relevant to an explanation of the practices of Muslims? Here again we touch on the issue of the accuracy and relevance of cultural and religious paradigms in explaining societal and political issues. According to Bernard Lewis, most *ulama* considered it impermissible for Muslims to live as a non-ruling minority.[12] Khaled Abou El Fadl, who graduated from the Near East Studies Center at Princeton, where Lewis taught for decades, disagrees, and shows how much more complex and opportunist were the answers given by *ulama*.[13] Most of them ruled according to specific historical cases and to social conditions, even if they agreed that no more than one condition absolutely had to be fulfilled: Muslims should be able to worship (*ibadat*), but not necessarily to follow the *sharia* (abstaining from *riba*, or interest). In short, the conditions settled on by most *ulama* for allowing Muslims to remain under non-Muslim rule correspond to what the West calls religious freedom.

As is so often the case, the impact of such theoretical and legal discussions on current practices is overemphasised by Western orientalists and contemporary Muslim fundamentalists. 'Real' Muslims act and live without waiting eagerly for the *ulama's* point of view. The idea that Muslims are reluctant to live as a minority is contradicted by facts. As we have seen, they have lived for centuries as minorities under non-Muslim rule. To believe that 'real' Muslims expect *fatwa* and theological decisions before making decisions relies on the usual overestimation of the impact on societies of religion in general and Islam in particular. Nevertheless, paradigms play a role in shaping not the social comportment but the *post hoc* discourse of legitimisation, particularly when the chosen attitude is challenged by critics, usually neofundamentalists calling for *hijra* or *jihad*, or by Western experts who always argue that a Muslim cannot be explained (much less understood) except through the lenses of *sharia* and Middle Eastern history. The mirror effect between fundamentalist *ulama* and Western orientalists does nothing to help open the debate. We shall focus here on paradigms of Muslims in a minority, not because they explain what is happening today, but because they may be reactivated by fundamentalists, militants, orientalists or liberal Muslims who must bow to the pressure of 'culturalism' and speak the language of religious representation and

12. Bernard Lewis and Dominique Schnapper (eds), *Muslims in Europe* (Social Change in Western Europe), London: Pinter, 1994.
13. Abou El Fadl, 'Striking a Balance'.

historical parallels to pass on their message. Paradigms do not explain what people do; they shape the way in which they express their situation, and particularly unhappiness about their situation.

HISTORICAL PARADIGMS OF MUSLIMS AS A MINORITY

We borrow the following categories from Mikel de Epalza, who studied the responses of the Mudejares of Spain to their new situation after the Christian *Reconquista* had been achieved in 1492.[14] They are useful in the sense that they provide a cluster of answers to a minority situation linked with historical conditions and theological interpretations.

Hijra, *or emigration*

Following the example of the Prophet, who left Mecca for Medina to avoid the rule of the pagans, *hijra* means a religiously motivated migration to a Muslim land from a territory that is no longer Muslim. Tens of thousands, if not hundreds of thousands, of Muslims left Andalusia for North Africa in the aftermath of the Christian conquest. The same phenomenon occurred regularly in Muslim history: northern Caucasians left Russian-occupied territories from 1873 onwards, for the Ottoman Empire; tens of thousands of Indian Muslims left India in 1921 to go to Afghanistan, and millions left for Pakistan after Partition; and millions of Afghans fled the Soviet invasion in 1980. The term *mohajir* (one who performed *hijra*) has positive religious connotations and is nowadays regularly advocated. The FIS 'emir' Belhaj called in 1990 for the return to their home country (Algeria) of North Africans living in France. In Britain a radical movement called al-Muhajiroun, headed by Omar Bakri Muhammad, calls for the emigration of all Muslims to a true Muslim land, while acknowledging that there is no true Muslim land – although for a while Taliban-ruled Afghanistan was one. The paradox is that a movement called the 'religious migrants' (Muhajiroun) operates from a non-Muslim country. The answer to this contradiction is simply to call for the conversion of the infidels.[15]

14. Mikel de Epalza *Jésus otage. Juifs, chrétiens et musulmans en Espagne (VIe-XVIIe siècles)*, Paris: Les Éditions du Cerf, 1987.
15. The program of this radical and sectarian movement includes the following paragraph: 'To bring the message of Islam to the unbelievers in the West, to

We touch here on the limitations of the *hijra* theory: What is a true Muslim land, in a time when many radical Muslims consider that all the regimes ruling Muslim countries are illegitimate?

The underlying issue is how to revive the traditional distinction between Dar-ul-Harb (the land of war) and Dar-ul-Islam (the land of Islam). If, as Abou El Fadl believes, the real issue is to what extent a Muslim can freely exercise his religious duties, then, as Tariq Ramadan, the grandson of Hassan al-Banna, states, there is more religious freedom for a Muslim in the West than in many 'Muslim' countries.[16] The entire religious geography of the Muslim world is subverted by the deterritorialisation of today's Muslim populations.

Jihad *to recover lost territories*

A *jihad* to recover lost lands was, according to Epalza,[17] a popular theme among Andalusians living in Morocco after 1492. It has recently been re-enacted by radical internationalist groups like Al Qaeda, which want to fight to recover lost or threatened territories: Bosnia, Chechnya, Afghanistan during the Soviet occupation, Kashmir and the southern Philippines. A line is thus drawn between those who consider *jihad* to be defensive (such as Abdullah Azzam, the precursor of Al Qaeda, did in the 1980s) and those who advocate a fight to the death against the West (Osama Bin Laden). The latter moved from the first to the second of these positions during the Gulf war. He expresses his fight as a total and global war against the Crusaders and the Jews. Offensive *jihad* is nowadays the dividing line between mainstream Islamists and radicals: Sheikh Qaradawi (an Egyptian Muslim Brother who holds a key position in the religious establishment of Qatar) endorses the Palestinian struggle (including suicide attacks) in the name of defensive *jihad*, while condemning the attacks on the World Trade

---

show them that this religion is both a doctrine and a way of life, which will allow them to understand Islam, to convert to Islam, or at least to accept it as a political regime.' (Mohamed Khaled Bayoun, 'Program of al-Muhajiroun', 1997.) See also *The Khilafah Will Dominate the World*, a booklet published in 2003 by al-Muhajiroun.

16. Tariq Ramadan, *Les musulmans dans la laïcité. Responsabilité et droits des musulmans dans les sociétés occidentales*, Lyon: Tawhid, 1994, p. 101.

17. Epalza, *Jésus otage*.

Center as simple murder of innocent civilians.[18] As we shall see, debates on the meaning and conditions of *sharia* pervade contemporary Islam.

Conversion to Christianity

Voluntary or forced, conversions were very important in sixteenth-century Spain. The topic remains a very sensitive one to this day and mass conversions are a thing of the past. But such events happened in Latin America with the Syrian–Lebanese immigration at the turn of the twentieth century (former Argentine President Carlos Menem is from a Sunni Arab family that converted to Catholicism); it is increasing in post-Soviet Central Asia (for example, Kyrgyzstan, where conversions of Muslims to Protestantism or the Jehovah's Witnesses are occurring by the thousands), and is not unknown among Western Muslims.

Ethnic and religious community (millet)

A religious community is formed when a minority group is defined by a religious marker, whatever its level of religious attendance and practice. In this case a religious marker defines an almost ethnic identity, which means that one is a Muslim by inherited community identity, whatever one's personal faith and religious practices. Such a community is ruled by its own regulations concerning personal status (marriage, divorce and inheritance). For instance the *aljama*, which means a local Muslim community, was recognised as such by Spanish law till 1525. This definition is symmetrical to that of the Ottoman *millet*, which was to last until 1856; a religious community of *dhimmi* (protected people) was allowed to retain its internal organisation and personal status in exchange for a contract of subordination and loyalty. This concept is nowadays enjoying a new lease of life, because it allows Muslims in Europe to be defined as an ethnocultural minority, blending a traditional Islamic legal concept with a modern one (minority group). It is another manifestation of the mutual reinforcement of conceptual categories taken from totally different intellectual frameworks. But

18. For an English version of the 27 November 2001 *fatwa* condemning the 9/11 terrorist attacks, see <http://www.unc.edu/~kurzman/Qaradawi_et_al.htm> (also the *Washington Post*, 11 October 2001).

it works. Many European Muslims nowadays rely on this dual concept of *millet*/minority group to ask for legal recognition of their
specific characteristics (such as the right to wear the *hijab* and be
provided with halal food, and, for most extremists, the right to
polygamy and to specific laws of inheritance), without of course
the derogatory status of both the *millet* and *aljama*, which defined
second-class subjects of the empire. The Turkish Islamist author Ali
Bulaç once called for the re-enactment of *millet* status in Turkey,
but this time acknowledging a new minority: the practising Muslims, in parallel with the *millet* of the 'Kemalists'.

Theological endorsement of Islam as a 'mere' religion

In the early twelfth century Sheikh al Mazari (died 1141) issued
a *fatwa* allowing Muslims to remain in Sicily for as long as their
religious freedom was guaranteed.[19] This development ushered in
a crucial moment in the history of Islam: it went so far as to make
Islam a 'mere' religion (that is, a set of rituals, beliefs and practices)
that could be exercised by a community of believers whatever the
social, cultural and political context. There need only be a legal
framework, set up by a state authority, which can be either Christian or secular, to ensure private and/or communal religious practice. This path has been reopened in very recent times by Western
Muslim thinkers as varied as Tariq Ramadan, Mohammed Arkoun
and Khaled Abou El Fadl, and fits with the common definition of
religious freedom in the West.

A call for Islamising 'Christian society'

A neat way to solve the conundrum of Islam as a minority would
be to convert enough non-Muslims to bring wider society into the
fold of Islam. Proselytism, or more precisely apologetic polemics, was
a constant factor of religious controversy in the (European) Middle
Ages. One only engages in polemics against symmetrical religions.
(Why bother to argue with a defeated religion?) The *Reconquista*
was full of elaborate polemics on both sides, Christian and Muslim,
each aiming to show the superiority of their religion by quoting

19. Khaled Abou El Fadl, 'Islamic Law and Muslim Minorities: The Juristic Dis-
    course on Muslim Minorities from the 2nd/8th to the 11th/17th Centuries',
    Journal of Islamic Law and Society, 1 (1994), pp. 149–56.

from the other's basic creed. Muslim proselytisers argued that the Gospels announced the coming of Muhammad (quoting John 14: 16, 26), while Christian theologians portrayed Muhammad as a false prophet. It is interesting to note that nowadays the mainstream Christian movements (except evangelicals, such as the group who manage answering-islam.org.uk) have abandoned such religious polemics (the Holy See no longer endorses such literature, nor do the European Protestants), while they are still put to lively use by modern Muslim preachers.[20] For example, the apocryphal Gospel of Barnabas, which is supposed to have announced that Muhammad will follow Jesus, has been regularly republished by Islamic institutions. (The last significant version was probably that printed by the Embassy of the Islamic Republic of Iran at the Vatican, which led to a diplomatic incident and the recall of Ambassador Hojjat-ol Islam Khosroshahi in 1985.)[21] In a more militant manner, the al-Muhajiroun movement has adamantly called for the conversion of British politicians and other leaders to Islam. There are also widespread rumours of other high-profile conversions to Islam (such as Jacques Cousteau and Princess Diana). It is noteworthy that modern Islamic fundamentalists are reusing the traditional religious polemics of the classical period about what is the best religion. Many booklets (for example, by Ahmed Deedat) and websites indulge in question-and-answer sessions or polemical critiques of the Gospels to show how Christian clerics have distorted the 'true' message or how Islam is far more coherent than Christianity. Many converts explain how they came to Islam after comparing both religions.

Conversely, most modern Christians do not care to compare other religions. They criticise Islam not for being 'wrong' but for not being secular enough. Contemporary fundamentalist Muslims see Europe as 'Christian', while most European Christians have endorsed secularism, care little for interfaith dialogue or polemics, and simply want Muslims to be as secular as they are. The only Christian groups to indulge in such polemics and wage an open fight for conversion are evangelical Protestants and the US Christian Right.[22]

20. From all obedience. Deedat specialised in anti-Christian polemics. See also *Islam and Christianism*, Istanbul: Haqiqat Kitabevi and Waqf Ikhlas, 1990.
21. For the Gospel of Barnabas, see Mikel de Epalza, 'Le milieu hispano-moresque de l'Evangile Islamisant de Barnabé (XVIe–XVIIe)', *Islamochristiana*, 8 (1982). On its present use, see *Islam and Christianism*, p. 17.
22. Barry Yeoman, 'The Stealth Crusade', *MotherJones*, May–June (2002) (<http://

Armed revolts

After the *Reconquista* sporadic armed struggles pitched certain Muslim communities against their new rulers. However, most Muslims in the West nowadays advocate integration, and use arguments about the absence of repression of Muslims and the voluntary settling of Muslims in the West to condemn any revolt in the name of Islam. But the radical fringe of Muslim youths in Europe does not shirk the call for a fight against the 'system', often using rhetoric borrowed from the Western ultra-left.[23]

The Moriscos and crypto-Muslims

The case of the Moriscos and crypto-Muslims, who apparently converted to Christianity (more or less by force) but retained some Muslim customs, makes little sense in the West now because there are no forced conversions and there is no longer any assimilation between the West and Christianity. Maybe a modern equivalent would be secular Muslims who are not believers but retain some customs, like abstinence from eating pork.[24]

These paradigms are used to reconcile traditions, history, religious law and contemporary situations by 'orientalists' and Muslim theologians, whether they are sceptical of or advocating the integration of Islam into the West. In this sense they are worth mentioning, but

---

www.motherjones.com/news/feature/2002/05/stealth.html>).   Websites by Christian fundamentalists are full of polemics with Islam (see <http://www.bible-koran.com/index.html>). It is interesting to the extent that, as we shall see in the conclusion, there is a real symmetry in the world between Islamic Salafism and Christian fundamentalism: they are widely engaged in missionary conversions and target the same people. Each of them sees the other as 'the other'. The Samuel Zwemer Institute in California is training Christian missionaries to convert Muslims all over the world and also extensively relies on religious polemics. See also the website <http://www.johnankerberg.org/Articles/apologetics/AP0700W2.htm>.

23. For example, the shootings and bomb attacks in France perpetrated in 1996 by a group led by a young Muslim of Lyon, Khaled Kelkal. See p. 316, this vol.

24. For instance, according to a poll conducted in France by INED (National Institute for Demographic Studies), 69 per cent of male immigrants born in Algeria declared that they fasted during Ramadan, while 48 per cent said

they do not exhaust the vast and complex array of iden\
tegies and discourses that shape the rooting of Islam in tl

ACCULTURATION AND IDENTITY RECONSTRUCTION

Acculturation does not automatically entail integration. It also leads to the creation of dynamic and fluctuating subcultures, one of the most visible being a so-called 'Muslim youth culture'. Even at the level of pristine and imported identity a reconstruction or multilevel approach has been under way. The Muslim population of foreign descent living in Europe displays tensions between five levels of identity (which are not necessarily mutually exclusive):

1. the transposition of an original, well-bonded solidarity group (based on geographical origin and/or kinship);

2. a larger 'ethnic' or national identity, based on a common language and culture, which can include solidarity-group identity, often duplicated with a common citizenship;

3. a neo-ethnic definition of Muslims, set by their genealogical ties with any kind of Muslim society, whatever their personal faith and religious practices, as sharing common sociocultural patterns in the anthropological sense (attitudes and values, but not language and literature);

4. definition of a Muslim identity based exclusively on religious patterns, with no reference to a specific culture or language; and

5. acculturation along Western lines, occasionally keeping the faith inside the home or, for some specific categories of youth, leading to the creation of a Western subculture, a marginal urban youth culture, sometimes recast into an ethnically described category (like the *beur* in France),[25] but where today's 'ethnicity' has little to do with their fathers' culture.

---

they did not believe and 64 per cent that they did not practise. This means that a majority of them saw fasting as some sort of cultural and communal custom, not as an act of faith (Michèle Tribalat, *Faire France. Une enquête sur les immigrés et leurs enfants*, Paris: La Découverte, 1995, pp. 96, 101).

25. The term *beur* is French slang (not derogatory) for Arab, but refers exclusively to young ethnic Arabs born in France and never to older ethnic Arabs living in France, nor to peoples from Arab countries. It expresses well the idea that

In all these levels of identity, what is absent is the explicit idea of a 'Muslim culture', which would be something other than, and more than, ethnic–national cultures or religion as such.

The crisis of pristine cultures

At the first level of identity, one can observe the strength of the solidarity of a 'native' group (based on kinship, village or district, caste, and so on), which has usually provided both the incentive for emigration and its direction. The Pakistani *biradari* (a patrilineal kinship group) is a typical example of the resilience of imported solidarity groups.[26] But here two caveats must be introduced. First, not all Muslim immigrants travel and settle within the protective framework of a solidarity group. The phenomenon is pervasive among South Asians in Britain, but is minimal among the North African Arabs settled in France, largely because the French-colonised countries have been transformed by the colonial factor to a greater degree than have former British colonies.[27] The host country also shapes immigrant identity. In France *communautarisme* (communitarianism) is not a norm and there is more pressure on immigrants to adopt ambient individualism.[28] The second caveat is about the longevity and nature of the *biradari*'s strength: it lingers only if the nature of the *biradari* changes. Traditional solidarity-group ties might fade away among the second and third generations, in favour either of Western acculturation or of a broader national and ethnic identity. (The shift is illustrated by the extension of the field of choice for spouses.) But, more interestingly, it might be reinforced if it is recast into a 'business' network or occupational association (restaurants, interest-free loans for members, hiring of newcomers

---

there is an 'ethnic' category whose definition is more social and generational than based on a different culture and religion. (There are neither rich nor old *beur*.)

26. Philip Lewis, *Islamic Britain: Religion, Politics and Identity among British Muslims*, London: I.B. Tauris, 1994, pp. 56–9, For a quotation from Fred Halliday on Yemenis in Britain, see p. 19 in the same volume.

27. However, the solidarity-group phenomenon has existed. Many Kabyles (Berber peoples from the mountainous coastal regions of Algeria) settled in Paris in the 1950s and were able to achieve some economic success (in cafés and restaurants) through such kinship and village networks.

28. On the impact of the host country's cultural and administrative traditions, see Emmanuel Todd, *Le destin des immigrés*, Paris: Editions du Seuil, 1994, p. 12.

by previous settlers, and so on), sometimes strengthened by a business relationship with the place of origin or fellow villagers living
in other countries. For instance, a citizen or a permanent resident
represents such value as a prospective spouse for a potential immigrant that families tend to marry their children to relatives (first
cousins) remaining in the country of origin, thus strengthening
traditional endogamy. If solidarity groups are successful enough to
favour business and social development, they retain their impact
among younger generations, but are shaped by new incentives and
a new environment.[29] Religious practices might here reinforce
the group link. Usually mosques are established when families arrive. There is a general correlation between the early established
mosques and solidarity groups.[30] This might lead to strengthening
of local solidarity groups, either imported or reconstructed, which
could also become the basis of a constituency for position and
power (such as elections for city council or for various community
associations).

Whatever the case, for the second and third generations solidarity groups are more reconstructed than imported. One tends to pass
from a 'real' community to an 'imagined' one, based on ethnicity,
nation or religion.[31] What is the role of Islam in the shaping of 'reconstructed identities'? Is Islam a global culture, extending beyond
the strict tenets of theology and rituals (meaning that, in this case,
to be a Muslim is not necessarily to be a believer)? Is it, on the contrary, a mere religion, which should be redefined solely on the basis
of its fundamentals, and should be clearly distinguished from national and ethnic cultures (meaning, for example, that a European

29. For both trends, see Philip Lewis, *Islamic Britain*, p. 66 (disaffection towards
   traditional solidarity) and p. 74 (resilience of a traditional solidarity that has
   become a power constituency). The obtaining of residence permits is also
   a factor in matrimonial strategy. A survey of Anatolian Turkish migrants in
   France showed that the rate of marriage between cousins (one in France the
   other in Turkey) tended to increase among immigrants and to be comparable
   with the rate in rural Turkey (16 per cent of Turkish migrants who arrived
   before 1975 were married to a cousin, but the figure is more than 30 per
   cent for those who arrived after 1985) (Michèle Tribalat, *De l'immigration à
   l'assimilation*, Paris: La Découverte, 1996, p. 81). This is because the residence
   permit is such a 'good' that it has to be maintained inside the family; but the
   number of divorces is also increasing.
30. Philip Lewis, *Islamic Britain*, pp. 56–8.
31. Benedict Anderson, cited in Philip Lewis, *Islamic Britain*, p. 164.

convert is more a Muslim than an (occasionally) alcohol-drink-
ing unveiled Algerian woman)? Or is Islam merely a marker of an
ethnic identity in modern multi-ethnic societies in which social
antagonisms tend to be recast into the language of ethnicity?

Islam is not taking (and cannot take) root in the West along
cultural lines imported from pristine cultures. These cultures usually do not survive the first generation as such, either fading away
or being recast along 'Western' lines. We are not addressing here
the fate of ethnic identities – what does it means to be an Arab
or an Italian in the United States? – but the destiny of a religion.
A 'universal' religion, which Islam is (as is Christianity), may be
embodied in a given culture but does not address a specific culture
or ethnic group. In countries of origin, Islam (like any universal
religion) is embedded in a given culture, through which the believer accedes to what he conceives as a universal religion. When
this culture is imported into the West or suddenly confronted with
another, it becomes an 'ethnic' culture (Arab, Persian or Indian, for
example) that shares Islam with others, or could even be understood without direct reference to religion (Lebanese and Syrians
can also be Christians).

To define a global Muslim identity means to delink Islam from
any given culture in favour of a transnational and universal set of
specific patterns (beliefs, rituals, diet, prescriptions and so on). In a
word, there is a strong relationship between deculturation and religious reformulation. When a religion is experienced not so much
by a minority as without relation to ethnicity and culture, it no
longer has social authority. What is the result of such a process of
deculturation? A 'mere' religion? A new ethnic identity? Another
culture? Could we speak of an universal Islamic culture? In what
sense do we use the term culture?

The reformulation of Islam goes along with its passage to the
West. To what extent can we speak of 'westernisation'? We shall see
below that westernisation may mean reformation and liberalism,
but not necessarily. It can also lead to a sort of neofundamentalism.
Young males who left the European suburbs to join Bin Laden in
Afghanistan or young girls who suddenly decided to wear a *hijab*
at school are not 'liberal'. What is evolving is not religion but religiosity – that is, the way in which believers build and live their
relationship with religion. As far as theology is concerned, there
is an ambiguity in the term reformism. The endeavour to purify

Islam of cultural influences and to redefine it along purely religious lines is as old as Islam; Shah Waliullah in eighteenth-century
India was explicitly trying to separate Islam from the surrounding
Indian culture. But the school he created (later called Deobandi)
has been profoundly embedded in a given culture, in which the
Persian and Urdu languages were the vehicle of an entire corpus.
Traditional fundamentalists, even those opposed to popular Sufism,
like Shah Waliullah, have been at ease with specific cultures. We
are not referring here to the pervasive, and questionable, conflict
between 'popular Islam' and '*ulama*'s Islam'. As pointed out by Nazif
Shahrani, this difference has been rather exaggerated and frozen.
On the one hand, ordinary Muslims indulging in 'popular Islam'
acknowledge that there is an Islam of the learned, and respect it.[32]
On the other hand, fundamentalist *ulama* have been the bearers of
'traditional Muslim cultures', as is obvious in Central and South
Asia. Sunni *ulama* in Central Asia (Afghanistan and Bukhara, Uzbekistan), where almost no secular culture existed till the 1920s,
used to transmit the tenets of Islam along with a traditional Persian
culture.[33] South Asian *ulama* shifted from the Persian language to
Urdu (which is nowadays identified with the Muslim culture of
the Indian subcontinent), and were instrumental in defining and
spreading the language and the culture associated with it, which
has never been exclusively religious. When *mullahs* come from
their South Asian *madrasas* to Britain, they identify still with the
fight to preserve a Muslim identity and the use of Urdu. But these
traditional *ulama*, whatever kinds of fundamentalist they might be,
are now on the defensive. How does one explain in Europe that
Urdu is the vector *par excellence* of Islam? It makes sense in the
Indian subcontinent, but not in Bradford. Traditional *ulama* are opposed by Islamists and neofundamentalists, who equate the idea of
a 'Muslim culture' with traditional and national cultures.

What is new in Western Islam is the crisis of the cultural reference in itself. Practising Muslims are embroiled in a struggle less to
promote a minority culture against a dominant one than to define
their own relationship with the very concept of culture.

32. Nazif Shahrani, 'Popular Knowledge of Islam' in Robert Canfield (ed.), *Tur-
co-Persia in Historical Perspective*, Cambridge University Press, 1992.
33. Books like the *Chahar Kitab*, widespread in Afghanistan, Tajikistan and Uzbekistan, are a typical mixture of religious teachings, literature, cosmogony,
Sufism and poetry.

The first generation of immigrants arrived with a pristine 'ethnic culture' (language, customs, religion, family patterns, diet, music). In countries of origin the different levels of identity (parochial, ethnic, national and religious) were not perceived to be in conflict with one another. Identity is 'experienced' as a whole, and this whole is precisely what we call a culture. Nevertheless, in immigration these different levels of identity might contradict one another. Collective identities have to be recomposed, even reinvented, because personal experience no longer fits with the largest group to which the individual is supposed to belong. It is clear that acculturation is working everywhere, but not in a simple way.[34]

An important element of collective identity is language. A cohesive ethno-national group might retain its language in emigration, especially if it is supported by an affirmative state policy of education, either domestic or directed towards the immigrants (as is the case for Turkey). But in many cases the mother tongue might be just as incompatible with the language of the host country as it is with that of the reconstructed identity group. Urdu is the common language of Muslims of the Indian subcontinent and of the republic of Pakistan. Hence a Pakistani Baluchi and a Mohajir from India may speak in Urdu when meeting in Karachi. But in London the children of the same Baluchi and Mohajir will converse in English. Urdu is no longer seen as a universal and supra-ethnic lingua franca but as a specifically ethnic idiom.

The use of mother tongues is fading, especially by the third generation. The young British-born citizens of Pakistani descent who travelled to Pakistan in 2002 to join Jayash-e-Muhammad or Hizb ut-Tahrir spoke only English during their trial.[35] In US mosques, 97 per cent of attendees speak English as their primary language.[36]

34. For the United States, see Yvonne Yazbeck Haddad and Adair T. Lummis, *Islamic Values in the United States: A Comparative Study*, Oxford University Press, 1987. For France see Todd, *Le destin des immigrés*; Tribalat, *Faire France*. For Britain, see Philip Lewis, *Islamic Britain*, p. 179. For other European examples (the Netherlands, Germany) see Bernard Lewis and Schnapper (eds), *Muslims in Europe*; Felice Dassetto (ed.), *Paroles d'islam. Indifus, sociétés et discours dans l'Islam européen contemporain*, Paris: Maisonneuve et Larose, 2000.
35. Khaled Ahmad, 'The Rise of the Hizb al-Tahreer', *Friday Times* (Lahore), 14 October 2002.
36. Council on American Islamic Relations (CAIR), *The Mosque in America: A National Portrait*, Report from the Mosque Study Project, Washington, DC: CAIR, 2001. This phenomenon also occurs because most of the mosques

In France, where the use of pristine languages is fading faster than elsewhere in Europe, the debate on Arabic-teaching in secondary schools is interesting. The majority of the teachers (often from Lebanon) favour the teaching of modern literary Arabic (that is, the language of the Middle Eastern media). It is nobody's mother tongue, and rather distant from the colloquial Arabic spoken by the Maghrebi families who settled in France. It can thus be used neither as a domestic tool of communication nor to keep in touch with peasant relatives still in Morocco or Algeria (not to mention the different Berber-speakers). But it does allow one to define a modern 'Arab' identity, the centre of which is the Middle East, and which is enhanced by satellite television. By contrast, a small but vocal group of social workers and anthropologists advocate the teaching of colloquial Arabic, in its 'Moroccan' or 'Algerian' forms. They stress the need for young people to be reinserted into a genealogy and a family's ethnolinguistic culture and tradition. Non-Arab Muslim students of Arabic, who are motivated by religion, prefer the teaching of Koranic Arabic. They are interested not in listening to Al-Jazeera but in devotion and salvation. They will learn Arabic privately or at evening courses. Conversely, many *beur* refuse to learn Arabic when they join secondary school and ask for instruction in English. They fear being pigeonholed as an ethnic group through language and lagging behind their non-Muslim fellows in the job market, due to their inferior command English. An issue apparently as simple as how to teach Arabic to Arabs turns into a debate about identity choices. In Germany, where the resilience of the Turkish language contrasts with the weakening of Arabic in Europe, new generations of Turkish migrants' children are nevertheless more at ease with German. As we shall see, Muslim preachers are increasingly relying on Western languages for their sermons for two simple reasons: they want to address the new generation, and they want to reach a multi-ethnic congregation. Elsewhere, when the Soviet Union collapsed in 1991 the *imams* of the two Moscow mosques, who were Tatars, decided to preach regularly in Tatar. However, they were opposed by Caucasian Muslims who wanted to retain Russian as the only common language of Muslims of the Russian Federation.

---

are multi-ethnic, and thus English is the only language mosque-goers have in common.

Although there is a resurgence of interest in modern literary Arabic among Muslim youths in Europe (thanks to satellite television), it has more to do with the recasting of identities and with globalisation than with the permanence of pristine cultures.

Such issues might be seen as artificial so far as individuals are concerned, because they experience and live the different levels (parochial, ethnic, national and religious; see page 122) together. But there is a growing 'obligation to choose' from different levels.[37] Islamic preachers (like those of the Tablighi Jama'at) denounce the concrete compromises elaborated informally by individual Muslims dealing with an alien environment. They shame 'Muslims' who compromise with the dominant culture. On the other hand, multiculturalism becomes a political issue. Human rights lobbyists, minority rights groups and some political parties (usually leftist, though not in France, while in Britain the conservatives are multiculturalist) lobby Western states to protect the cultural rights of minorities, which sooner or later obliges them to provide objective criteria for what a 'cultural' or ethnic or national community is. Political events, like the Gulf war or 9/11, impose constraints on individuals who are called upon to choose a side. And this is not to mention the ambient racism that imposes an identity from the outside. The logic of democracy also implies the emergence of lobbies and of pressure groups. To what extent could any of these identities be the basis for building a political constituency? And finally, through which identity might fundamentalist or Islamist influences make a breakthrough among Muslims living in Europe?

Neo-ethnicity

The term 'Muslim' is often used in the West in what I call a neo-ethnic sense, with no reference to faith and genuine religious practice. When speaking of neo-ethnicity, 'neo' means that the culture of origin is no longer really relevant, and 'ethnicity' that religion is not seen as a faith but as a set of cultural patterns that are inherited and not related to a person's spiritual life.[38] This ethnicisation may

37. As, for example, in the United States, where many sorts of application forms have 'ethnic' questions that must be answered.
38. The term 'Jewish' can also refer to non-believing and non-practising persons. In this sense it is also an ethnic marker, closer to a racial category. But the

also take the form of subgroups, often defined through the prism of colonial history: 'South Asians' in the United States (usually called 'Asians' in Britain), '*Maghrébins*' in France (who are called 'Arabs' or 'Middle Easterners' in Britain), 'Caucasians' in Moscow (who have the distinction of not being very white, contrary to the US view of 'Caucasians'). Neo-ethnicity means the construction of an ethnic group, which previously did not exist as such, through a limited set of differential patterns isolated from a more complex and diverse cultural background. This construction is carried out through the conceptual categories of the dominant Western systems of representation, which select what constitutes relevant differences as far as group categories are concerned. Racial patterns (skin colour), religion, language and geographical origin may (or may not) help in the West to define an ethnic group, which is not necessarily the expression of an imported and previously existing culture. Such Western categories are also changing according to countries and histories. The dichotomous racial category (white and non-white) that dominated the United States for more than a century gave way to a more complex and open perception of ethnic groups, in which ethnicity has replaced race. France traditionally has little taste for ethnic categorisation in the public and legal spheres.[39] A French person from the West Indies (an *Antillais*) will never be confused with a black African. But a new concept recently emerged in France, that of 'black' (in English) to qualify either 'black' youngsters from the suburbs or a 'black culture' emanating from trendy clubs. Britain has a law recognising 'races' (the British sense of the term is closer to 'ethnic group' than the US understanding of it).

---

symmetry stops there. A Jew who has turned Catholic is often still perceived as a Jew (for example, Cardinal Lustiger in France), a Muslim turned Christian will be less easily still dubbed a Muslim (for example, Carlos Menem, Nuriyev). Another difference is that Islam claims to be a universal religion not linked by definition to an ethnic group. Hence the association between Islam and ethnicity goes against the very concept of a Muslim community.

39. The publication in 1983 of a report from the Soviet Academy of Sciences on the ethnic composition of Europe created an uproar in France (including a protest by the very pro-Soviet French Communist Party) because it listed Alsatians as 'ethnic Germans'. (The uproar was even stronger in Alsace than elsewhere.) In 1991 a French law recognising the Corsicans as a specific 'people' was rejected by the constitutional council; 'regionalist' ethnic parties have never made a significant electoral advance except in Corsica, where they poll around 20 per cent.

Roughly speaking the West has carved out two categories to express minority groups in cultural terms: ethnicity and/or religion. (Sexual orientation is never linked to cultural patterns of behaviour, outside the choice of partners. Not all minority groups are built along neo-ethnic lines, but the same logic of discrimination versus minority rights will be applied.) Interestingly, the categories used to define neo-ethnic groups are usually forged by the host country and reappropriated by many among the concerned population. Neo-ethnicity is based not on a 'real' culture, but on a limited set of distinctive patterns that define the borders of the group, while not being antagonistic towards other traits of culture (language and cuisine, for instance).

In the West the category 'Muslims' is often used as a neo-ethnic definition in the following senses:

1. Every person of Muslim background is supposed to share a common Muslim culture, whatever his or her real culture of origin (Turk, Bosnian, Pakistani or Arab), which means that religion is seen as the main component of these cultures, a component that can be isolated and erected as a culture in itself.

2. This culture is attributed to everybody with a Muslim origin, whatever his or her religious practice or level of faith (that is, without any link to religiosity). In this sense, one could speak of 'non-believing Muslims'.[40]

3. This culture differentiates a 'Muslim' from an 'other', who, in the West, is defined as a member never of a religious community, but of a pseudo-ethnic group ('*Français de souche*', 'white', 'European'), reproducing patterns of colonial history.

Colonial history is full of ethnicisation of Muslims, whose antonym in modern times has never been the term 'Christians'. In colonial French Algeria and in Russian Central Asia, Muslims were differentiated from Europeans, to whom the term Christians was

40. In Lebanon, Syria, Egypt and the West Bank one's personal code is defined by religion, and there is no 'civil' marriage. So the Muslim personal code applies to anybody of Muslim origin, even an atheist. In this sense the concept of 'atheist Muslim' also exists in the Middle East. In Belgium in 1998 the decision to open the elections for a Muslim council to non-mosque-attending Muslims meant the creation of a category of non-believing Muslims.

never applied by the colonial authorities.[41] Religion was used to define one group (the Muslims), not the other, as if Muslim ethnic groups could not escape from the religious dimension of their cultures while Christians could. The same applies today in Western Europe. Nobody compares Muslims to Christians, except if the term Christians specifically refers to churchgoers. During the Balkan wars the term Muslim was more often used to qualify the Bosnians than the term Orthodox or Catholic for the Serbs and the Croats, following the official ethnicisation of the term by the Tito regime.[42] The same policy of ethnicisation is at work in China. The Hui from southern and north-western China have little in common except that they are Muslim, have been legally recognised as an ethnic group (*Hui min*) and not a religion (*Hui jiao*), which means that aversion to pork is explained as a cultural phenomenon, not as a religious interdict.[43] The same view is largely shared in Europe, where 'Muslims do not eat pork' is seen not as an affirmation analagous to 'Christians do not lust after each other's wives' (which they do), but rather to 'Englishmen don't eat frogs'.

Many Europeans are coping with Islam by using ethnic categories, and even when it is for the good (to create space for Islam), it is putting the clock back. A good example is to be found in an article in *The Economist* (8 August 2002) entitled 'Islam is Now Firmly Established in Western Europe: Don't Be Afraid of It', which is a positive agenda. But the journal, with the usual *Economist* sense of Anglo-Saxon superiority, states: 'Here, too, France and Germany lag. Neither yet has a body similar to Britain's 36-year-old Commission for Racial Equality.' Sure, but why should a religion be attributed to a race? The British Race Relations Act 1976 does not list Islam as a race. This means that nobody can use this law to complain of a religiously based act of discrimination. For example, a Sikh can sue for not being allowed to wear a turban – an ethnic

41. An interesting twist is the status of local Jews in French Algeria and in Russia. They were treated as natives so long as they were not explicitly integrated into the 'European' categories (but had to give up their specific personal law, in compliance with the *décret Crémieux* of October 1870).

42. Muslim with a capital M meant a member of an ethnic group, but with a lower-case m a follower of Islam.

43. Dru Gladney (ed.), *Making Majorities: Constituting the Nation in Japan, Korea, China, Malaysia, Fiji, Turkey, and the United States*, Stanford University Press, 1998, p. 127.

marker – but a Muslim woman cannot sue for being prevented
from wearing a *hijab* – a religious marker. The consequence is that
many British Muslims want to be recognised as members of a race;
that is, an ethnic group. This claim is often supported by secular
Muslims who want to promote minority groups on a non-religious
basis, thus revitalising historical clichés (such as 'Arab civilisation')
or Western racial concepts (such as 'Blacks and Asians' in Britain).
Ethnicisation of identity is popular on all sides (non-Muslims and
Muslims, secular and religious-minded people).

Although Islam is by definition a non-ethnic religion, many Islamic thinkers still promote the concept of 'Muslim culture' understood more in anthropological terms than by reference to a
cultural corpus of literature, fine arts and philosophy. The sociologist Muhammad Anwar, writing for a neofundamentalist institution about Muslims in the West,[44] states:

Religion is an important and sensitive part of ethnic identity and the
religious needs of different communities in Britain are very important.
These needs are equally important for the second and third generation of
British Muslims, born and brought up in a different cultural environment
from that of the first generation Muslim migrants, experiencing tensions
between minority and majority culture.

What is interesting here is not the ideas as such, which many anthropologists would share, but that the publisher is a Salafi institution, which by definition opposes the concept of culture as en-
compassing religion. It shows the extent to which a purely Western
typology is shaping the way even fundamentalist Muslims endeavour to recast Muslim identity in the West.

But what are the cultural patterns that are supposed to define a
Muslim ethnic identity? They do not come from precise ethnic or
national cultures (such as the Punjab or Egypt), but are made up of
what remains when these pristine cultures have vanished through
deculturation. The definition of Islam as a culture *per se* is possible
only after the process of immigration has disconnected religious
tenets from a given culture. This disconnection fits with Western
secularism, for which a religion is defined as a mere religion separated from other sociocultural fields. After this break Islam is then

44. Muhammad Anwar, *Young Muslims in Britain*, Leicester: Islamic Foundation,
    1994, p. 12.

re-objectified as a culture in itself and called to explain the social attitudes of Muslims (towards women, for example), under the pretext that Islam advocates living as a community. Tariq Ramadan exhorts young French Muslims to 'live out their faith and culture'.[45] But what is the meaning of culture here? Is it something larger than religion? In this case, is it linked with culture of origin? But which point of origin makes sense for a youth who has lost most of his or her links with other cultures? And if religion and culture are the same thing, why maintain the distinction?

The notion of a single 'Muslim culture' cannot survive analysis. If it refers to Islam as a religion it is redundant. The different Muslim populations have some elements in common such as diet and holidays, which are nothing more than the basic tenets of the rituals and beliefs, but in themselves they do not constitute a culture. What is beyond the strict tenets of religious rituals and beliefs refers to specific national or ethnic cultures, of which Islam is just a component, even if it is indistinguishable. It is difficult to find a common basis for an 'Islamic culture' outside the tenets of the religion. What about Muslim food, sports, dance, music, literature and even folklore? These elements are expressions either of a native, specific culture or possibly of ethnic groups defined as such from outside (Asians or Blacks in Britain, Arabs in France), but they cannot be part of the definition of a religious community. For instance, there are among Muslim populations living in France fewer cultural, sports or entertainment associations than among other, less numerous ethnic or national communities (Armenians, Portuguese, and so on). This is a consequence of the discrepancy between the ethnic or national cultures and Islamic religious standards of culture and entertainment. A Punjabi ballet makes sense, not an 'Islamic ballet'. For traditional believers, and specifically for those with a rural background, fidelity to national culture (diet, clothing, language) might equivate with fidelity towards Islam.[46] Sectarian affiliation might also mark out some cultural patterns linked with Islam – for example, a specific poetry and music for the Barelvis, associated with festivals and pilgrimages. But none of

45. Tariq Ramadan, *Islam, le face à face des civilisations*, Lyon: Tawhid, 1995, pp. 162–82.
46. The social background of Muslim migrants should never be underestimated, as stressed by Aziz Al Azmeh, *Islams and Modernities*, London: Verso, 1993, p. 3.

these specific cultures constitutes a 'Muslim culture' that would appeal to any Muslim. And if we return to the believers' viewpoint, the concept of 'Muslim culture' is a contradiction in terms. Neither Islamists nor neofundamentalists condone the idea of such a Muslim culture, because for them many aspects of it would simply not be Islamic, either because they are seen as 'un-Islamic' (for example, dance, music), or irrelevant to the definition of the *ummah* (specific language, the use of traditional medicine and so on).[47]

There is a contradiction between Islam and the concept of a contemporary Islamic culture. Many elements of what is seen by the actors as their Islamic culture are rejected by Islamists and neo-fundamentalists as 'customs' or national or ethnic culture: music[48] and specific rituals,[49] and all Sufi cultural practices. Communities that preserve music and poetry, like the Barelvis, come under heavy criticism from the rival group, the 'Deobandis', as well as from the Salafis.[50] Sufism, which is the basis of very lively Muslim cultures and also often of solidarity groups (which identify a village or

47. Traditional medicine is seen as part of the Muslim culture (Philip Lewis, *Islamic Britain*, p. 64). But it is a very ancient borrowing from the 'West' and is still called *tibb-i Yunani* (Greek medicine) in South and Central Asia.
48. For a protest by the Bradford Council of Mosques against the performing of *bhangra* music by a group that nevertheless claims to be Muslim, see Philip Lewis, *Islamic Britain*, p. 181.
49. Various newsgroups on the internet are full of discussions on this topic. In a post by Sayyd Aziz, entitled 'Culture or Religion?' (soc.religion.Islam, article 11020, 4 July 1995), all the burial rituals associated by traditional Pakistani Muslims with Islam (*qul, chehlum, khatm-i Koran*) were simply rejected as having no basis in Koran and Sunnah. Mohammed Atta stated in his will that he did not want to be buried according to traditional Egyptian custom, because it was not Islamic.
50. Speaking of culture, I used the word in an anthropological rather than a literary sense. Of course, this does not mean that there are not 'classical' literature and humanities in the Muslim world. There is a classical Arab culture. But in the present debate few actors refer to such cultures. In his book *The Malady of Islam* (New York: Basic Books, 2003) Abdelwahab Meddeb places in opposition Islamic fundamentalism and such a classical culture, which, like the classical Western culture, cannot be reduced to religion and belongs to the universal cultural treasury of the world. But the issue is the status of such a culture in the modern world. Arab 'humanities' are poorly taught in most of the Arab countries and seem to be absent from any curriculum available to second-generation Muslims in the West, except in the centres for Middle Eastern studies in some universities. In any case, the modern Islamic revival does not promote such literature.

district in Pakistan with a *pir*, or in Morocco with a 'saint'), is the arch-enemy of the neofundamentalists. It combines sectarianism, a cult of the saints, music, philosophy, and 'culture' pretending to be Islamic but with no basis in the Koran and Sunnah. The same discrepancy is still at work when second-generation immigrants make a breakthrough on the cultural stage in the West. Modern music and films produced by Muslim artists have nothing to do with Islam. *Bhangra* among Pakistanis living in Britain, *Rai* among Algerians, Egyptian films, with their mixture of romance and vio-lence – all express more an appropriation of modernity, and a syn-thesis between a renewed tradition and the tastes of new audiences, than the persistence of a historical culture.

In fact, the lowest common denominators in defining a Muslim culture are religious norms that can fit with or be recast along the lines of different cultural customs. Halal is a way to kill an animal, not a way to cook it. It is not linked with a culture and could perfectly well fit with global fast food.[51] The *hijab* is also more a concept than a given item of clothing. The way in which a Muslim woman can implement (or twist) the rule of concealing her hair, arms and legs can express either a given culture (Afghan *chadri*, Pakistani *burqa*) or a personal reappropriation of modernity (trench coat, headscarf and trousers for Turkish Islamist women or second-generation university students in Europe, not to mention the '*cha-Dior*' of the elegant upper-class ladies of Tehran).

Islamic culture is nonetheless often referred to as a set of an-thropological patterns and values. For instance, a specific relation-ship to the body is linked with Islam: reluctance to permit nudity, post-mortem examination and cremation; a stress on men's honour and women's chastity; and opposition to coeducation. All these traits might, of course, seem to be the internalisation of religious norms, but they do not make a culture as such, and they are shared by many other cultures. Some actors try to recast these 'cultural' norms in terms of values, which is also a form of westernisation. A value is an ideal norm, not a legal obligation. Tariq Ramadan,

---

51. In March 2002 a settlement agreement was signed between McDonald's and a coalition of Jews, Hindus and vegetarians who complained about the presence of beef in French fries. A group of Muslim organisations success-fully asked to be included in the settlement (<http://www.soundvision. com/info/mcdonalds>). In a word, Muslims just want to be able to go to McDonald's and remain good Muslims.

who still thinks the *hijab* is compulsory for any Muslim woman, speaks of it in terms of personal achievement, which should not be imposed but discovered through a process of deepening of the faith. Such an approach is more in line with Christian spirituality than with the classic legalistic approach of Islam.[52] To speak in terms of values instead of interdicts and obligations is also a way to recast a Muslim identity in terms compatible with a Western conception of religion. In Iran 'new theologians' also speak in terms of values (*arzeshha*), which is little more than the spiritualising of cultural norms, or giving a cultural form to universal norms. When speaking of the *hijab* as embodying a woman's chastity (instead of simply being God's commandment), does one mean that chastity is essentially a Muslim value, or that the *hijab* is just the Muslim way to enforce a value shared by other religions? Defence of values often goes along with social pressure inside the 'community' to enforce what is seen as a cultural heritage threatened by the pervasive influence of a free and almost depraved Western cultural environment.[53]

To sum up, we are witnessing an endeavour by many Muslim community leaders in the West, as well as reformist theologians, to express the difference between Islam and the West in terms compatible with and/or acceptable by the other (a Western non-Muslim). This is the methodological use of the neo-ethnic perception of Muslims in the West, which by definition insists on the legitimacy of recognising differences. But it contradicts the very definition of Islam as a universal true religion.

Why does the construction of Islam as the culture of a neo-ethnic group work if it has no religious basis? Precisely because it creates a common conceptual ground between Western categories and the strategy of would-be community leaders to reconstruct a

52. Tariq Ramadan (*Les Musulmans*, pp. 120–1) defines the *hijab* as a 'testimony of faith'. He considers it mandatory, but stresses that Muslim women should arrive at such a conclusion by themselves, without any external pressures.
53. It is a common view among Muslims that the West is technologically and politically more advanced but lacks moral values. See, for instance, CAIR, *The Mosque in America*, a report written by Muslims. On p. 31 it states: '99% of Muslims polled in the USA agree that "America is a technologically advanced society that we can learn from", 77% agree that "America is an example of freedom and democracy we can learn from", but 67% agree that "America is an immoral corrupt society".' All of the ambivalence of mosque-going Muslims about the West is embodied in these figures.

'Muslim' community on a basis that can fit Western cultural and legal categories of identities.

In Belgium, as we have seen, the government decided in 1998 to establish a Muslim representative council. As in France, a decision was taken first to put ballot boxes in mosques. Confronted with the protest of women's associations and secular Muslims, however, the Belgians also put boxes in city halls and schools. This move was interesting because it explicitly considered Muslims to be a neo-ethnic group: one could be a non–believing Muslim. Everybody of 'Muslim descent' was allowed to cast a vote, but converts were also added to the electorate, which means that the concept of Islam was forged on a complex and contradictory array of definitions: it is a religion for converts, but an ethnic and cultural identity for 'native' Muslims. Confronted by the same pressure, the French govern-ment decided to keep ballot boxes in mosques, precisely because it addresses believers in order to build a 'church', and not immigrants in order to constitute a minority group.

This ethnicisation of the category 'Muslim' is often spontaneous-ly reappropriated by Muslims, for different reasons. It fits with the modern Western concept of 'minority groups' and allows Muslims to surf the wave of multiculturalism. In this sense a change of name and garb is often a good way for converts to show they are Mus-lims and to be perceived as such. Cat Stevens became Yusuf Islam and wears long, loose shirts and trousers, but the conversion of Roger Garaudy is (rightly or wrongly) not seen as a change of identity because he wears the same suit and tie as he did before his conversion. On the other hand, the culturalist idea that cultures are inherited fits with the Muslim fundamentalist view that anyone born a Muslim is always a Muslim. Religious leaders can claim to speak for a community entirely comprising people of Muslim origin. Moreover Islam provides a convenient new marker of group identity among second-generation immigrants in Europe: it replaces pristine ethnic identities that are fading away, while giving a new sense and a new value to a 'difference' that is experienced in everyday life. But there is a contradiction in such a dynamic. The same marker, Islam, which is used to bypass ethnic differences in favour of a universal, purely religious and transnational identity, can also be turned around to designate a minority group defined on a neo-ethnic basis by the ethnic origin of its members, what-ever their personal commitment to faith. There is a confusion in terms between 'Muslim' and 'Arabs' in France, 'Asians' in Britain and 'Turks' in Germany. Islam is seen as an importation from the East and converts are perceived as exotic and strange. In the United States the Nation of Islam is explicitly based on a typical neo-ethnicity: being an African-American. In any case the confusion between ethnic, communal and religious belonging is taken as a fact. The multiculturalist discourse in the West pervades the Right and the Left; both stress that there are inherently different cultures, but draw different conclusions (the Right insists on preserving one's own values, the Left on making room for other values).[54] But an unintended consequence has been to put Muslims as a minority on the same footing as other minorities like 'gays and lesbians', a situation unacceptable to conservative Muslims, of course.

Neofundamentalists use Western categories in their quest for an 'objective' Muslim community and could 'Islamise' such categories by returning to traditional Muslim concepts such as the *millet*. The convergence between the traditional Islamic concept of *millet* and the Western definition of a minority group is facilitated because the derogatory status of the non-Muslim *millet* has been largely abolished by modern Middle Eastern states. In Lebanon, Palestine and Syria, Muslims and Christians do not view one another as inferior and are ruled by their own personal status. Each *tayfa* (the present term for *millet*) has its own court. In this sense Western concepts of multiculturalism and minority rights groups are called upon to promote a legal status for a Muslim community in the West, by stressing either the ethnic or the religious basis for such a community. Tariq Ramadan quotes approvingly the Austro-Hungarian Marxist philosopher Otto Bauer, who defended a non-territorial definition of ethnic communities to keep the Habsburg empire alive.[55]

In fact ethnicisation of religious identity is not just a by-product of Muslim immigration to the West, or simply a phenomenon to be found only among Muslims. A typical case is that of the

54. In the aftermath of the Rushdie affair, the then deputy leader of the British Labour Party, Roy Hattersley, wrote in an article for the *Independent* ('The Racism of Asserting That They Must Behave Like Us', 21 July 1989): 'The idea that we have a duty to applaud [Rushdie's] assault is a novel interpretation of the liberal obligation ... The proposition that Muslims are welcome in Britain if, and only if, they stop behaving like Muslims, is incompatible with the principle of a free society.'

55. Ramadan, *Islam*, pp. 162–82.

Pakistani Mohajir, meaning the Muslims who performed *hijra* from India to Pakistan after 1947. They came from diverse ethnic back-grounds, used Urdu as their lingua franca, but might speak different languages. The motivation of their choice to migrate was purely ideological: they wanted to live in a Muslim state. In this sense they were the harbinger of what would be a genuine Pakistani citizen-ship, one constructed out of religious and political choice, not out of an ethnic identity. It is why Urdu was chosen as the official language instead of Punjabi, although the latter is spoken by 64 per cent of Pakistanis. In Karachi in 1984 there emerged a party called the Mohajir Qaumi Movement; that is, the 'National Movement of the Mohajir' (renamed in 1997 the Muttahida Qaumi Movement, or MQM). Among second-generation immigrants from India reli-gious and political identity had become purely ethnic (MQM lead-ers were on the whole leftist and secular); this generation wanted to be put on an equal footing with Sindhis, Punjabis, Pathans and Baluchis, who are all Muslims. But by definition the Mohajir have no territorial basis; hence the MQM has logically been struggling to create a Mohajir province around Karachi. A religious marker (*hijra*) became in the end an ethnic one, but this ethnic group is a mere construction. The same is true, as we have seen, of the Hui in China and of Bosnians in Yugoslavia. We can also see how an Alevi identity is being constructed in Turkey. The Alevis, members of a heterodox Shia branch of Islam, never bothered to create a 'church' or an organised community. They are also established among Turks and Kurds (most of the latter speak a specific language called Zaza). But when in 1983 the military government made religious teaching compulsory at school, the Alevis were confronted with a complex choice: should they send their children to the official Sunni courses (and hence accept being considered to be Sunni Muslims), ask for a specific religious Alevi curriculum (hence acknowledging that Alevism is a religious denomination), or call for secularisation and separation of religion and state so as not to be obliged to 'choose' a religious identity? Some Zaza-speaking intellectuals even used the debate as an opportunity to call for the promotion of a Zaza ethnic identity, with a territorial basis in the province of Dersim.[56] We have here another example of the unintended consequences of

56. See Elise Massicard, 'Discovering Alevism, Covering Difference', *ISIM News-letter,* 6 (2000); Elise Massicard, 'Alevism as a Productive Misunderstanding:

a state policy that aims to control religion but ends up creating new community identities where religion is more a neo-ethnic marker than a personal commitment to a faith.

Other examples can be found in Christendom. The line dividing Protestants and Catholics in Northern Ireland, for example, is no longer based on a commitment to a faith; most Ulster Protestants are no longer churchgoers, while many IRA activists were Marxists in the 1960s and 1970s.[57] Christian Orthodox churches are based on an ethno-national constituency and territory. For example, the Macedonian Orthodox Patriarchate was created in 1967 after the Macedonians were recognised as an ethnic group, distinct from the Serbs and Bulgarians. Such communitarian affiliation has nothing to do with faith and religious practices, and is quite different from Europe's religious wars of the sixteenth and seventeenth centuries, in which the choice of a faith was largely ideological, going along with a different conception of salvation, authority, politics, economy, and so on. But nowadays when religion becomes the core marker of group identity, it does not necessarily go along with religious revivalism.[58] As we have seen, many secular or leftist intellectuals are struggling to make religion an ethnic marker. It is also a means by which they can secularise religion (as the Zionist movement did for Jews at the end of the nineteenth century). But why should religious fundamentalist leaders go along with the ethnicisation of religion? Because it is a way to give roots to a new and elusive constituency, and to improve visibility and social status.

To establish a minority with a status means also to designate or appoint community leaders, who can then negotiate with the authorities on specific issues (halal meat, building permits, chaplains for schools and gaols, religious teaching, participation in state ceremonies), all entailing a social, political and also financial dimension (for example, management of subsidies, wages, and revenues from

The Hacibektas Festival' in Joost Jongerden and Paul J. White (eds), *Turkey's Alevi Enigma: A Comprehensive Overview,* Leiden: E.J. Brill, 2003.

57. Elizabeth Picard, 'De la domination du groupe à l'invention de son identité' in Denis-Constant Martin (ed.), *Cartes d'identité,* Paris: Presse de la FNSP, 1994, pp. 157.

58. There is often confusion between religious visibility (new mosques, use of Arabic scripts) and actual practice. Bosnia is an interesting case where after the war the religious Party of Democratic Action (SDA) lost power to more secular parties.

halal food businesses). Thus in order to build as numerous a constituency as possible it is better even for a devout Muslim *imam* to define Muslims as a neo-ethnic community, which will enlist all descendants of immigrants from Muslim countries, whatever their personal choice or practices. A community based on mosque-goers would by definition be far less numerous.

The confusion between religious community and neo-ethnic group is also encouraged by Muslim states, which strive to use a 'reconstructed' Muslim community as a dual lever in dealing with Western non-Muslim states and with other Muslim states. The Turkish, Algerian and Moroccan governments are very actively involved in Europe in retaining control of their emigrants. But the changing patterns of citizenship have made this control less and less possible through traditional diplomatic and consular channels. Hence these countries play the religious card: Turkey sends *imams* who are state employees and members of the Directorate for Religious Affairs (Diyanet İşleri Başkanliği); Morocco and Algeria strive hard to supervise the 'Muslim' population in France by posing as 'Muslim' states as much as nation-states. Morocco supports the Fédération Nationale des Musulmans de France, while Algeria subsidises and indirectly appoints the head of the Grand Mosque of Paris. In a recent case in France, the Moroccan consulate in Bordeaux intervened to prevent the cremation of a French citizen (of Moroccan descent) who had explicitly asked in his will to be cremated. The consulate argued that a Muslim never ceases to be a Muslim, even if he expressly states other choices.[59] But the most notable attempt to use communitarisation as a tool of foreign policy comes from Saudi Arabia, which claims to represent all Muslims in the West and has created an array of institutions (like the Muslim League) to spread Salafism and foster non-assimilation. The issue of neo-ethnicity thus has political consequences that go beyond the definition of a minority group.

Islamisation, westernisation and changing sociological patterns

The idea that Muslim values are aligned with a specific set of traditional sociological patterns that survives immigration is often

---

59. Blandine Grosjean, 'Le Consulat marocain empêche l'incinération d'un français', *Libération*, 13 February 2002.

advocated to support the validity of the terms 'culture' and 'ethnic group'. The family is always seen as the core of Muslim identity, and most of the debate on the backwardness of Muslim societies concerns the issue of women. Muhammad Anwar, to whose book we have already referred,[60] states: 'The traditional family system among Muslims is the extended joint family.'

What does this mean? If it is supposed to mean that most Muslims in Europe live in extended families, it is not true. Does it mean that Muslims who do not live in extended families are not 'good' Muslims? Or that the extended family is merely a trait of traditional Muslim societies and has nothing to do with Islam as such? In this sense, to refer to the 'extended family' as a Muslim sociological pattern is simply irrelevant. Many values are thus ascribed to the elusive Muslim culture: respect for elders; close family ties; female chastity; strong conservative values concerning sexuality, pornography and censorship; priority of the observance of norms over freedom.

In France and Britain, social workers and observers have concluded that the 1990s ended with a trend of communitarisation if not ghettoisation among Muslims living in impoverished suburbs and neighbourhoods, a phenomenon accentuated in Britain by faith schools, with a consequent deepening of cultural differences. In this environment religious values are enacted by social pressure.[61] Social workers see an ethnic homogenisation of entire neighbourhoods, more social pressure to respect traditional values (such as chastity and the seclusion of women), an increase in endogamy and arranged marriages with a spouse from the village of origin,[62] more

60. Anwar, *Young Muslims in Britain*, p. 12.
61. For Britain, see Frank Dobson's proposal ('Open up Faith Schools', *Guardian*, 8 February 2002; Dobson is a Labour MP and former Health Secretary), which called for faith schools to be open to students of other faiths. Interestingly, in France there are very few Muslim faith schools (by contrast to Catholic or Jewish ones), but the result is that the brunt of the 'cultural' conflicts is borne by teachers from the public sector. These are mostly leftist, which means that on the one hand they are strongly secular and in favour of driving religion out of school, but on the other hand they are more open to the protection of minority rights. When they have to choose, contrary to their British counterparts, it is in favour of secularism over multiculturalism. They were the driving force behind the law banning the headscarf in schools.
62. Sylvia Rappi, 'L'éducation nationale se mobilise contre les mariages forcés' (The Teaching Community Mobilises against Forced Marriages), *Le Monde*, 8 March 2002. Note the confusion between 'arranged marriages' and 'forced

respect for collective celebrations like the Ramadan fast, and more young women wearing the *hijab*[63] – all of which is in line with the revival of Islam in Muslim countries.

But if one considers the sociological evolution of Muslims, whether in countries of origin or among migrants, the picture is different: most of the data show an increasing sociological westernisation.[64] Almost everywhere fertility rates are falling to European levels (Iran, Tunisia, Algeria, and of course within the immigrant community), with the exception of Saudi Arabia and Palestine. Everywhere extended families give way to nuclear families; in cities with huge housing problems, the inability to live as a nuclear family is seen not as an opportunity to revitalise tradition but as an unacceptable burden (hence social unrest in Algiers). Everywhere there is a growing generation gap. Young people are better educated than their parents, and many problems arise from the general crisis of authority, from juvenile delinquency to the rise of Salafism because, when returning to Islam, youths usually break with the cultural Islam of their parents (as we shall see). The lack of elders' and parents' authority over children is a common pattern among second-generation Muslims in Europe.

The status of women is at the core of the crisis. The media have tended to focus on cases that underline the plight of girls caught between two cultures. But if these cases seem to be increasing (forced marriages, the *hijab*, honour crimes, rape), it is because Muslim girls are increasingly escaping from their traditional position. The disruption of family patterns is particularly obvious in neighbourhoods in Western Europe that are often supposed to be experiencing re-Islamisation. A growing assertiveness among young people is as much a consequence of the erosion of traditional social patterns, coupled with a crisis in the process of integration (which came to attention in France in 1983 with the *beur* movement).[65] Radicalised

---

marriages'. (The former are seen as legitimate by the bride, while the second are imposed against her will.)

63. There is no reliable data to support the idea of a massive re-Islamisation. But the increase of tensions in impoverished neighbourhoods and the use of Islam as a tool of protest are widespread phenomena in Western Europe.

64. See Philippe Fargues, *Générations arabes. L'alchimie du nombre*, Paris: Fayard, 2000.

65. In 1983 second-generation Arabs, supported by civil rights and leftist movements, demonstrated in France's large cities, calling for integration.

Muslim youths (whether in terms of youth subculture or Islamic fundamentalism) are more a sign of the dissolution of traditional familial structures than of the steadiness of traditional Muslim cultures. Even sociological patterns that seem to manifest retraditionalisation may hide more complex strategies. Arranged and often endogamous marriages are a way to bring relatives to the West through family reunion. (A girl with citizenship or a residence permit, especially one who is educated, is not only very valuable on the marriage market, but has every chance of enjoying higher status than her putative bridegroom brought from the country of origin.) Even the wearing of a 'modern' *hijab* by some working women is a sign of the entry of women into the public space. Here retraditionalisation goes along with westernisation.

Muslim *imams* have long acknowledged that they have to struggle not so much to maintain values as to create and entrench values among an uprooted youth. Fighting drug addiction and petty delinquency is a favourite topic of their sermons. These preachers, as well as social workers, know that the disappearance of traditional values lays the groundwork for re-Islamisation, not the continuance of traditional structures. There is a discrepancy between so-called Muslim values that are promoted by community leaders and the underlying social structures they pretend to express and that have simply disappeared. Sometimes Islamic radicals are themselves a factor of unintended social changes. Patrick Haenni shows how Islamic militants in a suburb like Embaba contribute to the destruction of traditional patterns of loyalties and to the reshaping of the communal identity of the suburb in religious terms.[66]

Interestingly, nowhere has the imposition of 'Islamic' legislation been able to reverse the trend of social change. In Iran, where the legal age of marriage for a girl was lowered from sixteen to nine after the revolution, the real average age at marriage increased considerably to more than twenty-four during the 1990s. The re-Islamisation of Iran is going hand in hand with sociological westernisation (or, more precisely, with realignment towards Western demographic trends).[67] The call to respect Islamic 'values' is

---

66. Patrick Haenni, 'Banlieues indociles? Sur la politisation des quartiers péri-urbains du Caire', PhD dissertation, Institut d'études politique (IEP), Paris, 2001.
67. Marie Ladier-Fouladi, *Population et politique en Iran. De la monarchie à la République islamique*, Paris: INED, 2003.

articulated at a time when these values are under attack or do not correspond to sociological changes. Moreover, such a call is often a way to recast new social patterns into a traditional framework or simply to adapt to a changing world by adopting a defensive and reactive discourse, propounding 'ideal types' that are less and less borne out in practice by the actors concerned. For example, there has been a massive debate in France about the 'return of the headscarf in schools and in Muslim-populated neighbourhoods. But only several dozen manifestations of the 'headscarf affair' have gone to court in a decade, while nobody speaks about the increasing number of prostitutes and 'running girls'[68] of 'Muslim' origin. The stress on chastity, accompanying the voluntary wearing of the headscarf as a way of being respected by gangs of boys in poor neighbourhoods, says more about the crisis of traditional values and family structures than about the pervasiveness of traditional imported values. In parallel, Islam is sometimes advocated to justify attitudes that are a consequence of uprooting and westernisation. While genuine polygamy is fading away everywhere, the divorce rate seems to be increasing and has resulted in a rise in single-parent, female-headed households, a contemporary trend in low-income, non-Muslim neighbourhoods in the United States. It is, however, very much out of step with the image of a traditional Muslim family, where children are in their father's custody, and where divorced or widowed women return to their own families.

As we shall see, the revival of Islam among second-generation migrants leads to a recasting of the system of values (a stress on the couple and on the concept of responsibility, as opposed to the lack of responsibility among the older generation) and not a return to traditional sociological patterns (the extended family, poor female education, high birth rates). This also makes room for a recasting of 'Western values' and sociological changes in terms of neofundamentalism: the spouse is a partner, not just the mother of the children. One may contrast the traditional view of Iranian *ulama*, who see marriage as a mere contract, with the declaration of a martyr thanking his wife for her support and love, a formulation that might easily be found among Christians but not traditional Muslims.[69]

68. Young girls who have escaped from their school and family to live in the streets or in squats, and who occasionally work as prostitutes.
69. For the radical Islamists, see the interesting eulogy of an Al Qaeda fighter

In a totally different sphere, the rise of a business-minded Muslim middle class, quite at home with the free market and globalisation (having benefited from economic protectionism), but unhappy with the monopolisation by non-productive ruling élites of access to international markets (for example, Iran, Algeria) is also a by-product of globalisation.[70] Some preachers address the spiritual needs of this new modern and devout middle class, while legitimising its wealth.[71]

But the populations concerned experience such changes not in terms of purely sociological trends or of proactive adaptation, but as the negative consequences of westernisation. An omnipresent idea in sermons is that the dissolution of the 'ideal' family is a consequence of Western influence and not of deterritorialisation and adaptation. On the other hand, many in the West explain the Islamic revival by the irreducible permanence of 'Islamic' values and not as a reaction to sociological changes. ('Can Islam reform or adapt? Is Islam compatible with democracy, secularisation, the West, women's rights?' Such questions are a watchword of the public debate on Islam.) The consequence is that the fundamentalist (or at least conservative) Islamic discourse and the Western cliché of 'the clash of civilisations' find common ground in expressing

---

killed by US forces at Tora Bora, Afghanistan, in December 2001 (formerly at <http://www.azzam.com>, then on <http://www.islamicawakening.com/viewarticle.php?articleID=713>). Suraqah al-Andalusi was apparently a Spanish convert ('Arabic was not his mother tongue', and 'Andalusi' is an nickname obviously referring to Muslim Spain). The testimony of one of his comrades in arms says: 'One time we were speaking about families and I was telling him how difficult it always is to say goodbye to a tearful mother, not knowing whether you will meet her again in this life. He was silent for a while and then said, "No, brother, the bond between the wife and husband is a bond that is different than that of the mother and her son. It is something much stronger".' It is a clear shift from the traditional view of the Muslim family (and it also supposes that there is only one wife). For the changes in Iran, see Azadeh Kian-Thiébaut, *Les femmes iraniennes entre Islam, Etat et famille*, Paris: Maisonneuve et Larose, 2002.

70. On the Turkish MÜSIAD, see Gültekin Burcu, 'Instrumentalisation de l'Islam pour une stratégie de promotion sociale à travers le secteur privé. Le cas du Müsiad', DEA dissertation, Fondation Nationale des Sciences Politiques (FNSP), Paris, 1999.

71. Husam Tammam and Patrick Haenni, 'Chat Shows, Nashid Groups and Lite Preaching: Egypt's Air-conditioned Islam', *Le Monde Diplomatique* (English edn), September 2003.

problems linked with the passage to the West of Islam in terms of values, culture and religion, ignoring the sociological changes and the *de facto*, even makeshift westernisation of Islam.

To conclude, to speak in terms of a 'Muslim culture' based on specific sociological patterns does not fit with the sociological reality of the demographic and social evolution of Muslim populations. There is a discrepancy between the avowed values of a 'Muslim culture' and the sociological realities of everyday life for people of Muslim origin. As usual, cultural values are more preached than implemented. But this imaginary culture is too often taken at its own word by observers and politicians. With a slight time-lag, Muslim populations are entering the same patterns of sociological modernisation as the West, but this can occasionally be carried out through religious revivalism. In this sense the call to values has to be seen either as nostalgia for a disappearing social order or as a search for renewed foundations of personal religiosity in terms of purely religious values.

Protest youth culture

'Muslim' youth culture in Europe offers an interesting approach to the complex use of references to anthropological culture, social stratification, values, ethnicisation and changes in religiosity.

In Europe immigration has created, on the margins of society in inner cities or suburbs, a space of social exclusion largely populated by unemployed youth of Muslim origin. In the United States such a space is more likely to be populated by African-Americans and Hispanics. Spaces of social exclusion in Europe have recently been ethnicised through immigration, with occasional youth unrest and juvenile delinquency in Britain and France adding fuel to the debates on the integration of Muslims and on security. Such delinquency has often been presented as a symptom of the breakdown of integration, which is true – unemployment and racism have convinced many second-generation youngsters that they are not welcome. Nevertheless, the youth culture that spread in these spaces has little to do with Islam, but is a side-effect of acculturation.[72]

72. Jamaaluddin Haidar, a radical black convert living in Houston, Texas, wrote: 'I recently confronted one such gang that operates in the predominantly Yemeni community where I teach science and computer classes at the Islamic

Islam, on the contrary, provides a possible alternative identity to exclusion, and may also offer a path to a new respectability, as opposed to what is on offer from today's youth culture. 'Youth culture' is not the expression of a Muslim culture but of a Western 'subculture', grown in the suburbs, closer to the expression of black youth culture in the United States than to that of the Muslim countries of origin. The youngsters in question reject most of their fathers' values. They do not speak the original language or attend the mosque, but do eat at McDonald's, wear baseball caps, buy expensive clothes, fully engage in consumerism and breed dogs at home. Erasure of the culture of origin does not necessarily entail westernisation along the lines of the social mainstream, but the creation of a marginal protest culture (manifested in music, clothing, slang), which both adopts and subverts the symbols of the dominant Western culture, even playing on neo-ethnic identities (Asian, black, *beur*), which are no longer the expression of a given identity shared by parents and children. In France these young people used to be referred to as *beur*; their slang (*verlan*) itself is interesting, because it has nothing to do with Arabic, but is a legacy of a French tradition of 'outcasts' and thugs. It consists of an inversion of the first and final syllables of a word, in this case *à l'envers*, which gives *verlan*. Rap songs are based on quite literary written French; the music in competition with rap, *rai*, born in Algeria, is more a product of cultural hybridity.

Here there is a social category inventing its form of expression, culture and music, but it does not express a community. It expresses an age class, a period, a transition. It is by definition temporary and unstable, even if it does not necessarily mean that there will be an integration and homogenisation with mainstream social and cultural patterns. The striking fact is the ethnicisation of a space of social exclusion, although here 'ethnicity' has nothing to do with a 'culture' – it is the marker of social differentiation, of something that tends to replace the old class system.

school. I have observed this gang of thugs selling drugs across the street from the Masjid and the Islamic school. I have seen them spray graffiti on Muslim businesses. One gang symbol that they spray on walls is "A.W.A." and "Arabs with Attitudes" a play on the name of a group of California-based thugs turned "gangster" rappers – "N.W.A." or "N–ggers with Attitudes'" (<http://home.houston.rr.com/between/fset2.html>; the site is no longer online following the arrest of the owner in 2002).

Relationships between Islam and youth culture are complex. Preachers interacting with Muslim youths reject their 'Western' culture and criticise their entire way of living: food, music, drug habits and petty delinquency. For them, to be a born-again Muslim means a rejection of their habits. Born-again Muslims refuse to use the word *beur* or even 'Arab', and call for the exclusive use of the word 'Muslim'. Like their Protestant counterparts, *imams* ask the born-again to renounce their previous lives of sin. Gaols are known for producing born-again Muslims, but this is clearly linked to a high number of young Muslim detainees. On the other hand, in Western Europe at least, many such youngsters have used Islam as an occasional form of protest identity: calling for halal food at school, explaining Islam by attitudes that are more linked with their youth culture (rejection of women from public space, all-male gangs) or fasting during Ramadan as a sign of neighbourhood belonging (while they never pray and almost never go to the mosque.

Of course there are specific patterns of re-Islamisation in the suburbs – such as the *hijab*, beards and a growing visibility of Ramadan – that also contribute to the enhancement of neighbourhood identity and to a sense of solidarity. (It is quite common for non-Muslims to participate in *iftar*, the breaking of the day-long fast during Ramadan, as a form of socialisation, while, as we shall see, some young non-Muslims convert to Islam to join their friends next door in their quest for a protest identity.)

But this youth culture is definitely rooted in the West. Born-again Muslims are more prone to launch a halal McDonald's than a restaurant that serves couscous or traditional 'Indian' food.[73] The process of de-ethnicisation is clear. Re-Islamisation also regularly leads to the creation of a sub-ghetto inside a low-income neighbourhood. Some young people may join a small mosque under a self-proclaimed *imam* and disqualify other mosques as 'non-Islamic'. The conflict between generations remains at the heart of re-Islamisation and contributes nothing to the unification of the population by the building of a large faith community. As we have seen, most French and British Al Qaeda fighters came from low-income neighbourhoods. Khaled Kelkal, who was linked with the

73. In my home town there has been a shop selling 'halal Greek sandwiches'. Nobody is Greek and they serve doner kebabs.

GIA, was from the suburbs of Lyon, as was Mourad Benchellali, who was taken to Guantanamo Bay in the autumn of 2001, in the aftermath of US military operations in Afghanistan. After the second Palestinian intifada, in the autumn of 2000, half a dozen synagogues came under attack in precisely these sorts of neighbourhoods (France is one of the few countries, along with Israel, where working-class Jews live in close proximity to their Muslim counterparts), but the culprits were not linked to any Islamic movements. The fear that these Muslim youths could identify with Middle Eastern conflicts was at its peak in 1991 during the Gulf war, but has since receded. In fact political mobilisation for Palestine or Iraq remained at a very low level. (There have been no significant pro–Palestine demonstrations in Muslim-populated neighbourhoods in France, except in the larger cities, but with the participation of the Left and the antiglobalisation movement.) The Muslim youth of low-income neighbourhoods remain largely apolitical, as indicated by the low level of registration for elections

Towards redefining a religious community

A neo-ethnic definition of Muslims, although convenient in practical terms, also seems to many Muslims to contradict the universal message of Islam as the 'true' religion; they are willing to de-ethnicise Islam, in the name of its claim to be a universal religion. Converts, of course, do not feel at ease with an 'ethnic' religion. But beyond that, globalisation itself is de-ethnicising Islam. As we shall see, this can be played out in either 'liberal' or 'fundamentalist' terms. The endeavour to build a community whose sole criterion is religious faith presupposes the negation of any specific culture and ethnicity. This is explicit in the declarations and sermons of most religious leaders, and was the cornerstone of the acceptance of Black Muslims in the United States by mainstream Islamic clerics.[74] In this sense Islam is not only what the different Muslim ethnic groups have in common, but also what should appeal to 'whites'. New Muslim leaders in the countries of immigration base their actions on an Islamic reformism, and sometimes fundamentalism, by

74. See Moore, *Al-Mughtaribun*, p. 11. 'A key principle of this explicitly Islamic consciousness is that *religious* should prevail over *ethnic* identity.'

labelling as 'un-Islamic' many customs and habits from the pristine cultures, or at least by dissociating themselves from traditionalism. They advocate the use of the language of the new country, which is now the universal language. Through this contribution to the delegitimation of pristine cultures, Islamic reformism or fundamentalism is part of the process of acculturation, but it also offers a substitute identity.

In the next chapter we shall deal with the evolution not of Islam as such, but of the relationship between the faithful and their faith – that is, religiosity.

4
THE TRIUMPH OF THE RELIGIOUS SELF

The delinking of culture and religion is a fact. The attempt in the West to redefine a 'Muslim culture' on a neo-ethnic basis or as a translation of a religious code into a cultural idiom is a consequence of such a delinking, but it does not provide the social authority that goes with the very concept of culture. To live as a minority means experiencing Islam as only a religion. Even if Islam is an all-encompassing religion for the believer, such an integrative view is not supported by social authority. No allowances are made for Muslims to abide naturally and easily by the tenets of their religion. (For instance, meat is supposed to be halal in any Egyptian butcher's shop, but in Paris or London the believer must seek out a specialist halal shop.) Hence the implementation of binding religious obligations rests on the goodwill of the believer, not on any external cultural pressure or a state's legal system. To be a 'fundamentalist' Muslim in a non-Muslim society means experiencing secularisation; that is, the separation of church, or more precisely faith, from state. Religious norms have no relationships with social and political spheres; religion is *de facto* confined to the private sphere. Trying to externalise it does not mean changing society but joining others in building a community that is no more than a congregation of believers who follow their own rules of conduct. But, as we said in Chapter 1, the autonomy of both spheres is becoming increasingly visible in traditional Muslim societies, where believers, even when they comprise a demographic majority, resent the tensions between their faith and dominant cultural patterns – a fact that is acknowledged in the United States by many Christians, and even in Israel by orthodox Jews.

The weakening religion's social authority also entails a growing individualisation of religious practices. The definition of what it means to be a Muslim and the reconstruction of a Muslim community rest on the individual. The relevant dimension is that of religiosity – how believers experience and formulate their relationship to religion. Such an individualisation of Islam is pervasive and parallels the same phenomenon in Christianity: the stress on faith and values, the quest for a universal community going beyond cultures and nations, the importance of local congregations as a basis for socialisation, and alienation from a society seen as materialist and vain. But it is important to stress that such a move towards the individualisation of religion can lead to various forms of religiosity, from liberal Islam to neofundamentalism, passing through emotional pietism, moral conservatism, or humanistic and social propagandism. Individualisation of faith does not necessarily lead to a more secular and liberal way of life. Modernity does not automatically lead to liberalism and democracy, and secularisation could accompany a reconstruction of closed religious identities, a process we call communitarisation. In short, individualisation may lead either to liberal forms of Islam or to neofundamentalism. Instead of representing two clearly antagonistic traditions, the current debate between liberal and Salafi Islam offers two different responses to deculturation, uprooting and individualisation. The underlying common problematic is about reconciling the self with religion, in terms either of norms (Salafism) or values (liberal or ethical Islam). This process of reappropriation is what I call religiosity.

This explains why it is difficult to categorise contemporary expressions of religiosity. Is Wahhabism a conservative and apolitical school of thought, a counterweight to anti-Western radical Islam, as it was constantly perceived by the US government till 9/11? Or is it a radically anti-Western ideology, giving religious legitimacy to political terrorism? Did Wahhabism change during the 1990s? What are the relationships between Wahhabism and radical Islam? The fault lines are unclear. Some moderate but conservative Western Muslim leaders support the obligation for pious female Muslims to wear a *hijab*, yet firmly oppose Al Qaeda (as is the case with the Union of Islamic Organisations in France, the UOIF), yet some radicals target conservatives and liberals.[1] Sheikh Yusuf al-Qaradawi, a leading Egyptian Muslim Brother who graduated

---

1. A French Islamic terrorist group led by Khaled Kelkal began its terror campaign in France in 1995 by gunning down a conservative *imam*, Sahraoui, who was close to the Algerian FIS and considered to be a fundamentalist.

from Al-Azhar University and is a high-ranking cleric in Qatar, wrote *The Lawful and the Prohibited in Islam*, which in 1996 was banned by the French Ministry of the Interior (officially because it condoned wife-beating by Muslim men, but in reality because it was perceived to be the new radicals' 'textbook'), yet which the Salafis at the same time dubbed *The Lawful and the Lawful* because of its over-liberal views. The lines dividing liberals and conservatives in the West are blurred, according to many Muslim leaders. Sheikh Abdullah Hakim Quick (a black convert living in South Africa) wrote: 'Islam is the only organised way of life that can categorically oppose homosexuality, racism and secularism.'[2] In the West, and specifically in white South Africa, people who fight racism usually also oppose homophobia. (Laws banning discrimination against homosexuals often have been enacted in the West in the years after the introduction or strengthening of race relations legislation.) In France the Muslim intellectual Tariq Ramadan, who teaches philosophy in Geneva and has wide appeal with educated second-generation youth, is alternately labelled a liberal and modern thinker who praises citizenship and integration in the embrace of the French republic, and a fundamentalist and communitarianist leader who encourages Muslim girls to wear the *hijab*.[3]

More interestingly, many Muslim conservatives tend to recast Islamic legal norms into Western-compatible terms (cultures and values) but, contrary to Muslim reformers, their aim is not to water down Islamic legislation. On the contrary, they seek to enforce it in terms understandable by (if not acceptable to) non-Muslim Europeans. For example, the application of *sharia* norms on adultery is presented as the best way to fight AIDS, in the same way that conservative Christians advocate chastity.[4] Conservative Muslims align here with conservative Western Christians in their criticisms of an

2.   Hakim Quick, 'Seeking the Inner Muslim', <http://www.hakimquick.com/articles2.htm>.

3.   In a libel suit that Ramadan brought against a magazine in Lyon in November 2002, a Catholic priest testified in his favour and another one against him. He has been supported by a leading figure in a league that fought for decades against any form of religious interference in public life (the Movement against Racism and for Friendship among People, or MRAP), and by a secular leftist (and Jewish) journalist. His opponent, a Lebanese Christian, received the support of many French intellectuals.

4.   Hani Ramadan, 'La charia incomprise' ['The Misunderstood Sharia'], *Le Monde*, 10 September 2002. (Hani Ramadan is the brother of Tariq.)

over-permissive society: defence of marriage, distaste for coeducation (shared by many US Protestant fundamentalists), strong opposition to homosexuals marrying or adopting children, and support for harsher censorship of films and television.

But who, one is tempted to ask, speaks for Muslims? What is the Muslim community to which everybody refers? How does one pass from individualisation of faith to the enacting of a Muslim community? As we shall see, such an elusive community, which is no longer based on territory, state, culture or a given society, could only be virtual and established on a voluntary basis, unless specific legislation were passed to 'objectify' Muslims, as was the case with members of the various *millets* in the Ottoman Empire (and still is the case in Lebanon, Jordan and Palestine, and also India). Hence many conservative and neofundamentalist Muslims are using the multiculturalist idiom to obtain from Western states legal tools to define the community and draw sectarian borders.

THE LOSS OF RELIGIOUS AUTHORITY AND THE 'OBJECTIFICATION' OF ISLAM

Passage to the West changes the nature of religiosity because it entails:

1. the dilution of the pristine culture, where religion was embedded in a given culture and society;

2. the absence of legitimate religious authorities who could define the norms of Islam, coupled with a crisis of the transmission of knowledge; and

3. the impossibility of any form of legal, social or cultural coercion.

Religion is no longer embedded in cultural and social relationships. It has to be elaborated upon, not only for Muslims (how does one reconcile the ban on paying interest with the buying of a house, for instance), but also for non–Muslims, who are constantly pushing Muslims to be explicit on any currently important issue. (What does the Koran say about women or *jihad*? About terrorism?) It is difficult to remain a passive, silent and conformist Muslim in the West: every action has to be elaborated as a choice. The crisis of social authority accompanies an obligation to elaborate.

Fasting during the month of Ramadan in a traditional Muslim society is made easier by its social acceptance, even if it is avoided by many people. Whether by law or custom, working hours are adapted and fast-breaking (*iftar*) is announced by the firing of weapons or by an air-raid siren. *Iftar* parties are an opportunity for social gatherings (visiting family and neighbours, political meetings, or shows of allegiance to a leader or a notable). Religious formulas (such as *assalamu alaikum*) are often part of the vernacular language. (To say '*assalamu alaikum*' in Afghan Persian is vernacular, to say it in Iranian Persian is customary but conspicuously 'Islamic', but to use it when speaking French is to display an ostentatious, quite exotic and even provocative religious belonging.) In a Muslim society there are places to pray, food is supposed to be halal, and the calendar is in accord with religious celebrations (even in secular Turkey and Tunisia). This does not of course mean that people are regular mosque-goers, but it does mean that religious practice, casual or regular, is embedded in social authority and does not need to be elaborated upon and justified by the believer. Islam is part of the landscape. This means paradoxically that sin and transgression are also part of social life, as the penumbra of a familiar landscape.

But there is today a crisis of social authority in Muslim countries too. That *sharia*-based punishments have been introduced in recent years in Iran, Afghanistan (under the Taliban), Sudan, Pakistan and northern Nigeria means that these traditional Muslim societies have dealt for decades with transgressions of the *hudud* without feeling that their religion and societies were in danger. The first trial in modern times (to my knowledge) of homosexuals in Egypt, in 2002, could mean either that there was previously no homosexuality in Egypt or that a blind eye was turned to it. Meanwhile in the West the social authority of Islam has suddenly disappeared for Muslims. Ordinary believers must devise their own ways to be more or less good Muslims. As one British Muslim said, 'Living in a non-Muslim society, Muslims have to be careful of every step they take. They must be conscious of what they are doing at all times.'[5] Religious practice has to be elaborated upon. This, of course, does not apply solely to Islam. It is part of a wider process of 'minoritisation' and communitarisation of religious identities

5.   Fazeela Hanif, 'Being a Muslim in Great Britain', <http://www.mrc.org.uk> (2002).

which implies that even in countries where most people claim to be practising believers (such as the United States), any religious community nevertheless thinks of itself as being a minority group in a secular and materialist world.[6] A religious community, whether Muslim or Christian, is now perceived, even by its own members, as 'a voluntary group, whose existence depends on the adherence of individual members'.[7] What it means to be a believer must be stated explicitly.

Eickelman and Piscatori have coined the relevant concept of 'objectification of Islam', meaning that to be able to define Islam becomes a prerequisite for any born-again or practising believer, because Islam is no longer embedded in a culture and a social practice.[8] '*What is Islam?*', '*What does Islam say about ...*', '*Islam and ... [democracy, secularism, human rights, and so on]*' – these are common themes and titles of textbooks and sermons.[9] This is a novel development: I know of no classical works of theology with such formulations, and to my knowledge the word *Islam* does not appear in the titles of key religious works. Islam has become an object that must be apprehended as such.[10] The answers to such questions as those raised above (like 'What does Islam say about ...?') are less important than the approach they imply. Everybody who

6. The idea is summed up in an interview with Cardinal Poupard, a leading French Catholic figure (Marie-Noëlle Tranchant, 'Foi au singulier, culture au pluriel', *Le Figaro*, 28–29 December 2002, p. 17): 'An issue to be considered is that in countries which are sociologically Christian, Christians are a cultural minority.' It is echoed by a statement in a text of the al-Qur'an was-Sunnah Society of north America: 'A true salafi ... this makes him a stranger among people' (<http://www.qss.org/articles/salafi/text.html>).
7. Danièle Hervieu-Léger, *La religion pour mémoire*, Paris: Éditions du Cerf, 1993, p. 131.
8. Dale Eickelman and James Piscatori, *Muslim Politics*, Princeton University Press, 1996, p. 38.
9. If one considers the list of twenty-one books published in 1996 by the Tawhid publishing house in Lyon, France, five addressed the issue of Islam and the contemporary and modern world (*To be Muslim Today*; *Muslims in a Secular World*; *Islam Today*; *Three Problems of Islam in Contemporary World*; and *Islam, the Confrontation of Civilisations*), and three others the issue of faith.
10. This is an approach to be compared with 'objective Christianity', as defined by Michel de Certeau (cited in Hervieu-Léger, *La religion pour mémoire*, p. 91). What is new is not the comparison between Islam and Christianity (which is a cliché of the apologetic literature), but the construction of Islam as one religion among others.

asks these questions provides answers and thus participates in the process of objectification, whatever his or her academic credentials. The formulation, not the content, creates the meaning.

Even if the answer is integrative ('Islam is everything, from hygiene to politics'), which is the case for fundamentalism, merely to ask such a question presupposes that one is not living in a true Muslim context, which means that secularisation has succeeded.

Objectification of Islam is also reinforced by pressure from non-Muslims, especially in periods of crisis, when Muslims are summoned to answer questions such as, 'What does the Koran say on … [*jihad*, violence]?'. It is also the product of a mirror effect between Western societies and Muslim public opinion, which explains why non-Muslims are more inclined to listen to conservatives and fundamentalists than to liberal thinkers. Conservatives and fundamentalists give definite answers to the question 'What is Islam?', something that is more difficult for a Sufi, a spiritualist or a lay Muslim to do.

Even in Muslim countries the social authority of Islam is fading. 'True believers' are confronted with ways of life, images, films, cultural models, educational systems, consumer habits and economic practices that are heavily influenced by a secular and Western world.[11] As we shall see, this coincides not with a weakening of religious beliefs and practices but with a move towards rethinking what should be seen as 'true' Islam. Since the failure of the Islamist movements to rebuild from the top a true Islamic society, the only way to fight foreign influence has been to try to establish somewhere a sphere of true 'Islamicity', which means acknowledging the dominant secularisation, even when fighting it. There is a general feeling of an Islamicity not only besieged by hostile and dominant Western powers, but also undermined from within by Western influence. Hence the appeal in Muslim countries of Huntington's concept of 'the clash of civilisations'.

The Afghan Taliban, as usual, provide a good example. While they were ruling a profoundly Muslim country where Western

11. I use the opposition tradition/westernisation for the sake of expediency, but believe that there is a process of reappropriation and interaction between them (see Fariba Adelkhah, *Being Modern in Iran*, London: Hurst, 1999; Jean-François Bayart, *The Fictions of Cultural Identity*, London: Hurst, 2005). Traditional society or traditional Islam are often reconstructions made by the actors and by many social scientists (including me) along these lines.

influence had been at a minimum for historical reasons (the last episode being the Soviet occupation), and while they were on rather good terms, from 1994 to 1997, with the United States, they were nevertheless obsessed by the idea that the country might cease to be a true Muslim one. The destruction of the Buddhas of Bamiyan as a pagan symbol (after they had been spared in the previous fourteen centuries of Muslim rule); the arrest of aid workers of the Christian NGO Shelter Now International, who were accused of spreading religious propaganda; the imposition of 'emergency' teaching for Afghan children who had been taught by Christians (just to erase any residual Christian influence); and the imposition of the death penalty on any Muslim Afghan who had converted to Christianity or Judaism – all are clear signs of these obsessive feelings. Such paranoia seems odd to old Afghanistan hands like me, who remember the great tolerance of Afghans for other religions, and their profound faith. This faith has not been eroded by twenty years of war, so the new sense of fragility is linked with something other than the weakening of religious practices. The imposition of religious practices by force poses a problem that goes far beyond prohibiting evil and promoting good. It means that what is at stake is the link between religion and culture. The Taliban's targets were aspects of the traditional Afghan culture, from music to cockfighting. We are witnessing a two-pronged attack on 'traditional' cultures by both religious fundamentalism and globalisation. Fundamentalism is an agent and a consequence of deculturation.

The crisis of pristine cultures and the ensuing process of objectification of Islam means the new Muslim actors try to display a 'pure' form of Islam, not linked to any given society or culture, or adapted to any culture, which means by definition an Islam oblivious of its own history. More precisely, modern Islamic thinkers tend to 'de-Islamise' the history of the Muslim world by blaming foreigners or 'bad' Muslims for the trends and events that led to the decline of Muslim civilisation. This idea of a joint attack by western imperialism and domestic liberals is common among neofundamentalists. Iranian conservatives launched a campaign against 'cultural aggression' (*tajavoz-i farhangi*) in the early 1990s, targeting an emerging youth culture as well as liberal intellectuals.[12] Kemal Atatürk, whose

---

12. Ironically one of their targets, Abdolkarim Soroush, was in charge, after the 1979 revolution, of the 'Islamisation' of sciences at the University of Tehran.

systematic and brutal assault on traditional society traumatised many conservative Muslims, is said by Islamic activists to have originated from a family of Jewish converts (*dönme*).[13] Moreover many contemporary fundamentalist movements have entered politics by violently attacking syncretist or deviant Muslim sects. The Hojjatieh Society, from which many Iranian conservatives are drawn, was created in the early 1950s to fight the Baha'is, while the first large-scale political campaign launched by Maududi at that time was aimed at depriving Pakistani Qadianis of their status as Muslims. (Qadiani and Baha'i are religions that stemmed from Islam, but consider that Muhammad was not the final prophet.) The Tablighi Jama'at was founded in India in 1926 to purify Islam of Hindu and Christian influences. In this sense anti-imperialism dovetails nicely with fundamentalism, because it explains that deviation is a result of foreign influence. A common complaint among fundamentalists is that Christian missionaries are pursuing an aggressive campaign of conversion (which is true, incidentally – and Hindu, Jewish and Russian Orthodox activists complain of the same phenomenon).[14]

Another obsession, linked with the sense of being besieged, is apostasy. Salman Rushdie, for example, was branded an apostate. More interestingly, legal suits have recently been brought, not to punish apostates but to have them legally recognised as such, with the legal consequences entailed by this status. (Examples include Nasr Abu Zaid in Egypt and Taslima Nasrin in Bangladesh, as we shall see.) These trials are interesting because they introduce a new perception of apostates: they exist but cannot be eliminated, and so should be placed into a separate category of non-Muslims.

IMMIGRATION AND REFORMULATION OF ISLAM

Passage to the West offers a good opportunity to rethink an Islam rid of cultural and national particularities, which complements the dual movement of individualisation and reconstruction of a community on a purely religious basis. Individualisation is the consequence of the uprooting and dissolution of pristine social links.

13. See, for instance, an article entitled 'Adopting Secularism in Government is Apostasy from Islam' (20 July 2000), on the Hizb ut-Tahrir website (<http://www.khilafah.com/ home/lographics/category.php?DocumentID =13&TagID=3>).
14. See also n. 22, p. 115, this vol.

The new community may be purely ideal (with no ties other than faith), it may be based on traditional networks (retaining endogamous relations with the family remaining in the country of origin), but it always works as a reconstruction. Some actors would even acknowledge immigration as a positive factor, because by uprooting Muslims from pseudo-Muslim cultures and pushing them to recast their otherness in purely religious terms, it helps to promote a return to the true tenets of religion, however different they might be for those involved. This is the paradox of the new *mohajir* (migrant and/or exile), who can live a better Islam in a non-Muslim country because the homelands are only nominally Muslim and value hypocrisy above faith.[15] In this sense immigration is not seen only as a pragmatic quest for a better life; it is also presented as a positive opportunity to recast a religious identity in unequivocal terms. Tariq Ramadan goes so far as to write that a Muslim enjoys greater freedom to live up to his religion in the West than in most, if not all, Muslim countries.[16] There is no room for hypocrisy when social pressure in the West works against ostentatious practice. The same idea is expressed by a liberal US Muslim, Muqtedar Khan:

Indeed the opportunity for so many Muslim ethnicities to come together, undivided by silly nationalist agendas, has after a long time reproduced in microcosm a truly global Ummah. Now if this truly global Ummah can articulate a vision of Islam free from cultural artifacts, then we can begin to see a true turn toward an Islamic identity.[17]

Another liberal writes:

Ummah means a community built around certain values. For example, the founders of this country [the United States] left Europe and came here with certain values. They did not find room to implement those values in Europe, so they decided to find another place. They came here with their

15. In his book *Reflections of an American Muslim* (Chicago: Distributed by Kazi Publications; also posted on the internet at <http://islam-usa.com/>, 2002), Shahid Athar, a Pakistani-American, wrote of his frustration after visiting Pakistan: 'If a new Muslim or a "born-again" Muslim from the West visits a Muslim country, he will be shocked to see the dichotomy and hypocrisies in the preaching and practicing of Islam' (<http://islam-usa.com/r8.html>).
16. Tariq Ramadan, *Les musulmans dans la laïcité. Responsabilité et droits des musulmans dans les sociétés occidentales*, Lyon: Tawhid, 1994, p. 101.
17. M.A. Muqtedar Khan, 'Muslims in America: What Is the American Muslim Perspective?', *Washington Report on Middle East Affairs*, December 1999, p. 82 (<http://www.wrmea.com/backissues/1299/9912082.html>).

values to build this country. This is an Ummah, and not a nation, because nation is built around a piece of land, and not values.[18]

Interestingly the same idea appears on the other side of the spectrum, among radical fundamentalists like Abu Hamza of London. When asked if he favours *hijra* from non-Muslim to Muslim lands, he answered: 'I tell [Muslims in the West] to go into a Muslim environment, not a Muslim country, because in our countries [of origin] we have Muslims but we do not have Islamic states ... I say to Muslims get out of these societies ... I have to be the Moses in the house of the Pharaoh.'[19] This a clear definition of what I call deterritorialised Islam: the Dar-ul-Islam is where good Muslims convene; it is not a territory, it is an 'environment'. In this sense passage to the West is seen as positive by fundamentalists and liberals alike. Such a passage accentuates also the transformation of religiosity.

Crisis of religious teaching institutions

There is no clergy in Sunni Islam, but there has always been (at least since Nizam ol Molk's policy of building *madrasas* in the Seljuk Empire in the eleventh century) a corporation of the learned, the *ulama*, who had *de facto* hegemony on religious debate. This corporation of the learned has been in crisis since the nineteenth century for various reasons. With few exceptions (such as the nineteenth-century Egyptian reformer Rifaat al-Tahtawi), they remained aloof from the process of authoritarian modernisation led by lay rulers like Muhammad Ali. In the twentieth century no political actors (except among the Shias) and few of the intellectual actors of Islamic revivalism were drawn from the ranks of the *ulama*. They came instead from among modern intellectuals, who

18. Interview with Sheikh Taha: 'There Is No Justice with Dictatorship', *Muslim Democrat*, 4, 1 (2002), pp. 4–5 (<http://www.islam-democracy.org/documents/pdf/md_january2002.pdf>). Sheikh Taha Jabir Alalwani is president of the Graduate School of Islamic and Social Sciences, in Leesburg, Virginia.
19. <http://www.supportersofshariat.org/eng/abuhamza.html>, 17 October 2000; the site was closed after 9/11. The same interview appeared later as 'Who is Sheikh Abu-Hamza? A Conversation with Sheikh Abu-Hamza' at <http://www.angelfire.com/bc3/johnsonuk/eng/sheikh.html> (visited on 19 February 2004).

often had scientific training. The endeavour by many Muslim (and non-Muslim) states to establish an 'official clergy' led to the bureaucratisation of religious teaching and to a dearth of intellectual revivalism in the theological field. It also cut off religious studies from other fields of culture (literature and philosophy). The professionalisation of the religious curriculum (making religion a specific discipline) led to its deculturation, while the conservative re-Islamisation noted in Chapter 2 precipitated an intellectual sclerosis. 'Liberal' views expressed by state-sanctioned *mullahs* are not necessarily better elaborated than fundamentalist ones, and in any case no government wishes to promote an imaginative and provocative *alim* as a leading official cleric. Political and intellectual conformity complement each other.

There is a palpable uneasiness in the traditional big *madrasas*. Their role has declined, as has their prestige, due to the control exercised by political authorities (the dean of Al-Azhar University in Cairo has been a state appointee since Nasser's time). The fact that Al-Azhar has a growing percentage of African and South-East Asian (Indonesian) students may be more a sign of its decline than of continuing influence.[20] When the dean of the university, Sheikh Tantawi, refused in 1997 to make a statement on female circumcision, leaving that to medical doctors while nevertheless indicating that his daughter had not been subjected to it, he relinquished in a sense the moral and legal leadership he might have claimed for himself. Al-Azhar failed also to capitalise on its alumni to build an influential network; on the contrary, many graduates embarked upon independent religious careers, hiring themselves as preachers to a local congregation or opening their own teaching institutions (such as private religious schools).[21] Many clerics are reaching out to a new audience by leaving the closed corporate space of *madrasas* and religious seminaries to speak on radio or television, write in non-religious journals, serve as a kind of chaplain to lay associations (for example, Amr Khaled in Egypt) or teach at state universities. Thus they become participants in the contemporary blurring of lines between the religious and secular spheres. They leave behind the clerical world (and often clerical garb, as did Amr

20. Personal interviews at Al-Azhar University, March 2001.
21. Malika Zeghal, *Gardiens de l'Islam. Les oulémas d'Al-Azhar dans l'Égypte contemporaine*, Paris: Presses de Sciences Po, 1996.

Khaled) to address a lay audience, not as representatives of any religious institution but as individual thinkers and writers. By doing so they introduce traditional religious knowledge in a field largely populated by self-taught lay students turned *mullahs*, but they also endow them with legitimacy by acknowledging that religion no longer resides with a professional corporation. They put themselves beyond the control of their peers.

This explains the trials by religious courts in Iran of clerics like Mohsen Saidzadeh and Mohsen Kadivar. Their sin was not so much holding heterodox beliefs as having exposed those ideas in their professional capacity to a lay audience outside the traditional religious seminaries. Abdolkarim Soroush shares the same ideas but is a layman. He has been attacked, but not treated as harshly as Saidzadeh and Kadivar, who are seen by some clerics as traitors. Nevertheless, Iran is the only country where a religious establishment has the legal means to try to retain the monopoly on religious debate, and it has failed to do so. Everywhere else professional *ulama* either have to retreat or adapt in order to survive.

Traditional *madrasas* have also been bypassed by networks of private local ones, even if the latter (as in Pakistan with the Deobandi school) are offspring of the former. More modern institutions (modern in terms of living conditions and technical facilities, not of theology), such as teaching centres established by Gulf monarchies, attract educated young Muslims from the Middle East, while many born-again Muslims and converts prefer to join the private *madrasas* of Yemen and Pakistan (as did the US Talib John Walker Lindh). We mentioned in Chapter 2 the increasing numbers of private *madrasas* in Pakistan; the phenomenon is pervasive in Muslim countries where there is a crisis among state educational networks (as in Pakistan, Mali, Nigeria and Yemen) and where a policy of re-Islamisation has been effective through the initiative of religious political movements (for example, Indonesia with the development of the *pesantrem*, or boarding *madrasas*, especially those under the auspices of the Jemaah Islamiah, headed by Abu Bakar Bashir). On graduation from these schools, which have usually a shorter curriculum than traditional *madrasas*, graduates enter the job market. However, they can compete neither with graduates of the state religious universities, who are increasingly being awarded the monopoly of official positions (in Morocco, Turkey and Algeria), nor with graduates of non-religious faculties, who are supposed to master English and technical disciplines. This burgeoning of religious institutions entails a paradoxical declericalisation of the religious arena: new preachers are either self-taught or, on graduation from religious institutions, eschew sclerotic (and poorly paid) official positions to earn a living by investing in 'civil society'. Moreover the state's attempts to control the religious teaching system, coupled with the development of private *madrasas*, has boosted the privatisation of Islam by sending into the job market young graduates in religious sciences who have few vocational opportunities in the official religious bureaucracy. Because they have little education, generally in a single field (only in practical religious sciences, *ibadat* and *fiqh*), their sole hope of finding a job is not only to reproduce the system that trained them, but also to play on the delegitimation of secular intellectuals or of older and more traditional *ulama*. This entails first a push for the Islamisation of the bureaucracy, of justice and of society, which leads to politicisation of the movement; second, the development of and investment in a private religious sector (schools and mosques, but also businesses like Islamic banks, fashion emporia or food retailers); and finally the dismissal of competitors as bad Muslims.

Islamisation is accompanied everywhere by an increase in sectarian and religious feuds within the Muslim community. Competition for religious legitimacy means also competition for the right to say who is a good Muslim and conversely who is not. Privatisation entails the exacerbation of differences and anathema. It is not by chance that the increase in religious sectarianism in Pakistan (Sunnis versus Shias) came after the boom in the development of private *madrasas*.[22] In the 1980s, almost everywhere in the Muslim world (except Azerbaijan), tensions between Shias and Sunnis were at their peak. But these feuds are no longer contested within religious institutions, nor are they arbitrated by state power. They take place in the streets.

Religious debate everywhere is in everybody's hands. Even in Iran, where the clerical establishment has been able since the seventeenth century to exercise some kind of institutional control (for which it has been compared to the Catholic Church), the debate

---

22. See S.V.R. Nasr, 'The Rise of Sunni Militancy in Pakistan: The Changing Role of Islamism and the Ulama in Society and Politics', *Modern Asian Studies*, 34, 1 (2000), pp. 139–80.

is now to be found in the public sphere, where it features in numerous journals. The trend is stronger in Sunni countries, where the 'clergy' were no more than a corporation of *ulama* who had graduated from some kind of *madrasa*. The development of private *madrasas* changed the curriculum and, more precisely, led to its dissemination in a format that could be acquired independently of the *madrasas*, through self-education, pamphlets, informal discussion groups or websites. Information is easily accessible thanks to modern media, the universalisation of literacy, and cheap modes of communication (such as cassettes and the internet). The divide between intellectual and *alim* is blurred and because they have direct access to religious knowledge, many young educated people think themselves expert in religion. Religious knowledge is no longer linked to institutions. Moreover, the development of secular sciences has reduced the scope of what was understood as 'religious' knowledge. Before the development of modern educational networks, *madrasas* taught a universal knowledge, from philosophy, literature and poetry to mathematics,[23] but nowadays they teach 'purely' religious sciences (that is, a knowledge cut off from other fields). Religious fundamentalism (the literal interpretation of the revealed texts) has spread alongside the diffusion of a global secular and technical education, which tends to establish a clear division between religious and non-religious fields. In fact the establishment of purely religious schools left the dominant model of secular education in charge of all practical and scientific knowledge. In this sense too neofundamentalism parallels secularisation. Incidentally, the new Islamic thinkers and preachers (except for Saudis or Yemenis), whether fundamentalist or liberal, are rarely graduates of religious universities or *madrasas*. Abu Hamza, of London, is an engineer, as is Soroush; Jamal Badawi is a professor of management

23. I happened in 1981 to visit the personal library of an Afghan *alim*, Mirajuddin, from the Panjshir Valley in Afghanistan, who had studied in India for twenty years. The library contained hundreds of books that went far beyond the strict religious knowledge needed by a local *qadi*. None of the books was Western (printed in or translated from English), all belonged to the traditional Persian Sunni culture, and they included works of poetry, mathematics, alchemy, geometry (through an Arabic version of Euclid), 'Greek' medicine (Arabic translations of Galen or Jalinos), and dream interpretation (not Freudian). Most of the books were lithographs and some were handwritten. The library was burnt during the 1984 Soviet offensive. But I doubt that such eclecticism would have made sense to a young Talib of the next decade.

in Canada. In France all but one of the leaders of the main Islamic organisation (UOIF) graduated in non-religious disciplines.[24]

There is a trend, even among self-trained *imams*, to draw a new line between legitimate neo-*ulama* and 'the ignorant'. Nevertheless, everybody who touches on the subject aligns himself with the *ulama*. Sheikh Jamaal al-Din Zarabozo, who used to pronounce *fatwas*, delivered a speech entitled 'Speaking about Allah (SWT) without Knowledge',[25] the target of which was explicit. Yet he was attacked by disciples of the Saudi Wahhabi Sheikh al-Albani, despite claiming to be one of the Saudi sheikh's followers, having translated into English at least one of his books. But in 1999 Zarabozo made the mistake of saying that the Saudi sheikh had misquoted a Koranic verse, which triggered a counteroffensive.[26] What is interesting in such polemics is that the Saudi sheikhs, who graduated from religious *madrasas*, cannot stand the fact that young self-proclaimed *ulama* (and in this case a convert) claim to be their peers, even if they agree on the main issues. Zarabozo is called a 'newly arisen fresh newcomer', who brings a 'vulture culture'[27] by predation on more knowledgeable elders. Al-Albani himself reacted angrily: 'It is not allowed for a Muslim of the 14th century [Hegira] to begin giving fatwaas on the basis of some hadeeth, simply because he

24. Thami Breze, the chairman (in 2003), graduated in political sciences, and Fouad Alaoui, the secretary-general, in neuropsychology; the founder is an engineer, Mahmoud Zouheir. The exception is Cheykh Ahmed Jaballah, presently a member of the European Council of Fatwa. In general most of the *imams* who are French citizens do not have religious diplomas, whereas most of the foreign *imams* active in France have some sort of religious training from abroad. Hassan Iquioussen, the most famous video preacher (hundreds of recorded videotapes on topics pertaining to Islam and the daily life of a Muslim), has a degree in history. The dean of the Grand Mosque of Paris, Sheikh Hamza Boubakeur, is a cardiologist. Larbi Kechat, head of the largest mosque in Paris, graduated in linguistics.

25. Transcription of the audiotape *Usool al-Tafseer* (<http://islaam.com/Article. aspx?id=6>, April 2002). For Zarabozo's *fatwa*, see 'Fatawa from *Aljumuah* Magazine', to be found on the website of the Muslim Students' Association at the University of Houston, <http://www.uh.edu/campus/msa/articles/fatawa.html>.

26. For the reply to Zarabozo, see Abdullah Lahmami (comp.), *A Refutation of Some of the Statements of Jamal ud-Din Zarabozo*, Birmingham: Salafi Publications, 2002. This pamphlet, in PDF format, can be found at <http://www.salafipublications.com/sps/> (Article ID GRV130002).

27. Lahmani, *A Refutation*.

came across it in some book, although he does not know if it is saheeh according to the criteria of the people of knowledge of Hadeeth!'[28] But such pronouncements will have little effect on the popularity of Zarabozo. The problem for the Saudi *ulama* is that they have no way of preventing newcomers from acting as if they were *ulama* and peers. Living in the West (regardless of how strong their opposition to Western culture may be), the 'newcomers' are beyond the reach of the holy alliance between traditional *ulama* and Muslim states. The blossoming of young self-proclaimed preachers is a consequence of the deterritorialisation of Islam.

Religion has been secularised not in the sense that it is under the scrutiny of modern sciences, but to the extent that it is debated outside any specific institutions or corporations. Interestingly, the fact that there was a professional corporation of men learned in religion also allowed for some sort of 'secularisation'. Religious debates were addressed by the *ulama*, while the laypeople could manage their own lives; the mundane (*duniawi* in Persian) and the divine (*illahy*) were in states of *de facto* separation. But the crisis of the religious corporation once again brings religion back into the midst of worldly concerns, where it might be forever lost (swallowed by politics, as in Iran), or on the contrary overplayed and called upon to deal with the minutiae of daily or social life. This is related to the fact that a religion with the same conceptual framework (Protestantism) has given birth to the finest examples of religious indifference (the collapse of church attendance in northern Europe) and, at the same time, to charismatic fundamentalism (in the United States). The key lies not in the interpretation of scripture, which always has a *post hoc* dimension, but in a shift of religiosity based on the elusive distinction between mundane and divine.

Crisis of transmission

In Western Europe there is a clear generation gap between immigrants and their children. Many children reject their father's Islam, or think they can do better, not necessarily by being more faithful, but either by *thinking* more like a Muslim (criticising their father's

---

28. 'Some Points from a Question-and-Answer Session with Shaikh Muhammad Naasir ad-Deen al-Albaani', Muslim Students' Association at the University of Houston, <http://www.uh.edu/campus/msa/articles/tape_.html>.

set of beliefs) or, for a few radicals, by *acting* more like a Muslim (*jihad*).This crisis has an impact on several different levels. In impoverished European neighbourhoods, fathers who came thirty years ago as workers appear in their children's eyes to have failed. They have neither returned wealthy to their homeland nor succeeded in the host country, are often unemployed or have taken early retirement. For many second-generation Muslims, ambient racism strengthens the idea that keeping a low profile, being a law-abiding second-class citizen and avoiding conspicuous religious practices simply do not pay.The first-generation immigrants usually did not transmit their views on Islam or bother to establish private religious schools to do the job. Many foreign *imams*, hired by local congregations, do not speak European languages and cannot address the second generation. Children are usually better-educated than their parents, whose approach to religion they find unsatisfying. By contrast, as we shall see, Salafism provides youth with a rationale not to listen to their parents about what Islam is. Salafist preachers consider that the 'Islam' of the first generation of migrants has been mixed with local customs, folklore, superstitions and wrong beliefs; they prefer to teach those who are totally ignorant rather than those who have been exposed to falsehood and heresy.

But youths have another reason to bypass their parents' teaching on Islam and an elaborate curriculum in a religious school: they want the truth now. They are in search of a faith, not theological knowledge. It is a general feature of contemporary religiosity that truth is not linked with the acquisition of knowledge, or more precisely that such knowledge as there is can be immediately understood, especially when a charismatic leader is in charge. Young males who attend the Catholic World Youth Day do not then, as a general rule, join a seminary to spend years learning theology. The decline in enrolment at Catholic seminaries and theological universities is relatively proportional to the increasing number of young people who attend mass rallies to meet the Pope. It is not a contradiction, but a contrast between modern forms of religiosity and the classical conception of acquiring religious knowledge. (The Jewish Lubavitch movement, for example, stresses not the millenarian Jewish tradition of spending years in *yeshiva*, but the return to authenticity through the practice of simple rituals and codes.) Religion is experienced as faith and authenticity, not academic knowledge or scholarly training. The boundaries of religious identity are marked by signs of belonging (such as styles of clothing, wearing a *hijab* or growing a beard) and performative actions or declarations (such as dotting a speech with Arabic expressions).

This crisis of transmission is not confined to Muslims in the West. In Pakistani *madrasas* there is the same shrinking of the curriculum and disappearance of disciplines that were taught decades ago. This generation gap is embodied by the Taliban movement. Interestingly, its members always called themselves *taliban* (students) and not *ulama*, as if they acknowledged the gap between their studies and that of the generation before. Nevertheless, the title Amir al-Mumineen (Commander of the Believers) has been bestowed upon their leader, Mullah Omar, who has never been defined as an *alim*. Such an appointment sidesteps the entire traditional hierarchy of knowledge, which is based on the number of years devoted to study. (*Mutatis mutandis*, the same thing happened in Iran when Khamenei was appointed Guide instead of more learned grand ayatollahs.) The disappearance of a whole generation of learned people in Afghanistan and the promotion of half-educated junior *mujahedin* to senior positions are certainly consequences of twenty years of war, but the rise of young *taliban*, preachers and *imams* seems to be quite common in today's Muslim world. Needless to say, the generation gap has also been reinforced by the high rate of population increase during the 1970s and early 1980s. In any case, elders are no longer esteemed as models who should be emulated.

The rejection of traditional authority, which used to be embodied by the *ijaza*, or authorisation to teach given by an *alim* to his students, is explicit among many Islamic activists. Abu Hamza, former head of one the most radical mosques in 'Londonistan', wrote:'The people who have been bestowed ijaza give us nothing but headache ... What's the use of all this "Islamic" knowledge if it's not bringing anything positive to Muslim people and Islam?'[29] Activism replaces knowledge: Bin Laden is called 'Sheikh' by his followers and is dressed like a cleric, but he has never troubled to write a single sentence on real religious issues. (In fact there is little religion in his speeches, except for the use of symbolic words like *jihad* and *ummah*.)

29.   <http://www.supportersofshariat.org/eng/abuhamza.html>, 23 December 2000 (now at <http://www.angelfire.com/bc3/johnsonuk/eng/sheikh.html>).

But this rejection of hierarchical authority is not only a mat-ter of opposition to an older, supposedly more learned genera-tion. It corresponds, among fundamentalists, to a new relationship to knowledge, based on immediate accessibility, and to a percep-tion of the *ummah* as a community of equals, where charisma and not knowledge brings leaders to the fore. Mullah Omar has been credited by his fellow Taliban members not as being more learned than they were, but as having charisma.[30] Tablighi Jama'at preach-ing teams choose an '*emir*' from among themselves and pledge to obey him during the entire course of their missionary journey; but another *emir* can be chosen for the next journey.[31] When invited to attend meetings under the aegis of Jeunesse musulmane de France (which is not a radical organisation), I was struck by the efforts of the organisers to host a 'democratic' debate among the militants. Everybody had the right to speak and develop his or her point. Once again this had nothing to do with liberalism. The debate was not on free interpretation but on 'what the Koran really says'. Knowledge was not open to criticism but everybody was allowed to speak about the truth. Truth is transmitted between equals and brothers. The constant use of the term 'brother' is interesting. I am not an expert on 'medieval' or classical Islam, but I am not sure that this form of address was formerly as widespread as it is now.

A limited religious corpus

Newly born-again Muslims experience a sharp break with nomi-nal or cultural religion and thus want direct access to the corpus. Suddenly faith is their main motivation and it must be immedi-ately expressed in new norms and certitudes. Faith in a sense is direct access to truth, so the new believer is no longer interested in gradual access to knowledge. The knowledge he is seeking should fit with the sudden feeling of being in touch with truth. For us, as we shall see, the phenomenon of being born again (which differs from conversion) is a contemporary one in the sense that it is a way to enter into a religion that is not embedded in a given culture, and

---

30. Mullah Omar claimed that he was called in a dream by God to rid Afghani-stan of corruption. This charismatic dimension means a direct proximity with God that also makes theological knowledge irrelevant.
31. Barbara Metcalf, 'Contested Politics: Islam and Women: The Case of the Tablighi Jama'at', *Stanford Humanities Review*, 5, 1 (1996).

to reconstruct a self-evident truth from an intimate and personal experience, at a time when this evidence has been withdrawn from the social environment. The corpus usually ignores most interpretative works written during the classical period and all philosophical texts. This is linked to the lack of erudition and training of the new actors, but to a greater extent to the relationship they have with truth and knowledge. Because they can be true believers through behaviour and faith, why should they bother to turn truth into a complex corpus of theological studies? Truth is an experience re-enacted by rituals (for example, prayers and the sacralisation of daily life through rituals and uttering of given formulas).

Given the weakening of traditional networks for transmitting religious knowledge, the new actors need a corpus that provides them with what they need – norms and ready-made assertions – and is easily accessible in terms of content and medium. Such a corpus exists thanks to new media: booklets, websites and audio cassettes.[32] The extension of literacy has made printed and virtual material accessible. Such a corpus is abundant, normative, made up of small segments (a booklet, a cassette), and usually circular and repetitive. There is no gradation in learning.

This knowledge is also fragile because it lacks the imprimatur of a learned institution, especially when it is transmitted on the internet. The hierarchy of status between academic and non-academic knowledge (which has been more or less maintained for printed books through university presses, libraries, bookshops and reviews) disappears on the internet (as does the durability of 'established' knowledge – how does one keep track of the content of websites that are modified at will and may disappear overnight?).

The crisis of transmission is also due to new forms of transmission, or more precisely, as John Anderson notes, of the blurring of the divide between those who transmit and those who receive.[33] The circulation of such knowledge is horizontal, between equals, and not vertical, from learned people to students. This horizontal circulation is a characteristic of the internet. It also means the opening of formerly closed and private spheres of discussion to a

32. Dale Eickelman and Jon Anderson, *New Media in the Muslim World: The Emerging Public Sphere*, Bloomington: Indiana University Press, 1994.
33. Jon Anderson, 'The Internet and Islam's New Interpreters' in Eickelman and Anderson, *New Media*, p. 44. Eickelman has also written extensively on the topic.

public debating space. The very idea of professionalism in knowledge is ignored, although the corpus is presented as a technical one. (For example, how does one assert the validity of a Hadith?)

When we speak of a new corpus, we refer not to its content but to its medium and form. The religious knowledge circulating in mosques and on the internet is quite dogmatic and based on the same intangible principles. Quotations play an important role: a debate might simply be an exchange of quotations from the Koran or Hadith, with little reasoning or analysis. Such citations are always from the basic texts and seldom from commentators (except a few favourites like Ibn Taymiyya). Self-taught *mullahs* have mimetic relations with traditional *ulama*: they speak of knowledge, science and authority, and make use of a classical terminology, albeit applied to a reduced corpus. The authentication process for Hadith (*isnad*, or chains of transmission) is borrowed from tradition. There is no use of modern tools of exegesis such as linguistics and history.

In addition the lack of knowledge is often legitimised by schools of thought like the Wahhabis and Tablighi. There is a great deal of anti-intellectualism in all contemporary forms of religious revivalism, in Islam and in Christianity. The founder of Wahhabism, Muhammad Ibn Abdul Wahhab, wrote only one very small book, *Kitab al-Tawhid* (The Book of Divine Unity): why should a good believer try to learn more and go further? For the Tablighi faith is at stake rather than learning. Young born-again Muslims do not want to undertake years of study; they want the truth immediately. It is of little avail to lament the contempt for theology and philosophy among revivalist believers. This contempt is no accident but part of their religious experience.

Publications in the circulating corpus are often written in a Western language (English) to reach Western Muslims (who have easier access to the internet). In this sense translators play a significant role in selecting the books to be translated. But this use of English also favours English-speaking preachers, those living in the West or in countries where English is an official language (such as Pakistan and South Africa). Transmitters are often people with a minimum of experience, like Ahmed Deedat, who lived in South Africa. The aged Wahhabi sheikhs based in Saudi Arabia rely on their English-speaking disciples to be translated but also to be informed.

The corpus circulating in Western languages among young Muslims is undeniably eclectic. It may draw on orthodox Middle

Eastern institutions or on *ulama*: al-Qaradawi, Nadwi, Ghazali, and the Wahhabi sheikhs of Saudi Arabia. Sheikh al-Qaradawi's treatise *The Lawful and the Prohibited in Islam*, translated into French, can be found in any Muslim bookshop in France, as can *Riyadh as-Salihin*, a favourite book of the Tablighi. When young Muslims quote 'classical' authors, these are usually certain basic classics (such as those written by Muslim[34] or Bukhari)[35] and Ibn Taymiyya, and seldom anything more in-depth. Institutes located in the West but subsidised by Saudi and Gulf money publish directly to English (for example, the Islamic Foundation in Leicester, or the International Institute of Islamic Thought in Virginia). There are also prolific but peripheral preachers: Deedat, Quick, Bilal Philips and Zarabozo (many of them are Black converts, but not members of the Nation of Islam). In France, Hassan Iquioussen (a former student of history who specialised in videotaped conferences on Islam in French) and Tariq Ramadan (the grandson of Hassan al-Banna) are very popular preachers and lecturers. Whatever the academic credentials of these authors, the corpus circulates and is used free from institutional control, along with the works of self-taught preachers. There is no hierarchy, no order of knowledge, no gradation.[36]

What is often called the 'Wahhabisation' of the Islamic curriculum (namely reducing the corpus to only the Koran and Hadith, literally interpreted) does not necessarily mean that Wahhabi doctrine is replacing more traditional teachings. What it does involve is a diminution of the curriculum in terms of content and length of study. Neofundamentalism discards philosophy, literature, Sufism and any sort of sophisticated theology. The scripturalist approach (which says that one must adhere to the word of the Koran and the Sunnah) by definition nullifies centuries of interpretation and debates. It justifies the *de facto* shrinking of religious knowledge in relation to secular knowledge, not by recognising the prevalence of the latter (except in technical fields in the broadest sense), but by ignoring secular knowledge and relegating it to the purely technical sphere. Hence, in order to specialise in the religious sciences, religious schools have abandoned wider learning and left it entirely

34. Abul Husain Muslim bin al-Hajjaj al-Nisapuri, a student of Bukhari.
35. Abu Abdullah Muhammad bin Ismail bin Ibrahim bin al-Mughira al-Ja'fai.
36. See the lists of recommended authors on such websites as <http://www.islaam.com/Scholars.aspx>.

to secular schools. Paradoxically the creation of purely religious schools contributes to secularisation, because it means that religion is not an all-encompassing branch of knowledge, but a specific one. In parallel, religious teaching is based on a technical approach to religion (dos and don'ts) that presents *ibadat* and *fiqh* as a sort of code, not based on values and spirituality. This reflects a general trend, one not limited to Islam, in which we are witnessing the end of the 'humanities'.

THE RELIGIOUS MARKET AND THE SOCIOLOGY OF ISLAMIC ACTORS

At this point we face a methodological problem: What is the sociology of the actors about whom we are speaking? We are discussing neither Muslims in general, nor professional religious clerics, but actors who intervene in the public sphere in the name of Islam. We have quite an extensive understanding of this public sphere.[37] But what is the impact of these discourses and to what extent do they shape the evolution of religious thinking among contemporary Muslims? (They certainly contribute to shaping the perception of Islam by non-Muslims.) Who regularly surfs the internet? Who buys and reads the booklets to which we are referring? What is the real audience? These are certainly open questions. As Mamoun Fandy notes, in the Middle East there are serious limitations on access to information technology.[38] But two things are plain. First, the content of the websites is no different from the written literature (I have too few examples of spoken sermons, in which rhetorical and emotional effects certainly play a great role), which means that access to new discourses is not dependent on access to information technology. Second, the people who have access to the Web are those who largely shape the dominant Muslim discourse, and their Muslim opponents have to take into account the pervasiveness of these new discourses.

That said, conducting a relevant in-depth sociological study of Islamic actors is no easy matter. Sociology has less meaning because the uprootedness of Muslims may affect various social milieus or

37. In the sense defined by Eickelman and Anderson in *New Media*.
38. Mamoun Fandy, 'Information Technology, Trust, and Social Change in the Arab World', *Middle East Journal*, 54, 3 (2000).

blur the sense of belonging to a social milieu. Uprootedness is not linked with poverty or even with a lack of social integration. How it is experienced is what counts, and it is not based on quantitative parameters. Poverty and joblessness are less significant factors than the crisis in social expectations (implying also racism and anti-imperialism, where conflicts like Palestine or Chechnya awaken a sleeping Muslim identity). The generation gap is more important than socioreligious factors. Either we lack data, or a sociological approach provides few clues even if we know the role played by educated youths and converts. We lack a sociology of conversion to Islam, but I am not sure that classical sociology helps a lot. Most activists are students or university dropouts, but knowing this does not advance one's understanding of the situation, because the majority of the social group in question do not follow the same interpretation of Islam.

Another sociological approach would be to consider the religious market, where the commodities are, above all, meanings and symbols. Some entrepreneurs mobilise religious legitimacy to start private businesses. These include halal butchers, travel agencies specialising in pilgrimage, and Islamic fashion designers and manufacturers, banks, tourism (a recently opened five-star resort in Turkey claimed to be Islamic, with its segregated swimming pools and ban on alcohol), private schools, sports clubs (including martial arts), charities and undertakers. This religious market is globalised. It is fed by economic liberalisation, and by connections between diasporas in the West or elsewhere and countries of origin (travel agencies, pilgrimages and money transfers are good examples). In Muslim countries traditional *waqf*, or religious endowments, are no longer the link between religious and economic fields; *waqf* came largely under state control during the twentieth century. State bureaucracy, in most Muslim countries, has been an obstacle to the emergence of a native entrepreneurial class.

But a new generation of Muslim entrepreneurs has benefited from the wave of economic liberalisation that has swept a part of the Muslim world (for example, Turkey under Prime Minister Özal and Egypt after the *infitah*, or open-door, policy of Sadat). The development of 'Muslim' business has been one of the consequences of the westernisation of the economies of Muslim countries under the aegis of the World Bank and the International Monetary Fund (IMF). In Turkey the Muslim Industrialists' and

Businessmen's Association (MÜSIAD, where M now stands for 'Independent' instead of 'Muslim'), which has no particular links to a specific religious market, has encouraged its members to play an active role in sponsorship and charity. The emergence of a new class of independent entrepreneurs seeking to advance their social standing gave rise to new forms of patronage, like the *iftar* 'charity tables' sponsored by wealthy merchants in Egypt during Ramadan.[39] Economic liberalisation in countries such as Turkey and Egypt allowed many of these businessmen to be inserted into supranational networks and has considerably increased the scope of action for wealthy Muslims wanting to give to charity. Collecters for Islamic NGOs visit shopkeepers, bankers and entrepreneurs requesting that they give *zakat* directly to Muslim causes. There has been a tendency in the West, after 9/11, to see this practice as a means of financing terrorism, but it has a far larger scope.

These businessmen favour free enterprise and the free market; they have benefited from economic liberalisation and see the state as a liability (in terms of taxation, state monopolies and customs duties), not an asset. When they are religious-minded, they are better to stick with conservative neofundamentalism than revolutionary Islamism, because the anti-state political attitude of neofundamentalism fits better with their own anti-state economic views than with the statist and revolutionary approach of the Islamists. The businessmen want a smaller state. In this sense the trajectory of Iranian conservatives from revolutionary Islam to neofundamentalism is analogous to the evolution of the *bazaaris* (merchants), who, having benefited from a state-controlled economy (by playing on state subsidies, import quotas and multiple currency exchange-rates, for instance), now favour a more open economy in order to invest their newly acquired capital in industry or international business. As far as economics is concerned, neofundamentalism is congruent with the extension of the free market and the weakening of the state, while Islamists tended in the 1980s to be statist in terms of politics and economics. Neofundamentalism, which goes along with a distrust of state and nationalism, is better adapted to economic globalisation and the free market. (A good example is the

39. Haenni Patrick, 'Ils n'en ont pas fini avec l'Orient. De quelques islamisations non islamistes', *Revue du monde musulman et de la Méditerranée*, 85–6 (1999), pp. 121–48.

Bin Laden family business, which was built on a close patronage relationship with the Saudi royal family that allowed them to develop
a supranational holding.) Neofundamentalism brings Muslims a
kind of ethic of capitalism that features individualism, rejection
of conspicuous consumption and an apologetic attitude towards
wealth, which it says is a sign of God's blessing.

Distrust of an often corrupt state has entailed the adoption by
Muslims of Western forms of charity. The development of Islamic NGOs[40] shows that the charity business has taken root among
wealthy Muslims as an alternative to traditional forms of *waqf* and
the reliance on the state so prevalent in post-colonial systems. It
goes along with the development of a modern and transnational
class of wealthy Muslims. An Islamic banking system and private financial institutions also help to channel public savings into private
business (including some forms of speculative funds). As a result,
many of the sources of concern for Western authorities relating
to money-laundering and the financing of terrorism are simply
a consequence of globalisation and the westernisation of a pious
bourgeoisie, who are economically fully modern. The West has no
monopoly on 'compassionate conservatism'.

The religious market – that is, the manipulation of Islamic symbols and legitimacy – also has a political dimension: who will speak
for Muslims? The quest for social position is important because
it provides sociological legitimisation with all the attendant perks
(not necessarily in terms of wealth). In France, for example, some
mosques deliver their own halal certificates to Muslim butchers in
exchange for a fee of around 20 cents (US) per kilogram of meat.
Being recognised by the authorities affords more flexibility in buying land on which to build a mosque (for example, the city council
might guarantee a loan), and provides leverage to help members
of the community, by recommending them for jobs, for example.
At the other end of the spectrum, actors who have acquired some
legitimacy in the religious field (such as Iranian *mullahs*, Afghan or
Tajik *mujahedin* commanders, and the leaders of urban Islamist networks, as in Imbaba, a neighbourhood of Cairo)[41] can use it when
turning to business. In their new capacity they look after their own

40. Jonathan Benthall and Jerôme Bellion-Jourdan, *The Charitable Crescent: Politics of Aid in the Muslim World,* New York: Palgrave Macmillan, 2003.
41. Patrick Haenni, 'Banlieues indociles? Sur la politisation des quartiers péri-

wordly interests, even if they retain followers who have become
employees or clients.

INDIVIDUALISATION OF ENUNCIATION AND PROPAGANDA

Reconstruction of what it means to be a good Muslim in a non-
Muslim society essentially rests on the individual. The first reason
for this is that, as we have seen, neither the family nor the pristine
community suffices as a transmitter of traditional Islam. Traditional
hierarchies, including that of age, are irrelevant. The second reason
is the lack of social pressure that constrains believers individually to
reconstruct for themselves what it means to live a pious life, even if
on the 'religious market' they can choose between various models,
from the long white shirt and baggy trousers of the Tablighi to the
'tie and jacket with beard' attire of the modern Muslim Brothers. But many simple daily events create problems. Should one's
children attend the school Christmas party? Should one refuse to
shake the hand of a woman? Get a credit card? Eat cheese? Date a
non-Muslim woman? Requests for Islamic legal rulings, or *fatwas*,
are mushrooming among pious believers. But to whom should one
address such requests? Muslims in the West prefer to turn to new
bodies or personalities who have a direct experience of what they
are living, except for a few traditional *ulama* who develop an interest in modern issues (like the Syrian Sheikh Buti in bioethics).
Many websites issue *fatwas*. In London the Islamic Cultural Centre
in Park Road, Regent's Park, has a *fatwa* committee that gives religious legal advice, but of course cannot enforce the decisions or
impose sanctions.[42] But all this is by definition based on a voluntary approach: there is no way to enforce the *fatwa*. In the end the
believer decides, not the *mufti* or the *qadi*. Asking for a *fatwa* is a
personal issue, as is abiding by it once it has been delivered.

When fundamentalist Muslims in Europe push for recognition
of some elements of *sharia* for the Muslim minority, they cannot
escape the reality that it should be on a voluntary basis. A Muslim is

---

urbains du Caire', PhD dissertation, Institut d'études politiques (IEP), Paris,
2001.
42. See IslamOnline (<http://www.islamonline.org/english/index.shtml>), and
the links under the heading 'Fatwa Corner'. See also <http://www.fatwa-
online.com>.

somebody who says he or she is a Muslim, and not somebody who is a Muslim by origin.[43] When Muslim thinkers develop recommendations on how to live as far as possible according to *sharia* in a non-Muslim environment, such commitment relies on individual choice, which can be repudiated at any time.[44] It is up to the believer to decide, not to society or the law. However fundamentalist it might be, the norm always has to be shouldered by individuals.

Propaganda targets individuals, not groups

Islamists, when elaborating a political program, target groups, and more precisely social groups (impoverished neo-urbanites, students from the lower and middle classes, and so on). This remains congruent with their strategy of going to the polls; an electorate is always a collective and anonymous entity. But the new preachers target individuals, for the simple reason that they do not have a global political and social project, except implementation of *sharia*. Even the Taliban, who were ruling a 'real' country, never cared about implementing any economic or social program, but were exclusively concerned with *sharia*. In non-Muslim countries neofundamentalists do not make collective social demands (concerning wages, student scholarships, social justice) except where they relate to the religious community; they do not seek a coalition with other forces to push their agenda. They simply care about turning nominal Muslims into 'good' Muslims who strictly abide by the true tenets of Islam. As Sheikh al-Albani said (in response to the Muslim Brothers), 'establish Islam first in your heart';[45] then society can become Islamic. Islamisation addresses individuals. Propaganda techniques target individuals (in mosques or gaols, or

43. Such an issue illustrates the difference between 'corporate' Muslim minorities that enjoy a legal status, as in India, and atomised Muslim populations like those in Europe. In India the Supreme Court ruled in 1986 that *sharia*-based family law should be imposed on Muslims even if they turn to secular courts (Shah Banu case, 1986; a repudiated elderly woman was denied alimony from her husband).

44. Tariq Ramadan, for example, believes that the French Civil Solidarity Pact (PACS), which associates two non-married people, whatever their gender, is closer to marriage according to *sharia* than is the state legal status of a married couple (with one condition: it should be between a man and a woman), because it is a mere contract that imposes no allowances in case of separation.

45. Lahmani, *A Refutation*.

by door-to-door canvassing). It is not by chance that many conversions take place in prison (among either nominal Muslims or
non-Muslims).[46] By definition an incarcerated individual is cut off
from all social and family links.

A would-be born-again or convert is briefed by a small team
of propagandists and encouraged to change his life. He is rarely
sent to a higher centre of teaching. Follow-up is directly ensured
by those who (re)converted him. Born-again Muslims are encouraged to convert their entourage first, consistent with the parochial
dimension of many neofundamentalist groups (and, in extreme
cases, with the secrecy of operational networks). Individual *dawah*
is encouraged: manifesting a good example, behaving in a way that
shows the superiority of Islam, taking any opportunity to explain
one's religion to non-Muslims, converting relatives and friends, and
eventually breaking with one's non-Muslim former environment.

Neofundamentalist and contemporary spiritualist preachers
have one point in common: they stress not the worldly victories of
Islam but salvation and doomsday. Every believer should work for
God's satisfaction (*rezayat*) without expecting reward on earth, and
should behave as a good Muslim whatever the social environment.
Return to Islam begins with an effort of the self – taming passions
and emotions, showing modesty and dedication. There is little en-
thusiasm, even among radicals, for achieving worldly success – note
the deep pessimism that underlies Osama Bin Laden's world view.
Even millenarian movements like Hizb ut-Tahrir, which has a political goal (to establish the utopian Khilafat, or Caliphate), strive for
an imaginary agenda and are far removed from concrete politics.

Propaganda and organisation are sometimes expressed in terms
of modern marketing – that is, of a relationship between a seller
and a customer, who chooses between various commodities on
the religious market. In a paragraph entitled 'Muslim Preachers are
Salespeople', Shahid Athar writes:

Muslim preachers are salespeople, smiling and sweet-talking salespersons.
If salespersons fight and argue with the customer, do you think people will
buy the product. Salespersons are also persistent and never satisfied until
they have sold the product. Good salespersons are the one who provides
service for the product after they sell it. Thus, Muslim preachers should

---

46. Khaled Kelkal and 'shoe bomber' Richard Reid (re)converted to Islam while
in gaol.

continue to look after the customer. Good salespersons are friendly, so should Muslim preachers be friendly. '*God has purchased of the believers, their persons and their goods, for theirs (in return) is the garden (of Paradise)*' (9:111). Good salespersons should continue to service the product. As a result of our missionary work and guidance from God, if one becomes a Muslim, do we follow-up with that person? Do we help that person and support him or her in remaining a Muslim?[47]

Another noteworthy point in this quotation is that faith and conversion are perceived as inherently fragile, precisely because in the West it is difficult to remain a good Muslim.

This stress on the individual is particularly striking among radical militants who claim to fight for the *ummah*. Common among them is the belief that *jihad* is a compulsory individual duty (*fard 'ayn*), while traditionally it has always been considered a collective duty (*fard kifaya*), which means it rests on the shoulders of the group that is under threat.[48] The phenomenon of contemporary 'martyrdom' cannot be understood if we underestimate the prevalence of the self against collective political realisation. Why are suicide attacks not found in traditional Islam, when Taliban-like fundamentalism regularly occurred in the past? The 'reward in paradise' explanation is not very helpful. Why should Muslims have discovered only in 1983 that suicide attacks are a good way to enter paradise? The reference to the Hashshashin[49] proves that suicide attacks are linked not with mainstream Islam but with sects at the fringe of heterodoxy. They do not express the dilution of the self into the collective, but on the contrary mark an exacerbation of the self.[50] Al Qaeda involves no collective, no social group. The will of Muhammad Atta exhibits an exacerbated self, not the commitment of somebody who puts the group before his own life.[51] Al

---

47. Athar, *Reflections of an American Muslim*, <http://islam-usa.com/r22.html>. Punctuation, spelling and emphasis are as per the original.
48. Al Qaeda communiqué, 23 February 1998; see Chapter 1 of Rohan Gunaratna's *Inside Al Qaeda: Global Network of Terror* (New York: Berkley Books, 2003). For the Hizb ut-Tahrir, *jihad* is *ayn* too.
49. Bernard Lewis, *The Assassins: A Radical Sect in Islam*, New York: Basic Books, 2002.
50. See Farhad Khosrokhavar, *Les nouveaux martyrs d'Allah*, Paris: Flammarion, 2002. The Iranian martyrs of the Iran–Iraq War looked for death because they did not think the Islamic Republic could meet their expectations.
51. Atta's will can be found on the site of the US ABC News, <http://abcnews. go.com/sections/us/DailyNews/WTC_atta_will.html>. Simply writing a

Qaeda's cadres are individuals who join an imagined community only through death. Stories of volunteers who joined Al Qaeda in Afghanistan or fought in Chechnya stress the warmth and closeness of ties among volunteers. But it is a reconstructed collective. All these cadres have a story of isolation, rupture and quest for self. What we know of the recruitment of Al Qaeda members in Europe suggests that the organisation 'fishes' in places where 'born-again' Muslims gather, namely radical mosques.

Individualisation and innovation in the name of orthodoxy

By stressing individual actions, neofundamentalists regularly indulge in *bid'a* (innovation), which is normally abhorred by all fundamentalists. To include *jihad* in an individual's mandatory religious duties is to add a sixth pillar of the faith to the five admitted by orthodoxy.[52] Hizb ut-Tahrir declares Khilafat a compulsory religious duty, although this has never been stated by any classical theologian. Today, it seems, everyone feels qualified to issue a *fatwa*, which is also a clear innovation.

Non-radical conservatives point out how Bin Laden has strayed from the correct path. Sheikh al-Qaradawi issued a *fatwa* condemning the attack on the World Trade Center (which, incidentally, shows that certain well-known Muslim religious scholars did condemn the events of 9/11). But many neofundamentalists nevertheless added some norms that were not part of traditional *fiqh*. A good example is the question of Muslims marrying non-Muslim women. By tradition a man has to convert to marry a Muslim woman, but a woman from one of the religions of the Book is free to keep her religion when marrying a Muslim. Many contemporary preachers, however, warn against marrying Christian women,[53] arguing

---

will at the age of eighteen specifying how one should be buried shows a sort of exaggerated self-indulgence. It would have been easier to request burial according to Islamic ritual, without writing eighteen articles, replete with 'I' and 'my', reiterating what true Islamic burial was, as if nobody knew.

52. Mohammed Abd al Salem Farag, an electrical-engineering student at Cairo University, wrote a booklet the title of which is usually translated as *The Neglected Duty* (*al-Faridah al Gha'ibah*, although it should probably be read as *The Absent Obligation*), in which he considers *jihad* to be compulsory.

53. Examples of such pronouncements include: 'It is generally disliked to marry a non-Muslim woman, especially in a non-Muslim country, where it would be

that when Muslims are in a minority such marriages work to the benefit of Christianity or secularism. In doing so, such preachers flagrantly introduce a new form of *bid'a*. Innovation is permanent under the disguise of orthodoxy.

Another typical sign of individualisation is the sudden surge in *hisba* legal suits. *Hisba* is a traditional but never central concept of *sharia*. It means meddling, as an individual, in other people's behaviour, without being involved personally, to 'command the good and forbid the evil'. In Egypt, for example, a series of suits was launched in the late 1990s. In 1996 a lawyer, Semeida Abdul Samad, petitioned a civil court to declare void the marriage of Professor Nasr Abu Zaid, under the pretext that Zaid was an apostate (because of his critical approach to Islam) and thus could not marry a Muslim woman. The couple, of course, were unwilling to be divorced, but the court accepted the suit and declared the marriage void. A related action was launched against the feminist writer Nawwal al-Sadawi, whose divorce was requested by an attorney, Nabih al-Wahsh, in July 2001. Sheikh Yusuf Badri in 1997 sued the Ministry of Education for corrupting the youth of Egypt (on account of the

---

another factor that would affect the raising of one's children. As such, its general ruling in non-Muslim countries is that it is *makruh tahriman* (something from which one is strictly advised to abstain) and sinful. [*Fath al-Qadir, Radd al-Muhtar*]' (Sidi Faraz Rabbani, <http://www.sunnipath.com/Resources/Questions/QA00000578.aspx>.) 'A Muslim man is discouraged from marrying a non-Muslim woman if there is no Islamic State or if he is not living in an existing Islamic state, since the non-Islamic states do not recognize his rights as head of the family to raise the children Islamically. On the contrary, the children will most likely be brought up in their mother's religion, since the Muslim husband does not have his Islamic rights in his non-Muslim wife's country.' (<http://www.islamfortoday.com/interfaithmarriage.htm>.) 'My advice to all my brothers everywhere is, that they should not marry non-Muslim women and that they should be aware of the risks and end result of doing so. Rather, they should do their utmost to marry Muslim women and to educate and guide them to what is good. This is safer, especially at this time when evil and wickedness has increased. The *kuffaar* have today gained the upper hand over the Muslims, and women in the countries of the *kuffaar* have power and authority and dominate their Muslim husbands and try to attract them and their children to their false religion. And there is no power, no strength except with Allaah!' Shaykh Ibn Baaz, *al-Aqalliyaat al-Muslimah* [*The Muslim Minority*], Medina: Permanent Committee for Islamic Research and Fatwas, n.d., Fatwa 5, p. 29. This is a compilation of *fatwas* concerning Muslims living in a minority.

contents of new school textbooks) and the newspaper *Roz al-Yusuf* for indecency: he lost both cases. In June 1996 a group of lawyers and physicians, headed by a medical doctor, Munir Fawza, sued the Health Ministry for having banned female circumcision in government hospitals. They won in the administrative court but lost on appeal.[54] In Pakistan suits have been submitted by individual Muslims against Christians accused of slandering the Prophet.

In these cases two features stand out. First, individuals with no religious training took it upon themselves to decide what *sharia* meant. Second, the plaintiffs did not think of bringing their cases first to religious institutions (by requesting some sort of *fatwa*) but went directly to the civil courts. In a word, these individual initiatives bypass the religious establishment for the sake of *sharia*. Neofundamentalism goes hand in hand with individualisation and delegitimation of religious professionals in favour of religious-minded laypersons. In this sense it is also a factor in secularisation.

Is individualisation a gateway to liberalisation?

It is a truism that modernisation and democratisation in the West were assured by a shift from the collective to the individual.[55] Thus one would expect that Islam would have to undergo a similar process for it to become compatible with secularisation and democracy. What I try to demonstrate in this book runs largely counter to such an idea, for one very simple reason: individualisation of faith can also lead to fundamentalism, as witnessed in contemporary Protestantism. There is definitely a process of individualisation of faith and behaviour among Muslims, specifically those living in the West. There is a stress on the self, a quest for personal realisation and an individual reconstruction of attitudes towards religion. Faith is more important than dogma. In short, religiosity is more important than religion. Individualisation is a prerequisite for the westernisation of Islam and it has happened. Such a shift may lead to a critical approach to dogma, a quest for *ijtihad* (personal interpretation), a renewal of theological thinking – in other words, an Islamic Reformation.

54. J. Lancaster, 'Egyptian Court Overturns Decree That Banned Female Circumcision', *Washington Post*, 25 June 1997; see also *Al-Ahram Hebdo*, 2–8 July 1997.
55. C.B. Macpherson, *The Political Theory of Possessive Individualism: Hobbes to Locke*, Oxford University Press, 1962.

There are many Muslim thinkers who advocate the rehabilitation of such a critical approach, using the tools of modern intellectual inquiry such as history and linguistics. The key issue is not 'Can Islam be reformed?' There are many modern Islamic thinkers, whether laymen (such as Abdolkarim Soroush), or experts in Islamic law (like Khaled Abou El Fadl) or Koranic exegesis (such as Mohammed Arkoun). The issue concerns their readership: such thinkers do not meet the expectations of young born-again Muslims. If the reformers are to find a larger audience there must be a sociological evolution of Western Europe's Muslim population, but also an end to the present wave of neofundamentalism, fuelled by political tensions, which will exhaust itself through its inability to provide the Muslim community with long-term solutions. But the paradox is that contemporary neofundamentalism is based on the same process of individualisation as liberalism or the spiritualisation of Islam.

This process may lead to various formulations of what religion is and what it means. What is shared is enunciation rather than content. The discourse – the way in which the corpus is reappropriated and used by the actors concerned (interpretation in terms of values or legal norms) – varies considerably more than the corpus itself. In fact the ambiguity of the nineteenth-century Salafism of Jamal ad-Din al-Afghani was that by pretending to return to the Koran and Hadith as the sole corpus, it justified neofundamentalism (in the contemporary incarnation of Salafism, which is nowadays similar to Wahhabism) and liberalism (as exemplified by Saidzadeh in Iran). The difference between then and now is in the liberals' use of critical intellectual tools. It is interesting that few liberal thinkers try to build on the vast corpus of classical theology and interpretation.[56]

Moreover if conservative Islam does not undergo a reformation it may be as compatible with democracy as Catholicism has been since it was defeated in its face-to-face confrontation with modern secularism in late nineteenth-century France. Of course, in the United States the confrontation between state and religion is not the same as in Europe, but it is also a democracy based on a people among whom most believe that the laws of God are above those of men, and that there is a higher truth that is not decided by the

---

56. This is the main critique of the French-Tunisian thinker Abdelwahab Meddeb in his *Malady of Islam* (New York: Basic Books, 2003). An exception might be Khaled Abou El Fadl, who extensively used classical jurisprudence.

majority. By definition the Christian Right in the United States is undemocratic, as were the Communist Party in France and the Catholic Church at the turn of the nineteenth century. Democracy is neither an ideology nor a creed. It is a system of rules that can be recognised by people who adhere to an inclusive concept of society. In brief, democracy can function without democrats (or at least with relatively few of them).

As we shall see in the next chapter, neofundamentalism is a symptom and a tool of globalisation (that is, westernisation). It goes hand in hand with a process of individualisation that nevertheless constitutes a common ground between all forms of contemporary religiosity and more specifically the non-fundamentalist dimensions of individualisation, namely liberalism and spirituality, not forgetting other forms of self-realisation through Islam.

Individualism and the internet virtual ummah

Individualisation is clearly visible in many personal Web pages created and managed by individual, often isolated Muslims. These sites all have two traits in common: they reveal a 'self' and they reveal 'Islam'. The authors of the pages introduce themselves (by means such as a curriculum vitae, some very personal remarks, or sometimes a picture), but then the remaining the content and the links are devoted to revealing Islam, usually by simply referring to other sites. The virtual *ummah* of the internet is the perfect place for individuals to express themselves while claiming to belong to a community to whose enactment they contribute to the enacting of, rather than being passive members of it. (The original wording and spelling of the following extracts has been preserved.)

The purpose of this page, and all of my other pages, is to help the average web surfer gain access to information regarding Islam, Muslims, and other things I'm interested in sharing.[57]

Congratulations and Welcome to my official homepage. Only a tiny fraction of the world's population will ever have the experience of visiting this page. Hence, I suggest you appreciate your status amongst the privelaged few and enjoy your visit! ... Below are some links you might find useful and/or interesting.[58]

57. Asad on <http://www.geocities.com/CollegePark/6453/index.html>.
58. <http://umcc.ais.org/~maftab/>.

More About Me – Hobbies: Dedicated to presenting the pure teachings of Islaam, correcting misconceptions about Islaam and refuting the lies and distortions of enemies within and outside.[59]

Welcome to my page on Islam, where I hope that you will find many things of interest Insha'allah! I have many links to other Islamic pages so please check them out. I have spent a lot of time making this page in order for all us to gain more knowledge, and help us to keep to the straight path … I plan to add more information about Islam on these pages soon. So come and keep checking. If there is any topic that you would like to submit so that it appears on this web site then let me know and I shall do what I can inshallah. Jazak Allah Khair for visiting my web site.[60]

My name is Asad B., and I am a criminal prosecutor for the M. State Attorney's Office. I completed my law degree at the American University Washington College of Law in Washington, D.C. in May 2000. I earned a bachelor's degree in Political Science from the State University of New York (Binghamton University) in May 1997. I was recently married on June 17, 2001, to the most wonderful woman in the world, my beloved wife, Nadia Amin.[61]

Welcome to Zahra's Homepage on Islam! Jazak Allah hu Khayran for visiting. My name is Zahra. I am a Muslim, born and raised. My faith is Islam.[62]

Links and references may be very eclectic, but the contrast between the highly personalised website and the immediate jump into the virtual *ummah* of the internet is interesting, as if there was nothing standing between the individual and the virtual *ummah*. This includes conversion through the internet: 'I devoured anything I could get my hands on – WebPages, books, Quran, email lists. I ran out of reasons to NOT become muslim. I took Shahada on July 31, 2002 at Islamicity.com'.[63] There are many websites set up by converts who speak about their conversion, telling their life stories.[64]

59. <http://profiles.yahoo.com/abuubaydullah>.
60. <http://www.gzastorm.i12.com/islam/index.html>.
61. <http://www.geocities.com/CollegePark/6453/asadie.html>.
62. <http://www.geocities.com/Athens/Oracle/4321/main.html>.
63. <http://www.pacifier.com/~owlie/islam.htm>.
64. For example, stories of some converts can be found at <http://www.islam-fortoday.com/converts.htm#COTW>.

FAITH AND SELF

Faith (*iman*) has of course always been an important dimension in Islam, as in any revealed religion. But there is a clear stress on faith when contemporary Muslims speak of their religion. Faith means individual reappropriation of religion, a return to the inner self and a direct, unmediated connection to religion. The insistence on faith stresses the individual dimension of Islam in a non–Muslim environment. Faith is not supported by the social authority of religion. It is a personal matter and, more than that, it can weaken and vanish: faith is a face-to-face encounter not between God and individuals, but between individuals and themselves. 'How to live one's own faith', 'How to find peace?' writes Tariq Ramadan, but the peace is within oneself.[65] Fathi Yakan, a Lebanese Muslim Brother who played an important role in organising young Muslims in France, wrote a book (originally in Arabic, but since translated into French) entitled *What Does It Mean That I Belong to Islam?* (not *What Does Islam Mean?*). The answer is 'My belonging to Islam brings me the certitude that my existence makes sense.' The first chapter bears the title 'A Sincere Faith' and begins with a sort of credo: 'I must believe that …'.[66] The content is as usual perfectly orthodox, but the stress on the individual subject (*I, mine*) and internalisation of religion under the category of faith are typical of new forms of religiosity. Anxiety about the strength or the weakness of one's own faith, which has always been a typical Christian attitude, is now widespread among Muslims.[67]

65. Ramadan, *Les musulmans*, 2nd edn, 1998, p. 10.
66. Fathi Yakan, *Que signifie mon appartenance à l'Islam?* (transl. by Adam Hamid), Lyon: Tawhid, 1996. The English version is *To Be A Muslim* (online at <http://www.youngmuslims.ca/online_library/books/to_be_a_muslim/>). But the French translation is closer to the original title in Arabic (*Ma za ya'ni intima'i lil Islam*).
67. I never met an Afghan in Afghanistan who believed that the 'quality' of his faith was an issue, but many guidebooks for Muslims in the West insist on that dimension (Yakan's book *Que signifie mon appartenance à l'Islam?* insisted on the 'sincerity of faith'). Muhammad El-Mukhtar El-Channquiti (Shanqetee), a Saudi sheikh, is quoted as saying (in a conference): 'God! Bestow us a firm belief in You without any trace of doubt and a perfect faith without any trace of associationism' ('La croyance ferme en Allah', <http://www.cciq.qc.ca/cciqnew/view.asp?id=172#haut>). Repentance (*tawba*) is also a recurrent theme, which is linked with the shift from abiding by *sharia* to internalising its laws as a personal set of conducts.

In contemporary Islam, as in Christianity, there is a common type of born-again believer who suddenly crosses the boundary between a cultural or nominal religion to the status of 'true believers' or, more precisely, 'absolute' believer. A born-again believer is not simply a mosque-going Muslim or a churchgoing Christian. It is somebody whose faith suddenly becomes the central principle of their entire life. This is why born-again believers are often fundamentalists, because they cannot accept the grey area of a secular way of life between attendance at religious services. Prayers should accompany every activity; the ritualistic scansion of everyday life is a way to sanctify even menial activity. Salafist preachers regularly insist that prayers and formulas be uttered on every occasion.[68]

This quest for a personal religiosity may also bypass the orthodoxy of and even the boundaries between religions. In Iran the crisis of the established clergy and of political Islam undeniably led to a decline in religious practice, especially among youths. But many of them are trying to recast their quest for spirituality into new forms of religiosity, hence the sudden popularity of Sufism (which may or may not be related to traditional forms), and of religious eclecticism comparable to that of their Western counterparts (for example, interest in Buddhism or New Age religion). Although they cannot be compared with conversions from Christianity to Islam, there is an obvious surge of conversion to Christianity among young Muslims. Where professional Catholic religious orders (such as the Society of Missionaries of Africa, also know as the White Fathers) failed for a century, new Christian missionaries sometimes succeed. In Iran the assassination of an Armenian evangelist preacher in 1997 was a clear signal from the authorities that missionaries should cease their conversion campaign. Conversion to Christianity occurs in Turkey, among Muslims in the West, in Central Asia (Kyrgyzstan), and elsewhere. Sects are also flourishing, either very different from (such as Hare Krishna) or more or less linked with Islam. It is sometimes difficult to distinguish between a modern Sufi order and a religious sect (as illustrated by the Fethullah Gülen and Ahbash brotherhoods). Many converts came to fundamentalist

---

68. The book *Riyadh as-Salihin* (for example, Nawawi, Imam, *Gardens of the Righteous: The Riyadh as-Salihin of Imam Nawawi*, trans. by Muhammad Za-frulla Khan, 2nd edn, New York: Olive Branch Press, 1989), as well as Yakan's *Que signifie mon appartenance à l'Islam?*, are full of such recommendations.

branches of Islam having experienced Christianity, Buddhism and other religions, as illustrated by the case of John Walker Lindh, the young American Talib.[69] Even among neofundamentalists who are obsessed by legal norms, the mystical dimension of faith is central.

HUMANISM, ETHICAL ISLAM AND SALVATION

The sermons of certain *imams* and interviews with young Muslims indicate a fact of Islam that is quite absent from the pessimistic visions of radical Islamists like Sayyid Qutb.[70] This is the idea that Islam might bring happiness, or at least reconcile the believer with himself, by healing a self divided between faith and materialist aspirations, between tradition and modernity, between what sometimes seems a desolate life and the search for dignity and self-esteem. Such sermons are, of course, primarily addressed to an audience of young people who are experiencing uprootedness, alienation and racism, and vacillate between schizophrenic assimilation and hopeless revolt. But the message of these sermons also addresses the older generation, who, specifically in Western Europe, wonder what they have really achieved in their life, after lately acknowledging that they will not return to their country of origin, but will remain and even be buried in a non-Muslim society, unsure of the fate of their children. The sermons speak about salvation, ultimate ends, the value of life, and self-esteem. They portray a good Muslim as one who is obsessed not by legal norms, but by the meaning of norms, by values and ethics. They insist on social interaction, not on the strict following of norms; they acknowledge the non-Muslim environment as a matter of fact, not as a temporary, anomalous situation.[71] They pragmatically answer concrete requests for advice.

69. See Josh Tyrangiel, 'The Taliban Next Door', *Time*, 17 December 2001.
70. Imam Larbi Kechat, head of the Dawat mosque in Paris, is well known for his spiritualist sermons. For Islam as a way out of poor social conditions, see Farhad Khosrokhavar, *L'Islam des jeunes*, Paris: Flammarion, 1997. See also the various contributions in Felice Dassetto (ed.), *Paroles Musulmanes – Muslim Words*, Paris: Maisonneuve et Larose, 2000.
71. For example, Kechat advises his congregation to send their children to the Catholic Boy Scouts instead of trying to create a group that will not meet standards. The same attitude is implicitly endorsed by the numerous Muslim families who send their children to Catholic private schools instead of creating Muslim ones. There are in France fewer than ten Muslim faith schools to cater for the largest Muslim population in Europe.

But by definition they are confronted with situations that are the result of a brutal mixture of the merging of and confrontation between various values systems. Let us take an example:

Question: I am a white American girl who recently gave birth to a child whose father is a Pakistani muslim currently residing in the UK. We wish to marry so that our son can be raised in a proper muslim environment. Problem arising–This man has not told his father of our child. He is afraid his father will not allow us to be married because I also have another child from a previous time. His mother knows and is all for the marriage. I have tried to take on this religion as my own but it is hard because we are so far apart and I do not have that environment present in every day life. Can we defy his father if he does not allow us to marry just so that we can raise this child properly? Are there any surrahs in the Qu'ran or teachings in the hadiths to back up our decision to marry? Thank you very much. *Answer*: Since the child was born out of wedlock, the father is not considered to be the legal father of the child in Islamic law. However, since he is the biological father of the child, he should take moral responsibility of the child and rear him to the best of his ability. Now, if he wants to marry you to take care of you and his biological child, it is best he goes ahead. He should also explain the circumstances to his own father and request his blessings for this marriage. His permission is not necessary though laudable. He should try his level best in winning his father over and explain the situation to him – and Allah Ta'ala Knows Best.[72]

This case is interesting and quite common.[73] We have people who claim to be Muslims but experience and take responsibility for a situation largely inconceivable, or at least unspeakable, in a traditional Muslim society. A fundamentalist *mullah* could do nothing but condemn the sinners but, as we have seen, there is no way of punishing them. To expel them from the community (a solution that some Muslim, Jewish or Protestant preachers would advocate) would mean closing the door of the community to many people who still conceive of themselves as Muslim but cannot deal with the *sharia*. The answer of the *mufti* here is congruent with what almost any Catholic priest would say (and many Protestants or Jews): you are a sinner but it is best to consider life and moral duty

72. Mufti Muhammad Kadwa, 'Can we defy our parents to be married and raise our child born out of wedlock?', Ask the Imam, Question 5267, May 2002, <http://www.islam.tc/ask-imam/view.php?q=5276>. Spelling, punctuation and grammar are verbatim.
73. That the question might be a fake (which I do not believe) does not matter. Such situations do occur, and what is interesting is the answer of the *mufti*.

first, and God will deal with the rest. In a word, it is not for human beings to judge, but to help; this is a typical Christian answer. The same attitude is to be found, for example, in the work of Tariq Ramadan, who writes that the *hijab* is compulsory for Muslim women – here he remains in the fundamentalist fold against liberal theologians – but that it should never be forcibly imposed. Rather, it should be the result of the voluntary achievement of a personal quest for self-realisation and reconciliation with God; the *hijab* is 'a testimony to faith'.[74] In this sense the idea is not to dispense with the concept of law. The norm remains uncontested but is ascribed to a spiritual and personal itinerary, something more reminiscent of orthodox Sufism than of the Taliban's religious police. Ramadan speaks of a 'Muslim humanism'.[75]

I am unfamiliar with the *mufti* who wrote the *fatwa* above. He is probably not a liberal theologian, if a theologian at all, but a religious practitioner, someone who deals with real human beings and social situations. His answer is based on ethics and values, not on a legalist approach, nor on a theological reassessment of what the Koran says. It is the concrete experience of what it means to be a Muslim in a non-Muslim society, not theological modernisation, that triggers a change of attitude. Such a liberal and open moral attitude can exist perfectly well alongside orthodoxy (as is the case with most Catholic priests); the example of the Puritans and other born-again Protestants shows that opening the Revelation to everybody's understanding does not mean softening the law.

Such an approach is in line with the traditional concept of 'public good' (*maslahat*), which stresses the spirit and the meaning of law as opposed to a formal conception of it. The traditional view is expressed, for example, by al-Qaradawi: 'When this legislation [*sharia*] forbids something, it is for the sake of society and human beings' welfare, in order to make them better and to protect their properties, health, family, and honour in this world.'[76] But in this

---

74. Ramadan, *Les Musulmans*, 1994, p. 121. Recently in Tunisia, a new custom appeared: inviting friends and relatives for a party to celebrate a grown-up lady's decision to wear the *hijab* (personal observation), something congruent with the recent customs of some conservative religious colleges in the American Bible Belt to celebrate 'born-again virgins' (that is, unmarried girls who pledge to stop having sexual relations before their wedding).
75. Ramadan, *Les Musulmans*, 1994, p. 146.
76. Yusuf al-Qaradawi, *Le Licite et l'Illicite*, Paris: Al Qalamp, 1992. This is a

text he refers to a person as part of the social fabric (*society, family, honour, wealth* – all refer to a well-integrated member of a society), not as an individual *per se*, which is the way of 'Western' Muslims. For al-Qaradawi happiness is linked with social integration in a Muslim society; for a Muslim in the West it means self-achievement. Such a position opens the way to a more liberal approach to modern social and ethical issues, such as abortion, contraception and organ transplantation (see Sheikh Buti's commentaries). Traditional values are espoused, but linked to an ethical approach to life. Terms like *adab* (educated man's good manners), *fitrat* (man's nature) and *ekhlaq* (ethics; *ihlak* in Turkish) are given a new importance. Norms are reformulated in terms of values, and are subsequently 'negotiable', meaning that the issue is not to follow the letter but the spirit of the law.[77] Such a shift towards ethics appears also among modern Sufi orders, where the reference to ethics seems to play a greater role than sheer mysticism.[78]

Salvation is presented not so much in the context of doomsday, but as a way to escape a desolate life. When they preach to young nominal Muslims in impoverished European neighbourhoods, Muslim clerics resort arguments similar to those used by Salvation Army or Methodist preachers in a similar context with nominal Christians.[79] Salvation is as much a matter of worldly things as it

---

translation of the Arabic *Al-Halal wa'l-Haram fi'l Islam*, a book that has been derided by many Salafists for being too permissive. In 1995 the same book banned for a year by the French Interior Ministry for incitement to violence against women. One person's fundamentalist is another person's liberal.

77. Socialising with non-Muslims in countries where Muslims are in a minority is a big issue. Should one accept invitations to parties, dinners and weddings?

78. Ural Manço, 'L'Ethique du derviche et l'Esprit de la Confrérie: Le discours du cheikh Nakshibendi Mehmet E'san Cosan' in Dassetto (ed.), *Paroles d'Islam*.

79. Fathi Yakan is very explicit on that (see chapter 3, 'The Good Character'). See Khosrokhavar, *L'Islam des jeunes*, p. 196. When I was a young man, I witnessed Salvation Army teams working in a poor neighbourhood in my French home town. New recruits used to preach sermons, interrupted with hymns and 'hallelujahs', always based on the same topic: 'I was like you, drunk, stealing cars, spitting on my parents, escaping school, but one day I met Jesus, and since then I've been happy, clean and close to God.' Now Muslim preachers come to the same neighbourhood and preach in the same way, except there are no more hymns. But in some cases Islamic rap groups play the role of the chorus; singing is a way to make contact with urban youth.

is heavenly ones. We may witness the emergence of 'emotional preachers' (such as Kechat, Amr Khaled and Gülen), for whom feelings prevail over law in order to achieve repentance and return to a true faith. With tears instead of fear, we are far from the legalist approach of the neofundamentalists. Spiritualisation accompanies the individualisation of religion.

Ethics and moral values are propounded because the strictly legal approach does not work, or for neofundamentalists has to be recast as a code. In fact *sharia* as a legal norm does not survive as such in a non-Muslim environment. It has to be recast either in spiritualist and moral terms, or as a normative code of behaviour that draws a clear boundary between Muslims and non-Muslims. What makes the difference is relevant to defining what makes the *ummah*: the obsession with a boundary, which is at the centre of the neofundamentalist approach, is no longer relevant for the 'ethical' Muslim, where the real issue is centred on the self, not the community.

The values thus presented are not alien to the Muslim tradition. Patience, self-restraint, soft speaking, compassion and modesty are nevertheless put at the centre of individual religiosity rather than being a simple collateral dimension.[80] By the same token, old concepts are given a new life. The concept of *tawba* (repentance) is by definition taken from the Koran (title of Surat 9); it was used mainly by those of the Sufi tradition, but is now quite common among born-again Muslims who by definition have to repent of their previous life.[81] Such values may be held in common with

80. Yakan is explicit about this in Chapter 3 ('Morals') of his *Que signifie mon appartenance à l'Islam?* (<http://www.youngmuslims.ca/online_library/books/to_be_a_muslim/>).
81. See Abu Hamid Ghazali, Ibn Qayim Jawiya and Ibn Rajab Hanbali, *Sincere Repentance* (comp. by Abu Paryam Majdi Fathi al-Syed), London: Al-Firdous, 1995. There is nothing new in the ideas. What is new is collecting and publishing these quotations as a separate booklet. Tawba becomes central precisely because implementing legal punishments is less and less possible. Thus the return of the sinner to the mainstream relies on his or her repentance. The South African website Ask the Imam (<http://islam.tc/ask-imam/index.php>) is a good example of such a trend. *Fatwa*: 'i commited zina, im single, will he forgive me if i ask for toba? what dou'as to say, what can i do in ramadan that mite help forgive my sins, must i tell my future husband?' (original spelling). Answer: "If one fulfils the conditions of repentance, i.e. regret and make firm intention to reform, then surely Allah Ta'ala is Tawwaab (Most Forgiving)" (<http://islam.tc/ask-imam/view.php?q=4109>).

other religions or simply with other human beings, while religious laws ascribe an individual to a precise community. But to what extent does sharing common values simply dilute a religious identity? The debate about interreligious dialogue and finding common ground is a controversial one in every religion.[82]

ENUNCIATION OF THE SELF

The headscarf affair in France (where Muslim schoolgirls insisted on wearing the scarf inside the classroom) triggered uproar in many sections of French public opinion: militant secularists, social workers, members of parliament, 'clash of civilisationists' and most feminists. At first the scarf was perceived as the expression of a patriarchal society and as a burden imposed on women by men. But it very soon became clear that the schoolgirls concerned had not been forced to wear the scarf and chose to wear it as an expression of their faith and self. 'My body is my own business.'[83] This claim, typical of the women's liberation movement, was turned by educated and voluntarily scarfed Muslim women into a statement in favour of something that seems to be the opposite. Of course there is nothing in common between a Kabul woman under the Taliban, who was obliged to wear the *chadri*, and a female biology student from Ankara or the University of Paris, who is modern, independent and educated but wants to wear the headscarf as an expression of her self. Modern Islamists campaign not for the compulsory wearing of a headscarf or *hijab*, but for the right to do so,

82. The Reverend Jerry Vines, at the Southern Baptist Convention in June 2002, declared: 'Allah is not Jehovah' (Jim Jones, 'Baptist Pastor's Words Shock Muslim Leaders', *Star-Telegram* (Dallas and Fort Worth), 12 June 2002, <http://www.dfw.com/mld/dfw/3451104.htm>). Salafi Muslims oppose interfaith dialogue when it pertains to beliefs. ('But most of all, Muslim organizations and individuals must not compromise the message of Islam in the process of carrying out an interfaith dialogue' <http://www.islamonline.net/iol-english/dowalia/society-29-11/society1.asp>).
83. See Naheed Mustafa, 'My Body is My Own Business', *Globe and Mail* (Toronto), 29 June 1993. See also Sanna Negus, 'A Chosen Identity: Columnist and Social Critic Heba Raouf Espouses Social Equality without Feminism and Islamic Values without Islamism', *Cairo Times*, 3, 25 (20–26 January 2000), an article on Heba Raouf, a veiled journalist and sociologist, who left her husband and children for some months to study at Westminster and Oxford (see n. 21, pp. 216–17, this vol.).

playing on the modern concept of personal freedom rather than that of submission to God's law. One of the first moves of the AK Partisi in Turkey after its electoral victory in 2002 was to push for the freedom of women to wear the *hijab* at university, but not for its imposition. Muslims in Europe speak the language of freedom.

The meaning of the *hijab* (or headscarf) is worthy of further reflection, however. Most mothers of the headscarfed schoolgirls in France do not wear the *hijab*: it is often an adolescent kind of self-assertion in opposition to society, family and teachers. For many it is a purely transitional attitude: how many will still wear the *hijab* ten years later? For some girls, wearing the *hijab* in an impoverished Muslim-populated neighbourhood is also a way to escape the teasing and insults of idle young boys who have transformed the public space into a 'young males only' territory.

By the same token some converts or born-again Muslims wear a very visible form of attire to express their newly chosen identity (white cap, long white shirts and sometimes turbans). They use in Western languages coded Arabic expressions such as *assalamu alaikum*, *bismillah* and *jazakallah*, which are never so frequently heard in any 'native' Muslim language. They are staging their own selves, often to the verge of exhibitionism, which is also part of the expression of an exacerbated individualism.

The possibility of choosing between various traditions of dress and general appearance (whether in the West or the Middle East) gives a permanent meaning to individual choices of attire. In Iran looking permanently as if one has not shaved for a week means being a committed conservative (or a poor clerk with no choice), while in Pakistan wearing a long untrimmed beard with the upper lip carefully shaved indicates a fundamentalist. In Turkey modern Islamists wear suits and sport a small moustache (a longer one makes you a nationalist).

Quite logically, Islamic revivalism goes hand in hand with a modern trend: the culture of the self. As we have seen, a return to Islam is also equated with a sort of worldly salvation: to be at peace, to feel good, to regain self-esteem and dignity.[84] Hence the numerous

84. This is a general trend, but of course is more important to the Sufis. For an elaboration on the concept of 'practical Sufism', see Julia Day Howell, 'Indonesia's Urban Sufis: Challenging Stereotypes of Islamic Revival', *ISIM Newsletter*, 6 (2000) (<http://www.isim.nl/files/newsl_6.pdf>).

articles, papers and internet postings on 'How Islam is the best
solution for ...', followed by a list of contemporary social issues
(drugs, stress, violence, school problems, sexual relations). 'How
does one find peace?' wrote Tariq Ramadan.[85] Islam is presented as
a cure for suffering, with the aim of 'finding peace' ('Modern Stress
and Its Cure from Qur'an'),[86] which can extend even to mundane
concerns like keeping fit ('Health and Fitness in Islam').[87] The ban
on smoking, which is not new in Islam, is reformulated in modern
terms ('Smoking: A Social Poison',[88] a paper that tells about 'Harm
to the Environment' and of the 'Low Self-Esteem' manifested by
smoking). Psychology of the self is taken into account. An article entitled 'Psychological and Mental Health' by Professor Omar
Hasan Kasule (International Islamic University, Malaysia) explains
in 'Islamic' terms the issue of mental disorder.[89] His entire analysis
is based on the concept of 'personality'. The various sections of
the paper rely on modern categories ('Personality', defined as 'the
totality of behaviour of an individual with a given tendency system
interacting with a sequence of situations'; 'Enhancing the Positive';
'Discouraging the Negative'; 'Personal Failure'; and 'Causes of Personal Failure'), but the conclusion is that 'Forgetting Allah and ne-
glecting His command is the start of failure'. The melding of a
modern analytical approach with a Koranic moral conception of
norms is typical of the synthesis between modern objectivisation
of the self (the basis of the concept of psychology) and an ethical
and moral lecture on Islamic norms. Websites also offer 'Islamic'
goods, fashion, books, perfumes and other products. We are back
to Islamo-business, for which there is a demand that fits with a
modern consumer society.

Ethics are called upon to regulate this fully accepted consumer
society. An entire industry is developing to 'Islamise' this way of

85. Ramadan, *Les musulmans*, 1994, p. 10.
86. Shahid Athar (ed.), *Islamic Medicine*, <http://www.islam-usa.com/im14.html>.
87. <http://fauzynm.tripod.com/Nasihat/Nasihat96/nasihat96.html>. In To-
    ronto the Siha Health and Fitness Center is targeting the Muslim population,
    particularly women (<http://www.sihafitness.com/summary.html>).
88. By Muhammad al-Jibaly, published by the Salafi organisation al-Qur'an
    was-Sunnah Society of North America (a Salafi organisation) on
    <http://www.qss.org/articles/smoking.html>.
89. <http://www.crescentlife.com/articles/psychological_and_mental_health.
    htm>.

life, like the five-star Islamic hotel that opened in Turkey in 1999 (the Caprice Hotel, at Didim, on the Aegean coast).[90] The aim is not, as it would be in Iran or Saudi Arabia, simply to conform with rigidly imposed legislation, but to attract devout believers who also want to enjoy a good time at a recreational resort. Islam is in this case a marketing incentive, not a constraint. Consumerism regulated by ethics is a traditional pattern of the Protestant business ethic. An Islamic consumerism is emerging alongside a new Muslim work ethic adapted to modern entrepreneurs, embodied in the Turkish businessmen's union MÜSIAD.[91] This is just a symptom of the growth of a modern Muslim bourgeoisie, far from the bazaar and the bureaucracy, which were its traditional bases. Stress on work, family, ethics and modesty goes along with success stories: happiness on earth fits with heavenly salvation. Such a conception of happiness was found among the Protestant Puritans.[92] But it also means that this sort of re-Islamisation does not transcend social classes and socioeconomic divides. Islamic revival in the West helps to bypass ethnic identities, but conforms with socioeconomic diversity as reshaped by Western societies. In a word, Islamic revival is at ease with modern capitalism.[93]

This dilution of legal norms in favour of ethics and self-expression may find its zenith in the recent emergence of a 'Muslim gay' identity, on the model of Christian gays and lesbians.[94] It is an example of the process of westernisation that is also to be found in the 2002 trial of Egyptian homosexuals. In both cases, positively or negatively, the very concept of 'homosexuality' is presented as a legal concept, in terms of crime or of minority rights. Of course one can say that *sharia* has always condemned homosexuality, but

90. Interestingly, the 'women only' swimming pool at this resort is advertised on the Turkish-language part of the website, but not in the English-language section.
91. For an interesting comparison see Gültekin Burcu, *Instrumentalisation de l'Islam pour une stratégie de promotion sociale à travers le secteur privé. Le cas du Müsiad*, Paris: Presse de la FNSP, 1999.
92. Edmund Leites, in his book *The Puritan Conscience and Modern Sexuality* (New Haven, CT: Yale University Press, 1995), shows that Puritans were as interested in happiness as in salvation.
93. This would not have come as a surprise to Maxime Rodinson (*Islam and Capitalism*, Austin: University of Texas Press, 1978).
94. See the websites of Queer Jihad (<http://www.well.com/user/queerjhd/>) and the Al-Fatiha Foundation (<http://www.al-fatiha.net/>)

the 'object' has in fact not been constructed as such in the Muslim legal tradition, which cares about the circumstances of the act, not the nature of the actors. The way homosexuality is constructed today means the borrowing of two Western definitions (from sin to crime, from perversion to sexual orientation). To claim to be a believing gay Muslim cannot be understood if one ignores the shift of religiosity from objective and social norms to self-construction.

But the reading in terms of values is not necessarily permissive and liberal. It could also give birth to a Muslim culturalism, as we have seen previously, in which a set of conservative values (no premarital sex, no pornography) would define the Muslim community. Conformist and conservative values are reappropriated by pious modern middle-class urbanites, who stress family values over permissiveness. They particularly emphasise children's education, which leads many conservative Muslims in the West to discard or ignore the right to polygamy, which in a Western environment goes against familial stability and close supervision of children by the father. In fact the model of the 'good family' is close to the conservative Christian one. Hence Muslims call upon their Christian counterparts to join them to protest against pornography and blasphemy. (In the United States, the interfaith Alliance for Marriage, which opposes same-sex marriage, includes Muslims.) Although far from being radical in political terms, the views of this conservative middle class are often ignored or dubbed 'fundamentalist' by Christians and Jews. These conservative views are expressed through modern media (films, television and novels) that are ignored by the West. And one sees translated or distributed in the West 'Oriental' films and publications that seem to break with tradition in political or cultural terms (for example, Iranian 'new wave' cinema, or exiled Bangladeshi author Taslima Nasrin, who is under threat of death from a *fatwa* issued by Muslim fundamentalists in her home country). But one ignores an abundant local literature or cinema output, which is modern in terms of medium while extolling conservative norms adapted to contemporary tastes, speaking about love, family disputes, working women, children's education, and so on.[95]

95. On the Iranian 'popular' (that is, middle-class) literature, see Chapter 7 of Farhad Khosrokhavar and Olivier Roy's *Iran: Comment sortir d'une révolution religieuse* (Paris: Editions du Seuil, 1999), on an Iranian female writer, Fattaneh Hajj Seyyed Javadi, author of *Bamdade Khomar* (*Morning Hangover*), who writes in the tradition of Barbara Cartland, praising traditional family

We again reach a point where *sharia* is understood more in cultural (and social) terms (authenticity, respect for common values,
transmission of values) than in purely legal terms: norms are more
important than rules.[96]

RECOMMUNITARISATION AND CONSTRUCTION OF IDENTITY

The Muslim community is no longer based on territory and culture, but nor does it have a real social basis. Sociological analyses
of Muslims in the West show that they do not share specific patterns of behaviour and that they belong to different social groups.
Nowhere is there a Muslim vote: they vote as immigrants for the
first generation (usually leftist or democrat) and then according to
their social position, but not according to their creed (those who
have benefited or expect to benefit from upward social mobility
tend to vote more for the Right).[97] Ethnicity and/or social position
explain the pattern of marriage better than religious affiliation (the
insistence on some sort of endogamy is related to factors that are
more social and ethnic than strictly religious). As we have seen, it is
difficult to devise a sociology of born-again Muslims. (We tend to
focus on extremists because they make the news, but a sociology
of militants is not automatically relevant to the silent majority.) In
some cases the lack of social rootedness and the crisis of classical
social identities (such as working class) may explain why certain

values. We can also add Turkish writers like M. Inal and S.Y. Enler – see Ipek
Mercil, 'Les intellectuelles islamistes en Turquie contemporaine', PhD disser-
tation, L'École des Hautes Études en Sciences Sociales (EHESS), Paris, 2001.
About Bangladeshi writers, see Maimuna Huq, 'From Piety to Romance' in
Eickelman and Anderson, *New Media*.

96. For an original analysis of the claim for *sharia* as a quest for the respect of
cultural norms and not legal rules, see Beaudoin Dupret, *Au nom de quel droit?
Repertoires juridiques et reference religieuse dans la société Egyptienne musulmane
contemporaine* (In the Name of Which Law? Legal Repertoires and Religious Reference in Contemporary Egyptian Society), Paris: Cedej/Maison
des Sciences de l'Homme, 2000. A major issue is the need to understand why
sociological emancipation of women does not trigger a stronger feminist
movement among Muslim women: the call for *sharia* is not the monopoly of
fundamentalists. For Dupret, in many contemporary Muslim societies values
are seen as more important than laws, and *sharia* is more a set of values and a
cultural framework than a system of laws in itself.

97. The massive support from US Muslims for George W. Bush in 2000 seems
linked with an adherence to conservative moral views.

people identify themselves as Muslims while discarding other identities.[98] Such a community has no sociological basis.

But how does one reconstruct a community that by definition is a community of faith and not a product of history or society? Links to history have to be reconstructed. This is obvious in the issue of the Caliphate: should we consider that until 1924 there was always a Caliphate (the position of the Hizb ut-Tahrir), or should we discard any political construction that came after the time of the Prophet and his four successors? How do we assess the Ottoman Empire: as a true Muslim political construction or as a mere artefact in the hands of an ethnolinguistic group? What was the Golden Age of Islam? How do we assess Andalusia? Is the classical Arab culture a true Islamic culture? What about Averroës? Neither culture nor history provide a basis for reconstruction.

This community of faith is not to be taken for granted: it exists to the extent that believers identify with it. Hence the regular call (almost an imprecation) by the radicals: how can the vast silent majority remain silent in the face of what is going on in Palestine, Afghanistan and Chechnya?

Because the community is built on a voluntary basis, the issue of its boundaries is important. The stress on faith, and the will to create a community of faith rather than simply a cultural entity, means that *imams* are increasingly opposed to nominal conversions for the sake of marriage and insist on preliminary religious education.[99] As noted, Catholic and Jewish authorities are also less and less flexible on the

98. In the early 1980s violent social conflict erupted in French automobile plants, where the bulk of the non-skilled workers were Muslims. *En masse* they joined the communist-led Worker's Union (CGT), which in exchange pushed for the creation of prayer rooms in the workplace. But in the following years many Muslim leaders of the strikes gave up their 'working-class leader' identity for a purely Muslim one (Akka Ghazi, for example). By the same token some young Muslims who had joined a secular movement to promote Muslims of the second generation (*beurs*), sponsored by the Socialist Party in 1983, took a more religious turn after being frustrated by the unwillingness of the party to provide them with available positions at election times.
99. Mufti Ebrahim Desai, 'Muslim Guy Marrying a Sikh Girl ... Urgent Reply Needed', Ask the Imam, Question 5319, 30 March 2002, <http://www.islam.tc/ask-imam/view.php?q=5319>. A Muslim man is dating a Sikh girl. He proposes that she convert, but only verbally. The *mufti* answers: 'Accepting Islam is from the heart, not only verbally. Islam is a divine religion with a set of values and principles. Verbally accepting Islam to legalise the Nikah will not be valid.'

matter of conversions. Speaking of faith and insisting on moral values as a way to fight modern social and physical diseases from pornography to AIDS help to create common ground between different religious communities, especially in the most conservative milieus. But many conservatives and Salafis denounce such a close association on the grounds that it poses the danger of weakening group identity. Should a Muslim indulge in non-Muslim celebrations or even secular social events? Is it religiously permitted for children to attend a Christmas party at their school, to send greeting cards for the New Year, to offer gifts at Christmas? Neofundamentalists tend to limit interactions with non-Muslims as far as possible.[100] We have seen how some authors discourage Muslim men from marrying non-Muslim women. Such debates have occurred throughout Muslim history, but in situations in which Christians were in the minority. By contrast the Islamists were far less touchy about interacting with non-Muslims (Maududi, the founder of Jamaat-i-Islami, attended Hindu ceremonies, and the Foreign Ministry of the Islamic Republic of Iran used to send Christmas cards each year). The increasing rigidity of the interdictions is motivated by the fact that interactions with non-Muslims work to the detriment of Muslims in a minority. (A non-Muslim wife in a Muslim country has no choice but to raise her children as Muslims; in a country where Muslims are in a minority she will be more tempted to retain non-Muslim values and educational patterns.) Muslims have returned to the sense of being an endangered minority.

There is no means of giving this elusive *ummah* a political expression, for several reasons. One is that Muslims in a minority can play a political role either by joining or casting their votes for non-Muslim political movements (which they usually do), or by building an Islamic party that will remain a marginal, single-issue and sectarian entity (a choice made by Nation of Islam in the United States and some small marginal parties, like the Islamic Party of Britain and the Arab European League in Belgium). Many Salafists are pushing for the construction of a community of believers that would be built around a common language (Arabic), endogamy,

---

100. The Saudi television station Iqra broadcast, at Christmas time, many sermons on this issue. Jamal al-Din Zarabozo, from Los Angeles, published a *fatwa* on 'Celebrating or Participating in Holidays of the Disbelievers' (*Al-Jumuah Magazine*, 9, 2 (2002), <http://www.islaam.com/Article.aspx?id=112>), in which he stated that any form of participation amounts to *kufr*, or impiety.

social life and even a business community. Sheikh Abdul Rahman Abdul Khaliq put it in a straightforward manner:

Muslims of the West must be united in every matter. They must call to Islam and preserve their loyalty to Muslims and be disloyal to the disbelievers. Arabic must be their first language. Muslims should seek to socialise with, marry from and meet other Muslims in lectures, mosques, universities, picnics and general activities. Muslims must not be isolated from other Muslims.[101]

Violence is linked with the blurring of the community's boundaries. The sudden freedom that youths enjoy in the West is a concern for traditional elderly Muslims: how do they impose the norm? For lack of legal enforcement, one may resort to forced retraditionalisation (marrying girls as young as possible and within the community, committing honour crimes) or take to the streets (as in, for instance, the Rushdie affair). Hence the burgeoning of individual *fatwas* issued by petty *mullahs*. This rearguard action cannot stem the onslaught, but it is often stressed by Islamophobes to prove that Islam is linked to violence. It is sometimes even fashionable to be on the receiving end of a *fatwa*.[102]

But due to the lack of social authority and pressure, any form of recommunitarisation is in the end based on a personal choice. Muslims are those who say they are Muslim, and who define the ways in which they are Muslim by choosing what is available on the religious identity market.

The passive *ummah* comprises nominal Muslims, but radical groups reject the idea and tend to redefine themselves as the vanguard of the *ummah*. Because the *ummah* is a reconstruction, it depends on individual choices and free association of militants committed to the same ideal. In this sense there are as many *ummahs* as groups pretending to embody it. The *ummah* here plays the role of the proletariat for Trotskyist and leftist groups of the 1960s: an imaginary and therefore silent community that gives legitimacy to the small group pretending to speak in its name.

101. Abdul Rahman Abdul Khaliq, 'Priorities of Islamic Activities in the West', *Dar Ihyaa at-Turath* [*House for the Revival of the Heritage*], <http://www.islaam.com/Article.aspx?id=188>.
102. Daniel Pipes ('An American Rushdie?', *Jerusalem Post*, 4 July 2001) presents Khalid Duran, a controversial author, as the victim of a *fatwa* given by an unknown Jordanian sheikh.

5
ISLAM IN THE WEST OR THE WESTERNISATION OF ISLAM?

The reformulation of religiosity in Islam is mirrored in the other Western faiths, but this mirror effect extends also to institutionalisation and community-building. Islam tends to adapt to the laws and traditions of its host countries, even for movements that pretend to ignore or reject westernisation.

How can a Muslim community be built from a population that is merely Muslim? This is the challenge for Muslims in the West. There is, as we have seen, a permanent vacillation between two identity models: an ethnocultural community and a purely religious one (akin to a 'Muslim church'). Both models are entrenched in the Western conception of minorities and communities – 'church' (or more exactly 'churches') as a legacy of history, and 'multiculturalism' as a modern concept for dealing with ethnic diversity. The quest for recognition, whatever the scope of adaptation and concession, accompanies the quest for legal status, which is provided by existing legal models. Each Western country integrates Islam according to its own paradigms, and Muslim citizens tend to express their identity through these Western models, even if they oppose integration or if these paradigms theoretically contradict certain basic tenets of their beliefs (such as putting Islam on an equal footing with Christianity). Muslims in the West end up thinking in Western ways, even when they oppose Western values.

THE BUILDING OF MUSLIM 'CHURCHES'

In quest of modern communities

Neither individualisation nor the weakening of primary communal identities diminishes the sense of belonging to a community, but what does this mean concretely to Muslims living as a fractured and diversified minority in a non-Muslim West?

Any approach to community-building has to be constructivist. Community-building can be considered at three levels: the parochial level, in the framework of a local mosque and congregation, or of a student association; the national level, through the establishment of some kind of 'Muslim church' or a national council of Muslim associations in order to promote the interests of Muslim citizens of a given nation; and the universal level, that of the transnational *ummah*, to which the loyalty of the believer is directed. These three levels are not contradictory. A local congregation leader may participate in the promotion of a national Muslim identity while referring to the universal *ummah*, just as a Jew can be a good citizen and a supporter of Israel, or a Catholic can be a pillar of his parish while casting his vote for a Christian political party and supporting the Pope's supranational campaigns. Conflicts of loyalties are not new in history (for example, many French officers resigned when in 1905 the government sent the army to expel Catholic clerics from schools and monasteries). But the way in which the different levels are managed, separated and put on a hierarchical scale tells us much about the process of secularisation and westernisation.

While most Muslims at least pay lip-service to the concept of *ummah*, the manner of their participation in community activities is a good indication of their integration with the West. Roughly, we shall distinguish between those who try to inscribe forms of Muslim communalism in the framework of the host countries' regulations and customs, and those who pretend to ignore such limitations and endeavour to express their community as an ideal transnational and non-territorial entity. Liberals as well as conservatives take the former approach, while most neofundamentalists prefer to ignore the constraints of integration. The first approach corresponds to a westernisation in terms not only of institutionalisation, but also of secularisation, because it implies, more or less willingly, the two principal 'realms' (worldly and heavenly). But the neofundamentalist approach does not mean a return to the principle of Dar-ul-Islam. Instead of recreating a territorial Muslim entity, it necessitates a deterritorialisation of Dar-ul-Islam; it goes along with an abstract and theoretical approach to some sort of imaginary *ummah*, which is also an adaptation (even if this is denied) to the surrounding secularisation. We shall see in chapters 6 and 7 how neofundamentalism and radical Islam are the consequences of the deterritorialisation process.

The constructivist approach to building a community has two dimensions: an inward one, which consists of bringing at least a part of the Muslim population into the framework of a common local or national organisation, based on a common perception of what it means to be a Muslim; and an outward dimension, concerned with the surrounding society and state, looking either for confrontation or for recognition, which by definition should be negotiated and based on common values. Any Muslim community in the West is thus constructed, even unwillingly, through permanent interaction with wider society and, more precisely, by using patterns established by or for other Western religions. For moderates a Muslim may individually follow the law of his country of residence (by registering his marriage, for example) while abiding by Muslim rituals. In this sense the community may be experienced at two levels: the universal and purely ideal community of all believers (which takes no institutional form), and a local or national congregation, which is organised inside the legal framework of the host country. But for many neofundamentalists and radicals this community should not be 'negotiated' with a Western state. It is the community of all believers, regardless of borders or citizenship. A Muslim should not seek legal status such as would be bestowed by 'infidels'. This imaginary community is not bound by secular law, territory and borders, or given societies. It can be built on a transnational basis (through militancy, like Hizb ut-Tahrir, or via the internet); it can be implemented at the local level, as a closed community in a neighbourhood centred on a mosque, sometimes with the appearance of a cult. Farhad Khosrokhavar calls them 'neo-communes',[1] to the extent that they resemble the 'communes' of the 1960s and 1970s, when people of different geographical and social origins came together to live according to their beliefs. I have used the expression 'Islamised territories' because such a community incorporates in a common space people who decide to live according to their own code of behaviour.[2] But the term could also be applied to an existing territorial unit (for instance, a tribal territory in

1.   Farhad Khosrokhavar, *L'Islam des jeunes*, Paris: Flammarion, 1997.
2.   Olivier Roy, *The Failure of Political Islam*, Cambridge, MA: Harvard University Press, 1995.

Pakistan or a district of Cairo), whose members decide at a given time to express their own specificity in religious terms. It could also be a group of 'friends' who decide to live together with a specific purpose in mind (as did the 'Hamburg cell' that prepared the 9/11 attacks). Nevertheless, most Muslims in the West, when they care to build a community (which is not for most their primary concern), do so by referring to the legal and social categories of the host country, which would employ non-Islamic categories (for example, France's 1905 law on the separation of church and state).

The quest for legal status

Non-Muslim states and societies play a major role in shaping an elusive Muslim community. Even in the absence of a specific status for Islam, the rulings of courts on specific cases, by setting precedents, contribute to the shaping of a general legal framework in which the Muslim faith is integrated into the West. In France specific court rulings have determined the rights and limits for wearing a headscarf or *hijab*.[3] Muslims tend to adapt to this framework. Even if they disagree, they play along with the rules and utilise the courts when they consider that their rights have been infringed.

Achieving legal status can entail requesting a specific law on Islam, but such a choice has been made only by countries with a historical Muslim minority (including Austria and Russia, whose laws recognise Islam as a legal religion, but have no specific provisions regarding *sharia*; and India which, though secular according to its constitution, bestows a specific personal status on Muslims). The first modern European country to recognise Islam officially

3.   In 2004, the French parliament banned the headscarf in schools. In France a manager can fire a veiled Muslim employee if she is in visual contact with the customers, but not if she works outside their sight, while in Germany a Supreme Court ruling forbade the firing of a veiled saleswoman (10 October 2002), while a veiled schoolteacher could be fired (June 2001). In Britain a successful Muslim businessman sought to obtain recognition for polygamy (Jason Burke, 'Muslim Fights to Make Three Wives Legal', *Guardian*, 20 February 2000), invoking the *Human Rights Act 1998*. It is interesting that he advocates a law defending ethnic and religious minorities. In France, polygamy was legal for non-French citizens or citizens from former colonies turned 'French territories' (Comores) until 1993, when the law was restricted. Polygamy is now not recognised in metropolitan France. The colonial legacy does play a role.

was Austria (as a consequence of its Balkan possessions) in 1912. In this case the Muslim presence was originally linked with neither colonial possessions (Bosnia was not a colony) nor immigration, even if most Austrian Muslims are nowadays of Arab and Turkish origin. The Islamic Religious Community in Austria (IRCA, founded in 1979) was granted official status in 1988. No foreign *imam* may be accorded permanent status in Austria without IRCA permission (except the Turkish *imams* provided by the Directorate of Religious Affairs, or Diyanet İşleri Başkanliği), and Islam has been taught in state schools since 1982.

Otherwise, Western countries treat Islam according to their general laws on religion. Problems arise when religions have a specific constitutional status (in Germany the state pays the salaries of Catholic, Protestant and Jewish clergymen and collects religious taxes; in Britain the Anglican Church is the state church, as is the Lutheran Church in Denmark). But customs may also bestow pre-eminence on Christian religions through public holidays (Christmas, Good Friday, Easter) or official ceremonial protocols (where bishops and pastors appear with state officials). In every country most Muslim leaders ask for their communities to enjoy the same rights as the other faiths. By doing so, they put Islam into the fold of the general Western perception of what a religion is. For example, Friday for Muslims (although it has never been declared by classical *ulama* to be a public holiday) is equated with Sunday for Christians, and *imams* are considered to be professional clerics, which historically they never were; marriages performed by *mullahs* are considered religious marriages (while they are closer to a civil contract), and hence, for instance, French law forbids that they be performed before civil registration.

If we compare how Muslims organise themselves in different Western countries we may conclude that they express more the dynamics of the host country than of Islamic traditions. The issue of legal status sometimes overshadows the fact that the host country's habits and customs are the main driving factors for Muslims. Why are there so many Muslim 'faith schools' in Britain and so few in France? In countries with a tradition of faith schools, like Britain and the Netherlands, Muslims develop such schools, while in countries where state schools dominate (such as France) there are very few Muslim schools. This has nothing to do with law. French law on faith schools is rather elastic, as indicated by the growing

number of Jewish faith schools (which enrolled some 30,000 pupils in 2003). By contrast, there are almost no Muslim primary or
secondary schools. Muslims prefer to send their children to state
schools or, in impoverished neighbourhoods, to Catholic ones
because they are relatively free from violence.[4] In short, Muslims
react in the same way as most other French people. In Britain,
by contrast, faith schools have a long history and are seen as a
normal part of the educational system. There Muslims campaign
to benefit from the Race Relations Act (1976), which entails being recognised as an ethnic denomination, while in France their
leaders struggle to be recognised as a church, on the same footing
as Catholics, Protestants and Jews. In Belgium many Muslims wish
to be recognised as an ethnic (and even linguistic) group, aping
the decades-old Flemish–Walloon struggle.[5] An apparent paradox
is that secular France asks Muslims to organise in the framework
of a purely religious community, a church, while avowedly more
religious Britain (in the sense that it has a 'state' church) considers
group identity in ethnic and not religious terms. But the paradox
is misleading. By treating Islam as a 'mere' religion, France leaves
the choice of identity to the incumbent; one can refuse to be a
Muslim. However, by insisting on origin and culture, Belgium and
Britain impose a given and inescapable identity.

We touch here the most important factor that characterises the
delinking of religion and culture in Islam. The 'clash of civilisations'
debate, by ignoring this delinking, cannot explain what is going on
in the process of globalisation. It is by treating Islam as a mere religion that integration can take place. In the United States many
Muslims sought to emulate the 'Jewish lobby' by developing a centralised public-relations board, like the American Muslim Council
(founded in 1990), whose name is clearly derived from that of
the Jewish Council; the Muslim Public Affairs Council, in symmetry with the American Israeli Public Affairs Committee, which

4.   For instance, at Saint Maurond college in Marseilles, France, the vast majority
     of schoolchildren are Muslims.
5.   In Antwerp the European Arab League wants Arabic to be recognised as a
     state language, a unique demand in Europe, but clearly a consequence of the
     linguistic tussle between French and Flemish. One exists as a group only if
     one fights for a tongue. The 'Muslim' council has also explicitly been turned
     into a secular organisation by the state, which allows ballot boxes to be put in
     secular places such as schools or city halls.

endeavours to reconcile Islam and US patriotism; and the more vocal Council on American–Islamic Relations (CAIR),[6] which encourages Muslims to register to vote.[7] On its website CAIR uses typical US sociological categories: Muslims and converts are ethnically categorised as 'white', 'Afro-American' and so on. There are systematic references to US values related to gender, equality, community services and patriotism. A CAIR advertisement in the *New York Times* (23 February 2003) stated: 'The members of Santa Clara Muslim Girl Scout Troop #856 have made a pledge to serve their community, their country and God. The American values that we all cherish – like service, charity, and tolerance – are the same values that Muslims are taught to uphold in daily life.' The Muslim Public Affairs Council (MPAC), a civil rights and ethnic lobbying organisation, was founded in 1988. The Islamic Society of North America (ISNA), which is near to the Salafi school of thought, is more involved in trying to organise a religious life compatible with US standards (it provides a *fatwa* service).

The main difficulty for US Muslim organisations is resolving the conflicting demands of a purely ethnic identity and a purely religious one (the main proponents of the latter are more often from the Indian subcontinent). Muslims in the United States belong to three main ethnic groups: Arabs, South Asians and African-Americans (each comprising about a quarter of the Muslim population). Their political and social agendas are quite different, not to mention that most Arabs in the United States are Christians. The Nation of Islam is typically an endeavour to express in religious terms an ethnic divide, while many African-Americans convert to Islam precisely to escape such a divide and to merge into a universal community. A minority of Muslims vehemently oppose the integrationist approach, however, emulating the example in Britain of Sheikh Omar Bakri Muhammad, who considers as *kufr* (lacking in faith) the civil registration of marriages even if *nikah* (wedding ceremony) is performed,[8] and the Hizb ut-Tahrir.

6. <http://www.cair-net.org>.
7. See Chapter 3 ('Arab-American Identity and New Transnational Challenges') in Yossif Shahin, *Marketing the American Creed Abroad: Diasporas in the US and Their Homelands*, Cambridge University Press, 1999.
8. *Fatwa* by Omar Bakri Muhammad, 'The Islamic Verdict on Civil/Registered Marriages', Case No. Civil Marriages/M/F45, 9 March 2000, <http://www.mrc.org.uk/verdict.htm>.

It is nevertheless clear that till recently there was little pressure from grassroots Western Muslims to construct a 'Muslim community' at a national level. Most Muslims in the West, when engaged in religious activities, stress that local mosques are the centre of their community commitment. As previously mentioned, there is no 'Muslim vote' anywhere (though there are attempts to create one in some northern British cities), and there have never been massive demonstrations by Muslims in the West to gain recognition of a 'Muslim church'. The strategy of building a nationwide Muslim church is implemented by specific actors: community leaders whose social identity (and advancement) is linked with this constructivist approach. The issue of empowerment should not be underestimated – the establishment of a community group also means the building of a platform for the social promotion of community leaders. A sociological approach to understanding the latter may offer clues to explain this discrepancy between institutional leaders and grass-roots Muslims. Muslim institutions rarely represent rank-and-file Muslims, and tend to impose upon them concepts and paradigms that are often far different from those they would spontaneously support, such as compulsory veiling and systematic rules concerning halal food. In short, institutions are more fundamentalist than their flocks. For example, the French Interior Ministry established a Council of Muslim Faith (Conseil Français du Culte Musulman),[9] of which most members are Arabic-speaking Muslims who have come relatively recently to France as students, are often close to the Muslim Brotherhood and are quite separate from most of the up-rooted, French-speaking, second-generation Muslims. The reason for the choice is a convergent interest between the Interior Ministry and the chosen community leaders: both think in terms of organisation and of institutions. There is also an objective convergence between a bureaucratic state logic and the organisational strategy of the Muslim Brotherhood, probably to the detriment of a far more secular-minded, individualistic and liberal Muslim population.

A general stumbling block for Muslims in Europe is the building of a national body to represent all Muslims. It has never worked

9.   There is an interesting issue with the translation of 'Conseil Français du Culte Musulman'. The use of the term *culte* (faith or worship) systematically refers to a religion as a pure set of worshipping practices. A consequence of French secularism (*laïcité*) is a kind of reduction of religion to mere worshipping.

and probably never will work, for two main reasons. First, Islam is closer to Protestantism than Catholicism: there is no clergy and no church. Second, it is precisely the manner in which Islam has been entrenched from the grassroots level that prevents the building of an organisation for all Muslims. Grassroots organisations produce different categories of would-be leaders and notables, who are reluctant to give up their self-proclaimed status in favour of someone more learned in religion. Even if these more learned *ulama* exist (which is not certain), they are not geared towards local faith communities. As we have seen, the issue is not knowledge or authority but the very process of existing as a community.

Would-be leaders compete to represent such an elusive community. But their strategy can work only if they can mobilise enough Muslims and/or become recognised by the state as legitimate interlocutors. The process is complex, because the greater your recognition, the more you are criticised by hardliners for being an 'Uncle Tom' Muslim. CAIR is regularly castigated by radical young US Muslims for unabashedly defending the concept of being good and loyal US Muslim citizens, while at the same time being accused by the anti-Islamic activist Daniel Pipes of supporting terrorist groups.[10] Many radical leaders constantly oppose the search for a compromise with the Western legal system. In any case, it is clear that building a leadership and a Muslim community is carried out in a constant process of interaction with Western politics. In France, for example, when the government established the Council of Muslim Faith it chose to enlist the most conservative Islamic organisations (Union of Islamic Organisations in France (UOIF) and Tabligh) instead of coopting more liberal leaders. But even when relying on bodies with less authoritarian attitudes, most Western governments are usually eager to find a corporate body as interlocutor. In this sense, there is a policy of 'communitarisation from above', implemented by non-Muslim states, in parallel with the quest by Muslim organisations to be recognised as legitimate partners by the same non-Islamic states, while using any such legitimacy bestowed upon them to rally a constituency around them.

Another important dimension is that the legal status of various Islamic organisations in the West provides them with more freedom

10. Chris Suellentrop, 'Yes Related No. 3: The Pipes, the Pipes Are Calling', *Slate*, <http://slate.msn.com/id/2059069>, 28 November 2001.

and legal guarantees than they would have in most Muslim countries. Usually the law considers a local association as the legal basis for the ownership and management of the mosque, which prevents any sort of outside control. In this sense the autonomy of the preachers is not only endorsed but guaranteed by the law, even when authorities complain about this lack of control. Grassroots Muslim communities thereby benefit from legislation on freedom of religion. Radical sheikhs like Abu Hamza and Omar Bakri Muhammad were able to preach *jihad* freely in London until the end of 2002. These political cases notwithstanding, Western laws bestow a legal status to local mosques and associations when they solicit registration. Such entities are granted legal personality and do not depend on a centralised religious body. There may be some limitations for security or political reasons, but dissident Muslims are more assured of religious freedom in the West than in Muslim countries, as acknowledged by Tariq Ramadan.[11]

Local voluntary communities

A few mosques have been built in the West under state patronage, either Muslim or Western. For example, the Grand Mosque of Paris was erected by the state in 1926 in memory of the Muslim soldiers who died for France in the First World War; it is now run by the Algerian government. But apart from such cases, most mosques in the West have been established, often by using a building that was constructed for another purpose – a factory, a garage or even a church – by private citizens on the basis of imported solidarity groups (people originating from the same country and often the same region). For the first generation of migrants, sermons were in the pristine language or dialect. But the acculturation process led to a growing use of the host country's language, while younger Muslim militants oppose the confusion between pristine cultures and Islam. They strive for 'universal' mosques that all Muslims can attend solely on the basis of their faith and, often, intellectual affinity with the preacher. The personality of the mosque's *imam* is the key element in understanding of how the congregation is constituted. Congregations built around a mosque are progressively

11. Tariq Ramadan, *Les musulmans dans la laïcité. Responsabilité et droits des musulmans dans les sociétés occidentales*, Lyon: Tawhid, 1994, p. 101.

manifesting less and less of an ethnic dimension and becoming what could be called a community of spiritual affinity. Most of the mosques are operated by an association that is registered under the law of the host country (in France this is either a cultural or a religious association, depending on whether the 1901 or the 1905 laws are applied). Such mosques are the basic grassroots forms of association and community-building by Muslims in the West.

Most Muslims who attend the mosque are satisfied with that and do not strive to build a larger community. They construct their local congregation in the same way as other faiths, adding social and recreational activities such as after-school cultural and sporting classes. According to a survey, 55 per cent of US mosques run a soup kitchen for the poor, while almost none of these exist in France (religious communities tend to be involved in charity in the United States, while in France social services are more usually a state responsibility).[12] Mosques are also places for socialisation, especially in the United States, where people are quite willing to drive to a mosque. In Europe proximity to and location in an ethnic neighbourhood are more important. In Germany, Milli Görüs members refer to their local congregations as '*Islamische Gemeinde*' (Islamic parishes).[13]

Staffing mosques is an ongoing issue. The lack of training centres in the West led to the importation of *imams* from Muslim countries or to the appointment of self-styled preachers. Imported preachers tend to stress the use of 'Muslim' languages, mainly Arabic, as opposed to Western languages, but they have been unable to turn the tide of linguistic westernisation, especially in non-English-speaking Western countries. (It is easier to find a Saudi-born English-speaking *mullah* than one who speaks French or Dutch.) The gap between the expectations of the second-generation audience and the available preachers is growing, thereby leaving room for the different kinds of neofundamentalist or charismatic self-styled *mullahs*. Fearing that multiculturalism might not only create ethnic ghettos but also strengthen neofundamentalism, some Western states are considering incorporating Islamic religious teachings

---

12. Council on American Islamic Relations (CAIR), *The Mosque in America: A National Portrait*, Report from the Mosque Study Project, Washington, DC: CAIR, 2001.
13. Nikola Tietze, 'L'islam turc de la diaspora en Allemagne. Les forces des communautés imaginées', *CEMOTI*, 30 (2000), pp. 253–69.

into the mainstream state educational systems.[14] Hardly any leaders of mosques in the West have a religious degree from a Western teaching institution. They have a degree either from some sort of Middle Eastern religious institution, or in a lay discipline from a Western university.

Mosques are not the only form of reconstructed communities. For many youths, particularly those who come to study in the West, student bodies are often their first opportunity to socialise as a Muslim. Such associations are usually established at a specific university and then spread to a national level. The French Muslim student association is quite centralised (Associations des Étudiants Islamiques), as is usual for organisations in France. In the United States and Britain most large universities have their own Muslim students' association, which is often allocated a room and a website. Fuelled by a constant flow of students arriving directly from Muslim countries, the use of Arabic is more widespread among these students. After graduating from university, many of them become involved in building nationwide Islamic organisations (like the UOIF), which benefit from their organisational skills and nationwide connections. With a Western university background many of these community leaders have good political and organisational training, but often have problems establishing a working relationship with more traditional *ulama* and local *imams*.

Most Muslim student organisations have chosen to promote a faith community, not an ethnic one. In this sense they tend to 'Islamise' many nominally Muslim students who are simply looking for some sort of identity group or even student union, but feel alienated from mainstream 'white' associations. In France many young people from impoverished neighbourhoods spend years gaining little but the most minor degree from state universities, while more aware students enrol in prestigious and effective preparatory classes for graduate high schools (*grandes écoles*): this leads to a growing awareness of ethnic and religious particularities

14. The first faculty of Islamic instruction has been opened in the Netherlands, while the French government has considered for some time opening the Faculty of Protestant Theology in Strasbourg to Islamic instruction. As mentioned in Chapter 3, in Britain Labour MP Frank Dobson called for the opening of all faith schools to other faiths, with the same aim of bringing together the different teaching systems (Dobson, 'Open up Faith Schools', *Guardian*, 8 February 2002).

among alienated students, paving the way for Islamic student unions. Such groups either clash or ally with the mostly leftist and secular student unions when they enter the arena of student politics. In Britain the Hizb ut-Tahrir was expelled from campuses by a collective decision taken by the national union of student organisations, while in France an Islamic student association that attracted 7 per cent of votes in the 2001 university elections (with a very low turnout) joined forces with the leftist National Union of Students in France (UNEF) to take seats on university councils. But in both cases politicisation and religious sectarianism go hand in hand. Many community leaders in France (Larbi Kechat in Paris, Abdellah Boussouf in Strasbourg, and the entire leadership of the UOIF) come from student associations.

Student organisations also tend to promote among Muslims new (or, more precisely, non-traditional) forms of socialisation based on generational identity. 'Halal coeducation' and even 'halal dating'[15] bring together young men and *hijab*-wearing girls, sharing the same tasks (such as organising meetings, and printing and distributing leaflets), but of course avoiding any sort of sexual promiscuity. It is a way of acknowledging coeducation while introducing moral norms. This 'egalitarian' puritanism runs against the tide of sexual liberalisation in Western Europe but fits well with the Catholic Church and US Christian Right offensive to promote sexual abstinence and chastity among schoolchildren and university students. It is part of the convergence (noted elsewhere in this book) of religious revivalisms in all Western religions. It also allows young people to make matrimonial choices outside the traditional Muslim family circles of choice (such as first cousins, or girls from the village of origin or extended family). But such marriages bring together spouses on a more or less equal footing (in terms of age,

---

15. Khosrokhavar, *L'Islam des Jeunes*, p. 157. See also 'halal dating': 'They spend time talking over the phone or on the internet and even going on dates, though for Strict Muslims, a chaperone is always present … In halal dating, a clear understanding exists between the man and the woman that they are committed to marrying each other. They view the other as a life partner, not a hot prom date. Eventually they will obtain a marriage license and marry in a ceremony to which they invite their friends and family – a couple of American kids with "just married" written in soap on their car windows and soda cans tied to the bumper' (Asma Gull Hasan, 'Adventures in Halal Dating', <http://www.altmuslim.com/opinion_comments.php?id=P712_0_25_0_C>, 1 August 2002.

education and expectations), which is one of the basic elements of the definition of a modern nuclear family of the sort that is leading to a sharp and rapid fall in births.

By providing cadres for nationwide organisations, student associations also contribute to the reshaping of the Muslim community. As we have said from the outset, however, the promotion of young, educated and autonomous cadres by no means leads to liberalisation. Many of these cadres are Salafist, or at least morally conservative. They are far more ideologically minded than other middle-class Muslim professionals who work in faith communities, without having been re-Islamised through Islamic student organisations in Western universities. But they also contribute to the sociological westernisation of the Muslim population. Promotion of young leaders is, incidentally, a characteristic of Western Islamic organisations, which contrasts with the gerontocracy prevailing in Middle Eastern Islamic organisations after the revolutionary period of the 1970s. Of course Islamic student organisations do exist in the Middle East, but once they become official, as in Iran, they come under the supervision of 'elders', while more recent student movements are not specifically Islamic.

Western forms of socialisation among young Muslims, even when carried out in the name of religion, contradict most patterns of traditional behaviour and socialisation, stressing generational groups (and hence the generation gap), freedom to choose a spouse, gender mixing (even under the *hijab*), social activities in public that include women, and greater youth freedom. Even the concept of Islamic fashion is a contradiction in terms, but it works among educated, veiled young women. The spread of mosques and Islamic associations contributes to the development of a sense of belonging to a purely religious community, and induces forms of socialisation closer to their Western religious counterparts.

Westernisation of the expression of values

The West–Islam mirror effect goes beyond legal and administrative dimensions. It also touches the realm of values and ethics. While a few Muslims find in Western permissive society a way to revive a forgotten (or dreamt of) Muslim tradition of hedonism and freedom, most prefer to adjust to a Christian concept of values (as distinct from or even opposed to legal norms). The debate on homosexuality is a good example. A small but vocal group of gay Muslims want to be recognised as gays and as Muslims (a similar case has been made by Christian homosexuals). They express themselves in websites like fatiha.com or Queer Muslims.[16] They have, of course, aroused the ire of conservative *mullahs*, but, interestingly, the latter do construct the concept of 'homosexuals' in Western terms. For instance, Dr Muzammil Siddiqi, president of ISNA, wrote:

Homosexuality is a moral disorder. It is a moral disease, a sin and corruption ... No person is born homosexual, just like no one is born a thief, a liar or murderer. People acquire these evil habits due to a lack of proper guidance and education ... There are many reasons why it is forbidden in Islam. Homosexuality is dangerous for the health of the individuals and for the society. It is a main cause of one of the most harmful and fatal diseases. It is disgraceful for both men and women. It degrades a person. Islam teaches that men should be men and women should be women. Homosexuality deprives a man of his manhood and a woman of her womanhood. It is the most un-natural way of life. Homosexuality leads to the destruction of family life.[17]

The various concepts used here (person, family, health, protection of society, womanhood) are closer to conservative Christian values (and to the utilitarian moral conception of society) than to the *hudud* Koranic conception (it is forbidden because God has forbidden it and He knows best). By the same token, although he is clearly sympathetic to the position of the Salafis, Muzammil Siddiqi was able to say in his 1988 Ramadan address:

There are many good things in this [Western] society, but be aware of the social and moral problems that also exist here. Do not succumb to drugs, narcotics, and sexual perversions of fornication, adultery, homosexuality and pornography. Keep your families strong. Avoid divorces and breakdown of families. Protect yourself and your children from crimes, violence and gangs. Take care of your elderly. Teach your children how to be responsible citizens and good neighbors.[18]

16. <http://www.angelfire.com/ca2/queermuslims>.
17. Cited in B.A. Robinson, 'Islam and Homosexuality', <http://www.religious tolerance.org/hom_isla.htm>, 16 November 2002.
18. Muzammil Siddiqi, address to a congregation in Tustin, Orange County, California, during the month of Ramadan, 1998: <http://www.pakistanlink. com/religion/98/re-01-30.html>.

If an *imam* asks his congregation to care for the elderly and avoid divorce, it is simply because the elderly are cared for less and less and divorce no longer means the same in the West as in traditional Muslim societies. For a Muslim cleric to condemn divorce is particularly striking. Divorce at the husband's instigation is a pillar of the traditional conception of *sharia*, but in the West it means family breakdown. Thus the preacher adapts to the actual, rather than imagined, behaviour of his flock and stresses values that go against uncritical respect for the letter of the *sharia*, although he is certainly not a liberal. In this sense he speaks rather like a conservative Catholic priest.

It is not by chance that the same leader encourages interfaith dialogue: 'We must work with the people of other faiths for better understanding. Interfaith dialogue, and especially Muslim, Christian and Jewish dialogue, is very important in this country. We should support this dialogue for better relations and cooperation.'[19] Conversely the highest religious body in Saudi Arabia condemns any cooperation between Islam, Christianity and Judaism.[20]

The family accepted by conservative Muslims in the West is the modern nuclear family (father and mother with children, free choice of spouse, and women permitted to work and be educated) rather than the extended or polygamous family. The couple is emphasised as the basis of a modern Muslim family, and even the anti-feminist discourse uses the language of feminism.[21] Interestingly,

19. Siddiqi, Tustin address.
20. 'Unification of Religions', Fatwa No. 19402, by the Presidency of Administration of Islamic Research and Ifta, Riyadh, Kingdom of Saudi Arabia, under the General Supervision of the Grand Council of Scholars; Permanent Committee for Islamic Research and Ifta (Verdict), signed by Abdul-Aziz Ibn Baz (President), Abdul-Aziz Ibn Abdullah Al-Shaykh Abdullah (Vice-President), Salih Ibn Fawzan Al-Fawzan, Bakr Ibn Abdullah Abu Zaid; dated 25 Muharram 1418 H (May 1997). This *fatwa* appears on a number of websites; for example, <http://isgkc.org/interfaith1.htm>.
21. This is a growing phenomenon in all Muslim societies. See Sanna Negus, 'A Chosen Identity: Columnist and Social Critic Heba Raouf Espouses Social Equality without Feminism and Islamic Values without Islamism', *Cairo Times*, 3, 25 (20–26 January 2000), on Heba Raouf, an Egyptian former Islamist: 'The website magazine she edits is under the supervision of Yousef Qaradawi, a prominent Islamic jurist. And the response in Islamist circles to Raouf's emancipated views has been positive. "They have always been very understanding. There are some very articulate sisters," she says. Her strongest support, however, comes from her parents and her husband. Raouf married

legislation in Western Europe, even where polygamy is illegal as such, is usually quite flexible with regard to customary polygamy (most legal systems make no distinction between legitimate children and those born out of wedlock, and allow the latter to bear their father's surname), although very few Muslims take the opportunity to have more than one family. As we saw in the previous chapter, the French Muslim leader Tariq Ramadan went so far as to claim that the Civil Solidarity Pact in France, established for unmarried couples (and termed 'homosexual marriage' because it includes no gender condition) is closer to the concept of marriage according to *fiqh* (it is a contract rather than a sacrament, and imposes no maintenance payments in case of separation) than is the traditional Western marriage. The nuclear family is tending to replace the traditional extended family among Muslims not only in Europe but also in Muslim countries. A notable consequence of this trend is the stress on the relationship between spouses, to the detriment of that between parents and grown-up children. (How to choose a spouse and maintain a lasting relationship is a favourite topic of marriage counsellors who are flourishing on the Web.)[22]

Even radicals endorse such a sociological change in the perception of family. A document from azzam.com, a website founded in memory of Abdallah (or Abdullah) Azzam, the forerunner of Al Qaeda, extols the virtue of a *shahid* (martyr), Suraqah al-Andalusi (a pseudonym, probably of a second-generation Muslim living in Spain), who was killed fighting US troops in Afghanistan during the battle of Tora Bora in December 2001. One of al-Andalusi's companions remembers that, when discussing the pain of being separated from one's parents, he answered: 'No, brother, the bond

psychiatrist Ahmed Abdullah nine years ago, when she was 26, and she says she cannot overemphasise the importance of this marriage as an influence on her character. A couple of years ago she went to England to do research in Westminster and Oxford. "I left my family behind for eight months, and I got the full support of my husband for this," she recalls. Arguably, Raouf has successfully fulfilled the modern-day dream role of being a mother without sacrificing her career. Although some see her as the ideal modest woman, she's too humble to admit to that kind of image. "I'm like any other working woman of today," she says. "I'm not that different from those women who might read my profile"'

22. See Muntaqima Abdur-Rashid, 'Tips for a Happier Muslim Marriage', <http://www.islamfortoday.com/marriage_tips.htm>, which has advice such as 'Be a companion for your mate', and 'Share household duties'.

between the wife and husband is a bond that is different from that of the mother and her son. It is something stronger.'[23] Authentic or forged, the quotation clearly shows a departure from the traditional precedence of mother-son ties over those of husband and wife; the literature on martyrdom in Pakistan, Palestine and Lebanon extols the virtues of the martyr's mother, not of his wife. Along the same lines, many born-again Muslims in the West, specifically females, insist on choosing a spouse who shares the same values, rather than because of family ties. Young educated born-again Muslims in the West insist on establishing forms of virtuous gender-mixing, where (*hijab*-wearing) sisters and brothers socialise, work and have discussions together, even if some artificial and symbolic separation remains (no handshaking, girls seated on one side and boys on the other when meeting).

Muslims also tend to use the concepts of human rights and minority rights to promote their values, and consequently express these in a Western manner (equivalence of different groups with no hierarchy between 'true believers', People of the Book, polytheists, and so on). Women excluded from schools or jobs for wearing the *hijab* go to court in the name of antidiscrimination. There are occasional coalitions of different groups on specific issues: a British left-wing Labour MP, Keith Vaz, supported in 1989 the call for the banning of Rushdie's *Satanic Verses*, in the name of preventing an insult to a minority group, while a conservative faction of Anglican and Catholic priests, for whom this was a heaven-sent opportunity, tried to forge a sacred alliance against the profaning of religion in the name of art. (The affair of Scorsese's film *The Last Temptation of Christ*, it should be recalled, happened immediately afterwards.) Moreover antidiscrimination demonstrations in Western Europe have occasionally brought together homosexual groups and Muslim associations. Successive alliances between Muslim advocacy groups and the secular Left or Christian Right are sufficient indication of the complexity of identity levels that Muslims may express (or externalise) in the public sphere.

Islamic revival may thus be experienced according to Western and modern paradigms of social and professional behaviour, while

23. 'Azzam.com Correspondent Suraqah al-Andalusi Martyred in Afghanistan', <http://www.zavaj.com/azzam/suraqah_al_andulusi.html#brother>.   The original web page, at <http://www.azzam.com>, went offline after 9/11.

embodying a way of internalising such modernity. It is a common mistake to interpret any public expression of re-Islamisation as a traditionalist backlash or a sort of political statement. Even if mainstream Islamic revivalism is conservative (albeit in concert with Western conservative values), it may also disguise trends that are more secular in character. Re-Islamisation may encompass a wide range of motivations and meanings, and occurs alongside various and complex personal or collective strategies. It could be pure window-dressing in order to indulge safely in consumerism or entertainment, a way of combining modern activities and traditional social values. In Lebanon the modern *hijab* (worn with jeans and sneakers) is more an indicator of communal identity (Shia) than of religious practice, while by contrast in Turkey veiled and unveiled women are to be found in any professional or social milieu. A famous Turkish Islamist journalist, Abdurrahman Dilipak, wrote in the pro-Islamic daily newspaper *Akit* that he saw veiled Muslim girls 'singing, dancing, swaying and being ecstatic while attending Turkish pop-music concerts, trying to get close to the singers to embrace and kiss them'.[24] Islamic signs and symbols do not necessarily convey an Islamic content. Selling Mecca-Cola in France (2002) is more a manifestation of traditional anti-US feeling, castigating Coca-Cola and McDonald's, than of a return to religious practices. (Incidentally, orthodox *ulama* oppose the use of religious denominations solely for marketing purposes.) Shifting from wine to soft drinks is also among the habits of modern Muslim youths. Re-Islamisation can be transitional, in a personal life or in a society. Veiled women are not necessarily more decent or chaste (in Turkey sex scandals have blighted certain Islamic circles). And in Egypt, as Patrick Haenni has demonstrated, religious charities have been taken over by entrepreneurs and notables to enhance their social status. Not only does charity have nothing to do with radical Islam, but it also goes hand in hand with conservative and conformist social and political attitudes.[25] Businessmen are quick to capitalise on re-Islamisation to win a growing market share (for example, Islamic fashion or Islamic recreational resorts, as mentioned above).

24. *Akit*, 24 October 1997.
25. Patrick Haenni, 'Ils n'en ont pas fini avec l'Orient. De quelques islamisations non islamistes', *Revue du monde musulman et de la Méditerranée*, 85–6 (1999), pp. 121–48.

Re-Islamisation is synonymous with the weakening of traditional ties, with a growing individualisation and with adaptation to a new minority status in the West. Thus religious revivalism can work against political Islam, as we shall see in the following pages; it may accompany a revival of Sufism along the lines of Western forms of spirituality. It does not entail a change of society, let alone a polity, towards something 'more' Islamic; on the contrary, it involves a shift towards a more Western society. The various meanings of Islamisation parallel the opening up of the public sphere and the inability of the state to control or enforce it. Paradoxically, it goes hand in hand with the weakening of any normative religious reference and with disaffection with any form of 'established' Islam. It enforces and embodies the autonomy of social actors who take Islam into their own hands and bend it to their own purposes. It is more an assertion of a nascent civil society than a return to a holistic polity (which, incidentally, never existed).

NEO–BROTHERHOODS AND NEW AGE RELIGIOSITY

Globalisation also affects 'popular' Islam, by which we mean forms of worship that are not controlled by the *ulama*, but are not necessarily unorthodox (celebrating *ashura* among Shias, or practising *zikr* among Sunni Sufis). 'Popular' does not refer to 'lower'-class or rural populations; it concerns all social strata, as well as urban dwellers. Sufi orders are part of this popular Islam, even if they do not necessarily oppose the *ulama* in general (who may belong to Sufi orders). Popular Islam has a long history, but during the twentieth century it was squeezed between the reformism of the *ulama* (for example, Sheikh Ben Badis in Algeria), who branded it as superstition and folklore, and the Islamists, who associate popular Islam with a lack of political awareness (a tool of colonialism, as 'maraboutism' was described in Algeria), not to speak of neo-fundamentalists (the Afghan Taliban) and Wahhabis, who forbid all expression of popular Islam. We do not intend here to assess how it has survived (there is an extensive academic literature on contemporary popular Islam), but to stress some specific forms of revival, which are linked to estrangement from orthodox, political and/or official Islam. When emotional worship and ethical concerns are more valued than strict respect for *sharia*, then popular Islam might provide a religiosity that combines the authenticity of a non-fundamentalist tradition and a modern spirituality. In Iran, in reaction to the politicisation of the celebration of Ashura, which has been transformed into massive political demonstrations by the Islamic regime, many Iranians prefer to celebrate the day through local associations (*heyat*, or neighbourhood or professional guilds), where the 'big man' is not the *mullah* but the head of the association, and where rituals forbidden by the regime (such as self-flagellation) are re-enacted. By the same token *zurkhana* (gymnasiums where wrestling and certain religious rituals take place) and Sufi music had a revival among educated middle-class Iranians. In Egypt the Khalwatiyya and Shadliyya *turuq* (Sufi brotherhoods) are also thriving in rural areas and in towns.[26] Such popular Islam feeds spiritual needs that are ignored both by Islamism and neofundamentalism. It is therefore at odds with them, specifically when it takes the forms of neo-brotherhoods that intervene in the public sphere. But, as is often the case, such a 'return to tradition' may embody a more profound change in religiosity and correspond to forms of globalisation and westernisation.

We shall first address the case of neo-brotherhoods that offer an explicit Sufi dimension and later consider other sorts of communities and groupings, closer to modern sects and cults, even including neofundamentalist groups that strongly oppose Sufism but share many traits with the neo-brotherhoods.

Many contemporary *tariqat* (spiritual paths, whose followers form brotherhoods) have recently been founded or profoundly reshaped. They include, among others, Nurcu, Suleymanci and Fethullahci in Turkey; Muridiyya and Tijaniyya in Senegal; Muhammadiyya–Shadhiliyya in Egypt; Ahbash in Lebanon; Kaftariyya in Syria; and Ahl-i Haqq in Iran. Some made a breakthrough in the West, like the Naqshbandiyya–Haqqaniyya, now based in Chicago, and the Sammania (sammania.org). Creating new *tariqat* from ancient ones is certainly nothing new, but what we call a neo-brotherhood is not simply the offshoot of a traditional *tariqat*, and is shaped along new lines; it is usually derived from a traditional Muslim *tariqat*, but with some innovations.[27] The brotherhood is headed by a sheikh

26. Rachida Chih, *Le Soufisme au quotidien. Confréries d'Egypte au XXème siècle*, Aix-en-Provence: Actes Sud, 2000.
27. The term *neo-Sufism* is to be found in Julia Day Howell, 'Indonesia's Urban Sufis: Challenging Stereotypes of Islamic Revival', *ISIM Newsletter*, 6 (2000), p. 17, <http://www.isim.nl/files/newsl_6.pdf>.

(or *pir*), who is more a modern guru than a traditional Sufi master; he is often the founder of the brotherhood, or the founder's first successor, and his biography is disseminated by his devotees. He writes extensively (hundreds of books or, more precisely, booklets) and 'performs' his role at meetings or even on television. The sheikh is a public man who exploits modern media techniques.

His followers are recruited as individuals rather than as part of a family tradition; a neo-brotherhood recruits when traditional links of solidarity and communal ties have been broken. There is, moreover, no real initiation or gradation in membership. The follower learns the master's teachings by reading his writings and listening to his sermons (often on video). He has direct and complete, rather than progressive, access to knowledge, which is provided in a discursive form, not through spiritual exercises. Sometimes modern teaching institutions replace traditional *khanaqa* or *zawyat* (the Fethullah secondary schools, for instance). The disciple is not in regular contact with the *pir* or his deputies, but with an organisation that arranges public meetings with the *pir*. The brotherhood has an active public presence, using modern public-relations techniques (such as multiple websites, printed media, and appearances on television). Most of these brotherhoods have a policy of proselytising (increasingly among non-Muslims), and indulge in politics, but on a non-ideological basis, bargaining their ballots in favour of conservative but also somewhat secular and antifundamentalist political movements. They often reject the term *tariqat* in favour of *jamaat*, or 'community' (for example, Ahbash and Nurcu; the Fethullahci called itself successively *cam'at* and *cemyet* in Turkish script, and finally *birlik*, or 'union').[28] Proselytising works all the more effectively when the brotherhoods find a language in common with Western New Age cults or post-modern spiritualism (for example, the Haqqaniyya has been relayed in the West by Gurdjieff's disciples). A neo-brotherhood targets an individual who no longer has roots in

28. For the Nurcu, see Ahmed Akgündüz, 'The Risale-i Nur Movement: Is it a Sufi Order, a Political Society, or a Community?' in *Proceedings of the 3rd International Symposium on the Reconstruction of Islamic Thought in the Twentieth Century and Bediuzzaman Said Nursi, Istanbul, 24–26 September 1995*, 2 vols, Istanbul: Sözler Publications, 1997 (<http://www.sozler.com.tr/symposium/3/default.htm>). For the Fethullahci, personal interview with Latif Erdogan, head of the Endowment of Writers (a branch of the brotherhood), 1997.

a primary community and lives in a purely non-spiritual environment. It provides him with a new community often very similar to a modern cult, inward-looking and inclusive, which deals with all aspects of the newcomer's life (including his or her professional life). In more liberal versions it provides a kind of 'meditation club' where the member finds a spiritual added value to an otherwise ordinary life.[29] As Hakan Yavuz says of the Nurcu, 'The movement can be considered modern in that it espouses a world view centred around the self-reflective and politically active individual's ability to realise personal goals while adhering to a collective identity.'[30]

The shift from traditional brotherhoods to either modern sects or loose 'meditation clubs' highlights the entry of Sufism into modern forms of religiosity, what Danièle Hervieu-Léger calls 'the regrouping of practising believers' (*regroupement de pratiquants*), where members stress *their* primary community more than the universal community of believers, and define it through relationships with a charismatic leader and certain specific patterns of worship, without opposing members of other religious groups theologically (orthodoxy versus heresy, truth versus falsehood).[31] Members look for a form of religiosity best able to expresses their inner self and search for socialisation with people who share their quest for self-realisation. They stress the quality of their relationships inside the community, in order to create a positive environment for self-realisation and worship, but worship is seen more as part of self-realisation than as a quest for salvation. In short, they join because they enjoy it.

These brotherhoods remain largely centred around the sheikh, who employs modern technology to keep in touch with his followers without devolving any of his power. There are as few *khalifa*, or deputies, as possible and hence no 'layering' process (local branches seizing some autonomy under the influence of a *khalifa* who pays lip-service to the centre but introduces his own ways of doing things and, sooner or later, his own *selsele*, or chain of initiation). Neo-brotherhoods may break into different branches after the sheikh's death, but the use of email and the internet bestows

29. Howell, 'Indonesia's Urban Sufis', p. 17.
30. Hakan Yavuz, 'Being Modern in the Nurcu Way', *ISIM Newsletter*, 6 (2000), p. 7, <http://www.isim.nl/files/newsl_6.pdf>.
31. Danièle Hervieu-Léger, *La religion en miettes ou la question des sectes*, Paris: Calmann-Lévy, 2001, pp. 160–2.

on the sheikh a ubiquity that could only have come about as a 'miracle' in earlier times.

Joining a neo-brotherhood means entering contemporary forms of religiosity. This explains why such brotherhoods may attract converts and sometimes indulge in forms of syncretism quite distant from orthodox Islam.

Even if most of the Sufi orders established in the West were transplanted via immigration, they found a new constituency by adapting to the Western 'religious market' and the spiritual needs of their adherents, among them many converts. New Age Sufism appeared on the scene, for example, describing prayers as a breathing technique for better health.[32] Another form of 'westernisation' is the development (or revival) of women's 'sisterhoods' (for example, the Qubaysiyya in Syria, headed by Munira al-Qubaysi, is a Naqshbandiyya offshoot, which set up study circles – *halaqa* – in private houses). The Alawiyya, stemming from Algeria, also has *zikr* (Sufi incantations) for both genders. Once in the West, the Alawiyya grafted on a mystical pro-Islam tradition embodied by René Guénon; an Italian convert, Felice Pallavicini, has founded his own brotherhood. Followers of Pir Vilayat Inayat Khan (of the Chishti order, who was born in India in 1916 and educated in Britain) fit this pattern. Their website explicitly states: 'While honoring the initiatic [*sic*] tradition of his predecessors, Pir Vilayat is continually pioneering updated practices in keeping with the evolution of Western consciousness.'[33] Some brotherhoods seem to be exclusively made up of converts, such as the Murabitun, founded by a Scot, Ian Dallas, now Sheikh Abdalqadir al-Murabit. The brotherhood has opened a mosque in Granada, made a breakthrough among the Chiapas Indians in Mexico, and is struggling to replace the banking system by bringing back gold and silver as the standard medium of exchange.[34]

A distinction has to be made between the brotherhoods that remain orthodox (such as the Tijaniyya and Samaniyya), although they adapt to their audiences in the forms of communication they adopt, and those that turn towards syncretist New Age sects. But

---

32. Marcia Hermansen, 'In the Garden of American Sufi Movements: Hybrids and Perennials' in Peter B. Clarke (ed.), *New Trends and Developments in the World of Islam*, London: Luzac Oriental, 1997, p. 157.
33. <http://www.pirvilayat.org>.
34. <http://www.geocities.com/Athens/Delphi/6588/mundial.html>.

these are two poles rather than rigidly separate categories. Many are quite lenient over strict religious rituals like fasting and praying five times a day. They usually do not stress Islam as such, but prefer to refer to the universal dimension of their message,[35] and are structured along similar lines as many modern cults or sects (such as neo-Hindu groups): centred around the guru, playing on syncretism, using the internet and the English language, and relying heavily on conversions. Some Sufi orders, once established in the West, function like New Age religions, stressing a general spiritualist approach as opposed to strict compliance with *sharia*, insisting on well-being and happiness, and borrowing paradigms and metaphors from other fields. ('The electromagnetic field is the template in which the body is configured – the cells of the body. Actually the aura of light is a template in which the electromagnetic field is configured … Eventually we shall learn to heal with light.' This is a typical 'New Age' Sufi statement.)[36] Such orders are part of the New Age religious sphere, where syncretism, a focus on mind–body techniques, and charisma blur the theological divide.[37]

35. The introduction to Fethullah Gülen's biography on the website <http://www.fetullahgulen.org> at one time did not mention Islam at all: 'Known by his simple and austere lifestyle, Fethullah Gülen, affectionately called Hodjaefendi, is a scholar of extraordinary proportions. This man for all seasons was born in Erzurum, eastern Turkey, in 1938. Upon graduation from divinity school in Erzurum, he obtained his license to preach and teach. In addition to his great contribution to the betterment activities of education in Turkey by encouraging people to open private schools, he is renowned for his painstaking endeavors for the establishment of mutual understanding and tolerance in society. His social reform efforts, begun during the 1960s, have made him one of Turkey's most well-known and respected public figures. His tireless dedication to solving social problems and satisfying spiritual needs have gained him a considerable number of followers throughout the world. Though simple in outward appearance, he is original in thought and action. He embraces all humanity, and is deeply averse to unbelief, injustice, and deviation. His belief and feelings are profound, and his ideas and approach to problems are both wise and rational. A living model of love, ardor, and feeling, he is extraordinarily balanced in his thoughts, acts, and treatment of matters. 'Whenever I see a leaf fall from its branch in autumn, I feel as much pain as if my arm was amputated.'
36. <http://www.sufiorder.org>.
37. For a more precise approach, see in Peter B. Clarke (ed.), *New Trends and Developments in the World of Islam* (London: Luzac Oriental, 1997), the chapters by Peter Wilson ('The Strange Fate of Sufism in the New Age'), James Jervis ('The Sufi Order in the West and Pir Vilayat Inayat Khan; Space-age

Neo-brotherhoods tend to become global by putting down roots and recruiting outside their countries of origin while globalisation helps to set up 'a sacred space that transcends the nation state'.[38] Most of these groups are transnational and moving to the West. (The Turkish brotherhoods are nevertheless more pan-Turkist than universalist. They operate among the diaspora and, for the Fethullah, in the Caucasian and Turkic populations of Central Asia.)

It is worth mentioning the Mevlevi and the Helveti-Cerrahi, from Turkey, from where Sheikh Muzafar Ocak emigrated in 1980 to the United States. The biggest Naqshbandiyya branch in the United States seems to be the Haqqaniyya, which was founded in 1973 by Sheikh Nazim al-Haqqani, a Naqshbandi Turkish-speaker of Egyptian descent. Established in Cyprus, it is managed by al-Haqqani's deputy and son-in-law Sheikh Hisham Kabbani, who graduated from the American University of Beirut in chemistry, studied in Louvain (Belgium) and Damascus, and settled in Chicago in 1991, where he established a fast-expanding headquarters of the order. The branch began winning new converts after enrolling followers of Gurdjieff's protégé John G. Bennett, who died in 1974.[39] Many converts are African-Americans, like Sheikh Abdul Rashid Matthews, a dental surgeon who heads a mosque in Chicago.

Sheikh Hassan Cisse, grandson of the founder of the Senegalese Tijaniyya *tariqat*, has been building his brotherhood in the United States since the 1970s. It retains a more orthodox approach compared to New Age Sufism, and is gaining ground among African-Americans, some of whom study at the *tariqat*'s headquarters in Senegal. Interestingly, it thus helped to create a 'Black' transatlantic identity, which the creation of Liberia and the search for African roots among US Blacks failed to achieve. Here a neo-brotherhood is part of a global neo-ethnicity.[40]

Spirituality in Contemporary Europe-America') and Marcia Hermansen ('In the Garden of American Sufi Movements; Hybrids and Perennial').

38. About Tijaniyya, Ousmane Kane, 'Muslim Missionaries and African States' in Susan Hoeber Rudolph and James Piscatori (eds), *Transnational Religion and Fading States*, Boulder, CO: Westview Press, 1997.

39. David W. Damrel, 'A Sufi Apocalypse', *ISIM Newsletter*, 4 (1999), <http://www.isim.nl/files/newsl_4.pdf>.

40. Gary Bunt, *Virtually Islamic: Computer-mediated Communication and Cyber Islamic Environments*, Cardiff: University of Wales Press, 2000, p. 64.

Globalisation turns traditional brotherhoods into neo-brotherhoods by changing how they operate. Another example is the Kurdish Ahl-i Haqq *tariqat*. This movement is based on a specific creed (in which metempsychosis plays a role) and on an anthropological foundation (in which tribal and spiritual lineages are intertwined). But the passage to the West and the recruitment of many converts have profoundly altered the anthropological nature of the sect, leading to a schism into a traditional branch and a modern one in which membership is strictly personal and has nothing to do with belonging to a primary social unit.[41]

The Ahbash brotherhood in Lebanon, officially known as the Society of Islamic Philanthropic Projects, or Jam'iyyat al-Mashari' al-Khayriyya al-Islamiyya, was founded by Sheikh Abdallah ibn Muhammad ibn Yusuf al-Hirari al-Shibi al-Abdari (also known as al-Habashi, signifying his Ethiopian origins).[42] Its roots are in the Rifa'iyya brotherhood, but once established in Lebanon the brotherhood took an aggressively proselytising and militant stand, campaigning against political Islam and targeting especially the Muslim Brotherhood (headed by Fathi Yakan) and Wahhabis. The Ahbash brotherhood is supported by Syria, and one of its leaders, Nizar al-Halabi, was even assassinated in 1995 by a neofundamentalist radical Sunni group called Asbat al-Ansar. The brotherhood has recently moved into Western Europe. In France, for example, a strong branch is active around Montpellier and attracts many converts; one of its leaders is Abd Samad Moussaoui, the brother of Zacarias Moussaoui.

Another typical neo-brotherhood is the Fethullah Gülen movement, known as the Fethullahci. It is an offshoot of the Nurcu, who themselves have roots in the Naqshbandiyya. Strictly organised around its leader, the brotherhood is secretive about its internal workings, but has developed a remarkable public-relations system. Insisting on the importance of education, the movement has developed a network of secondary schools, first in Turkey and then in Central Asia, the Caucasus and the Balkans, slowly

41. Ziba Mir Hosseyni, 'Inner Truth and Outer History: The Two Worlds of the Ahl-i Haqq of Kurdistan', *International Journal of Middle East Studies*, 26 (1994), pp. 267–85
42. Nizar Hamzeh and Hrair Dekmejian, 'A Sufi Response to Political Islamism: Al-Ahbash of Lebanon', *International Journal of Middle East Studies*, 28 (1996), pp. 217–29.

extending towards the West. The curriculum includes modern sciences, computing and English. The brotherhood produces a newspaper, *Zaman*, which is widely distributed in local language versions throughout the Turkic world. (Interestingly, while the commonly held view in Turkey is that all Turkic languages are simply dialects of Turkish, the brotherhood, although largely pan-Turkist, dared to recognise Uzbek and Tatar as real languages.) Gülen is famous for his recorded sermons in which he begins weeping and addresses God directly, in the manner of certain US televangelists.

We may also add the Kaftariyya, headed by the present *mufti* of Syria, Sheikh Kaftaro. Its headquarters in Damascus is open to women and receives many students from all over the Muslim world, including converts.[43] As might be expected of a supporter of the Baathist regime, the Kaftariyya is anti-Wahhabi.

In Muslim countries most brotherhoods are apolitical or mainstream; they usually do not form alliances with Islamists, even if there is far less antagonism between them and the Wahhabis (many Islamist leaders have a Sufi background, including Erbakan, Hassan al-Banna and Maududi). In Turkey the Naqshbandi, Nurcu and Gülen provide a reservoir of votes more for centrist parties than for the Refah-Fazilet Partisi, although one-time Turkish Prime Minister Necmettin Erbakan was formerly a Naqshbandi. (He broke with the brotherhood after the death of his spiritual guide, Zahid Kotku, in 1980.)

In the West most neo-brotherhoods claim to provide a bridge between East and West, and present themselves as 'moderate' and pro-Western alternatives to Islamic fundamentalism. Fethullah Gülen met the Pope and launched a campaign in the United States (but his move was undermined in 2000 by a sudden backlash from the Turkish secular establishment, army and Supreme Court, who launched a suit against the organisation). Interestingly, many of these brotherhoods (such as Haqqaniyya, Sammania and Ahbash) are involved politically against Salafism and Wahhabism, and form alliances with Western governments and in some cases with Jewish, even Zionist, organisations. This cuts them off from a Middle

43. Annabelle Böttcher, 'L'élite féminine kurde de la Kaftariyya – une confrérie naqshbandi damascène' in Martin van Bruinessen and Joyce Blau (eds), *L'Islam des Kurdes*, Les annales de l'autre Islam 5, Paris: Inalco, 1999.

Eastern Arab audience, but enlarges their circle of sympathisers in the West. The Haqqaniyya is violently anti-Wahhabi and has met the American Jewish Council and pro-Russian Naqshbandi Chechens (such as Mufti Kadirov) to condemn Islamic fundamentalism.[44] A Sufi convert, Nuh Ha Mim Keller, has campaigned in the United States against the Salafis (and been attacked by them).[45] An Italian convert, Abdul Hadi Palazzi, made a plea for the right of Israel to exist as a Zionist state. Conversely, Salafi groups have regularly denounced such 'Western' Muslims.

The antagonism between Sufism and Salafism (or Wahhabism, or fundamentalism or orthodoxy) is a cliché in Islamology, but it seems that, in their contemporary guise, neo-brotherhoods and neofundamentalists have more in common in terms of religiosity than their opposition in terms of religion might suggest. They both address modern, insulated and mainly urban individuals and frame them within a closed community, explicitly conceived as an élite minority encapsulated in a largely secular and alien environment. Many contemporary religious groupings share these patterns, although they belong to very diverse schools of theology. Building a community of faith around a spiritual leader and certain specific beliefs or patterns of worship is not proper to the Sufi orders, whether traditional or 'neo'. We are clearly witnessing a trend towards the multiplication of 'faith communities' that may have nothing to do with *tariqat,* or may even strongly oppose the very nature of Sufism. Such groupings are more similar to contemporary sects. As Patrick Gaffney aptly notes after having studied preachers in Upper Egypt, 'What is being generated, in short, is a nascent sect, the stirrings of a separate self-justifying institution that does not aspire to unify the diverse and stratified segments of a whole society, but to create a cohesive new self-understanding of a particular interest group that is recent and restless.'[46] These

44. Conference of the Central Asia and Caucasus Institute, the American Jewish Committee and the Islamic Supreme Council of America, Johns Hopkins University, Washington, DC, 11–12 April 2000.
45. Nuh Ha Mim Keller, 'The Ijazas of Ibn Baz and al Albani', <http://homepage. ntlworld.com/masud/ISLAM/nuh/masudq6.htm>. (A list of works by Sheikh Nuh Keller can be found on <http://www.masud.co uk>).
46. Patrick Gaffney, 'Authority and the Mosque in Upper Egypt' in William R. Roff (ed.), *Islam and the Political Economy of Meaning: Comparative Studies of Muslim Discourse,* London: Croom Helm, 1987, p. 224.

transformations are not a legacy of Sufism as such, but are a new means of building a community as a subset of the *ummah*; such a community fulfils not only the spiritual needs of the follower, but also his very quest for a constructed social existence. It provides an answer to the weakening of communal ties and to the feeling of belonging to a homogeneous society, where religion and culture are embedded in social authority. In short, such subcommunities help to make sense of what it is to live as a minority. The Nation of Islam in the United States fits this pattern (and is heavily criticised by orthodox and Salafi Muslims).

Contemporary movements are also emerging that are not root-ed in the Sufi tradition (or any other), but have many patterns in common with neo-brotherhoods (a 'guru' and an inward-looking, closed community). They often become a sect or a cult. One example is the Minhaj-ul-Quran, which was founded in Lahore, Pakistan, in 1980 by Mohammed Tahir ul-Qadri (born in 1954 in Punjab Province), and has its roots in the Barelvi tradition of northern India. Qadri established a political movement (Pakistan Awami Tehrik) in 1989 and has a huge constituency in the Euro-pean diaspora. Another is the Tawba movement in Azerbaijan, es-tablished by a former sports teacher, which works to rehabilitate drug addicts.

The common denominator 'sect' may explain the strange sym-metry between some Sufi and anti-Sufi movements. In West Africa, for example, the Izalat movement of northern Nigeria has many features in common with a Sufi brotherhood. In Germany a move-ment called the Kaplanci considers its leader to be the new caliph of the entire Muslim world. It is strongly anti-Kemalist (Atatürk is dubbed by them a *dönme*, or superficially converted Jew) and anti-Western, but it recruits solely from among Turks living in the West.[47] The Aczmendi in Turkey (who wear loose black trousers and green headgear), the Darul Arqam in Malaysia, the Dawat-i-Islami in Pakistan, founded by a Barelvi Pakistani sheikh, Moham-med Ilyas Qaderi (who dress in white with a green cap) all share the same mixture of sectarianism, guruism, neofundamentalism and weird retraditionalisation, something not very different from certain contemporary Jewish communities.

---

47. After Kaplan's death in 1995, his son Metin Müftüoglu was involved in the murder of Kaplan's rival in 1997 and later gaoled.

Beyond intellectual and religious differences the ways in which faith communities are established share much in common not only with Muslims of diverse obediences but even with adherents of the main Western religions, from church to sect. However, history and psychoanalysis teach us that the more slender our differences from others, the more urgent our need to stress them.

6
THE MODERNITY OF AN ARCHAIC
WAY OF THINKING:
NEOFUNDAMENTALISM

If contemporary forms of religiosity among Muslims (and Christians too) have a number of patterns in common (individualisation, the quest for self-realisation, the rethinking of Islam outside the framework of a given culture, and the recasting of the Muslim *ummah* in non-territorial terms), how do we distinguish between open and liberal forms of Islam on the one hand and fundamentalist and radical ones on the other? From Pakistan's *madrasas* to Islamic bookshops in Paris or mosques in London, via hundreds of websites, a specific form of fundamentalism is spreading, which I call neofundamentalism.[1]

By neofundamentalism I mean a common intellectual matrix that can nevertheless be manifested in various political attitudes. If all radical Islamic groups are indisputably neofundamentalist in religious terms, many fundamentalist elements are simply conservative and law-abiding, even if they explicitly condemn the westernisation of Islam. I refer here not to a structured movement articulated around a coherent doctrine, but to a form of religiosity that has spread among different milieus. Moderate Muslims call it Wahhabism by referring to the official creed of Saudi Arabia, while most of those involved prefer to call themselves Salafis (that is, 'followers of the pious ancestors'). But others (like the Tablighi) reject such denominations and simply call themselves Muslims. Neofundamentalists by definition reject the idea that there can be different schools of thought and consider themselves the only true Muslims, refusing to be labelled as one specific group among the

---

1. Olivier Roy, *The Failure of Political Islam*, Cambridge, MA: Harvard University Press, 1995.

others. Their claim goes with their propensity for polemics and anathema among people who have a lot in common (for example, Salafis criticising Tablighi, and Wahhabis criticising self-proclaimed Western Salafis).

Without doubt the most-used nomenclature nowadays is 'Salafi'. The term Salafism was used at the end of the nineteenth century to designate a reform movement initiated by Jamal ad-Din al-Afghani. He strove to reform Islam in order to adapt it to the challenge of colonisation and westernisation. But Afghani was more an activist than a theologian. His call for a return to the true tenets of Islam was a means of castigating the backwardness of the religious establishment rather than an appeal for the implementation of *sharia*. In fact there is little in common between Jamal ad-Din al-Afghani and Mullah Omar, leader of the Taliban.

The historical Salafi movement was the forerunner of the Muslim Brotherhood and the Islamists, for whom it remains a reference point. In his book *Aux sources du renouveau musulman*, Tariq Ramadan advocates a return to the 'founding fathers', from al-Afghani to al-Banna, with a view to integrating Muslims in the West.[2] Salafism was originally meant to answer the challenge of the West. But 'Salafi' no longer refers to a global political project to reform and modernise Muslim societies. The idea is to ignore the West. Salafism is now associated with a conservative program of purifying Islam from cultural influences (from traditional Muslim societies as well as from the West). Contemporary Salafis have little in common with their predecessors, but much in common with the Wahhabis. They often explicitly condemn the traditional Salafiyya (see the work of the Yemeni Sheikh Muqbil).[3] Thus the use of the term 'Salafi' is historically misleading and I prefer the less elegant but more accurate 'neofundamentalism'.

Why 'neo'? The call for a return to the true tenets of Islam is not new. Rejection of sectarian affiliations, of the different schools of law, of theology and philosophy, in favour of a strict return to the Koran and the Sunnah is a perennial feature of Islamic fundamentalism. But there are some new elements that make a difference:

2.   Tariq Ramadan, *Aux sources du renouveau musulman*, Paris: Fayard, 1998.
3.   François Burgat and Muhammad Sbitli, 'Les Salafis au Yémen ou … la modernisation malgré tout' ['Salafis in Yemen or … Modernisation after All'], *Chroniques yéménites*, 2002 (<http://cy.revues.org/document137.html>).

contemporary neofundamentalism is coping with deterritorialisation – the end of Dar-ul-Islam as a geographical entity. Even if
it retains a traditional terminology, neofundamentalism explicitly
deals with a new situation. The discrepancy between, on the one
hand, its 'closed' terminology and vision and, on the other, the
totally new situation it addresses is not a contradiction. As we shall
see, neofundamentalism is even better adapted to globalisation than
many other forms of Islam. It has internalised and addressed the
changing forms of religiosity. It deals with a westernisation that is
now at the core and no longer at the frontiers of Islam. Conversely,
it is also dealing with a religion that is no longer embedded in a
given society and thus is open to reformation. There are, of course,
many other new elements, many of which we have already discussed (individualisation, the crisis of authority and knowledge). In
any case, the debate on the differences in formal identity of traditional forms of Islamic fundamentalism and neofundamentalism is
obscuring a profound mutation in religiosity.

SOURCES AND ACTORS OF NEOFUNDAMENTALISM

Neofundamentalism is not a structured organisation or even a precise school of thought; it is a trend, a state of mind, a dogmatic relation to the fundamentals of the religion. It thrives in very different
and even opposing contexts, from former Muslim Brothers to the
Tablighi Jama'at and Wahhabis. The main trend calls itself Salafi,
and includes the Saudi Wahhabis, even if many Salafis would not
accept being called by that name. (By the same token, Wahhabism
is not self-named; outsiders bestowed the term on the followers
of Abdul Wahhab.) The Salafi family includes most of the militant
groups, such as the Taliban in Afghanistan, or the Ahl-i Hadith in
Pakistan, but also more integrated and conservative associations,
like the different Ahl al Sunnah wal Jama'at in Britain and the
United States. The politically radical wing of neofundamentalism
includes the Qutbist movements of the 1970s (from Sayyid Qutb),
the Algerian GIA, Al Qaeda and the Pakistani radical groups like
Jayash-e-Muhammad or Sipah-e-Sahaba, which consider *jihad* to
be a personal religious duty, and are therefore often accurately referred to as 'Salafi-jihadist'.[4] Many independent and sometimes

4. The expression is common in the Pakistani press, but is now widely used

self-taught preachers are neofundamentalist, whether conservative or *jihadi* (such as Abu Hamza al-Masri and Omar Bakri Muhammad in London). Other less-known preachers have built their constituency mainly through the internet, and of these, interestingly many are converts and often black: Sheikh Zarabozo, Sheikh Quick, Sheikh Bilal Philips, Jamaaluddin Haidar and Sheikh Abdullah el-Faisal (a British Jamaican who was sentenced in 2003 to nine years in prison for his call to violence). They use English as their lingua franca. Salafi ideas are also to be found on many student websites, either collective or individual.

Two of the main neofundamentalist movements, the Tablighi and the Wahhabis, had till the 1960s a limited territorial basis (respectively the Indian subcontinent and Saudi Arabia), but gained a supranational worldwide audience through a policy of extensive propaganda.

The Tablighi, who do not refer to themselves as Salafi, launch short-term campaign tours by missionary teams comprising multinational lay preachers.[5] They instruct their members to avoid entanglement in local politics, to promote the veiling of women, to close coeducational schools, and to ban social interaction with non-Muslims, all the while insisting on prayers and piety. Knowledge of local languages has never been a prerequisite of *khuruj* (a missionary journey that all members are supposed to undertake at least once, on a model borrowed from the Mormons), although their propaganda is mainly oral and based on the team's exemplary manners and conduct (hence the importance of etiquette and dress codes). The internet and written publications are not the main media of propaganda for the Tablighi, which is based on verbal and door-to-door personal contact. *Ulama* do not play a role in the Tablighi movement.[6]

---

outside Pakistan by journalists; for Saudi Arabia, see Ehsan Ahrari, 'Whither Saudi Arabia?', *Time Asia*, 6 August 2002; for Morocco, see François Soudan, 'Le Sabre et le Coran', *Jeune Afrique L'Intelligent* (independent Paris news magazine), 12–25 August 2003.

5.   Tablighi Jama'at was launched in 1926 in Delhi by Mohammad Ilyas.
6.   Their core text is *Riyadh as-Salihin* (Gardens of the Righteous), written by the Syrian Shafi'i scholar Muhyi ad-din Abu Zakariyya' Yahya (born Sharaf an-Nawawi, 1233–78), which is a summary of 'dos' and 'don'ts'. Nawawi, Imam, *Gardens of the Righteous: The Riyadh as-Salihin of Imam Nawawi* (trans. by Muhammad Zafrulla Khan), 2nd edn, New York: Olive Branch Press, 1989.

By contrast, Saudi Wahhabism is centred around a cluster of learned sheikhs who rarely travel outside the Gulf states. They extend their influence through an intensive outpouring of *fatwas* and short conferences or lectures, spread through the internet, television stations (such as Iqra) or via cheap booklets. Their products form an important part of the curriculum of worldwide Muslim religious institutions that are subsidised by Gulf money. Through informal networks of disciples and former students, they reach a lay audience far larger than the *madrasas* in which they teach. But one should not exaggerate the 'Saudi' dimension of the Wahhabi; most of the best-known so-called 'Medina sheikhs' are not Saudi Wahhabis by birth, as we shall see.

Many recently created teaching networks have a Saudi connection, because their founders either studied in the Kingdom or have benefited from Saudi funding, directly or through one of the many institutions created or sponsored by the Saudis (such as the Rabita al-Alam al-Islami, or Muslim League, established in 1963). Scholarships and pilgrimages to Mecca continue to provide new recruits for Saudi-sponsored networks. Each Saudi embassy has a department of religious affairs responsible for funding Islamic institutions. Even if the Saudis do not openly promote Wahhabism, they push for the 'Salafisation' of teaching and preaching wherever they have a say. The reference to the classical Hanbali school of law allows them to reach beyond strict Wahhabi circles and thus avoid being seen as members of an extremist sect. Changes in the curriculum of the Pakistani Deobandi *madrasas* over the past thirty years are a good example of this Wahhabisation of more traditional schools of thought.[7] As we have seen, this process accompanies a contraction of the curriculum and therefore of the time spent in religious schools; there is less to teach, once one rejects all non-religious

7.   The personal library of an Afghan *alim* trained in a Deobandi school during the 1940s and 1950s included poetry, mathematics, dream-interpretation, alchemy, 'Greek' medicine and mysticism (personal observation at the library of Mawlawi Mirajuddin, Astana, Panjshir valley, in 1982; see also footnote 23, page 162). The curriculum of the *madrasa* included lay disciplines; in fact it covered a whole culture and knowledge. From the 1980s, in Taliban *madrasas*, the curriculum was reduced to purely religious matters, with an insistence on Hadith and *fiqh*. The extension of a secular educational system entailed a negative side-effect: religious schools gave up general teaching to restrict themselves to being purely religious occupational schools.

sciences, all schools of thought except that of Ibn Hanbal and most of the classical debates on Islam, in favour of *ibadat* (devotion), *fiqh* and Hadith.[8] Cycles of study are closer to Western curricula: from three to five years (and shaped and often named along the lines of US and British BA, MA and PhD courses), instead of the ten to twenty years an authentic *alim* used to spend in religious study. The main intellectual task of the sheikhs is to research *tafsir* (interpretation of the Koran) and Hadith (identifying and collecting authentic Hadith, as opposed to weak ones), and to produce *fatwas* and lectures or essays on what is licit or illicit. Devotion, rituals and law are the pillars of their conception of Islam.

The relationship between the Wahhabi clergy and the Saudi monarchy is ambiguous. Each needs the other, the monarchy for legitimacy, the clergy for funding and to ensure its religious hegemony in the kingdom (against Shias and other Sunnis). The clergy enjoy wide autonomy; it is dominated by the Sheikh family, while there are no members of the Saud family among the *ulama*. Some sheikhs are openly critical of the Sauds; a few have been gaoled (al-Awda, al-Hawali and Said al-Zuair), but the highest religious authorities always endeavour to negotiate the release of the detainees and corresponding political restraint on the part of the *imams*. The predicament of the Saudi monarchy is that the main contestation of its authority comes from within its basis of legitimacy: the Wahhabis. However regular the crackdowns against the dissidents, the *esprit de corps* of the Wahhabi clergy ensures a paradoxical freedom of expression. The amount of subsidies provided by the monarchy to radical religious groups is the object of polemics, but it is clear that mainstream Wahhabis, who can spread very fundamentalist ideas, are openly and directly subsidised by the monarchy.[9]

Another interesting case is that of the Hizb ut-Tahrir, a form of UFO (Unidentified Fundamentalist Object). Is it a neofundamentalist party? In a sense, no. The Hizb ut-Tahrir eschews the application of *sharia* as its top priority and retains many elements of its Muslim Brotherhood past, such as its use of the term 'ideology'; its

8. Sheikh Muqbil openly advocates short courses and self-teaching (Burgat and Sbitli, 'Les Salafis au Yémen').

9. See *Religious Freedom in the Kingdom of Saudi Arabia*, a report by the Saudi Institute, 30 January 2002, which gives a list of donations published by the official Saudi press, including Sheikh Bin Baz's official website (<http://www.binbaz.org.sa/aboutus_eng.asp>).

insistence on building an Islamic state in the form of a caliphate that will rule over the whole *ummah*; and its organisation as a po-litical movement (especially its use of cells). But it has become an uprooted and deterritorialised movement, with no thought of taking power in a given country. The caliphate it wants to establish has no territorial basis. Hizb ut-Tahrir uses pseudo-Koranic termi-nology, taken out of context, with no consideration of history and social circumstances. Its concept of Khilafat has little to do with the historical Caliphate; even if the party sees 1924 as the year when it ended, this does not mean that it wishes to revive the Ottoman political system. In fact, for Hizb ut-Tahrir the Caliphate is not a real geographical entity and has no territorial or sociological roots. It has to be established as soon as possible for the whole *ummah* and not on a specific territory. This global and abstract conception of the *ummah* is typical of neofundamentalism. The development of Hizb ut-Tahrir exemplifies how a former Islamist party turned neofundamentalist, even if it differs from all other neofundamen-talist movements.

Irrespective of their shared commitment to a strict return to the true tenets of Islam and the decontextualisation of religious prac-tices, neofundamentalists are divided. Wahhabis and Salafis dislike the Tablighis' 'innovations': for instance, the central concept of *khu-ruj*, or 'going forth', and the role of the sheikh (which means here not an *alim* but the group leader, who should be obeyed blindly, something similar to the relationship between monks and their elected abbot). They also criticise the Tablighi for their disdain of knowledge and their view that one does not need to be very learned to preach, a position similar to that held by many Protes-tant fundamentalists.

Wahhabis also openly scorn other preachers who call themselves Salafis (self-proclamation is common among all sorts of modern preachers). In the attacks by Medina sheikhs on 'deviant' schools there is often, beyond theological differences, an underlying vin-dication of a religious corporate establishment against newcom-ers, self-taught clerics (often converts) and independent preachers, who consider that one need not be highly educated to preach. (Sheikh al-Albani is particularly vehement in denouncing as igno-rant many preachers like Jamaal al-Din Zarabozo.)[10] Yemeni Salafis

10. Abdullah Lahmami, *A Refutation of Some of the Statements of Jamal ud-Din*

are, conversely, quite critical of the Wahhabis. Yahya al Hajuri, a well-known Yemeni Salafi, wrote a *fatwa* politically supporting the Taliban while calling them *maturidi* (a derogatory term meaning 'rationalist'). He also criticised Bin Laden for being a *jihadi* and a *takfiri*, in deviation from true doctrine.[11] Such important issues as *jihad*, *takfir* and leadership are surrounded by disagreement. The Taliban, despite their similarity to Wahhabis, never destroyed the graves of *pirs* (holy men) and emphasised dreams as a means of revelation, which is not a Wahhabi trait.

But what would a neofundamentalist corpus look like, and where would we find it? Perhaps one should set out by looking at several websites that are the most often referred to or are linked to each other. These are put up either by an organisation or by individuals (mainly students, as we shall see below). When searching for 'Islam' or *sharia* or suchlike on the internet, search engines often return Salafi sites among the first hits. Islamic bookshops, which are not necessarily Salafi but sell the products that are most in demand, are another good place to turn to. Whatever the neofundamentalist medium, the references one encounters are eclectic, from Ibn Taymiyya (thirteenth century), one of the very few 'classical' authors favoured by fundamentalists, to a cluster of contemporary Wahhabi sheikhs, and even some Islamist authors such as Maududi and Sayyid Qutb.[12] Contemporary preachers usually prefer to produce video and audio-tapes instead of books, and do so in Western languages, in order to address the largest possible audience, thereby transcending ethnic divides, and to address a new generation of Western-born Muslims (for instance the South African *mufti* Desai writes in English, as does Ahmed Deedat). There is therefore a huge amount of translation taking place (the Medina Wahhabi sheikhs always write or speak in Arabic). Any given text

Zarabozo, Birmingham: Salafi Publications, 2002. This pamphlet, in Adobe PDF format, can be found at <http://www.salafipublications.com>.

11. 'Yemeni Scholars Re-enforce the Call for Jihad', *fatwa* translated by Aqeel Walker and published on Political Islam Diffusion List, 25 January 2002. (This is published on a closed discussion list managed by Kamran Bokhari at the University of Austin, Texis.)

12. A significant list of selected scholars who are favourites of the Salafis is to be found on <http://www.islaam.com/Scholars.aspx>. Most of the listed scholars are contemporary, but some classical authors are also listed, such as Ibn Taymiyyah, as are some Islamists such as Maududi.

(such as a *fatwa* or a conference address) by a Wahhabi sheikh may appear in different translations on various websites. Such occurrences are also a good indicator of the popularity of a text or of a *fatwa*.[13] Translators – or, more precisely, people who are fluent in Arabic and a Western language – play a key role in making available Middle Eastern authors to a Western audience, such as Abu Maryam Isma'eel Alarcon, from the Salafi Society of North America. Pakistanis and South Africans, who usually have a better mastery of English than their Saudi counterparts, are spearheading this trend. Younger authors and those based in the West write directly in Western languages, which means that their impact may be restricted to a specific country for linguistic reasons, like Iquioussen in France who writes only in French, while others have a global audience. Some non-Wahhabi Sunni authors such as Abdul Fattah Abu Ghudda (died 1997, a former leader of the Syrian Hanafi brotherhood who wrote on 'Islamic manners') also have a large audience among neofundamentalists.

As usual the internet serves as a circulatory system of ideas that are reaffirmed by dint of repetition: the same set of references reappear again and again, while some authors are mentioned systematically.[14] The websites of students' associations are also a good vector for Salafi propaganda, specifically in the West. Most such websites are located in Western universities, mainly in the United States, Britain and Canada.[15] For instance, that of the Muslim Students' Association of the University of Southern California[16] has a page borrowed from the Department of Islamic Affairs of the Saudi Arabian embassy in Washington ('Understanding Islam and the Muslims', 2003). In 1999 the website of the Muslim Students' Association at the University of Houston[17] carried a lengthy

13. For instance, Sheikh Naasir-Ud-Deen Al-Albaanee (or Nasir ud-Din al-Albani), *Munatharah ma' tantheem al-jihad al-Islami*, audiotape, 2 vols. The English translation of this debate between al-Albani and an anonymous supporter of *jihad*, edited by a group supporting the former, is to be found on at least seven different websites (such as <http://www.muslimaccess.com/articles/jihad/albaani_jihad.asp>).
14. Those on the site <http://www.islaam.com/Scholars.aspx>.
15. The Muslim students' associations of the universities of Southern California and Houston are Salafi, for example, but others are not Salafi at all (such as those at Yale and the University of Maryland).
16. <http://www.usc.edu/dept/MSA/introduction/understandingislam.html>.
17. <http://www.uh.edu/campus/msa/home.php>.

question-and-answer session with Sheikh al-Albani (for example, is sex change surgery permissible in Islam, or body piercing?)

The most-quoted sheikhs are a handful of contemporary Wah-habis living in Medina, but many are not of Wahhabi Saudi Arabi-an origin and were initially trained outside the Kingdom in other schools of law. Examples include Nasir ud-Din al-Albani (from an Albanian Hanafi family, who died in 1999 and had spent much of his life in Jordan and Syria), his disciples Ali Abdul Hamid al-Halabi (Palestinian) and Salim al-Hilali (Palestinian, born in Hebron in 1957), Sheikh Muhammad Ameen ash-Shanqeeti (Mauritanian, a Maliki), Abdulwahhab Marzuq al-Banna (Egyptian, Shafi'i and Sufi milieu) and Abu Bakr al-Jazairi (or Al-Jaza'iry, an Algerian Maleki). Many became Wahhabi after they went to Saudi Arabia. Among the Saudi-born sheikhs, let us mention Mohammed Salih al-Munajjid (or Monjed, who owns the website islam-qa.com), Hammoud bin 'Uqla al-Shu'aybi, Saleh Bin Othaymeen (who died in 2001), Nassir al-Buraq (Barak), Salih Ibn Fawzan al-Fawzan, Sheikh Rabi' Ibn Hadi al-Madkhali (from a southern Saudi tribe) and Abdullah bin Abdur-Rahaan al-Ghudayan (born in Az-Zulfi, Saudi Arabia). Closely associated with the late grand *mufti* of Saudi Arabia, Sheikh Abdulaziz Bin Baz, they and their disciples staff the teaching insti-tutions they sponsor, such as the Albani Centre at Amman, Jordan, founded by Salim al-Hilali and Halabi. They also provide religious references and *fatwas* for a global audience. In France Abu Bakr al-Jazairi (Eldjazaïri) has replaced Yusuf al-Qaradawi (whose popu-larity declined when he condemned the 9/11 attacks) as the author of the most popular Islamic guidebook, *La voie du Musulman* (The Muslim's Path).[18] He is extensively quoted in the French version of the website islaam.com.

The grand *mufti* of Saudi Arabia, Sheikh Bin Baz (died 1999), re-mains an inspirational figure to these sheikhs, whose followers run active and well-produced websites.[19] They also support propaganda

18. The book, by Abu Bakr Jabir Al-Jaza'iry (al-Jazairi), is available in English as *Minhaj Al-Muslim [The Way of the Muslim]* (2 vols, London: Darussalam Pub-lications, 1998).

19. The following are some Salafi websites: <http://www.qss.org>, <http://www.al-sunnah.com>, <http://www.salafipublications.com>, <http://allaahuakbar.net>, <http://www.islam-qa.com> (<http://63.175.194.25>), <http://www.salafibookstore.com>, <http://www.al-manhaj.com> (strong-ly opposed to the Muslim Brotherhood), <http://www.fatwa-online.com>,

societies like the al-Qur'an was-Sunnah Society of North America,[20] or Ahlus-Sunnah wal-Jamaa'ah, based in Britain. The Open University in Alexandria, Virginia, and a publishing house in Leicester, England, are linked to this movement. The sheikhs quote each other, eulogise each other's students, and write in defence of those followers who are criticised or even arrested. Sheikh Naasir al-Aql wrote a booklet entitled *Ahlus Sunnah wal-Jamaa'ah* (published by the society of the same name) for the Muslims living in Britain; he quotes Safar al-Hawali and Fawzan al-Burak approvingly.[21] This last example demonstrates that the solidarity of ideas between the sheikhs goes further than political disagreement. Sheikh al-Hawali is considered a radical, critical of the Saudi monarchy and a supporter of the Taliban and Bin Laden (he took a more moderate stand after 9/11); with his colleague Sheikh Salam al-Odeh

<http://www.angelfire.com/home/niqabi4allah/page2.html>, <http://www.salafi.net> (in Arabic, by Sheikh Abdur-Rahman Abdul-Khaliq's followers, often criticised by other Salafis), <http://www.assalafi.com> (Atlanta, GA), <http://www.salaf.com>, <http://www.troid.org>, <http://www.islaam.com/Scholars.aspx>; and in French, <http://www.soubhannallah.com>, <http://www.assabyle.com/index.php?id=407> and <http://www.sounnah.free.fr>.

20. <http://www.qss.org>. The site is the expression of the al-Qur'an was-Sunnah Society of North America (QSS), which describes itself as follows: 'A well known organization in North America which adopts the Salafi Manhaj [method]. It was officially established in 1986 by Ihyaa ut-Turaath of Kuwait. It became independent from it in 1989. It was chaired by Mahmood Murad from 1986 to 1991, and by Muhammad al-Jibaly from 1991 to present. It holds annual conventions each year in December … It is well known to all the Salafi scholars overseas, and has written and verbal tazkiyah from many of them. Examples: QSS invited Sheikh Saalih al-Fawzaan to its convention in 1993. He asked Shakh Ibn Baaz for permission to attend, and the latter told us that he told him, "Yes, these are our Brothers and we know them, go to them!" Unfortunately, some personal circumstances prevented al-Fawzaan from attending. This year, Abu al-Hasan al-Misri al-Ma'ribee, one of the strongest students of knowledge of our time, asked al-Albani as to whether to accept an invitation to attend the convention. The latter told us that al-Albani gave us a strong tazkiyah and said, "By all means, these are our brothers. You must go to them!" Unfortunately, Abu al-Hasan was not granted a visa. QSS has many publications, in Arabic and English, which centre around the subjects of Aqeedah, Fiqh, Tarbiyah, and Manhaj. Examples, Tamaam ul-Minnah, Magnificent Journey, Celebrations in Islam, Imitation of Kuffaar, the Night Prayer, …' (2003).
21. Sheikh Naasir Al-'Aql, *General Precepts of Ahlus-Sunnah wal-Jamaa'ah*, London: Message of Islam, 1999.

(Awdeh), he was gaoled by the Saudi government from 1994 to 1999 but retained the protection of Bin Baz.[22]

The same mixture of political radicalism, Salafi rigour and closeness to the religious and even political establishment is to be found with the Yemeni Salafi school created by Sheikh Muqbil Bin Hadi al Wadi'i (died 2001), who was not a Wahhabi, but retained strong ties with such Wahhabis as Rabi Ibn Hadi and was buried close to Bin Baz. He established the Dar ul Hadith *madrasa* where the 'American Talib' John Walker Lindh studied. Two of his disciples, Mohammed al-Imam and Yahya al-Hajuri, came out strongly in favour of the Taliban and against the US intervention in Afghanistan and Iraq, while maintaing a working relationship with the Yemeni government. The leader of the Indonesian Jemaah Islamiah, Abu Bakar Bashir, also enjoyed the same sort of leniency from the government in Jakarta till the Bali bombings of October 2002.

In Pakistan the Ahl-i Hadith movement, with its military branch Lashkar-e-Toiba, has the same traits. It is part of the religious establishment, and its huge compound in Muridke, near Lahore, was built on a plot given by the then President General Zia ul-Haq. It has developed a high-level network of religious schools and helped sustain the Kashmir *jihad*. It also supported the Taliban.

In fact Salafis are well entrenched in many parts of the Muslim clerical establishment – Saudi Arabia, Yemen and Pakistan, and Western Muslim organisations.

THE BASIC TENETS OF NEOFUNDAMENTALISM

The neofundamentalists, and specifically the Salafis,[23] stress the absolute unity of God (*tawhid*): they oppose any sort of innovation (*bid'a*), associationism (*shirk*) and 'blind imitation' (*taqlid*). Hence they reject all accretions to a strict and literalist reading of Koran and Sunnah. The Salafis and Wahhabis support *ijtihad* (interpretation) as a way of bypassing the tradition of the different religious

22. 'We fear only Allah the almighty', stated Bin Baz on 16 October 1994. 'Sheikh Abdel Aziz Bin Baz defends Salman and Safar', *Mesanews*, 17 October 1994. See also Mamoun Fandy, *Saudi Arabia and the Politics of Dissent*, New York: St Martin's Press, 1999.
23. For a good summary in English of the Salafi view, see 'An Introduction to the Salafi Da'wah', on <http://www.qss.org/articles/salafi/text.html>.

schools, and not as a way of adapting to new situations.[24] They try to reduce the accepted Sunnah to what they see as the authentic Hadith (sayings of the Prophet), discarding many popular Hadith as being 'weak' (that is, inauthentic). Hadith (real or forged) have always been the way to open, enlarge and adapt the religious tenets of Islam to different situations and cultures. In this sense the Salafi 'reformist' approach consists of discarding pragmatic tools for adaptation and compromise. Neofundamentalists are obsessed by *bid'a*, or innovation, which for them amounts to heresy, even if the novelty is of no consequence or importance (hence a continuing debate on how to dress or brush one's teeth). The observer is often surprised by the time neofundamentalists spend discussing apparently mundane issues. They are prone to imitate the Prophet on all matters, including the most mundane ones, thus all actions, attitudes and behaviour should be referred to a religious norm. Neofundamentalists see religion as a code and life as a kind of ritual. *Tazkia* (purification of the self) is a key concept. This sacralisation of daily life is to be found across the spectrum of neofundamentalists (from the Tablighi to the instructions for Al Qaeda terrorists).

Neofundamentalists oppose the existence of different schools of law and consider themselves, by definition, to be the only 'true Muslims'. This entails a debate on *takfir*: should one declare infidel a nominal Muslim who does not follow the true path? Mainstream neofundamentalists oppose *takfir* and advocate *dawah* to return deviant Muslims to the true path.[25] Conversely the proponents of *takfir* usually support *jihad* as a permanent and individual duty, for the very reason that there is no longer a true Islamic ruler or even a true *ummah* that could call for *jihad*. Whatever their position on *takfir*, Salafi websites are replete with condemnations of 'deviant sects'.[26] They oppose the concept of 'national cultures' and local Islam and reject Sufism as *bid'a*.

24. That is certainly the big difference in the modern Shia or the Sunni liberal concept of *ijtihad*, which could allow some innovations rejected by the Wahhabis.
25. See *The Creed of Imaam Al-Albaanee on Takfir and Apostasy*, October 2000, <http://www.salafipublications.com/sps/downloads/pdf/MSC060006.pdf>.
26. The website <http://www.allaahuakbar.net> lists the following deviant Muslim groups (note the eclectic character of the selection): Ahmediyyah, Ansaru Allah, Moors, Warith-deen, Bahaullah, Nation of Islam, Shiites, Baatiniyyah, Boharas Dawoodi, Boharas Nusayris, Druzes, Agakhaani, Jamaat-

They also reject theology (*'ilm al-kalam*) because they see it as either redundant or constituting some sort of a 'rival' intellectual construction that ends by being a substitute for the true corpus. They oppose philosophy as well as literature. They consider that history is only the history of deviance and has no relevance except for teaching lessons about what is wrong. They logically ignore the concept of 'modernity'.[27]

They reject what they call *asabiyya* (identification with a sub-community, like a tribe, a nation, a race or an ethnic group) and *hizbiyya* (joining a political party, including an Islamic one). Consequently they dismiss the notion of an 'Islamic party', which puts them at odds with the Islamists.

Neofundamentalists advocate the strict implementation of *sharia*, with no concession to man-made law. By definition this pushes them to discard the modern state and to share a kind of modern 'libertarian' view of the state, which is considered a lesser evil but not as a tool for implementing Islam.

They consider that there is nothing positive to be borrowed from the West and nothing to discuss with Christians and Jews except calling them to Islam, although mainstream Salafis agree that one should treat non-belligerent infidels leniently.[28] Islam is for neofundamentalists an all-encompassing religion, but mainly in so far as the daily life of the individual is concerned. They reject the concept of 'Islamic ideology' that has been so prevalent among Islamists. They believe they should not borrow Western conceptual categories (like economy, constitution, political party, revolution or social justice), even by giving them an Islamic slant. Neofundamentalists do not care about social issues; they do not try to play on a specific social constituency, as the Islamists did. They refuse to

---

e-Islami, Sufism, Tableegi-Jamaat, Deobandism, Bareilwiyat, Naqshabandis, Ikhwani, Jihaadis, Qur'ânites, Qadariyyah, Khawariji, Jahmiyyah, Ash'ariyyah, Matrudiyyah, Murji'ah, Khalifites (19ers), Takfiris and Habashis.

27. See Jamaal al-Din Zarabozo, a US convert who became an *imam* in California. He delivered a speech entitled 'Modernism in Islam' (from an audiotape series available from Dar Makkah, Denver, Colorado). The speech is to be found on many websites, such as <http://members.cox.net/arshad/modernis.htm>). Says Zarabozo: 'The modernist movement as a whole (what it is based on) is from Bida' (innovation).'

28. See Eldjazaïri (Al-Jaza'iry), 'Comportement à l'égard des Infidèles' [Behaviour towards Infidels], *La voie du Musulman* [*Minhaj Al-Muslim*], Paris: Ennour, 2001, pp. 127–30.

take into consideration social sciences and philosophy (Islamists, on the other hand, do read Western philosophy, even if in a critical way or through abridged textbooks). Neofundamentalists use traditional Islamic legal categories (halal/*haram*, or lawful/prohibited) without endeavouring to modernise them or even admitting that the world has changed since the time of the Prophet.[29] They pepper their speeches and conversation with traditional religious terminology, and discuss at length classical topics like slavery, despite such subjects being outdated or irrelevant.[30]

Nevertheless, one should not underestimate the mystical dimension of neofundamentalism. The Islamists, busy with building an Islamic state, have a more worldly mindset and are driven by optimism. They believe one could build a truly positive Islamic society through the actions and determination of humankind. But the neofundamentalists, more aligned this time with the Qutbist approach, remain pessimistic. The world is an immense pitfall for the believer, and there is little he can achieve by himself. Neofundamentalists advocate total reliance on God and insist on faith (*iman*) and salvation.

This insistence on salvation is consistent with their focus on the individual. An extreme legalistic approach goes hand in hand with extolling faith, a stress on salvation, and even a kind of mysticism. Salvation is often linked with God's *riza*, or satisfaction. Radicals insist that action is more important than the result. Undertaking *jihad* is more important than victory, which is presented as a plus

29. See Zarabozo, 'Modernism in Islam': '1) everything in accordance with Qur'an and Sunna is Haq (truth) and what disagrees with it is false (some modernists disagree with this). Also, statements consistent with the Qur'an and Sunna are accepted; 2) Ijmaa (consensus) of the sahaaba (and early generations) is a hujja (proof) for all Muslims. Modernists say sahaaba are men and we are men, and even matters agreed on by them are open to ijtihaad; 3) anything in the Qur'an and Sunna cannot be opposed by 'aql, rational thought, opinion, or qiysas. This is supported in the Qur'an and is not open to discussion or vote. One modernist said cutting off the hand of the thief is a "Khomeini Islam" and is unethical.' Note the systematic use in English of Arabic technical terms.

30. The last chapter of Al-Jaza'iry's *Minhaj Al-Muslim* is entirely devoted to the rules concerning slavery, something one would not find in al-Banna or Khomeini. Given that the French translation of this work is one of most popular guidebooks for French born-again Muslims, one wonders what conclusions the reader could draw from this chapter.

but should not be the motivation of the warrior, hence the tendency among radicals towards sacrificial and even suicide missions. This is also consistent with the lack of a political program: the aim is to please God, not to achieve a specific agenda. It would be preposterous to think that man's will can achieve God's sovereignty on earth. The victory will come only when God decides.

Beyond their religious radicalism, neofundamentalists tend to ignore or despise politics, which paradoxically pushes them to accept the present political order without bestowing any legitimacy on it. Their religious radicalism pushes them towards political neutrality (except for the jihadists, even if they do not have a political agenda either). This may explain why they accept and even support regimes like that of Saudi Arabia, but also why they are more adapted to living in the West than true Islamists.

NEOFUNDAMENTALISTS AND ISLAMISTS

The main divide between neofundamentalists and Islamists is over the state and politics. While in theory they consider that Muslims should live under an Islamic state, the neofundamentalists reject the political struggle as a means of establishing such a state. They believe that an Islamic state should result from the re-Islamisation of the *ummah* and not be a tool for this re-Islamisation.[31] Political activism, according to neofundamentalists, overshadows the need to reform the self. The issue is not one of being either moderate or radical. Mainstream neofundamentalists oppose radical and moderate Islamists (including supranational jihadists as well as those who support a shift to democracy and multipartism). They condemn the very concepts of democracy, human rights and freedom, whereas Islamists try to show how Islam represents the best form of democracy (through the concept of *shura*, or consultation) and the best protection for human rights (including women's rights). Neofundamentalists refuse to express their views in modern terms borrowed from the West. They consider that indulging in politics, even for a good cause, will by definition lead to *bid'a* and *shirk* (the giving of priority to worldly considerations over religious values).

While Islamists consciously borrowed many concepts from Western political sciences (ideology, revolution, political party) or

---

31. See comments by Muqbil in Burgat and Sbitli, 'Les Salafis au Yémen', p. 7.

twisted some Koranic terms to give them a modern sense (Hezbollah, or God's party; *mostazafin*, or deprived people; and *hakimiyya*,
or sovereignty), neofundamentalists pretend to ignore the West and
to live in some sort of intellectual autarky. They refuse to borrow
anything from the West, considering this to be *bid'a*. Indeed they
reject the very concept of modernisation, which is coherent with
their refusal to admit that history has some meaning. Salafiyya is
not a 'movement' because 'a movement is meant to indicate something temporal or reactionary'.[32]

Mainstream neofundamentalists regard politics as irrelevant
while ever most Muslims have not been brought back to the true
tenets of Islam through propaganda. Reform of the soul should
precede reform of the state. Politics does not help to purify the
soul. Propaganda should take precedence over political action (the
Hizb ut-Tahrir shares this view), *dawah* (inviting people to Islam)
over *jihad*.[33]

Neofundamentalists feel no urge to build specific 'Islamic' institutions (from a constitution to a parliament) because that would
imply that *sharia* is not sufficient. When the Taliban ran Afghanistan, they cared nothing for building state institutions. For the Tal-
ibs the very concept of an Islamic state meant that something had
to be added to *sharia*. For neofundamentalists the aim of action
is salvation, not revolution. Their objective is the individual, not
society. One should first return to the true path as an individual
Muslim before taking political action: 'A true Salafi ... knows that
victory is not possible without true *tawhid* and that *shirk* cannot be

32. 'An Introduction to the Salafi Da'wah', <http://www.qss.org/articles/salafi/
    text.html>.
33. 'The Party defined its method of work into three stages:
    '*The First Stage*: The stage of culturing to produce people who believe in the
    idea and the method of the Party, so that they form the Party group.
    '*The Second Stage*: The stage of interaction with the Ummah, to let the Um-
    mah embrace and carry Islam, so that the Ummah takes it up as its issue, and
    thus works to establish it in the affairs of life.
    '*The Third Stage*: The stage of establishing government, implementing Islam
    generally and comprehensively, and carrying it as a message to the world.
      'The Party started the first stage in al-Quds in 1372 AH (1953 CE) under
    the leadership of its founder, the honourable scholar, thinker, able politician,
    qadi in the Court of Appeals in al-Quds, Taqiuddin al-Nabhani (may Allah's
    mercy be upon him).' <http://www.hizb-ut-tahrir.org/urdu/tareef/content.
    html>.

fought with the likes of it.'[34] There is even some arrogance, according to neofundamentalists, in striving to establish an Islamic State: the 'Ikhwan program' (that is, the Muslim Brotherhood) supposes

the purity of ones [*sic*] own soul, since it implies that we have fulfilled the conditions for victory to be granted to us, and deserve to be given establishment upon the earth – even though the kaafirs still have the upper hand over us. With such a negative attitude we shall neglect to cultivate our souls and neglect to take account of our own selves.[35]

Sheikh al-Hilali, in an often-quoted speech, states the priority: back to the Koran and the Sunnah according to the Salaf. In this speech there is not a word on *jihad*, politics, party, ideology, state, social action, and so on. But there is a constant theme: never imitate the unbelievers. Al-Hilali quotes one of the favourite Koranic *sura* of the neofundamentalists: 'Never will the Jews and the Christians be satisfied with you, until you follow their way' (Sura al-Baqarah 2. 120).[36] Quoting Shanqeeti, Sheikh Zarabozo writes:

The problem itself actually lies in the hearts and souls of the Muslims. The solution therefore lies in their turning sincerely to Allah, strengthening their faith and putting their trust in Allah, the All-Mighty, the All-Powerful, the one with control over all things. The one who truly belongs to Allah's party can never be overcome by any of the disbelievers, no matter how strong they seem to be. [1 Cf Al-Shanqeeti, vol. 3, pp. 452–457.][37]

The domination of the *kafir* is a consequence of the loss of the true faith. Sheikh al-Hilali writes: 'When the Muslims neglected the obedience to Allaah, He gave the Jews the power and they took Palestine, and when they were negligent about that which they were reminded of, Allaah established the Christians over them and they took Spain; and when they were negligent yet again, Allaah

34. 'An Introduction to the Salafi Da'wah', <http://www.qss.org/articles/salafi/text.html>.
35. Anonymous article (which nevertheless quotes Sheikh al-Albani) entitled 'The True Understanding of Politics in Islaam (as-Siyaasah)', <http://www.allaahuakbar.net/scholars/halabee/true_understanding_of_politics.htm>.
36. Sheikh Saleem al-Hilaalee, 'The State of the Ummah in the Light of the Prophecies of the Prophet (saw)', speech delivered at the Qu'ran and Sunnah Society Conference in the United States in 1993. This speech is to be found on many websites, such as <http://www.al-manhaj.com/Page1.cfm?ArticleID=144>.
37. Jamaal ud-Deen Zarabozo, 'The Plight of the Muslim Nation Today', <http://members.cox.net/ameer1/plightm.html>.

put the Christians in control in Bosnia.'[38] This means that victory will be bestowed by God only upon 'good' Muslims; it is pointless to opt for *jihad* before returning to the true tenets of the faith. *Sharia* is thus more important than state (the contrary was true for Khomeini, for example). As al-Albani states in *A Refutation of Some of the Statements of Jamal ud-Din Zarabozo*: 'Establish Islam in your heart and it will, in turn, be established for you in your land.' The ideas of the Islamists are often portrayed as some sort of deviant religious thinking. Sheikh Muqbil blasts 'Suroorism', while Salafi publications denounce Bannaawism, Qutbism and Suroorism.[39]

Nevertheless, beyond this clear-cut condemnation of the Islamist agenda, relations between Islamists and neofundamentalists are ambivalent. Their analyses of the state of the *ummah* are not very different: the *ummah* is in a state of despair, and Islam is politically and culturally besieged by the West. The enemy is the West. They differ on how to respond, however. The neofundamentalists' answer is usually *dawah* (or *da'wat*), sometimes *jihad*, but never political action. The Islamists' answer is the 'Islamic state'.

The ambivalence of their relationship is reflected in the Wahhabi condemnation of Sayyid Qutb.[40] Paradoxically his books are found everywhere and mentioned on most neofundamentalist websites. He fascinates Islamists and certain neofundamentalists for different reasons. His political message of revolt and action appeals to radical Islamists, but his more pessimistic views on the modern world, his radical contempt and hatred for the West, and his mystical approach resonate more with neofundamentalists, who are obsessed by Hell and salvation.[41]

38. Hilaalee, 'The State of the Ummah'; see also <http://www.al-sunnah.com>, <http://www.geocities.com/Athens/Forum/1424/ummahprophs.html>, <http://www.ummah.net>, <http://groups.yahoo.com/group/jewstoislam/message/344>.
39. See <http://www.salafipublications.com>, which in 2004 contained thirty-three articles opposing Qutubis (Qutbists) and Suroorists.
40. Sheikh Uthaymeen (Othaymeen), for instance. See <http://www.allaahuakbar.net/jamaat-e-islaami/qutb/shaikh_muhammad_ibn_saalih_on_sayyid_qutb.htm>.
41. The 'Qutbist' movement, from Farag to Islambuli, is more similar to neofundamentalism, even if it has regularly been categorised as Islamist for its political involvement. However, neither the Qutbists nor Bin Laden ever cared to build a true political movement, and they never cared about the day after (for example, the assassination of Sadat, or 9/11). It is not by chance

Logically the condemnation of any sort of Islamic politics entails a more vocal rejection of non-Muslim politics. Most neofundamentalists vow to remain aloof from '*kafir*' politics. 'Ruling by Kufr is Haram', wrote Sheikh al-Masri (a Saudi Salafi who is close to Hizb ut-Tahrir). But such a radical rejection of political involvement does not necessarily mean open revolt. It may signify an apolitical position, a neutral and even indifferent attitude towards politics, which can also mean tactical accommodation (for example, Sheikh Muqbil in Yemen) or participation at the local level (in municipal affairs). Neofundamentalists agree not to endorse any Western political system, but debate whether interaction with such systems is permissible.[42] This ambivalence is, as we shall see, at the core of Western distrust of neofundamentalists. On the one hand, they express a rejection of the West that goes beyond that of the Islamists; on the other hand, they do not wage a political struggle and are open to accommodation.

But the dividing line between Islamists and neofundamentalists tends to be blurred by the individual paths of many Muslim Brothers, who have given up political activism, disheartened by the stalemate or even by the advanced age of their leaders (for example, in Egypt). Others adopted a neofundamentalist agenda mainly because that was where the momentum lay. The Taliban saga in Afghanistan had an impact on Pakistani politics, where the Jamaat-i-Islami (whose ideology was very close to that of the Muslim Brotherhood) jumped on to the neofundamentalist bandwagon by joining the Muttahida Majlis-e-Amal (MMA, a coalition of pro-Taliban movements). Having won the elections in the North-West

---

that the survivors of the Qutbist movement joined Bin Laden and not the Islamist movements.
42. See, for instance, the position of the Hizb ut-Tahrir as shown by 'The Ruling on Participating in Parliamentary Elections' (<http://www.islamic-state.org/leaflets/030425RulingOnParliamentaryElections.htm>), about Yemen, in which participation is allowed only if it is a means of finding a springboard for '*dawa'at*' (*dawah*). Omar Bakri and Abu Hamza (in London) both oppose participation in '*kufr* politics' and refuse to participate in British elections. A posting by 'truth1' on the 'Islam.com Discussion Forum' on Tuesday, 25 November 2003 (<http://www.islam.com/reply.asp?id=285378&ct=6&mn=285378>), expressed a rather common view:'For over 50 years there's been Hypocrite Muslims in the U.K. participating in the Kufr systems and what have they achieved, 2 MP's? There is not a single Muslim in the House of Representatives nor the Senate. What impact do you hope to achieve?'

Frontier Province in October 2002, the MMA has since been pushing for a purely neofundamentalist agenda – implementing *sharia*, banning television and films, and so on – but without bringing into question the central federal state. Some other Islamists turned neofundamentalist when their prospects of exercising state power faded because of political repression or the migration of militants to countries where Muslims are in a minority. Moreover, in the course of searching for jobs or political asylum they became internationalised and thus deprived of a specific national political environment (while the Turkish Islamists have maintained a local presence). Some are employed by neo-Salafi institutions, under the umbrella of the Rabita. The grandsons of Hassan al-Banna, Hani and Tariq Ramadan, are a good example of the diffusion of the Muslim Brotherhood to the diaspora. Born in Switzerland and citizens of that country, they express the two faces of modern Salafism: Hani is a neofundamentalist and Tariq seeks some sort of accommodation between a 'Muslim community' (defined by its culture and values) and a secular Western environment.

In any country social advancement and political empowerment can entail a shift from revolutionary Islam to a more conservative and neofundamentalist approach, as embodied by the conservatives in Iran.

While the Muslim Brotherhood may become Salafi, some neofundamentalists, conversely, may put an end to their 'splendid isolation' and engage in social activism, even if they are still reluctant to become involved in state politics. This is the case in France with members of the Tablighi Jama'at who consented to join the Conseil Français du Culte Musulman, while in Yemen dissidents aligned with Sheikh Muqbil also engaged in social activities.[43] The categories we are using in this book are not permanent labels to be stuck on people. One should not neglect personal trajectories: a former Islamist turned Salafi might adopt a more open and flexible Muslim identity. Labels do not give a fair account of the complexity of personal paths and histories.

Conversely, Muslim Brothers who have shunned the quest for an Islamic state do not necessarily become neofundamentalists. Many, like Sheikh al-Qaradawi, have become a kind of conservative liberal. By that I mean that they insist on ethical values more than

---

43. Burgat and Sbitli, 'Les Salafis au Yémen'.

on a strict adherence to *sharia*, reject violence and accept debate. Al-Qaradawi is not a neofundamentalist, although he has been read as such by many born-again Muslims through the widespread translations into Western languages of his book *Al-Halal wal-Haram fil Islam* (The Lawful and the Prohibited in Islam). Nevertheless, his recent more conciliatory approach towards the West (he issued a *fatwa* condemning the terror attacks on the World Trade Center) has antagonised many of his latter-day admirers. Negative critiques of al-Qaradawi's book are recurrent in Salafi sites and have increased since 9/11.[44] He is considered too liberal and permissive; his book became jokingly known as *Halal wal Halal* (The Lawful and the Lawful).[45] One should remember that the book was briefly banned in France in 1995 for being too radical.

This confusion between Salafis, moderate conservatives, Muslim Brothers and even some liberals is reflected in many of the websites of Muslim associations in the West, which might juxtapose Salafi lectures with advertisements and invitations concerning social events that are quite contrary to the Salafi approach. We touch here the complexity of the religious sphere that we have referred to under the appellation 'post-Islamism'. Let us take an example. The website of a local Muslim community in Canada, the Islamic Information Society of Calgary,[46] promotes 'karate for brothers and sisters', women's soccer (although indoors) and the sermons of Bin Baz and Othaymeen. One might guess that women's soccer would not be the sort of entertainment approved of for women in Medina. It may mean that the people who manage the different pages of the website simply do not follow the same philosophies, but apparently they get along with one another.

The blurring of the divide between Muslim Brothers, neofundamentalists and conservatives has political and strategic dimensions. How does one assess the threats or possibilities of finding stabilising

44. See different critiques from Sulaymân ibn Sâlih Al-Kharrâshî, Sheikh 'Abdul-Hamîd Tamhâz and Sheikh Othaymine, <http://www.sounnah.free.fr/sommaire_news.htm> (in French); Bin Laden is condemned too.
45. See <http://www.allaahuakbar.net/jamaat-e-islaami/qaradawism/reading_in_qaradawism.htm>. The site quotes Muqbil and Ibn Uthaymeen against al-Qaradawi. It is interesting to note that the Salafis tend to have the same habit as did the Soviets, labelling a 'deviation' with the name of the thinker (Suroorism, Qaradawism, Qutbism).
46. <http://www.iisc.ca>.

elements among conservative Muslims? What is the role of Saudi Arabia? The reciprocal instrumentalisation of Saudi Arabia and Muslim Brothers to counter Arab nationalism, communism and Iranian Islamism in the 1980s has in fact paved the way for more radical movements.

If we consider that most violent Islamist groups share some sort of neofundamentalist outlook, the issue of violence should be addressed.

NEOFUNDAMENTALISTS AND RADICAL VIOLENCE

The main divide between mainstream neofundamentalists and radical groups has to do with *jihad*: Is it compulsory? Is it an individual duty? Is it now time to engage in a *jihad* against the enemy? And who is the enemy? Of course the radicals all conclude that *jihad* is a permanent and personal religious duty and that 'the Crusaders and the Jews' are the enemy, as Bin Laden put it. On the other side of the coin, the Salafi mainstream *ulama* consider *jihad* a collective rather than an individual duty.[47] They also believe that even if there is *jihad*, there are rules of conduct during war that should be

47. '*Question*: Is jihaad in this time a collective or an individual obligation? What is the difference between the two and what are the conditions for them both? *Response*: Jihaad, primarily, is a collective obligation and, as such, if it is undertaken by sufficient enough people it is no longer obligatory upon the rest. For this reason the Prophet, (sal-Allaahu 'alayhe wa sallam) would fight jihaad himself and send out detachments and raiding parties while the rest of the Muslims would remain behind to take care of other affairs and needs. However, jihaad could become an individual obligation if the Imaam calls upon whoever is fit and suitable for it … The Prophet (sal-Allaahu 'alayhe wa sallam) said: "If you are called to go to fight, then answer the call." It also becomes an individual obligation if an enemy attacks any of the Muslim lands. It becomes an individual obligation on the Muslims to repel the enemy and save the country from them, as happened in Afghanistan. The third situation where it becomes an individual obligation is when a man is either amongst the ranks of the Muslims fighting the enemy or when the Muslims are lining up in preparation to fight the enemy. At this time he must not desert them or flee but rather, he must fight with his brothers and be steadfast. Other than in these situations, jihaad is Sunna and is one of the most virtuous of deeds. Indeed it is the best action that man can undertake because its virtue, over and above other deeds, has been mentioned in texts.' Sheikh Ibn Baaz, *al-Aqal-liyaat al-Muslimah* [The Muslim Minority], Fatwa 1, p. 24, cited at <http://www.fatwa-online.com/fataawa/muslimminorities/0000822_1.htm> ('The Obligation of Jihaad'). Grammar and punctuation are as per the original.

respected.[48] Sheikh al-Albani is clear on that topic: *jihad* might be an individual duty only for people belonging to a specific threatened group (Chechen, Afghans), but it needs a leader (*emir*) and an organisation. There is no question of asking individuals from all over the world to go to fight in some remote place:

> We said that jihad is two kinds: *fard kifayah*, which only a small group of Muslims can do, and if a group do it, the rest of the Muslims are not questioned about it. This kind of jihad, individuals can do on their own. *Fard 'ayn* which *all* the Muslims have to do it in a specific area. To do this kind of jihad, do we not need an Ameer to lead the Muslims?[49]

He went further, stressing the priority of *dawah* over *jihad*:

> History repeats itself. Everybody claims that the Prophet is their role model. Our Prophet (*salallaahu'alayheewasallam*) spent the first half of his message in making da'wa, and he started with it not with jihad. The Prophet (*salallaahu'alayheewasallam*) first raised his companions with Islamic education like he educated them to say the word of truth and not be afraid of it, he (*salallaahu'alayheewasallam*) also taught them the Islamic teachings. We know that our Islam today is not like it was when Allah revealed 'today I have completed your religion', many things have indeed been added to Islam, do you not agree?[50]

Jihad may have a pedagogic effect in purifying the soul, but it is not an aim in itself. The priority of *dawah* over *jihad* is the watershed between mainstream neofundamentalists and radical groups. Most of the Wahhabi *ulama*, the Tablighi Jama'at and even the Hizb ut-Tahrir consider that *jihad* is not on the agenda, except for defense.

On the other hand, many Wahhabi sheikhs openly supported radical groups that were at odds with the Saudi monarchy yet still benefited from official complacency. The sheikhs Awda and al-Hawali, although openly supportive of Bin Laden and the Taliban, have been defended by Grand Mufti Bin Baz.[51] They were

48. Al-Qaradawi and the new grand *mufti* of Saudi Arabia, Abdoul 'Aziz ibn 'Abdillah ibn Mohammed al-Sheikh, issued *fatwas* condemning the attack on the World Trade Center. The Islamic brigade of the Bosnian army had rules of engagement that clearly forbade attacks on monks and civilians, and mistreatment of prisoners. Conversely, the GIA and Bin Laden consider any targets legitimate.
49. Al-Albaanee, *Munatharah ma' tantheem al-jihad al-Islami*.
50. Al-Albaanee, *Munatharah ma' tantheem al-jihad al-Islami*.
51. 'Sheikh Abdel Aziz Bin Baz defends Salman and Safar.' See also Fandy, *Saudi Arabia and the Politics of Dissent*.

freed from gaol in Saudi Arabia in 1999. Al-Hawali adopted a more
moderate stand after 9/11. The sheikhs Hammoud bin 'Uqla al-
Shu'aybi (died January 2002), Saleh Bin Othaymeen (died 2001),
Nassir al-Buraq and Salih Ibn Fawzan al Fawzan also supported
the Taliban.[52] Shu'aybi's role came to light when the attack on a
Riyadh housing compound in May 2003 was attributed to some
of his disciples: Ali al-Khudair, in his fifties, Nasser al-Fahd, in
his forties, and Ahmad al-Khalidi, in his thirties, were drawn together by their belief in the ideas of Shu'aybi, who was based in
Buraydah, a town famous for its strict piety. But during his life
he spent only two weeks in gaol and two years under house arrest, although he regularly criticised the Saudi monarchy. Another
Wahhabi Sheikh Naser Bin Hamad Al-Fahad wrote a *fatwa* approving the use of weapons of mass destruction against the 'Kafer'
(*kafir*).[53] He went into hiding before the US attack on Iraq. An
anonymous Saudi who conducted a videotaped conversation with
Osama Bin Ladin mentioned that Sheikh Sulayman Ibn Nasir al-
'Ulwan had handed down a *fatwa* refusing to condemn the 9/11
terrorist attacks.[54] Although less well-known than the other Saudi sheikhs (al-Albani, Munajjid and Bin Baz), he is spoken of on
an equal footing with them in some Salafi–Wahhabi websites.[55]
In Yemen, Yahya al-Hajuri (a disciple of Sheikh Muqbil) also
wrote a *fatwa* in support of the Taliban, while strongly opposing
the 'Qutbists'.

The Hizb ut-Tahrir position against the launching of *jihad* is
purely tactical. The organisation believes that the time has not yet
come for *jihad*, but that it is a compulsory duty for any Muslim.

52. In a series of *fatwas* issued in September and October 2001, Sheikh Hammoud bin 'Uqla al-Shu'aybi, opposing the US campaign in Afghanistan, declares 'anybody who supports infidels against Muslims is himself an infidel'.
He previously stated that 'Afghanistan … is the *only* country in the world in
which there are no man-made laws and legislation' (so much for Saudi Arabia). 29 November 2000, 2d Ramadan, 1421 hijri. <http://www.geocities.
com/raehatu_almisk/taliban_fatawa.html>.
53. 'Resalat fi hukm estekhdâm al-eslahat al-damâr al-shamâl zed al kufâr' (rabi
al awal 1424), <http://www.al-fhd.com>. The domain name for this website
seems to be still registered, but it is currently not in use.
54. An English translation is available at <http://www.beliefnet.com/story/95/
story_9556_1.html>.
55. For example, <http://www.al-islaam.de/hp/Frage___Antwort/frage___ant-
wort.html>. See also <http://www.jimas.org/books.htm>.

Thus the choice of whether to use or reject violence is not linked with the basic tenets of neofundamentalism. It is a political decision, formulated (after the decision to use lethal action has been made) in religious terms, which could even be considered as *bid'a*, or innovation (the perception of *jihad* as *fard*, or individual duty, is typically a *bid'a*). There is not necessarily a 'theology of violence'. When *ulama* take a position on violence, it is usually for political reasons, even if they cast their choice in terms of a religious discourse. *Ulama* from the same school of thought may take divergent positions on violence.

We have seen how mainstream Salafis reject the ideas of Sayyid Qutb.[56] But others who are strongly opposed to 'Qutbism' for religious reasons nevertheless support *jihad*, terrorism and Al Qaeda for purely political reasons (hatred of the West). In short, there is no systematic link between a radical political position and theological thinking. This is particularly obvious among the Saudi Wahhabis, of whom some will hold very radical positions even though their religious thinking differs not at all from that of their more moderate colleagues. Moreover, even in case of strong political disagreements, the corporate solidarity and *esprit de corps* of the *ulama* maintain ties and protection. The ambivalence of the Saudi establishment has probably been the most puzzling discovery by the US administration following 9/11.

WHY IS NEOFUNDAMENTALISM SUCCESSFUL?

The spread of neofundamentalist influence raises many important questions. How can such a narrow and unsophisticated vision take root among modern educated Muslims? How can it spread among quite different sociological milieus, from Taliban Pashtun tribesmen to the wealthy Saudi Arabian middle class, moving through impoverished suburbs of Western Europe or Morocco while reaching a supranational intelligentsia and even converts? What explains the plasticity of the neofundamentalist matrix?

56. See, among many other texts, 'Abu A'laa Mawdudi, Qutb and the Prophets of Allaah' (<http://www.salafipublications.com/sps/downloads/pdf/NDV080001.pdf>), which attacks Sayyid Qutb and Muhammad Suroor. Official Wahhabis are eager to draw a clear-cut line along religious grounds between radicals and moderates.

A tool of deculturation

Neofundamentalism is both a product and an agent of globalisation, first of all because it embodies in itself an explicit process of deculturation. It rejects the very concept of culture, whether conceived of as arts and intellectual productions or as an integrated system of socially acquired values, beliefs and rules of conduct, as defined by anthropology. It looks at globalisation as a good opportunity to rebuild the Muslim *ummah* on a purely religious basis, not in the sense that religion is separated from culture and politics, but to the extent religion discards and even ignores other fields of symbolic practices. Neofundamentalism promotes the decontextualisation of religious practices. In this sense it is perfectly adapted to a basic dimension of contemporary globalisation: that of turning human behaviour into codes, and patterns of consumption and communication, delinked from any specific culture.[57]

An ongoing debate among neofundamentalists concerns culture: beyond faith, how to define a purely religious system of behaviour and norms, decoupled from any surrounding culture. Culture is either redundant or misleading, and has no value in itself. It is at best obscuring and at worst distorting the true tenets of Islam.

The rejection of 'cultural Islam' – appraising deculturation. The primary targets of the neofundamentalists are the so-called Muslim cultures; Western culture is a secondary objective. However, the West is not rejected in favour of any sort of 'Islamic culture'.

---

57. For many globalisation means westernisation; for others it means Americanisation (a typical view in France, where McDonald's is considered to epitomise US culture). In both cases the globalisation process is seen as acculturation; that is, the adopting of a new culture (Western or US culture). But I believe that what circulates under the name of US or Western culture is less a specific culture, with a content (art, literature), than a form comprising codes and products of consumption. The English language, which has become the world medium of communication, is not the vector of *the* English culture (Shakespeare *et al.*), but a tool of communication that could convey different systems of representations. The debate on multiculturalism in the West is rarely a debate on languages, at least from the side of English-speakers, for whom diversity is expressed in English. Many British and US liberals or multiculturalists are, for instance, very critical towards the way Québécois or the French try to preserve their languages. But the same people will, at the same time, condemn the French refusal to allow schoolgirls to wear the Islamic *hijab* (which is seen as a rejection of multiculturalism).

Neofundamentalists consider Islam not as a form of culture but as a 'mere' religion that loses its purity and holistic dimension if embedded in a specific culture. Islam, as preached by the Taliban, Wahhabis and Bin Laden's radicals, is hostile even to cultures that are Muslim in origin. Whatever such fundamentalism has destroyed – Muhammad's tomb, the Bamiyan statues of the Buddha or the World Trade Center – it expresses the same rejection of material civilisation and culture.

Neofundamentalists dream of a *tabula rasa*.[58] They do not value the classical great Muslim civilisations such as the Umayyad or the Ottoman Empire. They also reject the different religious schools as well as Sufism, which have been so instrumental in the 'nativisation' of Islam. How can we study Yemen without considering the rift between Zaydism and Shafism, or Central Asia without taking into account the role of Hanafism and Sufism? Neofundamentalists reject local Islams (such as the Egyptian and the Moroccan) and wage a relentless war on folk customs and even learned traditions, religious or secular. For instance, they oppose any cult of the 'saints' (*zyarat* in Central Asia and *moussem* in North Africa, a religious pilgrimage in which people come to pray to the local patron saint), and even the celebration of the Prophet's birthday (Al-Mawlid).[59] They reject Sufism and mystical practices (*zikr*), and any form of artistic performance associated with a religious practice (*qawwali* music in Pakistan, for example), with some exceptions such as religious songs unaccompanied by musical instruments.[60] They reject

58. 'Islam is a religion. But, to many Malays, Islam is a culture. It is a practice handed down by their fathers, and their father's father before that. It is something they do out of habit rather than out of the education they have received. That is why the converts or the "Born Again Muslims", if I may be permitted to use this phrase, make better Muslims.

    'Converts learn the religion from scratch and throw away their old beliefs on becoming Muslims. The Born Again Muslims re-learn the religion and are able to differentiate between Islam and the Malay Adat, and are brave enough to reject what is unIslamic though they run the risk of being branded fanatics.' Anonymous article ('Ethnic Culture versus Islam') cited on <http://www.themodernreligion.com/ugly/culture.html>.

59. See Imaam 'Abdul-'Azeez bin Baaz, *Fataawaa al-Islaamiyyah*, vol. 1, n.p., n.d., pp. 131–2), cited on <http://www.al-manhaj.com/Page1.cfm?ArticleID=131> ('Ruling on Celebrating the Prophet's Birthday'). Illustrations of the different statements made in this paragraph could be found on the websites mentioned in n. 19, p. 241, of this chapter.

60. On worshipping at graves and playing music, see Shaykh Munajjid (<http://

specific burial rituals.[61] Quite evidently they also forbid participation in pagan or secular celebrations. For example, the popular Persian Nowruz festival (21 April) was banned by the Taliban,
and the Saudi Council of Fatwa ruled against a traditional festival
(*Grayqaan* or *Quraiqa'an*), in which children from the Gulf coast
used to knock on doors and collect treats.[62]

The Taliban went very far in their struggle against traditional
Afghan culture. As is the practice of all neofundamentalists, they
first targeted 'bad Muslims', while Western culture came only second. They had quite good relations with the United States till the
autumn of 1997 and did not bother to expel Western NGOs, later
turning anti-US for purely political reasons. Instead they took
a hard line on Afghan customs and culture. They banned music,
films, dancing and kite-flying (because someone climbing a tree
to remove a kite might end up watching, even inadvertently, an
unveiled women in an adjacent house or garden). Pet songbirds
were outlawed because they might nullify a believer's prayer by

---

www.islam-qa.com/Books/Muharamaat/english.shtml#3>). In Iraqi Kurdistan the group Ansar al-Islam desecrated the graves of Sheikh Husam al-Din,
Sheikh Baha al-Din, and Sheikh Siraj al-Din, known guides of the Naqshbandi order, in July 2002. The head of the group, Mullah Krekar, is a permanent resident of Norway (another good example of the relationship between
neofundamentalism and globalisation).

61. Among others the Pakistani customs of *qul, chehlum, khatm-i Koran* (recitation
of the Koran at certain periods after a person's death) are rejected as non-
Muslim ('But rites like "Qul" and "Chehlum" are all of Hindu origin to
which the ignorant Muslims have taken a fancy. Similarly, Qur'an reading
meant to transmit reward to a dead man's soul is against the Prophet's example.' Nawawi, Imam, *Gardens of the Righteous: The Riyadh as-Salihin of Imam Nawawi*, trans. by Muhammad Zafrulla Khan, 2nd edn, New York: Olive Branch
Press, 1989, Chapter 162.) In his will, Muhammad Atta asked not to be buried 'according Egyptian customs' (that is, followed by third- and fortieth-day
commemorations), 'because it has no basis in the Qoran and the Sunnah'.
62. Fatwa 15532, 24/11/1413 AH (1993). The council considered this to be a
Shia celebration (even if Sunnis also participate). Why forbid such a custom
in the 1990s? Maybe because it is too similar to Halloween, the spread of
which is another sign of globalisation? It is interesting to note that the Islamic regime in Iran never banned traditional culture, or *nowruz*, even if it
demoted such culture in favour of religious ceremonies. After some debate
Ferdowsi Street in Tehran was not renamed. Ferdowsi, or Firdausi, was a classical tenth-century Persian poet, who wrote the *Shahnama* (Book of Kings),
in which there is no reference to Islam. In general, all Islamists acknowledge
the concept of culture, although they stress its religious dimension.

distracting him. Moreover the Taliban destroyed the statues of the Buddhas, not in opposition to Buddhism *per se*, but (apart from Islam forbidding representation of the human form) because these statues were not linked with any current religion in Afghanistan. Even if such statues had no religious meaning, or a negative religious meaning, they would still have had to be destroyed. For the Taliban religion must have the monopoly of the symbolic sphere. Life should be entirely devoted to preparing oneself for the hereafter, and this can be done only through abiding by a strict code of conduct and ritual.

This onslaught on traditional culture also touches social structures. Neofundamentalists attack traditional and accepted social stratification, even if it has some sort of religious legitimacy. In Yemen the Salafis decry the privileged status of the *sayyid* (the descendants of the Prophet).[63] In Senegal local Wahhabis (young Saudi-educated *taliban*) oppose the brotherhoods (Muridiyya, Tijaniyya, Layen) that play a pivotal role in Senegal's society and politics. Fighting Sufism is a common concern for neofundamentalists (even if many brotherhoods are quite fundamentalist). This goes beyond refuting the mystical and allegorical approach of Islam; the social dimension of Sufism is also under attack. A researcher studying the Nigerian Izala (a neofundamentalist group), which targets the Sufi brotherhoods, perceptively points out that 'the shift from Sufism to anti-Sufism entails a re-orientation of a communal to an individualistic mode of religiosity and seems to be more in tune with the rugged individualism of capitalist social relations'.[64]

In this sense the Salafis strike at the anthropological dimension of culture: the symbolic system under which bonds of human social relations are expressed and transmitted. The Taliban undermined the legitimacy of traditional tribal elders and of *ulama* (many *ulama* were older and more knowledgeable than Mullah Omar, who was not from a big tribal family) and explicitly rejected customary tribal law (*pashtunwali*).[65] In Pakistan, as well as in northern

63. Shelagh Weir, 'A Clash of Fundamentalism: Wahhabism in Yemen', *Middle East Report*, 215 (2000).
64. Mohammad Sani Umar, 'From Sufism to Anti-Sufism in Nigeria' in L. Brenner (ed.), *Muslim Identity and Social Change in Sub-Saharan Africa*, London: Hurst, 1993.
65. 'Supreme Leader of Afghan Taliban movement Mullah Muhammad Omar has outlawed forced marriage of women and the offering of a female as

Nigeria, local Salafis vow to replace state law and customary law with *sharia*. This onslaught on tradition goes hand in hand with the emergence of a new leadership and often with the recasting of traditional solidarity groups (clans) into more ideologically motivated groups: leaders and notables, as well as newcomers and competitors, recast their struggle using current political idiom.[66] Many fellow travellers of the neofundamentalists are motivated by social and economic strategies as well as by the fear of damnation – politics makes a comeback, even if this is not acknowledged as such by the protagonists.

Neofundamentalists do not articulate an antimodernist reaction from among traditional sectors of society. They are actors of deculturation and change inside traditional societies. Neofundamentalism contributes to the collapse (or the adaptation) of traditional societies and paves the way for other forms of westernisation and globalisation, including in the economic sphere. But it also appeals to uprooted people.

This deculturation is all the more effective when traditional societies have already been destabilised by different processes of modernisation such as migration, the free market and education. Neofundamentalists use deculturation as a tool for propaganda, while other *ulama* are confounded by it. Traditional fundamentalist *ulama* have been the bearers of 'traditional Muslim cultures', as is obvious in Central and South Asia. Sunni *ulama* in Central Asia (Afghanistan and Bukhara), where almost no secular culture existed till the 1920s, used to transmit the tenets of Islam and of a

---

compensation in a blood feud, officials said Saturday. A decree banning the two traditional practices in the Afghan society was issued Friday, they said. Omar ruled that no family shall force the widow of one of its male members to marry another member of the same family against her will. The decree also forbids the practice of offering a woman to the heir of a murder victim as blood-money or compensation.' (Agence France Presse (AFP), 12 September 1998.) The last-mentioned custom was a traditional way to settle blood feuds. Forbidding it means that one has to look for another code of law, which, given the Taliban's policy, could not be state law (*qanun*) but only *sharia*.

66. Olivier Roy, 'Groupes de solidarités au Moyen-Orient et en Asie centrale. Etats, territoires et réseaux', *Les Cahiers du CERI*, 16 (1996); Patrick Haenni, 'Banlieues indociles? Sur la politisation des quartiers péri-urbains du Caire', PhD dissertation, Institut d'études politique (IEP), Paris, 2001. I also benefited from the unpublished research of Selma Bellal (Université Libre de Bruxelles) on the GIA in Algeria.

traditional Persian culture.[67] Such traditional Muslim cultures were able to bypass ethnic and linguistic identities in favour of a universal civilisation, even if it was 'regional'. Neither Persian nor Urdu was seen as an 'ethnic' language before the appearance of modern nation-states. In the course of decolonisation, South Asian *ulama* shifted from Persian to Urdu, which is nowadays identified with the Muslim culture of the Indian subcontinent; these *ulama* have been instrumental in defining and spreading Urdu and the culture associated with it, a culture that has never been exclusively religious. These kinds of traditional fundamentalists had no problem with the concept of culture. They experienced religious reformism in the framework of a specific culture that they use as a tool for proselytising and education, and for bypassing local ethnic or linguistic divides. Later, in the wake of labour migration, when such *mullahs* travelled from their South Asian *madrasas* to Britain, they were still identifying the fight to preserve a Muslim identity with the use of Urdu and the preservation of their pristine culture. But these traditional *ulama*, to whatever category of fundamentalism they might belong, are now on the defensive. As we saw in Chapter 3, in the passage to the West traditional Muslim cultures ceased to represent a universal civilisation and turned into merely 'ethnic' cultures.[68] Traditional fundamentalists are at a loss how to deal with deculturation, while neofundamentalists consider this deculturation as an almost positive factor that permits the decontextualisation of Islam.

Interestingly, neofundamentalists are consequently very critical of attempts to define a 'Muslim minority' in the West in cultural terms. They reject the neo-ethnic model (which states that Muslims in the West should be considered an ethnic group with a specific culture, whatever the diversity of their origins), because 'culture' is for them redundant – it is either irrelevant or part of the religion. An incident illustrates this stand. In 1988 the Bradford

---

67. As mentioned in n. 33, Chapter 3, popular books like the *Chahar Kitab* are a typical mixture of theology, literature, cosmogony, Sufism and poetry.
68. In the Chinese province of Xinjiang, Uighur restaurants during the 1980s advertised 'national cuisine' (*milli ash*), which meant the food was halal: religious meaning superseded ethnic identity. (It seems from my personal observations that such restaurants now simply advertise themselves as 'halal'.) But in New York such an Uighur restaurant would be first of all a 'Uighur' ethnic restaurant, halal or not. Immigration dissociates ethnicity and religion.

Council of Mosques opposed the performance of *bhangra* music in schools. This music is a creation of young 'Asian' bands mixing Punjabi and Western rhythms, some of which explicitly assert a 'Muslim' identity (the group called Fun-da-mental claims to be Islamic), but the Council of Mosques considered that what they were doing was simply not Islamic at all.[69] In France Islamic militants reject *rai* (a hybrid of North African musical styles) as immoral, but sometimes resort to rap music to spread the message among the young. *Banghra, rai* and rap all express a Western youth subculture and a creolisation of musical traditions. In this sense they combine to express a reconstructed westernised protest of Muslim identity.[70] Neofundamentalists conversely cannot accept this recasting of Muslim identity into cultural terms. For them the only themes that can define such a community are purely religious and they should not be borrowed either from Western or pristine identities. By contrast modern youth culture is a combination of both. Neofundamentalism rejects subcultures that are a by-product of acculturation, creolisation and recasting of cultural elements taken from pristine cultures into the dominant culture, even if these subcultures use the term Muslim.

Neofundamentalists push for the use either of the language of the host country (generally English) or of Arabic, but not of pristine languages. In Moscow during the *perestroika* era the *imams* of the two recognised mosques, who were Tatars, decided to use the Tatar language instead of Russian, but met with the opposition of their non-Tatar congregations (Caucasians and Central Asians), who campaigned for the use of Russian, the only language they had in common.

Neofundamentalists therefore are not interested in creating or asserting a 'Muslim' culture. They reject the concept, even if they sometimes use the term to find a common language with Western

---

69. Philip Lewis, *Islamic Britain: Religion, Politics and Identity among British Muslims*, London: I.B. Tauris, 1994, pp. 180–1.
70. A radical rap song called 'Dirty Kuffar' appeared on a website run by Saudi dissident Muhammad al-Massari (Antony Barnett, 'Islamic rappers' message of terror', *Observer*, 8 February 2004). In France a rap CD released in 2003, entitled *La conception*, is marketed by publishing house Tawhid (in Lyon) with the comment: 'La conception est un CD de RAP dont les paroles sont empreintes d'une éthique musulmane' (*La conception* is a rap CD whose words are impregnated with a Muslim ethic).

societies, where the language of multiculturalism is the main idiom through which we deal with otherness. Conspicuous by their absence are neofundamentalist novelists, poets, musicians, filmmakers or comedians. By stressing the gap between culture and religion, by striving to establish a pure religion, separated from secular and lay elements, neofundamentalists contribute to the paradoxical secularisation of modern society, because they isolate religion from the other dimensions of social life that they would like to, but cannot, ignore or destroy.

From culture to code, from collective identity to individual worship.   How do neofundamentalists conceive of religion? As we have seen they insist on *sharia, fiqh,* Hadith and *ibadat* (rituals of worship). For them religion is above all a strict code of explicit and objective norms of conduct, the respect for which is a prerequisite for salvation. Neofundamentalists produce many books, websites and videos explaining what should be done and what is forbidden, as well as collections of *fatwas* issued to adjust the code to new situations arising from living in non-Muslim societies. There is thus a strong link between the collapse of the social authority of norms and the obsession with such norms. Such a need for a permanent elaboration of norms governing every field of activity arises from the fact that they are no longer internalised as cultural patterns, but have to be defined as explicit and external rules about how we should act, think and feel – such norms are no longer 'natural' or obvious. We have seen how the passage of Islam to the West entails a need to 'objectify' Islam, to redefine and reconstruct it in explicit terms. Neofundamentalism presents a clear answer to this challenge. The objectification of religion is often embodied in the believer's body, while the personage of the Prophet provides a timeless model of behaviour. The Taliban, as we know, enforced a strict code of mimetic dressing and behaviour (physical imitation of the Prophet); for them religion is reduced to a code of rituals and of 'dos' and 'don'ts'. Norms aim to sanctify everyday life. All gestures or actions, including the most mundane, have to be made under a specific norm and experienced as devotion (for example, by uttering prayers or *sura*).

Norms have always been an issue in Islam, but because they are no longer embedded in a given everyday culture, in customs and social authority, every action, every move and item of social conduct has to be thought upon and elaborated: 'Living in a non-Muslim society, Muslims have to be careful of every step they take. They must be conscious of what they are doing at all times.'[71] How should one wake in the morning, dress, eat, sit, walk, speak to another person, and so on? Sheikh al-Albani wrote extensively on the obligation to wear a beard and the sort of beard it should be.[72] Among the documents left by the 9/11 hijackers was a small guidebook giving precise instructions about which prayer or *sura* to utter at every step of the mission (embarking on a plan, going to sleep). Tablighi Jama'at published an almost obsessive list of gestures, deeds and sentences. It lists, for instance, twenty-six norms on the etiquette of eating and drinking: 'Always use three fingers when eating … always drink water while sitting with the right hand and in three pauses.'[73] The book *Riyadh as-Salihin* is full of such recommendations (see Chapter 3, called 'The Book about the Etiquette of Eating'). Thus there is an expanding process of *fatwa* production: when social norms are no longer the product of a given culture, every step and action of daily life has to be elaborated under an explicitly formulated norm.

Interestingly, this has some impact on the status of women, which in traditional Muslim societies is usually seen as low due to the combination of a patriarchal structure and legal Islamic norms. But as every anthropologist knows, there is always a gap, some leeway between avowed norms and real practices. Women are transmitters of traditions and actors who can strive to bend these traditions and deploy a strategy of reappropriation, especially when the transmission is oral and thus not in the hands of an all-male corporation of the learned.[74] Tradition maintains a space of ambiguity. Conversely the establishment of a univocal system of explicit norms reduces

71. Fazeela Hanif, 'Being A Muslim in Great Britain', Moon Research Centre (UK), was published on <http://www.mrc.org.uk> (hard copy in possession of author).
72. The Web page <http://www.uh.edu/campus/msa/articles/tape_.html #face> (Muslim Students' Association, University of Houston) is full of such explanations.
73. The text is called *Six Points of Tabligh*, and the chapter concerned is 'Desired Manners of Eating and Drinking', apparently written by Maulana Mohammad Ilyas, the founder of the movement. It has appeared on different websites, such as <http://www.almadinah.org> (now closed) and <http://www.noornet.com/tabligh/Booksix.htm>.
74. Eva Rosander, 'Introduction: The Islamization of Tradition and Modernity'

the autonomy of actors in favour of compulsory and standardised attitudes. The Taliban deprived Afghan women of the small space of autonomy provided by traditional society. But born-again Muslim women, as well as women who fall under a neofundamentalist-imposed social order, have to reconstruct and recompose their way of being a woman by dealing with strict regulations. A woman's body is reshaped by norms. The dress issue becomes central in modernised societies, while traditional ones offer some compromise between norms and customs.

This is a good indicator of how neofundamentalism is a tool for the foundation of an artificial social order that deliberately ignores the gap between explicit rules and practical conduct. Any action has to be explained and elaborated. Discourse precedes action. The logic of neofundamentalism is embodied in the question it addresses to nominal Muslims (a common technique when a Tablighi team knocks at the door of an 'ordinary' Muslim): 'Is your behaviour coherent with your faith?' And the answer is by definition negative: no human behaviour can be reduced to explicit norms. The guilt that goes with that acknowledgement, coupled with the constant reminders of Hell and salvation, is a strong inducement to turn one's mind to *haram* and halal.

What is reconstructed here is not only religion: it is the self itself, in some sort of permanent representation and staging of the self. Believers (and especially converts and born-again Muslims) act in such a way as to stage their own faith: a sort of 'exhibitionism' is often manifested among many neofundamentalists, who use deliberate markers of their own religious identity (specific dress and also terms, usually Arabic ones, frequently occur in their speech – brother, *jazakallah*, *bismillah*, and so on). This stress on the individual and interest in the self is quite modern. Many non-Muslim sects (such as Hare Krishna) transform individuals into actors who perform their faith using the street as a stage. The individual has to be 'constructed'. This construction is based on a set of markers with little content but with high differentiation value (from beards to toothbrushes).

Because it addresses individuals in search of the self, neofundamentalism has a strong appeal for disfranchised youths. It gives sense

in David Westerlund and Eva Evers Rosander (eds), *African Islam and Islam in Africa: Encounters between Sufis and Islamists*, London: Hurst, 1997, p. 7.

to generational conflict: by discarding the religion of the elders as 'cultural' Islam, it valorises the quest of youth for autonomy (and even rupture) *vis-à-vis* their parents and family (as we shall see, many Al Qaeda militants split from their Muslim families.) To be a *talib* (that is, a student) and not an *alim* (a learned scholar) is seen as positive, as shown by the denomination retained by the Taliban. The social and generational dimensions of neofundamentalism should never be underestimated.

By freeing the believer from the bonds of pristine societies, families, tribes, social status and ethnic solidarities, but also from the bonds of brotherhoods, religious institutions and traditions, neofundamentalism favours individualism, or more precisely it sacralises the experience of individualisation. By appealing to youths over the heads of their parents, by ignoring *ulama* in favour of a direct approach to the texts, and by encouraging a personal return to the true tenets of Islam, neofundamentalists contribute to the promotion of the individual as opposed to any sort of group or hierarchy. The individual who has severed his links with any previous social group is prized. Nevertheless, it does not reject the idea of community or *ummah*: such a community has to be reconstructed, starting with individuals.

Neofundamentalists, contrary to Islamists, are not concerned with social issues, because they care only about individuals and not existing societies. As one scholar puts it,

The exclusive focus of the Tablighi Jama'at is individual. It has been assumed that an individual can sustain his/her moral character even in a hostile social environment. It is on the basis of this assumption that the Jama'at does not seem to have concerned itself with issues of social significance and has not addressed itself to the problems of reforming political and social institutions while transforming individuals.[75]

This stress on the individual and indifference towards social issues is to be found in most Christian neofundamentalist revivalist denominations (the Universal Church in Brazil, for instance, as well as the Christian Right in the United States).

Neofundamentalists strive to construct, from a collection of individual born-again Muslims, a true *ummah* – that is, a homogeneous

---

75. Mumtaz Ahmad, 'Great Movements of the 20th Century No. 3: The Tablighi Jama'at', <http://www.icna.org/tm/greatmovement3.htm>.

community of equals, delinked from their natural milieu and devoted to the sole aim of practising a true Islam. Such a constructivist approach to the concept of a religious community recurs among
new forms of religious revival everywhere.[76] The new community
is based on a personal, individual and voluntary adherence, not on
an inherited cultural legacy. The weakness and the strength of such
communities is that they do not exist outside free and personal
choices. Norms and transgression are two sides of the same coin:
how does one enforce the norm if there is no external authority?
Implementation of norms is in everyone's hands. Fanaticism is one
of the consequences of being insecure about the limits of the community. Disillusionment with political instances of religious control
has caused the responsibility for keeping the true path and maintaining the integrity of the community to be devolved to all of that
community's members. Hence the permanent display of normative
attitudes. Telling others what is right and wrong (*amr bilma'aruf* ...)
is not new, but it has suddenly become a permanent and individual
duty, because there are no longer any obvious social rules. Living
in the West compels Muslims, as we have said, to reiterate norms
and to impose them upon every detail of daily life. Mention of
damnation and Hell is also a way to enforce rules upon individuals
who are not under social pressure. Insistence on salvation is also a
consequence of the individualisation of religious discourse.

The audience.   Neofundamentalism does not target communities
with ties to a culture of origin but is aimed at individuals who have
doubts about their faith and identity. In the West it appeals to an
uprooted, often young and well-educated but frustrated and already
disgruntled youth. For such uprooted individuals, fundamentalism
offers a system for regulating behaviour that can fit any situation,
from Afghan deserts to US college campuses. No wonder neofundamentalism attracts the losers from deculturation. But 'loser'
should not be understood in purely socioeconomic terms: it is not a
matter of poverty but of self-identity. Neofundamentalism has even
made a breakthrough among an educated middle class that is not
revolutionary and is looking for respectability while experiencing

76. About French Christians: 'such communal aspirations thrive on the very
    ground of individualism'. Danièle Hervieu-Léger, *La religion pour mémoire*,
    Paris: Éditions du Cerf, 1993.

some form of acculturation. In Egypt and Pakistan, for example, neofundamentalism reaches many workers returning from the Gulf states.[77] They engage in grassroots activities where charities, business and social advancement are heavily intertwined with what could be called a parallel Islamic economic sector.[78] In Europe neofundamentalism attracts second-generation Muslims who have broken with the pristine culture of their parents but do not feel integrated into Western society, although they have mastered its languages and consumption habits. Neofundamentalism also suits Muslim university students and school dropouts, and sometimes former drug addicts, who find in it discipline and a new community. It also attracts young converts. Gaol is a recruiting ground because it entails isolation, loneliness and a severance of social ties that favours self-reflection. The breakthrough of neofundamentalism (the Salafi or Wahhabi version) in tribal societies is also striking (for example, in northern Nigeria and northern Yemen, and among Afghan and Pakistani Pashtuns), as we shall see later.

In this sense neofundamentalism is unwittingly working to adapt Islam to modern models of individualisation and the free market, as did the US brand of Protestant fundamentalism.

Neofundamentalism as a product and a tool of globalisation.   Neofundamentalism valorises the uprootedness of uprooted people. By pretending to ignore the cultural context and by providing a code of conduct that functions in a similar manner in any part of the world, it is a perfect tool of globalisation. It works along the same lines as globalisation – individualisation, deculturation and deterritorialisation – and promotes a reconstructed identity based on the homogenisation of patterns of conduct.

Religion, conceived of as a decontextualised set of norms, can be adapted to any society, precisely because it has severed its links with a given culture and allows people to live in a sort of virtual, deterritorialised community that includes any believer. The religious

77. Mariam Abou Zahab and Olivier Roy, *Islamic Networks: The Pakistan-Afghan Connection*, London: Hurst, 2003; Malika Zeghal, *Gardiens de L'Islam. Les oulemas d'Al Azhar dans l'Egypte contemporaine*, Paris: Presses de Science Po, 1996; Muhammad Qasim Zaman, *The Ulama in Contemporary Islam: Custodians of Change*, Princeton University Press, 2002, p. 148.
78. Haenni, 'Banlieues indociles?'; Fariba Adelkhah, *Being Modern in Iran*, London: Hurst, 1999.

community is decoupled from real societies and, in this sense neo-fundamentalism acknowledges the secularisation that affects them. It nevertheless maintains the usual fundamentalist claims that in Islam there is no separation between religion and state, and that Islam is an all-encompassing religion. But it does that simply by ignoring the real world and building an abstract community where it is for the individual to experience, in his or her self, a totality that no longer exists. Wherever the true believer is, he remains in touch with the virtual community by sharing the same portable kit of norms, adaptable to any social context. The internet is also a perfect paradigm and tool of this virtual community. Halal is not linked, for instance, to a specific cuisine and can be considered a part of the new global cuisine.

Food versus cuisine[79] is a good example of the opposition between code and culture. Neofundamentalists care nothing for cuisine. Anything that is halal is good, whatever the basic ingredients and the recipe. When they open a restaurant it never promotes Ottoman or Moroccan cuisine, but halal food, and more often than not will simply offer the usual Western fast-food products. Similarly, halal dress can be based on Western raincoats, gloves, fashionable scarves (*cha-Dior*, as the Iranians joke), and so on. Halal is thus a code that is adaptable to any culture. Objects cease to have a history and to be culturally meaningful; once chosen they meet a normative requirement and do not refer to a specific culture. Such a view probably creates the great divide between neofundamentalists and European opponents of the US 'cultural' hegemony (the *alter-mondialiste* movement of José Bové in France, for instance). For the neofundamentalist the hamburger is seen as culturally neutral as long as it is made along the lines of a religious norm (halal).[80] By the same token a successful Muslim businessman in France launched in 2003 a soft drink called Mecca-Cola, whose foremost quality is that it looks almost exactly like Coca-Cola, except that

79. Warning and reminder: the author of this book is French.
80. On the request of Muslim organisations to be included in a protocol of agreement with McDonald's, see <http://www.soundvision.com/info/mcdonalds/>. On the protest from the radical sector against IFANCA (Islamic Food and Nutrition Council of America) for allegedly declaring McDonald's halal, see 'IFANCA Puts Label of "Halal" on McDonalds Exports to Muslim World', *New Trend Magazine*, 21 September 2003 (<http://www.newtrendmag.org>).

the marketing appeals explicitly to Islamic values (and is aimed at supporting the Palestinians).[81]

Modern food is a matter of code, not culture. In the United States today sushi can be served with pasta, and 'Asian cuisine' combines Chinese, Vietnamese, Japanese and Thai elements. Islamisation of the global cuisine simply means using halal food, just as 'health food' is based more on the selection of ingredients than on the invention of new recipes.[82]

But at the same time, precisely because it is based on a reconstruction, neofundamentalism has to borrow the different elements it uses to rebuild the body and the daily life of a true Muslim, either from an imagined tradition (for example, the turban, or the Pakistani *salwar* and *kameez*, whose origin had more to do with the Roman *camisa*) or from Western sources (raincoat and gloves for women). In this sense neofundamentalism accords with the modern makeshift cultural patchwork where 'the social life of things'[83] depends only on the meaning bestowed on them by consumers/ actors. The religious market is part of the global market.

Deterritorialisation: the end of Dar-ul-Islam

Neofundamentalism refers to an imaginary *ummah*, beyond ethnicity, race, language and culture, on that is no longer embedded in a specific territory. Geography is as irrelevant as history. Nowhere is there a country where state and society are ruled only by the true precepts of Islam. The failure of political Islam has also alienated many neofundamentalists from the political scene in the Middle

81. It is interesting that one of the few attacks from Islamic militants against McDonald's came not from neofundamentalists, but from Islamists, who still retain the concept of national heritage. Qazi Husseyn Ahmed, leader of the Pakistani Jamaat-i-Islami, said in a speech: 'We will boycott them, the Pepsi and Coca Cola, and McDonald burger. This is forbidden – the Kentucky chicken and the McDonald burger is forbidden for the Muslims. There are people present here who can make such foods which are better than this McDonald burger and Kentucky chicken. Why should we allow from abroad these things?', Voice of America, 25 October 1998.

82. See M. Ariff, I. Azad, A. Benkhelifa and N. Driscoll, *Authentic Etiquette of Eating and Hosting from the Qur'aan and Sunnah with 150 Recipes from around the World*, Path to Knowledge Publishing, 1999.

83. As defined by Arjun Appadurai in his book *The Social Life of Things: Commodities in Cultural Perspective* (Cambridge University Press, 1988).

East. Afghanistan under the Taliban was briefly seen as a model, but the fall of the regime and, in the aftermath of 9/11, the US military pressure on any would-be 'Islamic liberated territory' have dashed any hopes of equating a given country with Islam. In this sense the 'war against terror' has accentuated the deterritorialisation of Islam. As we have seen, many neofundamentalists consider that true Muslims are living as a minority everywhere, in Muslim or in non–Muslim countries, erasing the concept of a physical frontier between the two worlds. Abu Hamza, a veteran of Afghanistan and *imam* of one the most hard-line mosques in London, put the matter bluntly, as we saw in Chapter 4 (page 158). There is no promised land. More precisely the whole earth is the virtual land of the *um-mah*. Meanwhile, *hijra* does not mean a territorial or a geographical movement; it is a social one, and has to be made within the society in which one lives. Living in the West is a way to extend the *ummah* beyond a strict geographical definition

Neofundamentalists came to the same conclusions, but for different reasons from those of many liberal and even conservative Western Muslims. It is irrelevant to consider Dar-ul-Islam as a purely territorial concept. Both groups use the Puritan paradigm of virgin lands, whereby settling in a new country allows one to live one's religion better.[84]

Many radical US Muslims (especially African-American converts) also consider that one should both remain in the United States and boycott a non-Muslim system (voting, inviting elected or government officials to religious celebrations or community gatherings, and so on). This is, for instance, the constant position of Kaukab Siddique, head of Jamaat al-Muslimeen, who is a pillar of *New Trend Magazine*'s website. This site supports such gaoled African-American Muslims as Imam Jamil, and mixes Koranic and leftist terminology ('bring up the oppressed – mustadafeen').[85]

84. See the quotation by Sheikh Taha Jabir Alalwani on pp. 157–8, Chapter 4. Sheikh Alalwani, president of the Graduate School of Islamic and Social Sciences in Leesburg, Virginia, is not a neofundamentalist: 'There is no justice with dictatorship.'
85. For instance: 'Muslims in America must understand the people among whom they live and be witnesses to the truth without taking sides with any of the misled forces at work here. America has serious problems which only Islam can solve. Among them: Drugs and crime interlinked, hooked to the burgeoning prison industry. Racism which persists in spite of laws against

The main difference here between liberals and conservatives on the one hand, and neofundamentalists on the other, is that the former opt to take Western citizenship and be fully integrated into Western countries, while the latter insist that Muslims should remain deterritorialised and not identify with the countries in which they are living:

It is not permissible to celebrate independence day or any similar occasions, because that entails imitation of the kuffaar. From another angle it is also a kind of innovation. So these celebrations combine sin and bid'ah (innovation) ... This 'asabiyyah (tribalism) that is appearing nowadays in most countries, where people form factions on the basis of race, colour or homeland, is akin to the ancient tribalism that existed between the tribes of Aws and Khazraj; it is one of the leftovers of jahiliyyah [ignorance].[86]

Hizb ut-Tahrir believes that Muslims in the United States are not considered and should not consider themselves true US citizens: 'Our Brotherhood is Real and their Citizenship is False.'[87] Khaled Kelkal, the first French Islamic radical to carry out a terrorist action in France, said in an interview given before he engaged in terrorism: 'I am not French, I am not an Arab, I am a Muslim.'[88]

There is a mirror effect between the deterritorialisation of Muslims in the West and the way they view the Middle East. The latter is no longer a promised land. On the contrary, it is a depleted and desperate place. It is the guilt at having left more than the hope of returning that drives sympathy for those suffering there. *Ummah* is no longer a territory. It brings together those who have cut their links with a given territory, in this case the Middle East.

---

discrimination. The breakdown of the family. The debate between pro-"choice" and pro-"life" groups. The fragmentation of the truth between Republicans and Democrats. The exploitation of women under cover of "freedom".' Imam Jamil, speech at Johns Hopkins Hospital, Baltimore, Maryland, on 11 November 2003 <http://www.newtrendmag.org>. The reference to *mustadafeen* is on the information page for *New Trend Magazine*'s website <http://www.newtrendmag.org/ntmfinfo.html>.

86. 'Question #34749: Various Questions about 'Asabiyyah (Tribalism) and Nationality', Islam Q&A, 21 March 2003, <http://63.175.194.25/index.php?ln=eng&ds=qa&lv=browse&QR=34749&dgn=4>.

87. <http://www.hizb-ut-tahrir.org/english/culture/new_messages_01/1.htm>.

88. Interview with Dietmar Loch, published in *Le Monde*, 7 October 1995 (the text was published after the killing of Kelkal).

How is this virtual *ummah* to be endowed with existence? The Caliphate as proposed by the Hizb ut-Tahrir also fits the model of a virtual world. Of course the idea, for the radicals, is that sooner or later Muslims will cease to be a minority and the world will convert (or be converted) to Islam. The three stages defined by Hizb ut-Tahrir (see note 33, p. 248) bypass the issue of putting down geographical, territorial and national roots. There is not a word on concrete strategy or proceedings, or on the location of this Caliphate. Nevertheless the Caliphate (Khilafat) should rule directly over all Muslims and not over a given territory. It is not a re-enactment of a historical institution, but a deterritorialised fancy.

But most neofundamentalists have no such a utopian political program. They consider the *ummah* as simply comprising all believers who follow the true path, wherever they are. To bring them together means to push them to behave in a similar fashion and have the same way of life. Such a virtual community could be enforced by the use of one language (Arabic) but few really advocate it.[89]

The imagined space pertains to a purely religious community, surrounded by a hostile or indifferent secular world. This faith community can be embodied in a local grouping (a congregation, a neighbourhood, a province) encapsulated in a society whose norms are rejected (what we call an 'Islamised territory'). It can also be enacted through an imagined *ummah*, whose frontier has to be defended by a *jihad* that can be waged everywhere, precisely because the community has lost its territorial definition. The 'peripheral' *jihad* (from Bosnia to Kashmir) is a means of making the *ummah* concrete: if one is fighting on a frontier, it means that there is something within that frontier. Finally, the faith community can be established in cyberspace, as a *virtual* ummah. There is a permanent relationship between these three levels: the micro (a local community), the macro (the imagined *ummah*) and the virtual (the internet).

Neofundamentalists and Muslim life in the West

By inducing believers to identify with an abstract, deterritorialised and homogeneous egalitarian community of believers,

89. Dr 'Abd al-Rahmaan Aal 'Uthman, 'Rulings on Speaking Languages other than Arabic', *al-Bayaan* magazine, 152, Rabee' al-Aakhir 1421 AH (July 2000), pp. 8–15. (Reproduced at <http://63.175.194.25/words/speaking_other_arabic/speaking_other_arabic.shtml>.)

neofundamentalism provides an alternative group identity that does not impinge upon the individual life of the believer, precisely because such a community is imagined and has no real social basis. The individual can take part in a little-valued but real social life among non-believers. Restricting religion to an imagined space allows one to live *de facto* in a secular world (that is, the real world, on which the believer has little leverage). But the negative side is that non-Muslim societies are also full of *haram* things. Avoidance is a prerequisite for maintaining a true religious life. Neofundamentalists reject both assimilation and integration.

As we have seen, most mainstream conservative Muslims, and specifically those who are sympathetic to the Muslim Brotherhood, advocate integration without assimilation. They strive to organise Muslims into a visible and active community, with institutions and establishment figures, involved in education and social services (such as after-school lessons for children with learning difficulties, and literacy courses). The UOIF (Union of Islamic Organisations in France) and Milli Görüs in Germany advocate such a policy. They want to be recognised by the authorities and consequently promote debate and negotiation. They often advocate the 'Jewish' model (as they see it) to mobilise the Muslim community. They are legal-minded and willing to negotiate over community issues (the *hijab*, halal food or consultation on ethical issues). They may evolve into a sort of Muslim church in Europe, which will pose little or no security threat, but will push for conservative moral and social values, putting an end to the alliance between a multiculturalist but liberal European Left and the first generation of migrants.

Neofundamentalists oppose this approach. They see the presence of a Muslim minority in the West as transitory; it should give way either to *hijra* or to the spread of Islam. The issue is clearly stated in a question-and-answer session with Sheikh Ibn 'Uthaymeen (Othaymeen):

Question: Muslim women and their daughters in western countries where there are Muslim minorities face very difficult circumstances in that education and work are mixed environments. We are caught between two possibilities. Either we cut-off our provision, stay at home and beg and as a result sink to a very desperate material condition, or, alternatively, wear our Islaamic *hijaab* and study and work in those societies which do not differentiate between mixing and separation. What is your esteemed opinion concerning this matter?

Response: Concerning this very crucial issue, I believe that it is obligatory for a Muslim to patiently adhere to and persevere with Allaah's religion and not to be of those whom Allaah describes, saying: {And of mankind are those that say, 'We believe in Allaah.' But if they are made to suffer for the Sake of Allaah, they consider the persecution of mankind as Allaah's punishment...}, [Soorah al-'Ankaboot, Aayah 10]. A Muslim must be patient and if it is not possible to gain a livelihood except by what Allaah has forbidden, namely through the mixing of men and women, then this livelihood must be abandoned and another sought from another direction or from another country. Was Allaah's land not vast enough for you to emigrate therein?[90]

Sheikh Muqbil holds a similar view.[91] Another official Saudi sheikh declares:

There should be a legitimate need for taking the nationality, such as the benefits for which the Muslim has settled in the kaafir country being dependent upon his taking the nationality. Otherwise that is not permissible for him, because taking the nationality is an obvious manifestation of befriending the kuffaar, and because it involves speaking words which it is not permissible to believe in or adhere to, such as approving of kufr or man-made laws.[92]

There is a distinction to be made between the neofundamen-talist *fatwa*-makers living in the West and those in Saudi Arabia. The Saudis are more prone to support the traditional ban on Muslims living indefinitely in non-Muslim states. But the *fatwa*-makers living in the West can hardly advocate *hijra*.[93] In any case, all are

90. Shaykh Ibn 'Uthaymeen, *al-Aqalliyaat al-Muslimah*, Fatwa 14, p. 74.
91. 'Shaikh Muqbil discusses conditions for living among the disbelievers: "Therefore I think that it is not permissible to live in these lands (i.e. the lands of the disbelievers in the West) except for dire necessity, or for a person who goes there inviting to Allaah, glorified is He and Exalted is He (i.e. working in Da'wah). And (along with this) he can protect himself from the Fitnah (trials, evil temptations), and the Fitnah of the women, and the Fitnah of the Dunyaa (worldly things)".'Al-Imaam Muqbil bin Haadee Al-Waadi'ee; Source: Tuhfatul-Mujeeb 'an As'ilatil-Haadhir wal-Ghareeb, question no. 26, translated by Aqeel Walker, at <http://www.salafnotkhalaf.com/forum/top-ic.asp?TOPIC_ID=259>.
92. Sheikh Khaalid al-Maajid, 'Question #14235: Ruling on Muslims taking on European nationality', Islam Q&A, <http://63.175.194.25/index.php?ln=en g&ds=qa&dv=browse&QR=14235&dgn=4>.
93. Some nevertheless carry it out. For example, Jamaaluddin Haidar, a black convert from Houston, Texas, lives in a poor neighbourhood and opposes the gang lifestyle of young Muslims: 'For me, *hijrah* is most definitely the answer.

opposed to any sort of integration and want to organise the Muslims as a separate community, almost on a ghetto model. Sheikh Nasir al Aql, widely quoted by Salafists in Britain and the United States, warns believers not to imitate 'unbelievers' by citing one of the favourite Koranic verses of the neofundamentalists: 'And never will the Jews and Christians be pleased with you until you follow their religions' (2. 120).[94] They consider Christendom to be on the move, at a time when most Christians, especially in Western Europe, see their religion and civilisation as declining.[95]

For neofundamentalists the only way to preserve a community based on respect for the true tenets of Islam is to avoid interaction with the non-Muslim dominant society. They look askance at educating females and strongly oppose coeducation. Many suggest leaving non-Muslim schools to establish purely Muslim ones.[96] Many scholars recommend not marrying non-Muslim girls, even though they acknowledge that *sharia* does allow the taking of Christian and Jewish wives. Once again neofundamentalism is part of religious innovation in the very name of preventing the community from innovating:

My advice to all Muslims is that they should not marry anyone who is not a Muslim. A Muslim man should do his utmost to marry a Muslim woman because that will be good for him, both in the life of this world and in the Hereafter and good for his children as well. With regards to marrying kuffaar, if they are not from the People of the Book, the Jews and Christians, then, according to clear text and consensus of the scholars, it is forbidden. According to a consensus of the scholars, it is not permitted for a Muslim to marry Buddhists, communists, atheists and so forth.[97]

It has now become a mandate and indeed a mission' (<http://home.houston. rr.com/between/fset2.html>). The website is no longer active; hard copy in possession of the author.

94. 'Causes which Lead to Muslim's Imitation of the Kufaar', Islamic Propagation, Information and Resource Center, Pennsylvania, 1994, <http://www. allaahuakbar.net/jihaad/plotting_of_kuffaar_against_islam_and_muslims. htm>.

95. 'Christian Missions: The New Crusades', *Islamic Times* (Manchester), <www. mrc.org.uk/crusade.htm>.

96. 'We must make a pledge to never send our children to the schools of the kuffar', Jamaaluddin al-Haidar, al Bayan, <http://home.houston.rr.com/ between/fset2.html> (hard copy in possession of the author).

97. Shaykh Ibn Baaz, *Al-Aqalliyaat al-Muslimah*, Fatwa 5, p. 29, quoted at <http:// www.fatwa-online.com/fataawa/muslimminorities/0000822_5.htm> ('Marrying Non-Muslim Women').

But the argument opposing interfaith marriage is based on a modern definition of marriage: 'Marriage does not consist merely of sexual relations ... It is a relationship which has deep social, moral and emotional implications.'[98]

Neofundamentalism strictly forbids participation not only in non-Muslim religious ceremonies, but also in any social event that does not have a Muslim content: Christmas trees for schoolchildren, burial of a Christian friend or colleague, social gatherings in general.[99] Socialisation is restricted even in trivial matters:

If they [Christians] congratulate us or give us best wishes, we can return the greeting to them. However, to give them best wishes on the occasion of their religious festivals is completely forbidden. It is prohibited, for example, to give them best wishes at Christmas or on the occasion of any other of their festivals because to wish them well by affirming their festivals of disbelief is to be contented and happy that these are their festivals. In the same way that it is prohibited to wish them good health over a drink of wine or any other prohibited subsume [*sic*], it is also forbidden to wish them well by affirming their religious rites.[100]

Neofundamentalists are also reluctant to abide by Western legislation ruling personal status. Some strictly oppose registering marriages with the civil authorities. The radical Sheikh Omar Bakri Muhammad declared: 'The civil marriage contract is prohibited (Haram) to be involved in for Muslims from an Islamic perspective ...'.[101] Sheikh Othaymeen states:

98. 'Why Muslim Man Should Not Marry a Non Muslim woman'. This text circulates without attribution on various websites (for instance, <http://groups.yahoo.com/group/ajnabiclub/message/19>; it is also distributed by the Sound Vision Foundation, Bridgeview, Illinois).
99. Jamaal al-Din Zarabozo, 'Celebrating or Participating in Holidays of the Disbelievers', *Al-Jumuah Magazine*, 9, 2 (1997), <http://www.islaam.com/Article.aspx?id=112>; Badr al-Suhayl, 'The Danger of Mixing with Disbelievers and Evildoers', *al-Bayaan* magazine, 152, Rabee' al-Aakhir 1421 (July 2000), pp. 34–9, cited at Islam Q&A, <http://63.175.194.25/words/natural/natural.shtml>.
100. Shaykh Ibn 'Uthaymeen, *al-Aqalliyaat al-Muslimah*, Fatwa 22, p. 81. It should be mentioned that, contrary to this opinion, the embassies of the Islamic Republic of Iran used to send Christmas cards to non-Muslims (but of course calling Jesus a Prophet and not the Son of God).
101. Among the nineteen reasons for this prohibition is the following: 'Contrary to Islam, a civil marriage does not permit a man to enforce sex on his wife or to discipline her.' Sheikh Omar Bakri Muhammad, 'The Islamic Verdict

It is not permissible for a Muslim to follow, either in his worship or in his dealings with others, other than what is laid down in Islaamic law. Divorce is one of those issues which is dealt with by Islaamic law in the most complete manner. It is, therefore not permitted for anyone to go beyond or transgress the limits set by Allaah (*Subhaanahu wa Ta'aala*) concerning divorce.[102]

But the sheikh adds that one can register the divorce. It is typical of the form of non-antagonistic aloofness promoted by apolitical neo-fundamentalists: organising one's life as a Muslim in a non-Muslim environment without causing affront. At the opposite end of the spectrum, Tariq Ramadan invites French Muslims to subscribe to the Civil Solidarity Pact (PACS, nicknamed 'the homosexual marriage', a civil contract that gives legal status to couples irrespective of their gender) – although of course for Muslims a marriage should be between people of different genders – because, as a civil contract, it is closer to the *nikah* according to *sharia*. This example shows that equally 'sincere' Muslims, facing the same problem, may advocate two completely different responses.[103]

Conservative and non-violent neofundamentalists may nevertheless play according to the legal rules of Western countries; they may register mosques, charities and schools, and they may cast their vote (although many reject taking citizenship) and participate in public debate, while rejecting the concept of democracy, as traditionalist Christians can also do. But these Muslims object to any cultural compromise. Such an attitude is a source of many social problems, but they are not a serious security threat so long as such people are allowed to live their segregated communal lives without interference from Western authorities.

---

on Civil/Registered Marriage', 9 March 2000, <http://www.mrc.org.uk/verdict.htm>.

102. Shaykh Ibn 'Uthaymeen, *al-Aqalliyaat al-Muslimah*, Fatwa 12, p. 73, quoted at <http://www.fatwa-online.com/fataawa/muslimminorities/0000920_2.htm> ('Divorce Procedures in Non-Muslim Countries'). The sheikh continues: '*Question*: If it is necessary by law to register a divorce or to follow registration procedures with the official authorities in the country where he is living, then, after he has divorced according to Islaamic law, should he go and formally register it with those authorities? *Response*: There is no objection to him registering it but it should be done according to Islaamic law. He should say that he has divorced his wife so and so, the daughter of so and so, according to Islaamic law and then it can be entered in the register of those people.'

103. Personal account of some of Tariq Ramadan's conferences in Paris, 2000.

Islamised territories

Neofundamentalists distrust the state. Their quest for a strict implementation of *sharia* with no concession to man-made law pushes them to reject the modern state in favour of a kind of 'libertarian' view of the state: the state is a lesser evil but is not the tool for implementing Islam. As a Hizb ut-Tahrir internet posting says: 'Abiding by the rules of shariah will achieve the domination of the shariah rules.' This clearly means that the responsibility for implementing *sharia* is on the shoulders of the believer, not on the state.[104] Individual Muslims who have found the true path should unite to establish a community of true believers, which will be extended by means of *dawah* and/or *jihad*. Such a community has no need of a territory; it can be virtual, as we have seen. Nevertheless, neofundamentalists (as well as many Sufi brotherhoods) tend to establish local territorial communities where they can live among their coreligionists and follow their own rules, whatever the overall social and political environment. Such communities can either comprise voluntary groupings of born-again Muslims, who perform some sort of 'domestic' *hijra* in order to create a favourable environment, or can be based on a specific social segment (often a tribe or a clan) that joins a neofundamentalist movement (or brotherhood).

Islamic neighbourhoods. The members of a local community, or Islamic neighbourhood, of true believers regard it as the first step towards the establishment of a whole polity, a result of their exemplary attitude, or simply an opportunity for the 'saints' (the happy few who will be saved) to remain aloof from impiety and corruption.[105] This view is not far from that of the sixteenth-century Puritans, who travelled great distances in order to establish a free local community, a free society. Social life is part of the religion and is central to all Muslims – there is no withdrawal from social life, no anchoritism. In this sense living in an almost closed community is

104. <http://www.khilafah.com> (20 July 2001). The text is no longer on the website, but hard copy is in the possession of the author.
105. The idea that only a minority of Muslims will achieve salvation is common among neofundamentalists; the 'saved' ones (after a quotation from the Koran) belong to the Firqatun-Nâjiyah (the Saved Sect). (For one of many references see <http://salafi.homepage.dk/manhaj/savedsect.html>.) This is somehow congruent with the Calvinist view of predestination: faith and deeds are not sufficient to gain salvation.

not a sign of failure; rather, its objective is first to preserve Muslim identity in the West and then to provide a cornerstone for social reformation in Muslim countries. That is what Abu Hamza meant when he said, 'Go to a Muslim environment, not a Muslim country, because in our countries we have Muslims, but we do not have Islamic states.'[106] Neofundamentalists stress the need for an immediate and personal implementation of religious duties and permanent devotion. A closed community creates a positive environment in which to achieve this.

What form can such a community take? This can remain rather vague: people who visit the same mosque, or even just those who contact each other via the internet (to receive a *fatwa*, to find a spouse, to exchange views, to buy books). Let us turn now to consider the community with a territory. In the West neofundamentalists play on *de facto* ethnic segregation in many poor neighbourhoods: fanning out from the congregation of a local mosque, they buy or rent houses and flats in the neighbourhood and strive to re-create a particular social environment with its own mores and pressures (on women, for instance, who have little choice but to wear the *hijab* in this public space). In France such neighbourhoods are often under the influence of the Tabligh. In Britain the trend has been re-enforced by the growing number of Muslim faith-schools.[107] Many impoverished districts, in the West as well as in Muslim countries, are fertile ground for this neofundamentalist propaganda. In this case the 'other' they are confronted with is more often urban youth subculture, with its drug-related violence spreading among the same 'ethnic' Muslim groups.[108]

Some *imams* call for the voluntary establishment of such communities, instead of simply taking advantage of *de facto* segregation, which may limit the *dawah* (preaching or propaganda) to ethnic

106. <http://www.angelfire.com/bc3/johnsonuk/eng/sheikh.html>.
107. Frank Dobson, 'Open up Faith Schools', *Guardian*, 8 February 2002.
108. Jamaaluddin al-Haidar states: 'We must maintain a tough, uncompromising, no-nonsense posture towards those unruly youth who have gone astray and have brought shame on the Muslim community ... One gang symbol that they spray on walls is "A.W.A." and "Arabs with Attitudes" a play on the name of a group of California-based thugs turned "gangster" rappers – "N.W.A." or "N–ggers with Attitudes". This gang of so-called Muslims had begun to hang around the Islamic school and intimidate and beat up some of our Muslim students.' <http://home.houston.rr.com/between/fset2.html>. Hard copy in possession of the author.

and social ghettos instead of reaching out to the whole population. Jamaaluddin al-Haidar, in Houston, after complaining of the spread of drugs and violence among second-generation Muslims, writes:

Muslims in America are not positioned to declare jihad to establish Allah's sovereignty in America. As Muslims, we are a weak and divided minority whose mission can only be to act as 'warners' and to call the people to Islam through preaching, dawah, and our exemplary character and lifestyle (i.e. establishing 'model' Islamic residential communities and business districts).[109]

But until now there has been no such middle-class religious neigh-bourhood anywhere in the West. The few Islamic spaces are mapped by ethnic segregation.

Interestingly, this policy of establishing local Islamic communi-ties in a secular or Christian environment is also found in some traditional Muslim societies. Tribal areas, villages and refugee camps can become 'Islamised spaces', where fundamentalism is part of the recasting of local identities into religious ones. The Embaba neighbourhood in Cairo (which was studied by Patrick Haenni)[110] and the Ain al-Hilweh Palestinian refugee camp in southern Leba-non are good examples of this trend. During the 1990s the latter came under the control of the Asbat al-Ansar (or Usbat al-Ansar) organisation. Excluded from the Oslo Accords and convinced that there would be no return to Palestine, many refugees abandoned their Palestinian national identity and now identify with the glo-bal *ummah*. They thus turned their uprootedness into a positive

109. <http://home.houston.rr.com/between/fset5.html>. Hard copy in posses-sion of the author. For a comparable project of a utopian urban neighbour-hood, in Pakistan: 'The Jamaat does operate a small community, in Mansura, on the outskirts of Lahore. A few hundred people live in a large, peaceful compound which contains the Jamaat's offices, a large mosque, several small schools and a hospital. Now the party has far grander plans. Jamaat's new city will be called Qurtuba, a "city of knowledge" that will focus on education. The party has bought 2,000 acres of land in an open area of countryside about 30 minutes drive south [of] Islamabad. Here it plans to build primary and secondary schools, undergraduate colleges and postgraduate study cen-tres. There will be mosques, libraries, gymnasiums and playing fields. The party has begun to sell plots of land for people to build their own homes in the community ... Many of the plots have been bought by ex-pat Pakistanis living in Britain, Europe or the US.' Rory McCarthy, 'Building for an Islamic Future', *Guardian*, 21 February 2003.
110. Patrick Haenni, 'Banlieues indociles'.

transnational identity.[111] This shift from national to transnational identity is a typical pattern of neofundamentalism in the West. Globalisation is also at work, levelling the differences between the West and the Middle East.

Islamic emirates and Islamo-tribalism. A phenomenon that has recently developed in Muslim countries is the transformation of a given territory, at a subnational level, into an Islamic entity, directly connected to the outside world by religious and economic networks. *Ulama* and traders are tools and agents of local autonomy. These spaces are more often than not hewn from a tribal society. From the late 1980s to the electoral success of the MMA (a coalition of religious parties) in the North-West Frontier Province of Pakistan in the autumn of 2002, the tribal areas straddling the Afghan-Pakistani border saw the emergence of Islamic emirates that usually overlapped with a tribal identity. In Nuristan, Afghanistan, as early as 1984, the Kati tribe declared its territory an 'Islamic state', under the leadership of Mullah Afzal (supported by the Pakistani Ahl-i Hadith movement). The Safi tribe of the Pech Valley also became an Islamic emirate under Jamil-ur-Rahman, who was supported by, among others, the Yemeni Sheikh Muqbil.[112] The Afghan Taliban launched their movement in 1994 from a local tribal zone and with the financial backing of a guild of freight operators, who were running transportation from Afghanistan to Karachi. In Pakistan some Pashtun tribes threw out the state administration, rejected customary law and declared *sharia* the only law.

Islamic assertiveness is also a tool for recasting a traditional opposition to the state in terms that are ideologically acceptable to a wider audience. Self-proclaimed Islamic territories are burgeoning in parallel with an unprecedented tendency of the Pakistani state, since the 1990s, to re-establish its control over tribal areas. In this sense neofundamentalism is a symptom of the recasting of tribal identities in modern ideological terms. The Tehrik-e-

---

111. 'The Alleged Relocation of Fundamentalists from the Caucasus to the Middle East', <http://www.nnjv.btinternet.co.uk/TER_checharab280502.htm>. See also Bernard Rougier, 'Dynamiques religieuses et identité nationale dans les camps de réfugiés palestiniens du Liban' ['Religious Dynamics and National Identity in Palestinian Refugee Camps of Lebanon'], *Maghreb-Machrek*, 176 (2003).

112. Burgat and Sbitli, 'Les Salafis au Yémen'.

Nifaz-e-Shariat-e-Mohammadi (Movement for the Implementation of the Sharia) in Malakand, Pakistan, founded in 1994 by Sufi Mohammad, and in 1998 the Islamic Tehrik-e-Taliban in northern Waziristan both announced the implementation of *sharia* law.[113]

This Salafi breakthrough among tribes seems to be part of a process of detribalisation and changes in local leadership, but this hypothesis must be tested in the field.[114] The Saudi Wahhabi Ikhwan of the early 1920s were voluntarily detribalised tribesmen who chose to bypass tribal affiliations in favour of an ideological commitment, as did the Taliban. Many contemporary Saudi radicals retain a tribal link (at least through their name). Several al-Ghamdi and al-Shehri (the names of two tribes) are to be found among the ranks of Al Qaeda. The leader of the attack on Mecca's Grand Mosque in 1979, Juhayman al-Utaybi, was also from a large tribe. (Because most Saudis are originally from a tribe, retaining that tribe's name and coming from the tribal area can be significant.) Does the pro-Al Qaeda Ansar al-Islam group in Iraqi Kurdistan belong to this category of tribal Salafis? This has yet to be confirmed.

Salafis are ambivalent towards tribes. They explicitly condemn tribal customs and tribalism as such (calling it *asabiyya*), but do not hesitate to appeal to tribal identity. (The Taliban in Afghanistan played the Pashtuns off against other groups, and Sheikh Muqbil condemned tribalism yet praised the tribes that supported him.)[115] In Yemen, a Salafi group called the Aden-Abyan Army was created by Abu al-Hassan (Zain al-Abdin Abubakr al-Mihdar), from the

---

113. 'Taking their lead from the Afghan Taliban militia, a Pakistani tribal group has publicly destroyed televisions to cleanse society of "un-Islamic" influences. The Sunni fundamentalist movement in the semi-autonomous North Waziristan Agency held a public ceremony where they set fire to three televisions and a video machine on Sunday, the *Dawn* daily reported. Local religious leaders had also drawn up a code of behaviour which forbids music at marriage functions, drug pushing and other acts believed to promote "obscenity" in the undeveloped rural community.' AFP Islamabad, 31 July 2001.

114. Thirty years ago, it was Marxism that benefited from the crisis of the tribal system. In Afghanistan the Khalq faction of the Communist Party recruited from among many of the same tribes that are now filling Taliban's ranks. Marxists were also well established among southern Yemeni tribes and in Pakistani Baluchistan.

115. Burgat and Sbitli, 'Les Salafis au Yémen'.

Mihdar tribe, in the early 1990s. It called for other tribes to join it, 'following the Mihdar and Yazidi tribes'.[116]

The victory of the MMA in Pakistan's North-West Frontier Province (in the autumn of 2002) shows how this tribal basis can be transcended to give way to a real political movement, but still with a 'community' and local vision:

Nearly four months after forming the government in the NWFP single-handedly, the Mutahidda Majlis-e-Amal (MMA) announced its draft Shariah package on 21st March, choosing Friday, the Muslim holy day, to honour its pre-election promise ... Shariah would be the supreme law in the province, Chief Minister Durrani told TFT, emphasising that future legislation will refer to the Quran and Sunnah as guiding principles and all provincial laws will be brought in conformity with the Shariah.[117]

Elsewhere in the world there are other examples of such 'Islamised territories'. The northern states of Zamfara, Sokoto and Kano in Nigeria imposed *sharia* law in 2000. In the former Soviet republic of Dagestan, in the district of Buynaksk, a cluster of villages around Karamakhi declared themselves in 1996 an Islamic territory. It gave asylum to the Arab Al Qaeda militant known as Khattab, who married a local girl. The feud between local 'Wahhabis' and other Muslims, according to a local observer, is connected with the generation gap and clan-based rivalries.[118]

This feature of Islamic territories is well illustrated by brotherhoods in Africa. The town of Medina Gounass in the Casamance region of Senegal was founded by Thierno Amadou Seydou Ba in 1935. The inhabitants, mostly Peuls and Hal Pular, settled there from other areas, as did the sheikh, who came from the Tijaniyya brotherhood. The town is ruled as a fundamentalist emirate. *Sharia* law prevails there; women are veiled and secluded. A conflict with the state erupted in 1975 over new regulations concerning cotton marketing, and at the time of writing there was still no Senegalese state administration in the town, whose economic development is

---

116. 'Abu al-Hassan and the Islamic Army of Aden-Abyan', Yemen Gateway, <http://www.al-bab.com/yemen/hamza/hassan.htm>.
117. Iqbal Khattak, 'Shariah and MMA in NWFP', *Friday Times*, 27 March 2003.
118. Nabi Abdullaev, political editor of *Novoye Delo*, Makhachkala, in *Transitions On Line*, March 1998, <http://www.ijt.cz/transitions>. Hard copy in possession of the author.

largely linked with emigration and gifts to the sheikh (presently Ahmed Titan Bad) from emigrants.[119]

Far from being isolated, Islamic territories are well connected to the surrounding world, but try to avoid and bypass the state. These local communities are often linked to the global world by networks (familial, diasporic or ideological), which may also nurture economic ties (*hawala*, a South Asian practice that consists of simultaneously depositing money in one country and withdrawing it in another without going through the banking system, but using family and clan connections). This combination of economic and social links is not specific to neofundamentalism, of course, but can provide a social and economic basis for its diffusion. These networks support a parallel economy and may occasionally give some logistical support to radical militants (but also to charities, mosques and *imams*).

THE NEW FRONTIER OF THE IMAGINED *UMMAH*

There is a clear parallel between territory and politics. Islamists act on a territorial basis (national or regional) to win over a state. Neofundamentalists (and many brotherhoods) reject the state and are deterritorialised. Deterritorialisation and statelessness go together. But how does one re-create a concrete *ummah*? How does one reunite Muslims? Is the ideal community of Muslims definitely virtual or confined to a small sect?

For instance, it is remarkable that neofundamentalists never sought to mobilise the annual pilgrimage to Mecca either for propaganda purposes or to stir up feelings of belonging to the *ummah*. (The 1979 attack on Mecca's Grand Mosque was carried out by Saudi dissidents; the Shia upheavals in 1987 were sponsored by the Iranian security services.) It was as if contemporary neofundamentalists simply had no desire to take action on what remained of the territorial centre of the *ummah*. This lack of real presence and activism among pilgrims should not be attributed solely to the efficiency of the Saudi security services. It has to do with neofundamentalists and radicals having no interest in the 'real' *ummah* (that is, the millions of ordinary pilgrims who bring to

119. Ed van Hoven, 'Medina Gounass: The End of a Religious Isolate', *ISIM Newsletter*, 4 (1999), p. 25.

Mecca all the diversity and complexity of the 'real' Muslim world). They believe that only the vanguard minority of true Muslims is the real *ummah*. This disconnection between activists and societies living in the real world is probably the Achilles heel of the neo-fundamentalists and radicals. For neofundamentalists there are two ways to build a true *ummah*: *dawah* and *jihad*. The failure of Bin Laden to destroy the might of the United States and the retaliation that has ensued have convinced many that *jihad* is not the answer. The traditional preaching movements (such as the Tablighi) find in Bin Laden's failure a confirmation of their refusal to enter into politics. Conversely, the same US retaliation is encouraging new militants, who do not necessarily share the neofundamentalist agenda, to enter into *jihad*. The split between pro-*dawah* and jihad-ists is growing, whatever may be their ultimate views on Islam.

In a sense neofundamentalists live in an imaginary world, whatever their political options. The Tablighi behave in the same way whatever the cultural and sociological environment, as if they were on an isolated planet. The Hizb ut-Tahrir speaks of Caliphate or Khilafat without any historical nor geographical consideration, as if the Caliphate was some sort of dream. The cyber-Muslims set their minds in another world.

The jihadists, on the contrary, are confronted with the real world. They choose to fight. But even jihadist geography relates to some sort of imagined world. Jihadists always ignore the concrete sociocultural context of the people they want to help; they disregard their culture, national interests and politics. They fight at the periphery of the Muslim world, from Bosnia to Kashmir, through Chechnya and Afghanistan, in the very confines where the Muslim warriors of the first century AH had to stop their victorious advance. But these confines are also the remnants of fallen empires and the fault-line between North and South (or rich and poor countries): they are related to modern wars and politics.

This imagined *ummah* can be expressed in historical paradigms (the Ottoman Empire), in political myth (the Caliphate), in legal Muslim categories (Dar-ul-Harb and Dar-ul-Islam) or in modern anti-US rhetoric (anti-imperialism), but it has never fitted with a given territory. *Jihad* in a sense gives life to a new territorialisation. If I am fighting in Afghanistan or Bosnia to protect the *ummah* against the encroachments of unbelievers, it means that there is something worth protecting on one side of the battle line. But glancing over his shoulder the *mujahid* sees nothing but *kafir* in the lands that he is supposed to protect. As we have seen, nationalism is the principal driving force throughout the Middle East. Radical militant jihadists fight at the frontier to protect a centre where they have no place. They fight not to protect a territory but to re-create a community. They are besieged in a fortress they do not inhabit. This empty fortress syndrome is related to the pathological dimension of their *jihad*.[120]

Contemporary *mujahedin* are pessimistic because they know that there is no longer a fortress to protect, that the enemy is in the fortress. Such pessimism certainly has to do with the proliferation of suicide attacks.[121] Fighting is above all a spiritual journey. It is the ultimate proof of the reform of the self.

120. Bruno Bettelheim and Philip Douglas, *The Empty Fortress: Infantile Autism and the Birth of the Self*, New York: The Free Press, 1967.
121. Some suicide attacks are rational in the sense that the cost-effectiveness ratio cannot be matched by a 'classical' military operation. The destruction of the World Trade Center is a good example. But what about the suicide bombers of Casablanca (April 2003), who blew themselves up to destroy 'soft' and almost irrelevant symbolic targets (a Spanish restaurant, and a Jewish cultural centre that was closed for Sabbath at the time of the attack)? These targets could have been destroyed simply by throwing bombs or by using car bombs. The suicide dimension here is not tactical or instrumental here: it is the aim in itself.

7

ON THE PATH TO WAR: BIN LADEN AND OTHERS

The early 1990s saw a dramatic change in patterns of Islam-related violence. Political violence, which till then was associated with Islamist movements, passed into the hands of neofundamentalist groups (with the relative exception of the Israeli–Palestinian conflict). From the GIA in Algeria to terrorist bombings in France (1995–6), the various Al Qaeda terrorist attacks, the Jemaah Islamiah operations in Indonesia, the Taliban's support for Bin Laden and the radicalisation of Pakistani religious networks, a wave of terrorist actions took place, following an agenda that was no longer associated with the 'Islamic revolution'. These organisations are not related to a state, have no state agenda, work at an internationally and primarily target the West and its symbols rather than local governments.[1]

This shift began almost unnoticed, because in the previous two decades neofundamentalism had been seen by the United States, its Pakistani and Saudi allies, and many Arab regimes as a strategic tool for fighting communism, radical Shiism and even Arab leftist nationalism (from the PLO to Baathism). In 1980 two events caused great concern in the West and among Muslim conservative states – the Soviet invasion of Afghanistan (27 December 1979) and the radicalisation of the Iranian revolution, which turned openly anti-Western and called for the toppling of conservative Arab regimes,

---

1. The GIA could to some extent be considered an Islamist movement, because it targeted the Algerian state (and people). But there is now clear evidence that many GIA leaders were instrumentalised by military security and intelligence officers (*le pouvoir*) who were playing a complex game aimed at retaining power. (Mohammed Samraoui, *Chroniques des années de sang*, Paris: Denoël, 2003. Samraoui is a former high-ranking Algerian officer.) Whatever its background, the GIA retained a strict neofundamentalist program (*sharia*, with no real political program).

which Khomeini dubbed 'renegade'. The assassination of President
Sadat of Egypt in October 1981, followed by a wave of terrorist
and suicide attacks on Western targets (such as those against French
and US troops in Lebanon in 1983–4), persuaded many in Arab
ruling circles to try to divert Islamic Sunni radicalism against communism and radical Shiism.

The war in Afghanistan provided a great opportunity; thousands
of Muslim volunteers went to Afghanistan to fight the Soviets. For
Pakistan and Saudi Arabia, which organised the scheme, and the
United States, which approved of it, the idea was to turn potentially anti-Western Islamic fundamentalism against the communist
camp. The Saudis were also trying to undermine Iranian prestige
among the Islamists by promoting their own brand of fundamentalism. Simply put, the idea was to promote an Islamic fundamentalism closer to the Wahhabi school of thought, which was official
in Saudi Arabia, strongly anti-Shia and socially conservative.

The Pakistanis had a further agenda. General Zia ul-Haq used
the Afghan war to make Pakistan a close ally of the United States
and the regional vanguard of Sunni Islam. Zia felt from the onset
of the war that the USSR would withdraw sooner or later and that
Soviet Muslims would win their independence.[2] Obsessed by the
Indian threat, the Pakistani ruling élites hoped to gain some strategic depth by establishing a new sphere of influence stretching
from Kabul to Tashkent. The only common denominator of this
area was the Sunni Muslim identity of the diverse ethnic groups
living within it. This was also the sole source of legitimacy for Pakistan, which was created on the basis of being a 'Muslim country.'

The main supporters of the scheme (which involved sending Islamic volunteers to Afghanistan) were the director of Inter-Services
Intelligence (ISI), General Abdur Rahman Akhtar (in charge from
1979 to 1987), his successor, General Hamid Gul, and the Saudi
prince Turki al-Faisal, head of the Ministry of Intelligence. They
found support from various Islamic organisations in the Middle
East (such as the Muslim Brotherhood) and from the Pakistani
Jamaat-i-Islami. Interestingly, they were dealing with people who
were explicitly seeking to overthrow regimes in the Middle East
(for instance, Ayman al-Zawahiri, a doctor who was one of the first
Arabs to arrive in Peshawar, Pakistan, in 1980). The CIA was not

2.   Personal interview with General Zia ul-Haq, Islamabad, July 1988.

in charge (accusing Bin Laden of having been a CIA agent is non-sense) of the program, but it did not oppose the scheme or worry about its negative consequences.

Whatever the impact of the volunteers on the course of the war in Afghanistan, the international strategic landscape changed dramatically around 1990. The failure of the Iranian revolution to export itself and the collapse of the Soviet Union made the Islamic card redundant for the United States. Nevertheless, nothing was done to disband or monitor the militants who remained in Afghanistan. The US attitude had more to do with benign neglect than Machiavellian strategy. Eagerness to claim absolute victory in Afghanistan, bureaucratic inertia, lack of concern and expertise, overconfidence in the Saudi and Pakistani security services, obsession with 'rogue' states at the expense of non-state movements – all explain why nobody in Washington cared. But the two allies of the United States, the Saudis and the Pakistanis, had domestic and strategic reasons to maintain their ties with these Islamic networks (essentially because they were a tool of legitimacy and regional influence). Despite the first bombing attack on the World Trade Center in 1993, it was only in August 1998 that Bin Laden was identified by Washington as enemy number one, but no concrete steps were taken against him. The official US policy on the Taliban was still to drive a wedge between it and Bin Laden.[3] The 9/11 attacks changed the whole picture.

Around 1991 the Islamic networks supported by Saudi Arabia and Pakistan turned openly anti-Western. This development was partly the result of a change in the strategic landscape. The militants (rightly or wrongly) saw the fall of the USSR as a consequence of the Afghan *jihad*, and this encouraged them to train their fire on the one remaining superpower, the United States. That the

---

3.   Assistant Secretary of State Karl Inderfurth met Taliban officials regularly and always asked them to 'bring Bin Laden to justice', without questioning the existence of the Taliban regime. (He met the Taliban Information Minister, Mullah Amir Khan Muttaqi, in Pakistan in July 1999, and in October of that year met the Taliban representative in Washington, DC, Abdul Hakim Mujahid: Barry Schweid, 'U.S. presses Taliban to give up Bin Laden', Associated Press, 26 October 1999). See also Petra Mayer, 'Afghanistan: Bin Laden's Whereabouts Unknown', Radio Free Europe/Radio Liberty, 17 February 1999   (<http://www.rferl.org/features/1999/02/f.ru.990217141528.asp>). US-sponsored sanctions against the Taliban were aimed not at bringing down the Taliban regime but at persuading it to expel Bin Laden.

latter considered itself not a hegemonic power but a benevolent broker or peacekeeper (at least before the neoconservatives came to power under President George W. Bush) should not conceal another trend. The 1990s saw a continuing expansion of the US military presence in the Muslim world. Bin Laden became openly anti-US during the first Gulf war (1990–1) and tried to fight the US intervention in Somalia.

The February 1993 attack on the World Trade Center indicates that Bin Laden had decided to target the United States directly in the aftermath of the Gulf war. But it would be erroneous to conclude that he would not have targeted the superpower had the latter not been involved in Saudi affairs. It would be a mistake also to consider that the main strategic goal of Bin Laden was to topple the Saudi monarchy. He had fashioned a global strategy of confrontation with the West during the anti-Soviet war in Afghanistan. The *jihadis* who flocked to Afghanistan did not become anti-Western after 1991 – they had always been so.[4] They did not see themselves as auxiliaries of the West against communism but as opponents of both West and East.

Nor did it matter to the radicals that many US interventions were made on behalf of Muslim populations (in Afghanistan, Bosnia, Kosovo and, in a sense, Somalia). In fact the extension of US power throughout the world is mirrored by the call for the defence of an imaginary *ummah* that is everywhere and nowhere. This mirror construction of US might and its arch-enemy is expressed by the cliché of the decade: the clash of civilisations. Without going into detail, let us mention that the concept is shared by

---

4.   All westerners, like me, who encountered the so-called 'Arabs' inside Afghanistan during the war of resistance were struck (sometimes physically) by their hostility. The Arabs constantly asked the Afghan *mujahedin* commanders to get rid of the 'infidels' and to choose only good Muslims as supporters, and called for the expulsion of Western NGOs. The situation was so tense that in many areas the *mujahedin* had to intervene to prevent physical assaults on westerners. Commander Massoud established two separate guesthouses in the Panjshir, one for Arabs, the other for westerners. The greatest hostility was expressed by Algerians (especially towards the French, of course) and African-American converts. The least hostile were the very few Turks (I travelled for a whole week with two very interesting and devoted Islamic Turks, one of whom was killed in action in Panjshir in September 1987). The main beneficiary of the US assistance, Gulbuddin Hekmatyar, never hid his strong anti-Western position.

neofundamentalists (even if they prefer to speak in terms of religion). The political expression of the West is for them the United
States, not Europe. They care little or nothing for the latter, although many Islamists tried to exploit the transatlantic divide, and
nothing for Russia either. Al Qaeda's support for the Chechens
has never translated into a terrorist attack against Russian interests
elsewhere in the world, surely the acid test of their commitment to
their coreligionists in the Caucasus. As we have seen, Al Qaeda has
no strategic vision. It fights against Babylon, against what it sees as
evil, the United States and its ally Israel. Most of Al Qaeda's targets
have no military or strategic value: a nightclub in Bali, a Spanish restaurant in Casablanca, a synagogue on the Tunisian island
of Jerba.

AL QAEDA AND THE NEW TERRORISTS[5]

Al Qaeda is an organisation and a trademark. It can operate directly,
in a joint venture, or by franchising. It embodies, but does not have
the monopoly of, a new kind of violence. Many groups (such as
the Kelkal network in France) are acting along the same lines without necessarily having a direct connection with Al Qaeda. In the
pages below we shall concentrate on Al Qaeda but also mention
other groups and actors, focusing more on new patterns of Islam-
related violence than on Al Qaeda itself.

The strength of Al Qaeda is that it is made up of veterans of the
Afghan wars, who know each other and have developed an *esprit
de corps* in the Afghan 'trenches' (*sangar*) or training camps. This
comrade-based solidarity between people from different countries
has been translated into a flexible and mobile international organisation where the chain of command duplicates personal ties. The
weaknesses of Al Qaeda are, first, that it needs a sanctuary to create
such a spirit of brotherhood and, second, that the uprootedness

5.   There have already been many books and papers on Al Qaeda. The most
     important ones include: Rohan Gunaratna, *Inside Al Qaeda: Global Network
     of Terror*, London: Hurst, 2002; Jessica Stern, *Terror in the Name of God: Why
     Religious Militants Kill*, New York: HarperCollins, 2003; Jason Burke, *Al Qae-
     da: Casting a Shadow of Terror*, London: I.B. Tauris, 2003; and Marc Sageman,
     Understanding Terror Networks, Philadelphia: University of Pennsylvania Press,
     2004.

of these militants make it difficult for them to establish a social and political basis among Muslim populations in areas where they do not benefit from the support of some sort of indigenous subcontractors.

The first wave: from Abdullah Azzam to Al Qaeda

The forerunner of Al Qaeda was the Office of Services (Maktab al-Khidamat, also called Bayt al-Ansar, or House of Auxiliaries) established in the early 1980s in Peshawar by Abdullah Azzam, a Palestinian Muslim Brother with a Jordanian passport (a refugee of 1967), who broke with the PLO in protest against its nationalist and secular stand. Azzam (correctly) understood that nationalism was superseding the religious dimension in the Palestinian *jihad* as in all Islamist movements in the Middle East. He concluded that the only legitimate *jihad* was for the sake of the entire *ummah* and picked the Afghan resistance against the Soviet invasion as the exemplary model. Azzam was not an ideologue or a theologian. He was an activist whose thinking revolved entirely around the concepts of *jihad* and *ummah*. Nor was he a Salafi or a Wahhabi. He used to quote all the classical schools of law and to debate using the traditional concepts of the classical *fiqh*. When extolling *jihad*, Azzam held an intermediary position between the classical view that *jihad* is only a collective duty and is not a pillar of Islam, and the view of the modern jihadists, for whom it is both a pillar of the faith and a personal duty.[6] In this sense he was not a

6. For an English translation of Azzam's work, see 'Join the Caravan', <http://www.religioscope.com/info/doc/jihad/azzam_caravan_3_part1.htm>. Azzam states that *jihad* comes just after *iman* (faith), which makes it a pillar of Islam, but maintains the difference between 'offensive' *jihad*, which is *kifaya* (collective), and 'defensive' *jihad*, which is *ayn* (compulsory for individuals). However, he considers *de facto* that the contemporary *jihad* are all defensive:
    '*Defensive Jihad*
    'This is expelling the Kuffar from our land, and it is Fard Ayn, a compulsory duty upon all. It is the most important of all the compulsory duties and arises in the following conditions:
    '1) If the Kuffar enter a land of the Muslims.
    '2) If the rows meet in battle and they begin to approach each other.
    '3) If the Imam calls a person or a people to march forward then they must march.
    '4) If the Kuffar capture and imprison a group of Muslims.'

neofundamentalist and requested (vainly) that the volunteers going into Afghanistan not meddle with Afghan religious customs.

Did Azzam have a coherent long-term strategic view when sending young Muslim volunteers into Afghanistan? Not necessarily. Of course the ultimate goal of *jihad* is to provide the *ummah* with a secure territory. But Afghanistan was seen by Azzam less as a frontier that had to be defended than as a training ground to breed the vanguard that would spark an overall resistance against the encroachments of the infidels on the *ummah*. The first virtue of *jihad* is to magnify the faith and commitment of believers, whatever its real success on the ground. *Jihad* is a religious duty first: 'Jihad is the most excellent form of worship, and by means of it the Muslim can reach the highest of ranks.'[7] *Jihad* in Afghanistan was aimed at setting up the vanguard of the *ummah*, not at creating an Islamic state there. Nor did Azzam favour supporting a given Afghan faction; he seldom interfered in *mujahedin* politics and earned great respect among the Afghan fighters. He eschewed terrorist attacks (including targeting civilians) and restrained his activities to the Afghan battlefield, avoiding strikes on Soviet interests outside Afghanistan.

The shift to the Al Qaeda of the 1990s was done under Bin Laden's supervision after Abdullah Azzam died in a mysterious car bombing in Peshawar in November 1989. His death, which is still shrouded in mystery, was beneficial to Bin Laden, who took charge of what remained of the organisation, sidelining the would-be heir

---

From 'Defence of the Muslim Lands:The First Obligation after Iman', <http://www.religioscope.com/info/doc/jihad/azzam_defence_3_chap1.htm>.

7.   Azzam, 'Join the Caravan': 'Establishment of the Muslim community on an area of land is a necessity, as vital as water and air. This homeland will not come about without an organised Islamic movement which perseveres consciously and realistically upon Jihad, and which regards fighting as a decisive factor and as a protective wrapping. The Islamic movement will not be able to establish the Islamic community except through a common, people's Jihad which has the Islamic movement as its beating heart and deliberating mind. It will be like the small spark which ignites a large keg of explosives, for the Islamic movement brings about an eruption of the hidden capabilities of the Ummah, and a gushing forth of the springs of Good stored up in its depth. The Companions of the Prophet were exceedingly few in number compared to the troops who toppled the throne of the Persian Kisra and overthrew the Caesar of Rome.' A well-known website, azzam.com, for years promoted international *jihad*, but after Azzam's death it reflected far more extremist views than those held by Azzam.

of Azzam, his son-in law, Abdullah Anas.[8] The transfer of power was undertaken with the obvious blessing of the Pakistani and Saudi sponsors, who maintained their support for Bin Laden till 1998 in the case of the Saudis, and 9/11 in that of the Pakistanis. The United States ceased even to monitor closely the chain of events after February 1989, and woke up belatedly in August 1998 – ten years of neglect that would prove very costly.

To enhance their legitimacy and belittle the role of Abdullah Azzam, Bin Laden's disciples developed a kind of 'foundation myth': the battle of Masada, or 'the Lion's Den' (a camp near Jaji that was besieged by Soviet troops in June 1987, during the sacred month of Ramadan). According to the legend, Bin Laden and a handful of fighters succeeded in breaking the siege. Many of the founding fathers of Al Qaeda participated in the battle (such as Enaam Arnaut, a Syrian-born US citizen; Ayman al-Zawahiri; Abu Zubair al-Madani, who was killed in Bosnia in 1992; and the Saudi Abu Abdurrahman, or Hassan as-Sarehi).

Tens of thousands of militants went to Afghanistan through the Islamic networks for training and *jihad*. They were called 'Arabs' by the Afghans and 'Afghans' by their compatriots after they had returned to their country of origin. The three prominent nationalities among the 'Afghans' (if we exclude the Pakistanis who were not under Bin Laden's control) were the Saudis, the Egyptians and the Algerians. If we consider the ratio of militants to population, the Saudis are clearly overrepresented in Al Qaeda's ranks.[9]

8. There is a theory that Azzam was killed by the ISI to prevent first a rapprochement between him and Massoud, and second the appointment of his son-in-law (the Algerian Boujema Bounouar, who went by the *nom de guerre* Abdullah Anas) as his successor. Anas having been trained in Panjshir alongside Massoud, the story could make sense, although there is no evidence other than the testimony of Bounouar, as collected by Judith Miller; see Stephen Engelberg, 'One Man and a Global Web of Violence', *New York Times*, 14 January 2001.

9. There are many contradictory estimates of the number of 'Afghans', but I cannot see how more than 50,000 volunteers could have gone into Afghanistan. It also depends how we define a sojourn in Afghanistan. Some (and not only Islamic volunteers) spent just one day and claim to have participated in the war. For a plausible sample to estimate the proportions of nationalities, the best sources are the many lists of martyrs; see, among others, Imtiaz Hussain, 'Osama Prepares List of Arab Martyrs of Afghan Jihad', *Frontier Post*, 13 May 2000.

Interestingly there were almost no Syrians, no 'actual' Palestinians (that is, those living in West Bank or Gaza; the Palestinians in Al Qaeda all came from refugee families), no Iraqi Arabs (Iraqi 'Afghans' were all Kurds) and very few Turks. It is also important to note that there were no 'real' Afghans among the 'Afghans', and no Iranians at all. Al Qaeda did not circumvent the Sunni/Shia divide. Many of the volunteers were killed in action. Some stayed in Afghanistan or Pakistan after the Soviet withdrawal in 1989, while others returned to their own country and helped to establish more radical splinter groups from the mainstream Islamist movements.

In Algeria many 'Afghans' were among the founders of the FIS – Said Mekhloufi, Kamar Eddine Kherbane and Abdullah Anas, for example. The 'Afghans' were even more numerous in the radical GIA, of which all the first wave of leaders had returned from Afghanistan: Tayyeb el Afghani (killed in 1992), Jaffar el Afghani (killed in 1994) and Sherif Gusmi (killed in 1994). The founders of the FIS had been with Commander Massoud and the GIA's founders with Gulbuddin Hekmatyar. In Yemen, Sheikh Tariq al-Fadli founded an Islamic Jihad organisation, while Zayn al-Abidin Abu Bakr al-Mihdar created the Aden-Abyan Islamic Army. In Jordan, Khalil al-Deek established the Army of Muhammad, while in Libya, Abu Shartila, alias Abu Tariq Darnaw, heads the Mohammed al Hami battalion. In the Philippines, Abubakar Janjalani (killed in 1997) launched the Abu Sayyaf Group (named after an Afghanistan veteran killed in action). Abu Hamza al-Masri (the Egyptian Mustafa Kamel) lost one eye and a hand in Afghanistan and ended up as a radical *imam* in London, where he founded the Supporters of Sharia. Ibn ul-Khattab, one of the youngest volunteers for Afghanistan, joined the Chechen resistance, where he played an important role in triggering the second war in August 1999. He was reportedly assassinated by a Russian secret service poisoned letter in 2003.

Less often the Afghanistan veterans came from existing organisations and gave them a more radical twist when they returned to their home countries, as did Riduan Isamuddin (also known as Hambali), who joined Jemaah Islamiah in Indonesia. From Egypt, Muhammad al-Islambuli, brother of the murderer of Sadat, went to Afghanistan, as did Sheikh Omar Abdurrahman (sentenced in the United States for the first attempt on the World Trade Center) and his sons. The Saudi Hassan as-Sarehi was charged in Saudi Arabia with the 1995 attacks on the National Guard barracks (he denied any involvement). Leaders of the Egyptian Gama'at Islamiya, Fuad Qassim, Mustafa Hamza and Ahmed Taha, are also 'Afghans,' as is Ayman al-Zawahiri, leader of Egyptian Islamic Jihad, who co-signed Bin Laden's communiqués in early 1998. Mehat Muhammad Abdel Rahman, suspected of being the leader of the group responsible for the massacre of European tourists in Luxor in September 1997, was also an 'Afghan'. Nevertheless, all the Egyptian 'Afghans', while still claiming to belong to the Gama'at and Islamic Jihad, developed a more radical line, which ended in a split with the parent organisations after 9/11.

The 'Afghans' make up the majority of the Harakat ul-Ansar movement presently fighting in Kashmir, and whose training camps were bombed on 21 August 1998 by US missiles in the Afghan province of Khost, in retaliation for the bombing of the US embassies in East Africa. Sipah-e-Sahaba also sent many of its members for training in Afghanistan (which provided a training group for many Pakistani activists). Spending time in Afghanistan was a kind of rite of passage for young Pakistani students of religion; it was even added to the curriculum by some *madrasas* (such as Haqqaniyya at Akora Khattak in 2001).

Other former 'Afghans' played a role as individuals, not as members or founders of organisations, as did, for example, Abu Messaab (a Syrian), a former writer for the London-based GIA journal *Al Ansar*. Others moved with alacrity into building an international terrorist network, like the cell that perpetrated the first bombing of the World Trade Center in February 1993. Ramzi Ahmed Yousef, Muhammad Salameh, Ahmed Ajjaj and Wadih el-Hage (convicted for the bombing of the US embassy in Nairobi, Kenya) also spent some time in Afghanistan. Others returned to the country in which they were living and started to recruit new members (for example, in France, among second-generation Muslims).

Finally a hard core of veterans remained closely connected with Bin Laden, following him in his peregrinations from Saudi Arabia and Somalia to Yemen and Sudan: Muhammad Atef, alias Abdulaziz Abu Sitta, alias Abu Hafs al-Misri, a former Egyptian police officer (who would become the father-in-law of Bin Laden's son); Sulaiman Abu Ghaith, Bin Laden's spokesman; and Ayman al-Zawahiri. In any case, many 'Afghans' remained in touch with one another, wherever they went. Such personal connections could at any time be reactivated, or new recruits could be sent to

Afghanistan, under the patronage of veterans. Moreover, the volunteers in Afghanistan experienced a concrete internationalisation based on personal contacts, the brotherhoods of comrades in arms, friendships and affinities. They learned to know other people and other languages, and travelled elsewhere to meet their former comrades, as did Ramzi Ahmed Yousef when he travelled to the Philippines. Converts found in Afghanistan a new community and brotherhood with which to identify, as John Walker Lindh stated when he was captured in Kunduz.

But between 1989 and 1996, no individual organised or directed the Arab militants in Afghanistan. Some Islamic NGOs (such as the International Islamic Relief Organisation, or IIRO) had their own centres (in Kunduz, for instance); some local *mujahedin* commanders kept their 'Arabs' with them and received direct support from the Gulf or Pakistan (like commanders Mullah Afzal in Nuristan and Jamil ur-Rahman in the Pech Valley). When the Taliban took Kabul in September 1996, they were quite upset to see the mess in Afghanistan and were happy to hand the monopoly of organising the Arab volunteers to Bin Laden, who, after travelling successively in Yemen and Sudan, had been expelled from Sudan in May 1996 to Jalalabad, in Afghanistan (and was a guest of Haji Qadir, the brother of Abdul Haqq, who would become a key ally of the United States in 2001).[10] It seems the Pakistanis introduced Bin Laden to Mullah Omar. The label 'Arab' was applied to all foreigners who were not Pakistani or Central Asian. These last two groups had their own organisations (such as the Islamic Movement of Uzbekistan, and the many Pakistani groups, including Sipah-e-Sahaba, Harkat-ul-Mujahidin, Lashkar-e-Toiba, and so on). Bin Laden, with the help of al-Zawahiri, reorganised the volunteers, and put them into training camps (Darunta and Khalden) and residential compounds for cadres (and their families). As a result, any Islamic volunteers (except Pakistanis or Central Asians) who went to Afghanistan between 1997 and 2001 were necessarily enlisted by Al Qaeda.

The volunteers were cut off from Afghan society and organised into two categories: an infantry battalion that fought alongside the Taliban against the Northern Alliance, and more gifted Western

10. The expulsion of Bin Laden from Sudan also meant that the United States did not request his extradition; the French had in 1994 taken Carlos from the same Sudanese government.

Muslims were trained to go return to Europe and the United States to perpetrate terrorism. While the initial action of Al Qaeda was the first bombing of the World Trade Center in 1993, it was only in 1998 that it became well known in the West when the creation of the 'World Islamic Front for the Struggle against Jews and Crusaders' was announced, followed by the bombings of US embassies in East Africa.

Al Qaeda's first-generation members shared common traits: all came from a Muslim country and had a previous record of political activism; almost all went directly from the Middle East to Afghanistan. They had little experience of the West, and had a traditional way of life (traditional marriages, and their women kept at home).

From the early 1990s a new breed of militants slowly emerged. The change was embodied by two leading figures who participated in anti-US terrorist attacks, namely the first World Trade Center bombing in February 1993, and the attack on the US embassy in Kenya in August 1998. Ramzi Ahmed Yousef was born in 1968 in Kuwait, of a Pakistani father (from Baluchistan) and a Palestinian mother. He did not identify with a given country (although he used to call himself a Pakistani). His name (an alias) means 'secret'; it is almost a choice of identity. He was educated at a vocational training school in Wales between 1986 and 1989 under the name Adul Basit Mahmoud Kareem, graduated in electronic engineering, and then went in 1990 to Afghanistan to wage *jihad*. There he met the brother of the founder of the Philippine Abu Sayyaf Group (Janjalani), who invited him to his country. Yousef left for Baghdad, acquired an Iraqi passport, returned to Peshawar, met Ahmed Ajjaj (a Palestinian refugee in the United States), and settled in New Jersey. He left the very day of the first attack against the World Trade Center, stayed in Karachi with an extremist Pakistani anti-Shiite group, the Sipah-e-Sahaba, then returned to the Philippines, where he was involved in a plot to hijack aeroplanes and kill the Pope. Finally he was arraigned in Karachi and extradited to the United States.[11] The second example is Mohamed Saddiq Odeh (Awadh or Howeyda), a Jordanian citizen, born in Saudi Arabia of a Palestinian family. He received a degree in architecture in the Philippines in 1990, was trained in Afghanistan in the same year,

11. David B. Ottaway and Steve Coll, 'Retracing the Steps of a Terror Suspect' *Washington Post*, 5 June 1995.

and went to Somalia in 1992 to join the Sheikh Hassan radical Islamic group. Odeh married a Kenyan wife, acquired a Yemeni passport, settled in Kenya and was involved in the bombing of the US embassy there in 1998.

This new breed was above all largely uprooted and more westernised than its predecessors, had few links (if any) to any particular Muslim country, and moved around the world, travelling from *jihad* to *jihad*. The flying *jihadi* was born, the *jihadi* jet set.

The second wave: Western Muslims

The second wave of Al Qaeda militants operating internationally was characterised by the breaking of their ties with the 'real' Muslim world they claimed to represent. If we exclude most of the Saudis and Yemenis, as well as the 'subcontractors' (militants from local organisations that act under the Al Qaeda label in their own country), most Al Qaeda militants left their country of origin to fight or study abroad (usually in the West), breaking with their families. They lived separate from society and rarely integrated with a new community, except around some radical mosques. They were cultural outcasts, in their home countries and their host countries. But they were all westernised in some way (again, except for the Saudis and Yemenis); none had attended a *madrasa*, and all were trained in technical or scientific disciplines and spoke a Western language. If we include the logistical networks, some held Western citizenship (the alleged 9/11 conspirator Zacarias Moussaoui was born in France). Most of them (except, again, the Saudis) became born-again Muslims in the West after living 'normal' lives in their countries of origin. The mosques of Hamburg (Al Quds), London (Finsbury Park), Marseilles and even Montreal played a far greater role in their religious radicalisation than any Saudi *madrasa*.

Thus, far from representing a traditional religious community or culture, these militants broke with their past (and some with traditional Islam altogether). They experienced an individual re-Islamisation in a small cell of uprooted fellows, where they forged their own Islam – as vividly illustrated by Muhammad Atta's refusal to be buried according to tradition, which he dubbed un-Islamic.[12]

12. Muhammad Atta's will in English can be found at <http://abcnews.go.com/sections/us/DailyNews/WTC_atta_will.html>.

They did not follow any Islamic school or notable cleric, and sometimes lived according to non-Muslim standards. They were all far more products of a westernised Islam than of traditional Middle Eastern politics. However old-fashioned their theology may seem to Westerners, and whatever they may think of themselves, radical Euro-Islamists are clearly more a postmodern phenomenon than a premodern one.

Even if many of these militants come from the Middle East, they are not linked to or used by any Middle Eastern state, intelligence service or radical movement, as had been the case with the militants of the 1980s. With a single, transitional exception,[13] they are part of the deterritorialised, supranational Islamic networks that operate specifically in the West and at the periphery of the Middle East. Their background has nothing to do with Middle Eastern conflicts. Their groups are often mixtures of educated middle-class leaders and working-class dropouts, a pattern common to most West European radicals of the 1970s and 1980s (Germany's Red Army Faction, Italy's Red Brigades, France's Action Directe). Many became 'born-again' Muslims or gaolhouse converts, sharing a common marginal culture.

Roughly there are three main categories: students, who came from Middle Eastern countries to study in the West; second-generation Muslims, who were either born in the West or came as infants; and converts. The students (for example, the World Trade Center pilots) are usually middle or upper class, and all were educated in technical or scientific disciplines. The second-generation Muslims emanate from the working class and disfranchised urban youths. The converts are a more complex category. Most of the individuals who gravitate towards these three categories are 'new Muslims', either born-again or converts.

We will now try to summarise what these new militants have in common, using a sample based on those individuals involved in or indicted for international terrorism since the 1993 World Trade Center attack.[14] International terrorism is taken to mean attacks

13. Khaled Kelkal's network in France (1995) was set up by an Algerian, Ali Touchent, who might be either an emissary of a GIA *emir* (Zeytuni) or, more probably, an agent of the military security services. (See Samraoui, *Chroniques des années de sang*, p. 230.)
14. In the list referred to (which is pending judicial decisions; inclusion in the list does not necessarily mean an individual is a terrorist) are included: Abdel

that are committed outside the homeland of the perpetrators, and are not state-sponsored.

DETERRITORIALISATION

Our militants operate globally, travelling widely, settling in various countries that have little connection with their homelands and learning foreign languages. Zacarias Moussaoui, a French citizen of Moroccan descent, studied in Montpellier, learnt English and settled in London, where he became a born-again Muslim. Muhammad Atta and the other 9/11 pilots came from the Middle East, settled first in Germany, learnt German, and then went to the United States. Djamel Beghal, who was living in the Paris suburb of Corbeil, settled in Leicester, in the English Midlands. Ahmed Ressam left Algeria, where he was born, for Marseilles and later for Corsica (1992–4), before settling in Montreal, where he scraped a living from casual jobs and theft. He became a born-again Muslim at the As Sunnah mosque and went to Afghanistan in 1998. Back in Montreal, he was contacted by a Mauritanian, Mohambedou Ould Slahi, who funded his preparations to attack Los Angeles International Airport in December 1999. Ould Slahi used to live in Duisburg, Germany, where he attended university and launched an import business.

Al Qaeda is an international organisation, even if its centre till 2001 was in Afghanistan. Its local networks were built with the aim of targeting a specific objective and organised around 'hubs',

Sattar, Ahmed; Abderrahman, Ahmed; Ait Idir, Stephane; Akhnouche, Yasin; al-Fadli, Tariq; al-Maqdisi, Sheikh Abu Muhammad; al-Shehhi, Marwan; Amrouche Laurent; Atmani, Said; Atta, Muhammad; Attar; Bahaji, Said; Bakri Omar; Beghal, Djamel; Ben Mustafa Khaled; Bensakhria, Mohamed; Binalshibh, Ramzi; Budiman, Agus; Cazé, Christophe; Dahmane, Abdesattar; Daoudi, Kamel; Darkazanli, Mamoun; Derwish, Kamal (alias Ahmed Hijazi); Djaffo, Xavier; Dumont, Lionel; al-Deek, Khalil; el-Hage, Wadih; al-Mihdar, Zayn al-Abidin Abu Bakr; el-Ouaer, Rachid Bouraoui; Essabar, Zakariya; Hammadi Redouane; Ibn ul-Khattab; Isamuddin, Riduan; Jabarah, Mohammed Mansour; Jarrah, Ziad; Kamel, Fateh; Kherchtou, L'Houssaine; Khalfaoui, Slimane; Khedr, Ahmed Sayyid; Loudaini, Ahmed; Mohammed, Khalid Sheikh; al-Motassadeq, Munir; Moussaoui, Zacarias; Odeh, Mohamed Saddiq; Omary, Mohammed; Ouldali, Khaled; Rechouane, Abdesslam.; Ressam Ahmed; Sheikh, Omar Saeed; Walker Lindh, John; Yousef, Ramzi Ahmed; Zammar, Mohammed Haydar; Zubayda, Abu.

none of which was in a Middle Eastern country. The 9/11 attacks were prepared in Hamburg, Spain and Kuala Lumpur by four students based in Hamburg (an Egyptian, Muhammad Atta; an Emirati, Marwan al-Shehhi; a Yemeni, Ramzi Binalshibh; and a Lebanese, Ziad Jarrah). The members of the Hamburg support cell for 9/11 fitted the same patterns. They met at the Al Quds mosque in Hamburg. London probably served as the main global centre for propaganda and the recruitment of would-be terrorists who were dispatched to Afghanistan.

Relations between militants and their country of origin are weak or non-existent; we are facing not a diaspora but a truly deterritorialised population. Almost none of the militants fought in his own country, or in his family's country of origin (except some Pakistanis). Two cases are especially relevant: those of the Palestinians and the Algerians. One would expect a Western-based born-again Muslim of Algerian or Palestinian origin to be eager to wage *jihad* in his country of origin, both Algeria and Palestine being battlefields. But I do not know of a single instance of such a return from the diaspora. The French Redouane Hammadi and Stephane Ait Idir, of Algerian origin, carried out a terrorist attack in Morocco (1995); Fateh Kamel and Ahmed Ressam (both Algerians) tried to blow up Los Angeles airport. None of the Algerian militants in Al Qaeda came directly from Algeria. Links with Al Qaeda were built up through Algerian immigration, not by way of the GIA's headquarters or other groups within Algeria. Conversely, the campaign of demonstrations in Algeria, from 1999 onwards, has been carried out in the name of democracy, human rights and defence of the Kabyle (Berber) identity, not of *sharia* or an Islamic state.

All of the Palestinians in Al Qaeda (such as Mohamed Odeh and Abu Zubayda) come from refugee families (either from 1948 or 1967). None of them tried to return to Palestinian-Israeli territory. There is a trend among uprooted Islamic Palestinians towards a 'de-Palestinisation' of their identity in favour of the *ummah*, as is obvious in the Palestinian refugee camp of Ain al-Hilweh, in Lebanon, where Salafi groups are on gaining ground, as we saw previously.

The same is true of the Egyptians: how does one explain the discrepancy between the high number of Egyptians in Al Qaeda's leadership and the decrease in religious violence in Egypt? Clearly this time it is the leadership inside Egypt that has cut links with the internationalists.[15]

Some personal trajectories are particularly instructive in highlighting the internationalisation of Islamist militants. Ramzi Ahmed Yousef's life has already been discussed. Mohammed Mansour Jabarah, who was born in Kuwait, went to Canada when he was twelve years old and later became a Canadian citizen. He was allegedly the intermediary between Al Qaeda and Jemaah Islamiah in Indonesia.[16] It is interesting to note that (as was the case with Khalid Sheikh Mohammed and Abu Zubayda, other Al Qaeda Kuwaitis) he never attempted an operation in Kuwait. Amor Sliti, a Tunisian-born Belgian citizen, was a frequent worshipper at the Finsbury Park mosque in London, spent years in Afghanistan with Bin Laden, and helped the murderers of the anti-Taliban commander Massoud to travel to Afghanistan. Sliti married a Belgian woman and gave his very young daughter in marriage to an Afghan *mujahid*.

Wadih el-Hage, a US citizen, has been indicted for helping in the attacks on the East African US embassies in 1998. A Lebanese Christian who converted to Islam, el-Hage also lived for a while in Kuwait and went to the United States in 1978 to study city planning at South-Western Louisiana University. He married an American, fathered seven children, and went off to help the *mujahedin* fight the Soviet Union. Then, in the early 1990s, he worked in Sudan as Bin Laden's secretary. By 1994 el-Hage had moved to Kenya and helped to establish an Al Qaeda cell in Nairobi – the same unit that allegedly plotted the embassy bombing there. El-Hage returned home in 1997 and took a low-level job as manager of the Lone Star Wheels and Tires shop in Fort Worth, Texas. Also indicted in the case was Ali Mohamed, a major in the Egyptian army. He went to the United States in 1986 and continued his military career. He joined the US army and was eventually assigned to the John F. Kennedy Special Warfare Center at Fort Bragg, North Carolina. Within a year of his 1989 discharge, he was training Al Qaeda members in Afghanistan and Sudan and travelling the world for Bin Laden, delivering messages and conducting financial transactions.

15. See Chapter 2, this volume.
16. Richard C. Paddock, 'The Making of a Terrorist', *Los Angeles Times*, 22 January 2002.

Born March 1960 at El-Harrach, in the suburbs of Algiers, Fateh Kamel moved to France, and later settled in Canada in 1987. He took citizenship, married a woman (Nathalie B.) from Gaspé, Quebec, and opened a business in Montreal, importing Cuban cigars. Kamel went to Afghanistan in 1990 and then to Bosnia, where he met members of the Roubaix gang (see page 316). He was extradited from Jordan to France in April 1999 for allegedly being the '*emir*' of the Roubaix network.

L'Houssaine Kherchtou, born in Morocco in 1964, went to Corsica after graduating from university, settled in Milan where he headed the Islamic cultural centre, and went to Afghanistan in 1991. He was arrested in Kenya for his role in the 1998 attack on the US embassy there.

Beyond these examples, a general rule is that, except for a few Pakistanis and Yemenis, no Al Qaeda member left Europe or the United States to fight for Islam in his homeland or that of his family.[17] As we have seen, none of the Algerians involved in international Al Qaeda terrorism came from a GIA stronghold in Algeria; they all became radicalised in Europe (like Ahmed Ressam). The foreigners sentenced in Yemen in January 1999 for kidnapping included six British citizens of Pakistani descent (including the son-in-law of Abu Hamza, the Egyptian-born former *imam* of the Finsbury Park mosque) and two French Algerians. No Britons of Yemeni descent were involved in the case. The two young Muslims sentenced in Morocco for shooting tourists in a Marrakech hotel in 1994 were from French Algerian families. Omar Saeed Sheikh, convicted in Pakistan for the kidnapping of Daniel Pearl, is a British-born citizen of the United Kingdom. He is one of the few who returned to his family's country of origin.

All these examples bear out how activists of Middle Eastern origin have hardly ever undertaken missions in the region or with a regional objective. They have struck global targets, in most cases from the West.[18]

17. The Yemeni exception is Kamal Derwish from Buffalo, Colorado, of Yemeni descent. Derwish was killed by a CIA missile in October 2002 in Yemen, alongside Ali Qaed Senyan al-Harthi, who masterminded the attack on the destroyer USS *Cole*. But the other members of the so-called Lackawanna group (all US citizens of Yemeni descent) were caught in Pakistan.
18. One partial exception is Abu Mussab al-Zarqawi, a Jordanian. He never went to the West, even if his path in the Middle East is also 'deterritorialised'. He

RE-ISLAMISATION IN THE WEST

Many activists, whether settled in the West or studying there, became born-again Muslims and turned politically radical soon after,
while still there (for example, the 9/11 pilots, Ressam, Trabelsi,
Daoudi and Kelkal, and alleged would-be pilot Moussaoui). Many
of them were not known for being very religious-minded until they became born-again in the West.[19] Re-Islamisation occurs
never through the social pressure of the neighbourhood, family or
community, or on return to the country of origin, but as the result
of an individual quest that usually leads to a personal meeting with
an Afghan veteran in a mosque headed by a neofundamentalist
preacher. A number of mosques are known to be used for that purpose: the Hamburg Al Quds mosque (led by Moroccans) for the
9/11 pilots; London's Finsbury Park mosque for Daoudi, Djamel
Beghal, Bensakhria and many others (Christophe Cazé corres-
ponded with Abu Hamza); the Brixton mosque (whose chairman,
Abdul Haqq Baker, is a moderate) for Moussaoui and Reid; and
the Montreal Assuna-Annabawiyah mosque for Ressam. Gaols are
also recruiting centres for, among others, converts.

The lives of the leaders of many such mosques have followed a 'deterritorialised' trajectory. Abu Hamza became a born-again Muslim
in Britain. He originally came from Egypt to study civil engineering, attained British citizenship and returned to Islam after meeting
veterans from Afghanistan.[20] Abu Qatada, whose real name is Omar
Abu Omar, is a Palestinian from Jordan who was granted political asylum in Britain in 1993. He wrote editorials for the Algerian
GIA journal *Al Ansar*, while audiotapes of his incendiary sermons

fought in Afghanistan, joined the Kurdish Ansar al Islam pro-Al Qaeda group
in Iraq, and killed a US diplomat in Jordan. He has also been accused of having links with two Western Al Qaeda cells in Britain and Germany (<http://
www.theage.com.au/articles/2003/01/27/1043533989987.html>), and in
Italy (Risa Molitz, 'Suspected Terrorists Arrested in Italy', ABC News, 3 June
2003). In 2003 he became the figurehead of the internationalist radicals
fighting the United States in Iraq.
19. An interesting case is that of the two Britons from a Pakistani family, Asif Mohammed Hanif and Omar Khan Sharif, who blew themselves up in Tel Aviv
(April 2003). Though not part of Al Qaeda, they are part of the same category
of radicals. See Cahal Milmo, Justin Huggler, Nigel Morris and Arifa Akbar,
'The Trail of Death that Led from Britain to Israel', *Independent,* 2 May 2003.
20. Peter Ford, 'Why Do They Hate Us?', *Christian Science Monitor,* 27 September
2001.

were found in the Hamburg apartment of Muhammad Atta. Sheikh Omar Bakri Muhammad leads the al-Muhajiroun group, linked with Hizb ut-Tahrir, while Abdullah el-Faisal, a Jamaican convert, was convicted of inciting racial hatred in his violent anti-Jewish sermons. Young converts can travel throughout Europe, going from one such mosque to another, ignoring ethnic divides and speaking English everywhere (just as Catholic clerics and monks in the Middle Ages, going from one monastery to another, spoke Latin).

All of these preachers and organisations target second-generation Muslims, explicitly playing on their sense of being victims of racism, exclusion and loneliness in the West, and hence are very successful among Blacks or non-Muslim members of the underclass, as well as gaoled petty criminals. They offer a valorising substitute identity: members of the vanguard of internationalist jihadists who fight the global superpower and the international system.

There is now an interesting reverse trend: the export of radical Islam from West to East. During the 1990s proportionally more and more Islamic radicalism in Muslim countries has been organised in and from the West, as in the case of Omar Saeed Sheikh (see above). Raed Hijazi, arrested in Jordan for allegedly attempting to blow up a hotel in 1999, is a US-born Muslim who studied business at California State University in the late 1980s and joined a group in Sacramento called the Islamic Assistance Organisation.

An interesting phenomenon that has nothing to do with Al Qaeda is the spread of Hizb ut-Tahrir (the Liberation Party). This radical fundamentalist organisation, now based in London, spread to Central Asia, Pakistan and the Middle East from its British hub. In April 2002 three Britons were arrested in Egypt, allegedly for making propaganda on behalf of Hizb ut-Tahrir: Reza Pankhurst, Ian Malcolm Nisbett and Maajid Nawaz. None of them has any connection with Egypt, and two are converts.[21]

UPROOTING AND ACCULTURATION

Many activists are Western citizens. Syrian-born Mohammed Haydar Zammar is German, as is Said Bahaji; Ahmed Sayyid

---

21. 'Egypt: Opening of Trial of Three Britons and 23 Egyptians Raises Unfair Trial and Torture Concerns', Amnesty International Press Release, News Service No. 186, 18 October 2002.

Khedr and Fateh Kamel are Canadian. Nizar Sassi, Redouane Hammadi, Stephane Ait Idir, Moussaoui, Kamel Daoudi, Ahmed Loudaini, Khaled Ouldali and many others are French. Wadih el-Hage, Khalil al-Deek, Raed Hijazi, Kamal Derwish (alias Ahmed Hijazi, killed in Yemen), and all the members of the 'Lackawanna Six' group are citizens of the United States. Omar Saeed Sheikh is British. Amor Sliti is Belgian. Abu Mesaab is Spanish, as are two other Guantanamo Bay detainees, Ahmed Abderrahman and Abdesslam Rechouane.

None (except for the Saudis) was educated in a Muslim religious school and Jarrah even attended a Lebanese Christian school. Most of them studied technology, computing or town planning, as the World Trade Center pilots had done. Mohamed Saddiq Odeh studied architecture (in the Philippines); Khalid Sheikh Mohammed graduated from North Carolina Agricultural and Technical University in Greensboro in 1986. Daoudi was a computer engineer, employed by the French municipality of Athis-Mons. Omar Sheikh studied at the LSE. Munir al-Motassadeq studied electronics, al-Zarqawi supposedly biology. Omar Khan Sharif, who perpetrated a bomb attack in Tel Aviv, studied at London University. Many so-called *imams* and sheikhs such as Abu Hamza al-Masri and Omar Bakri Muhammad also studied science and technology.

Many activists cut their family ties when joining groups associated with Al Qaeda. This is congruent with the generation gap that is the hallmark of neofundamentalism, but it is particularly striking in the case of these individuals. While Islam stresses respect for one's parents, many of Al Qaeda's operatives have an uneasy relationship with theirs. The 9/11 pilots broke such links years earlier, although Ziad Jarrah returned to Lebanon in February 2001 when his father underwent open-heart surgery. Conversely, Abdullah Azzam stressed that one should seek the advice of one's parents before embarking on *jihad*. The new breed of activists cares little for such niceties. They adopt a way of life that is opposed to tradition: they are either too westernised (seeing women outside marriage) or too Islamic (regarding their parents as 'bad' Muslims).

Whatever their level of faith and religious commitment before becoming radicalised, most of these militants undeniably behaved in a more Western than traditional way, to the extent the parents and friends of those who had been arrested or died in a terrorist action all advanced the same explanation: 'They were irreligious; they had to be prodded to mosque. They drank. They smoked. They went clubbing and chasing girls.'[22]

Many militants married a 'Western' girl, or at least a Muslim woman from another country. Omar Khan Sharif, from a Pakistani family, married an Arab; Motassadeq a Russian; Fateh Kamel a Quebecker; Djamel Beghal a Frenchwoman; Kamel Daoudi a Hungarian; Amor Sliti a Belgian; and Slimane Khalfaoui a French-woman. Daoudi even met his Hungarian wife through the inter-net; she asked for a divorce three years later when he suddenly asked her to don the *hijab*. Jarrah lived with and married a Turk-ish woman, Aysel Senguen. Their tumultuous five-year relation-ship (love, break-ups, quarrels, reconciliation, abortion) was the everyday story of a modern couple.[23] Abdessatar Dahmane, one of the two Tunisians settled in Belgium who murdered Ahmed Shah Massoud, took his wife, Malika el Aroud (a Belgian citizen born in Tangier, Morocco), to Afghanistan. She wrote a book in French, telling how her husband behaved like a 'modern' man (sewing the buttons on his shirt because she hated doing such tasks).[24] Converts underwent the reverse trend: Lionel Dumont married a Bosnian and Jose Padilla an Arab (his second marriage). Bypassing racial and ethnic divides is a characteristic of radical neofundamentalists.

Most of these militants eschewed a traditional Muslim marriage, which favours a union from within a kinship group (and prefer-ably between first cousins), or at least an arranged marriage, which was normal among Al Qaeda's first generation. Its second genera-tion all chose their own partners without familial interference. But there are also many single men in Al Qaeda and no women, which is a significant difference from the Islamist movements (the Mus-lim Brothers, Hamas, FIS, Islamic Jihad and Hezbollah have many female members).

22. Amy Waldman, 'How in a Little British Town Jihad Found Young Converts', *New York Times*, 24 April 2002.
23. Dirk Laabs and Terry McDermott, 'Prelude to 9/11: A Hijacker's Love, Lies', *Los Angeles Times*, 27 January 2003.
24. Malika el Aroud, *Les soldats de lumière*, n.p., 2003; see a review (in French) by Jean François Mayer, '"Les soldats de lumière": Une autre image du jihad', <http://www.terrorisme.net/p/article_50.shtml>.

THE PERIPHERAL *JIHAD*

The peripheral character of Al Qaeda militants is also reflected in the geography of their chosen battlefields, which exhibits a paradox: most Al Qaeda fighters are ethnic Arabs, the majority being Saudis, Egyptians, Algerians and Jordanian-Palestinians. But Al Qaeda has been conspicuously absent from Arab lands, at least before the US occupation of Iraq, with the exception of the Khobar Towers attack, the bombing of USS *Cole* and the October 2002 murder of Laurence Foley, the USAID representative in Jordan. Nor have these militants cared much for Arab conflicts (although the US occupation of Iraq is attracting some Al Qaeda fighters). Osama Bin Laden paid only lip-service to the Palestinian cause till late 2001, while plans for the 9/11 attacks were initiated well before the second Palestinian intifada. Most of the terrorists involved arrived on US soil in the spring of 2000 and the decision to attack had been made that January, which shows that it was not a reaction to the escalation of the Israeli-Palestinian conflict. Instead of fighting in the Middle East, Al Qaeda and its ilk have been conducting military *jihad* in the West (New York, Paris and London), in Bosnia, Kosovo, Somalia, Chechnya, Afghanistan, Central Asia, Pakistan, Kashmir, the Philippines, Indonesia and East Africa – but not in Egypt, Israel/Palestine, Lebanon, Syria, the Gulf states or Algeria. The radicals who in the spring of 2004 engaged in violent actions in Saudia Arabia are Saudis with a Saudi agenda; they targeted Western interests in the Kingdom nevertheless. More Al Qaeda Arabs went to Indonesia and Malaysia than to Palestine or Egypt.

This is not just because Arab states take their own internal security seriously. Logically the recommunalised Muslims of the West are fighting at the frontiers of their imaginary *ummah*, and are doing so because what agitates them most are the consequences of their own westernisation. All of the literature and websites linked to Al Qaeda emphasise and publicise the 'peripheral' *jihad*, from Bosnia to the Philippines. Most *jihadi* websites are based in the West or in Malaysia. This is not only because of censorship; it is because the people behind them live in the West. While Al Qaeda's campaign against US interests has constantly grown, and hundreds of Islamic militants have been arrested or tracked down in Europe, Islamist violence in the Middle East has steadily decreased since the Luxor killings of 1997. (I believe that the violence in Iraq and Israel-

Palestine is primarily motivated by nationalism rather than religion, even though religion may easily accompany nationalism.)

The decision to wage a peripheral *jihad* was reached because the locations of such *jihads* seem like 'virgin lands' that have relatively poorly organised resistance movements. Thus foreign volunteers can hope to influence not only their local comrades in arms but also society as a whole. This is certainly not the case in areas like Israel/Palestine or other Middle Eastern countries, where nobody is likely to accept a lecture from a Western Muslim. The periphery is more receptive to the *jihadis'* millenarianist dream. But in Bosnia as in Afghanistan many local fighters, specifically Sufis, were antagonised by Salafi and Wahhabi propaganda.[25] Ultimately no foreign *jihadis* have been able to impose their religious agenda on any Muslim society, though it would be fair to concede that they have played significant military roles in conflicts in Chechnya, Bosnia and Kashmir.

The Bosnian connection[26]

Not only Al Qaeda, but also many other radical networks from the West and the Middle East have set up support networks to send volunteers to many parts of the peripheral *jihad*. Bosnia probably has the greatest diversity among networks that have sent volunteers. Maktab al-Khidamat opened an office in Zagreb in 1992, as did the International Islamic Relief Organisation later. The first fighting group was headed by a Saudi, Abu Abdul Aziz, who had also fought in Afghanistan and Kashmir (according to some sources he was of Indian Muslim descent). The town of Zenica, home of the Bosnian 7th Battalion (a military unit with a pronounced Islamic identity), became the headquarters of the Islamic volunteers, who joined the Bosnian 7th Corps. In 1993 they established a purely *jihadi* unit, the El Mujahid brigade, made up of foreign volunteers and some Bosnians who had split from traditional

25. In 1993, during the Bosnian war, the Islamic 7th Battalion split between its Bosnian Sufi components and the Wahhabi volunteers headed by the Saudi Abu Abdul Aziz. See Xavier Bougarel, 'Les réseaux transnationaux Islamiques en Bosnie Herzégovine' in Xavier Bougarel and Nathalie Clayer (eds), *Le nouvel islam balkanique. Les musulmans, acteurs du post-communisme 1990-2000*, Paris: Maisonneuve et Larose, 2001.
26. See Bougarel, 'Les réseaux transnationaux Islamiques'.

Balkan Sufi Islam. The London office of an NGO helped to send volunteers to Bosnia. Many Europeans went to fight there, among them the Roubaix gang (Mouloud Bouguelane, Lionel Dumont and Christophe Cazé, a doctor who led the group). They were linked, through Said Atmani, to the Fateh Kamel and Ressam group in Montreal .

Many second-generation Western Muslims and converts fought in Bosnia: Abu Musa al-Almaani, born to Turkish parents in Germany and adopted by a German family, was killed on 21 July 1995.[27] The Frenchman Xavier Djaffo, known as Massoud al-Benin Djaffo (whose family came from Benin but were Catholic), a close friend of Zacarias Moussaoui, was also killed in 1997.

Some survivors, like Lionel Dumont, attempted for a while to stay in Zenica, where they established a local Islamic community, which was finally disbanded under government pressure. The *jihadis* never changed Bosnian society.

The Chechen connection

After the fall of the Taliban, many would-be *jihadis* endeavoured to go to Chechnya, including volunteers from France, one of whom was arrested in Georgia in December 2002. He is a French citizen, born in France of Algerian parents, and thought by police to be a former supporter of the Algerian FIS. Also arrested were other second-generation French Muslims, one of whose brothers has been detained in Guantanamo Bay. The latter case reveals that any *jihad* will do for such militants. Opting for a given *jihad* has nothing to do with ethnicity or linguistic ability, or probably with strategic considerations either.

Other European volunteers follow the same paths. Two German nationals were killed in October 2002 (Tarek B., from Schorndorf, born in Tunisia and married to a German, and Mevlüt P., born in Turkey).[28]

---

27. See the picture in azzam.com, as reproduced in Bougarel, 'Les réseaux trans-nationaux Islamiques', p. 442.
28. 'Kämpfer für den Kaukasus, Deutsche Islamisten werden auch für den Krieg gegen Russland rekrutiert: In Tschetschenien starben jetzt zwei Muslime aus der Bundesrepublik', *Der Spiegel*, 45 (2002), p. 134.

Other jihads

In Kashmir many Britons of Pakistani descent have been killed in action, but in January 2002 two Dutch Moroccans from Eindhoven were also killed: Ahmed el Bakiouli (twenty years old) and Khalid el Hassnaoui (or Massnaoui, twenty-one). There is also one case in Israel in which two Britons of Pakistani background (Asif Mohammed Hanif, twenty-one, and Omar Khan Sharif, twenty-seven, born in Derby) blew themselves up in a suicide attack in April 2002. They are an exception in the sense that they are the only second-generation *jihadis* to have gone to Israel to fight. (Curiously, they were among the few to have had harmonious relations with their families.) Will Iraq play the same role in the future? In any case, the rift will remain between the foreign volunteers, motivated by global *jihad*, and the local actors, motivated by nationalism.

As we have seen, in a globalised world the natural field of *jihad* is everywhere.

THE WESTERN–BORN OR SECOND–GENERATION MUSLIMS

If many leaders and activists (such as Djamel Beghal and the World Trade Center pilots) came to the West as students from abroad, they recruited or were helped by second-generation European Muslims. There is a general pattern of radicalisation in Europe. A politicised middleman from the Middle East (usually with an 'Afghan' background) contacts a group of local friends, often involved in petty delinquency or drug abuse, whose ethnic origin is less relevant than their sense of isolation and uprootedness, and who find in radical Islam a positive protest identity, even when they have no previous record of religious practice (and this includes by definition the converts). Most of the French Muslims who joined Al Qaeda are from impoverished suburbs, even those who later did well professionally. The motivation to join Al Qaeda is not necessarily born out of poverty. There are as many well-educated and well-integrated young men who are drawn to Al Qaeda as there are jobless outcasts. What is at stake is more the reconstruction or recasting of a lost identity than the expression of a depressed social or economic situation. The same is true, incidentally, of radicals from the Middle East: why did Saudi Arabia provide the highest number of terrorists (*per capita*) and Bangladesh the lowest? (I have yet to hear of a single Bangladeshi international terrorist.)

The perpetrators of terrorist attacks against European tourists in Marrakech in 1994 were two young unemployed French Muslims, Redouane Hammadi and Stephane Ait Idir, of Algerian origin and from the impoverished Cité des 4000 district in La Courneuve, a Paris suburb. Neither spoke Arabic. They became radicalised under the influence of a Moroccan college teacher working in France, Abdelilah Ziyad, who had gone to Afghanistan in 1992 and, on his return, had robbed several banks before leaving for Morocco.

In 1995 the first series of non-state-sponsored acts of Islamic terrorism in France was carried out by a network of French Muslims from the suburbs of Lyon. The terrorists were led by French-born Khaled Kelkal, who had become a born-again Muslim in gaol. The group organised deadly bomb attacks on the public transport system between August and October 1995. Kelkal was killed by the police on 28 September that year. In March 1996 shooting erupted between police and a group of young men in Roubaix, leaving four dead. This group was ethnically mixed: it comprised two converts, Christophe Cazé (a doctor) and Lionel Dumont (from a poor working-class family), along with French-born Muslim Mouloud Bouguelane and two Franco-Algerians, Omar Zemmiri and Hocine Bendaoui.

The Beghal network, uncovered in the summer of 2001, exhibits a range of typical profiles. The leader, Djamel Beghal, is an Algerian, married to a Frenchwoman, who became a French citizen. Kamel Daoudi came as an infant to France, was brought up in a typical suburban area, and studied computing. Nizar Trabelsi, a football player, was known as a petty drug-dealer. But the group also included four converts, Jerome and David Courtailler, Johann Bonte (Beghal's brother-in-law) and Jean-Marc Grandvisir. In October 2003 a French Caribbean convert, Willy Brigitte, was arrested for allegedly plotting a bomb attack in Australia in connection with the Pakistani movement Lashkar-e-Toiba.

The Frankfurt network, which allegedly planned to target the football World Cup in France in 1998,[29] also comprised second-generation French Muslims who became born-again in London.

29. Xavier Ternisien, 'Comment naissent et vivent les réseaux d'Al Qaida en Europe', *Le Monde*, 4 January 2003.

Slimane Khalfaoui, arrested in November 2002 in Montfermeil (another impoverished suburb of Paris) for allegedly planning a bombing in Strasbourg, converted his brother-in-law, Nicolas Belloni, to Islam. Two of the French prisoners in Guantanamo Bay, Nizar Sassi and Mourad Benchellali, come from a notorious neighbourhood of Lyon (Les Minguettes), which has been the scene of youth riots and political protests since the early 1980s.

THE CONVERTS AND THE 'PROTEST CONVERSION'

Far from being a marginal phenomenon, the number and role of converts in radical Islamic networks have been growing since the early 1990s and are another indicator of the globalisation and westernisation of Islam. Converts from Western Europe (whose existence was well known in there but only discovered by US authorities with the case of John Walker Lindh) match patterns similar to the second generation of Muslim militants, with some added specificities. We can draw up four categories, which may overlap and which constitute what I call 'protest conversions':

- politicised rebels, who find a cause in Islam and are fascinated by the anti-system and anti-imperialist dimension of radical Islam, while the classical radical left failed to challenge the ruling order (examples here are Christophe Cazé, Lionel Dumont, and probably the Spaniard Luis Jose Galan);

- religious nomads, who found their way into Islam after tasting different religions on the religious market (John Walker Lindh and David Hicks);

- former drug addicts and petty thieves, who find in Islam an escape from an impoverished life, as well as a supportive milieu and a new brotherhood (Jerome Courtailler and Richard Reid); and

- Blacks, Latinos and persons of mixed race who find in radical Islamic groups a rebuke to racism and a way to fight a system they reject (Jose Padilla, Richard Reid, Johann Bonte and Jean-Marc Grandvisir).

A few are from the middle class, usually the leaders like Christophe Cazé, a French doctor who was killed 'in action' running a police roadblock in Roubaix in 1996; John Walker Lindh, who is not a leader, is also middle-class. But many belong to the same milieu as their Muslim friends; they live in impoverished neighbourhoods and are working-class dropouts – for example, Jose Padilla, Richard Reid and the Frenchman Lionel Dumont – who converted Islam because 'the Muslims are the only ones to fight the system'. Many are from racial minorities (such as Blacks, specifically from the Caribbean) that find in radical Islam a truly non-racist environment. To convert to Islam today is a way for a European rebel to find a cause; it has little to do with theology.

More than 100,000 converts to Islam live in France, but most converted for practical reasons – to marry a Muslim woman, for example. For converts and for those who are born Muslim, radicalisation remains an ultra-minority attitude. There follows an unscientific attempt to describe the profiles of some radical converts.

Looking again at the groups we studied earlier, we find converts not only among the rank and file but also among the leaders of all the main radical networks (including Kelkal's group). In the Beghal network one finds David Courtailler, a former drug addict who went to Brighton in 1990, became a Muslim there, travelled to Afghanistan in 1997, and was gaoled in France in 2004.

The Frenchman Jamel Loiseau was found dead on the Afghanistan–Pakistan border in December 2001. His father, Said Belhaji, is a non-practising Algerian Muslim who migrated to France, and his mother is French. Loiseau was converted by the Tabligh.

In the United States Jose Padilla (born 1970) is the son of Puerto Rican immigrants. Now called Abdullah al-Muhajir, he had done poorly in school, joined street gangs, been convicted for mostly minor crimes and held a series of minimum-wage jobs, and then become a Muslim in Florida in 1993. On his marriage license Padilla's race was listed as black. He went to Egypt in 1999, married an Egyptian woman, left for Afghanistan and was arrested in May 2002 when returning from Egypt through Zürich.[30]

So-called 'shoe bomber' Richard Reid was born in 1973 in the London suburb of Bromley, the son of an English mother and a Jamaican father. He fell into a life of petty crime and in the mid-1990s was gaoled for a string of muggings, for which he served time

30. Manuel Roig-Franzia and Amy Goldstein, 'A Bomb Suspect's Search for Identity: In Padilla's Metamorphosis into Al Muhajir, Fla. Provided a Turning Point', *Washington Post*, 15 June 2002, p. A01.

in a number of prisons, including Feltham Young Offenders' Institution in west London, where he is said to have converted to Islam.

David Hicks, an Australian born in 1976, was a school dropout who became a drug addict. He went to Japan, and then joined the Kosovo Liberation Army through the internet, attended Bible courses back in Australia but became a Muslim. At one time he was married to an Australian Aborigine (the search to bypass the ethnic and racial divide is common among radicals). He went to Afghanistan and ended up in gaol in Guantanamo Bay.[31]

The story of Hiram Torres is also emblematic, because it encompasses three of the categories we have defined.[32] Torres disappeared after 1998 but his name was found in the records of Harkat-ul-Mujahidin in Kabul after the US military victory. He was of Puerto Rican origin, and, according to a former schoolmate, 'His dream was to be part of a revolution somewhere'. He moved through the 'Bible, Koran and the Bhagavad-Gita', dropped out of college, left for Bangladesh and Pakistan, and cut his ties with his mother.

An interesting case is that of Christian Ganczarski, a Polish-born German national who was arrested at Charles de Gaulle Airport in June 2003 on suspicion of involvement in the Jerba synagogue bombing of April 2002. Shortly before the blast, Ganczarski allegedly received a call on his mobile phone from Tunisian suicide bomber Nizar Nawar, whose family lives in France.

To conclude, the variety of categories of converts indicates that the trend is probably durable, and for as long as radical Islam is seen as the vanguard of an absolute opposition to so-called US imperialism, more and more converts will join. But the role played by converts in different radical organisations shows also that ethnicity has nothing to do with radical neofundamentalism.

THE SUBCONTRACTORS

Al Qaeda finds 'subcontractors' in countries where local radical groups have a genuine base (such as Indonesia, Saudi Arabia and Pakistan) or, in other Muslim countries, among radicalised young

31. Raymond Bonner, 'A Drifter's Odyssey from the Outback to Guantanamo', *New York Times*, 4 May 2003.
32. David Rhode and James Risen, 'Missing New Jersey Man's Name Turns up in Kabul', *New York Times*, 6 February 2002.

denizens of run-down inner cities and suburbs who are trying to make and impression by identifying with Al Qaeda (for example, the Casablanca group).

In Indonesia, Saudi Arabia and Pakistan, Al Qaeda is not the source of radicalisation; there already exist several indigenous radical networks with their own history. But some of them have decided to act on behalf of Al Qaeda or to join forces against a common enemy (the United States, the West, the Saudi monarchy). As a social basis these groups enjoy different circles of support: members, sympathisers, fund-raisers, contacts in the government apparatus, certain members of the clerical establishment, and so on. Interestingly, this phenomenon occurs in the countries where an autonomous *madrasa* system is pervasive and growing.

In Pakistan, Omar Sheikh, a leader of Jayash-e-Muhammad who kidnapped Richard Pearl, enjoyed a close connection with the ISI (Pakistani security services) and with Al Qaeda through Khalid Sheikh Mohammed.[33] The kidnapping and murder of *Wall Street Journal* reporter Daniel Pearl was probably a joint venture.

The Indonesian Jemaah Islamiah seems to act only as a subcontractor. Hambali, who masterminded the bombing of a Bali nightclub in October 2002, went to Afghanistan around 1988; he met Moussaoui and Khalid al-Midhar in Kuala Lumpur before 9/11. But he is not an Al Qaeda operative. He belongs to a genuine organisation with its own history and agenda. Nevertheless, the agendas of Al Qaeda and Jemaah Islamiah coincide. Jemaah is not an Islamist movement but a neofundamentalist one that is striving for a supranational caliphate in South-East Asia.

In Saudi Arabia the May 2003 attack on residential compounds inhabited by expatriates in Riyadh was also perpetrated by Saudis, apparently linked to the late Sheikh Hammoud bin 'Uqla al-Shu'aybi. However, the names of many of those arrested indicate that they have a specific tribal background (from the Asir area in the south and al-Jouf in the north). In particular, the name al-Ghamdi (that of a southern tribe) is common to three of the 9/11 terrorists and Riyadh attackers. The complex relationship we have already seen between neofundamentalism and tribalism seems to be at work again. But at least this shows that the radicals in Saudi Arabia have a

33. Mariam Abou Zahab and Olivier Roy, *Islamic Networks: The Pakistan-Afghan Connection*, London: Hurst, 2003.

genuine social basis. They are more Saudi citizens than members of Al Qaeda. Other subcontractors have a far more localised and narrow social basis, more reminiscent of their Western counterparts.

The Casablanca group, whose members killed forty-four people in an attack on a Spanish restaurant and a Jewish cultural centre on 16 May 2003, comprised friends from the same poor slum area of Sidi Moumen. Some of them had tried in vain to migrate to France to find work but been expelled. They coalesced around a local leader and created a small, closed group, most of whom died in the operation. The explosive devices were provided by an outsider from Fez. The group may have been in contact with a French convert living in Tangier. This case is almost symmetrical with those of the different groups operating in France in the 1990s: local young men who jumped from joblessness and petty delinquency to political radicalisation through the influence of an outsider with a political connection.

The attack on the synagogue on Jerba fits the same pattern: a local isolated group directly linked with an international network (Nizar Nawar acting under the instructions of outsiders). In a sense both attacks (Casablanca and Jerba) could have happened in any European country, following the same patterns.

If it is quite understandable for a small local group to claim Al Qaeda's name and style (franchising), why should a more entrenched and structured organisation, like the Indonesian Jemaah Islamiah, act as subcontractor to Al Qaeda? It is interesting to note that these subcontractors, from Indonesia to Pakistan and Morocco, did not target the state authorities. When they set up terrorist attacks they are always against symbolic Western targets, with absolutely no strategic importance: nightclubs, restaurants, de luxe hotels (such as the Marriott in Jakarta), cultural centres and compounds for expatriates, but never a police station, a governor, a state bank. For them the state is probably no longer a valuable target. They act from the local to the global, ignoring the state. Even Saudi radicals, who undoubtedly target the Saudi regime, in the spring of 2004 attacked mostly foreign locations and people.

THE FUTURE OF AL QAEDA

It should be clear that Al Qaeda has little to do with a true underground revolutionary movement. It acted against all the rules of clandestine action, as defined by decades of revolutionary experience (for example, the Comintern) and by the standards of any modern intelligence service. Secret agents and operatives are supposed not to know one another and to meet only to set up operations or deliver information. Procedures for meetings are quite complex, anonymity is respected, and no chance should be taken that might reveal links between the underground agents. Al Qaeda's cadres do exactly the opposite. Theirs is a network of friends, of mates, a kindred community based on an easy brotherhood, not only where everybody knows everybody, but where they travel and live together. The Hamburg cell is a good example.[34] They shared apartments and bank accounts, participated in the wedding parties of their friends (Binalshibh is shown on a video speaking at Said Bahaji's wedding in October 1999, after being trained in Afghanistan), and signed their friend's will (Muhammad Atta). All this is absolute heresy in terms of classical clandestine operations. Nor did Al Qaeda build a strong political organisation. Al Qaeda is not a communist party, or the PKK, the IRA or ETA. There is no political branch, union, women's organisation, student branch or press, and there are no fellow-travellers. The 'masses' are left on the pavement, watching some sort of apocalyptic video game played by Al Qaeda. In this sense Al Qaeda is more a mafia or a sect than a professional underground organisation.

The Afghan sanctuary allowed members to meet, train and forge *esprit de corps* and links; in a word, to coalesce a ragtag collection of activists into a cohesive and disciplined organisation. A specific dimension of Al Qaeda was the solidarity of its veterans; many young radicals, who met first as a Western group of discontented friends and acquaintances, turned into an efficient cell only after having lived in Afghanistan. International connections followed this experience: Ramzi Ahmed Yousef and Abubakar Janjalani, and Zayn al-Abidin Abu Bakr al-Mihdar (founder of the Aden-Abyan Army). Moreover, a distinctive pattern of Al Qaeda was that personal links between veterans of the Afghan *jihad* had turned into an efficient but flexible chain of command. But this sanctuary has disappeared. Unless it can be re-created elsewhere (the new 'Talibanistan' emerging in North-West Frontier

34. For a good article based on an interview with Aysel Senguen, Ziad Jarrah's girlfriend, see Laabs and McDermott, 'Prelude to 9/11'.

Province in Pakistan, for instance), Al Qaeda will have to adapt to a new situation.

After 9/11 and the campaign in Afghanistan, the terrorists are facing two new problems with immediate consequences for their ability to act in or from Western Europe. First, there is no longer a sanctuary in which to build the links. It is becoming far more difficult to become organised and to contact the leaders. Second, the 'demonising' of Islam that has put the Muslim population in the West on the defensive may have made some individuals more radical, but has globally persuaded Muslims living in the West to clarify their position on terrorism and to advocate greater integration into mainstream society in response to 'Islamophobia'. European authorities have usually responded positively to that quest for recognition, contributing to the isolation of radicals. Isolation among the European Muslim population and alienation from them are the main challenges for the radicals.

Consequently two new patterns of Islamic radicalism are developing. The first is 'franchising': local groups, based on local solidarities (neighbourhood, family, university) and with few or no ties to Al Qaeda take the label and act according to what they see as Al Qaeda's ideology and strategy. The second is a quest for allies and support beyond the pale of Islamic fundamentalists. The radicals try to find allies and fellow-travellers at the expense of the purity of their ideological message. They may one day find support among the European ultra-left or certain other 'liberation' movements (for instance, former Baathists in Iraq, or ETA in Europe). Both trends are in line with the globalisation of Al Qaeda.

One of the issues in this quest for allies is the choice to be made between the national level and the global. Until 1998, every time internationalists joined a movement of national liberation (from Palestine to Afghanistan and Bosnia to Chechnya), it was the national movement that succeeded in imposing its agenda on foreign volunteers, even if it borrowed some tactics (such as suicide bombing). That was the pattern in the 1970s when hundreds of leftist secular militants left Europe and Japan to fight in Bolivia (Régis Debray), Palestine (Japanese Red Army) and Lebanon (Red Army Faction). But we see now a trend in which some 'national' movements identify with global organisations. The Taliban movement, for example, committed political suicide when it refused to dissociate itself from Bin Laden after the August 1998 terrorist attacks on US embassies in East Africa. Jemaah Islamiah would not have been repressed as it was by the Indonesian authorities had it not directly attacked Western interests. This is also a consequence of the 'failure of political Islam' and the demise of the 'Islamic state' paradigm. Globalisation is a pessimistic answer to the failure of national projects.

Internationalism versus nationalism is not a consequence of a reading of the Koran but simply the revival of a radical phenomenon of the 1970s. Thirty years ago, many of today's radicals, specifically in the West, would have joined radical leftist movements, which have now disappeared or become 'bourgeois' (like the Revolutionary Communist League in France). Nowadays only two Western currents of radical protest claim to be 'internationalist': the antiglobalisation movement and radical Islamists. But their constituencies are quite different. Islamist radicals will not be able to find a stable and lasting constituency, precisely because their appeal is based on uprootedness and the generation gap. To find allies radical Islam has to be less and less Islamic. To put down its roots among Muslims, it has to become less and less radical.

It is clear that Al Qaeda has 'Islamised' an existing space of anti-imperialism and contestation. Its militants are activists, with little ideological formation or few ideological concerns. Al Qaeda is heir to the ultra-leftist and Third Worldist movements of the 1970s. The European extreme Left, if existent, is no longer active in depressed housing estates and degraded inner cities. Islamist preachers have replaced far-Left militants and social workers. Many of the young people in these neighbourhoods find in radical Islam a way to recast and rationalise their sense of exclusion and uprootedness. Many radical preachers mix the Koran with almost Marxist statements. Abu Hamza and Abu Qatada deride integration. 'The West has greatly oppressed our nation,' declared Qatada. 'To strengthen the roots of religion in our nation is to reject the Western ideology.'[35] They tell the young that there is no hope of making their way in Western societies except through violence.

What are the implications of this trend? The reasons why some people rebel will not disappear overnight, nor will reasons for returning to Islam. But rebellion and re-Islamisation should not be confused. Many returns to Islam are transitional and the revolt still lacks a strategic perspective.

35. CNN, 29 November 2001.

We have already noted the main failure of Al Qaeda: the lack of genuine strategic goals. Its aim is to destroy the United States, but the backlash has been severe, from Afghanistan to Iraq. Even if the United States is trapped in a new form of hubris (reshaping the Muslim world), it is not on the verge of collapsing.

An important debate among Muslim radicals has yet to be satisfactorily resolved. Bin Laden has called for *jihad* and has failed. Moreover, US troops are everywhere, and the main Muslim movements of national liberation are taking the brunt of the unholy antiterrorist alliance: Chechens and Palestinians are losing international support. Innocent Muslims living in the United States are suffering prejudice. Many radicals who share the ideas of Al Qaeda are discussing its strategy (or lack of it). The debate is reminiscent of that between Leninist and ultra-leftists organisations in the 1920s and 1930s: should one call for immediate revolution throughout the world, or first secure 'socialism' in one country, while campaigning among the 'masses' to win their hearts and minds, before calling them to arms? There is talk among many militants that they should revert to *dawah* (preaching; that is, propaganda and, in a sense, political action) instead of *jihad*. Postponement of *jihad* does not necessarily mean moderation, but implies a return to some sense of reality and pragmatism: one has to deal with the real people. The purity of the neofundamentalist message will be lost in the very process of re-Islamisation. To maintain purity means living in a ghetto or a closed community. To 'address the masses' means entering into the real world of politics and compromise. Whatever the tensions, the decision among many European governments not to exclude the so-called fundamentalist movements from political dialogue is positive and pushes those movements towards moderation and compromise. The policy of integration works so long as the call to arms is no longer heard or listened to. Al Qaeda's dream of mobilising the *ummah* around *jihad* is self-limiting. The movement is a security threat, but it lacks a strategic agenda.

8
REMAPPING THE WORLD: CIVILISATION, RELIGION AND STRATEGY

In the West the debate on Islam crosses the lines between the various political and religious schools of thought. Secularists and feminists strongly oppose 'fundamentalism', and, although they are mostly from the Left, often end up supporting authoritarian but secular regimes against Islamists (from Algeria to Saddam's Iraq). Other leftists, as secular as the former but who defend the Third World and promote multiculturalism in the West, campaign to see the wearing of the headscarf allowed in European schools. An Anglican bishop might side with a Labour MP to condemn Rushdie's *Satanic Verses*. Many anti-imperialist militants, although supposed to promote women's rights, supported the Taliban when it came under US attack. Some Jewish community leaders allied with the US Christian coalition, whose support for Israel relies on the dream of a conversion to Christianity of the Jews who will survive Armageddon (which means that a good Jew is either dead or Christian). Leading homosexual politicians like the late Pim Fortuyn may join Catholic bishops and neofascists in saying that Islam is incompatible with the West. Conversely, many bishops, orthodox Jews and conservative Muslim leaders may unite to oppose gay rights. The same Christian Right that unleashes smears on the Prophet Muhammad shares with neofundamentalist Muslims the conception that religion encompasses all aspects of the believer's life. A rightist French essayist might write a book claiming that radical Islam is a US plot to destroy Europe,[1] while others would claim that President Chirac opposed the war in Iraq to placate

---

1. Alexandre Del Valle, *Islamisme et États-Unis. Une alliance contre l'Europe,* Lausanne: L'Age d'Homme, 1999.

French Muslims. In France the extreme-Right National Front can call for the expulsion of Muslims and for support for Saddam Hussein against the United States. The usual fault-lines (Left/Right, nationalist/universalist, secularist/religious) are increasingly irrelevant in explaining current alignments, which are often conjectural and elusive, in the debate on Islam. The idea that 'Islam is the issue' might also be shared by leftist secularists and conservative Catholics. The Israeli-Palestinian conflict can be read in the French suburbs as a metaphor for the exclusion of disfranchised second-generation youths, who may attack a local synagogue but cannot locate Jericho on the map and do not bother to express their views in the streets of Paris, where no pro-Palestine demonstration has ever attracted more than 20,000 people, half of them secular leftists. Social tensions in a remote Paris suburb are read according to a global idiom, without any intellectual coherence: Third World versus US imperialism, Muslims versus Jews, Arabs versus Israelis, youth versus police. The references come from a disparaged intellectual matrix: anti-Semitism has more to do with the European brand,[2] for which a Jew is always a Jew, than with traditional Islam (where a converted Jew ceases to be a Jew).

This is a time of great intellectual confusion, when historical and cultural paradigms, even insignificant or irrelevant ones, are marshalled to explain complex modern political and ideological trends. (For instance, suicide bombers may be referred to as 'Hashshashin', in reference to a twelfth-century heretic sect, while the modern use of suicide attacks was pioneered, if that is the right word, by Sri Lanka's Tamil Tigers, a nationalist–Marxist liberation movement.) Islam has become the focal point of a debate largely born after the collapse of the USSR, which would have arisen anyway. Where is evil? What is the meaning of the 'West'? How does one link morality and politicals? How does one establish a relationship between a given society, a culture, a religion, a political system and a territory? How does one visualise threats in terms of territory? How does one remap the world, in terms of sense and meanings?

To send an army, one needs a territory and a visible target. But borders and frontiers are no longer territorial. There is no wall defending the enemy, an enemy that is more often than not too

---

2. As we have seen, the biggest source of anti-Semitic literature in Islamic bookshops is European (for example, *The Protocol of the Elders of Zion* and Roger Garaudy).

elusive to be named and targeted, an enemy who if he is shadowy is sometimes merely our shadow. It is interesting to note the linguistic contortions that are entailed by the use of such clear-cut terms as 'axis of evil' or 'terrorism'. Their deployment is usually followed by a debate on definitions (what is terrorism?), by counterstatements and by denial ('We don't fight against Islam', 'Islam is a moderate religion, but ...'). The looseness of such definitions, either vague ('terrorism') or precise in appearance only ('radical Islamism', 'Islamic terrorism') brings home the difficulty in defining the enemy or simply the 'other'. The 'us or them' battle cry is not supported by a clear-cut conceptual definition of the 'them' (except among those who claim that 'Islam is the issue' – they are wrong but coherent). Manichaeism is central to the discourse but does not find a basis in reality. The issues of territory and mapping underpin the debate.

CULTURE, RELIGION AND CIVILISATIONS: THE CONUNDRUM OF CLASH AND DIALOGUE

The concept of the clash of civilisations is predicated upon a little-debated premise: that civilisations and cultures are based on religion.[3] Many opponents of the clash-of-civilisations theory promote instead a 'dialogue' between civilisations and push for interfaith dialogue and multiculturalism. But they share the same premise: there are distinct cultures, each based on a specific religion.

Here is not the place directly to challenge the concepts of culture, civilisation and religion, even if I merely point out that they follow a variable geometry more adapted to what is to be proved than to fact. Is the West best defined by Helleno-Christianity, Judaeo-Christianity, Christianity or Protestantism? Does Islam define a whole civilisation from Morocco to Indonesia, or refer only to the Arab world?[4] In this case what it is the relation between the 'Islamic' and 'Arab' parameters? Another problem is the constant confusion between correlation and causality. When Max Weber

3.   T.S. Eliot expresses in verse the conventional wisdom: 'Ultimately, antagonistic religions must mean antagonistic cultures; and ultimately religions cannot be reconciled.'

4.   In *What Went Wrong: Western Impact and Eastern Response* (Oxford University Press, 2002), Bernard Lewis speaks of Islam in general, but makes reference almost solely to the Middle East.

wrote *The Protestant Ethic and the Spirit of Capitalism*, he wanted to study a range of correlations, but not to make Protestantism the cause of capitalism or the reverse. He did not say that Catholics are ill-equipped to practise modern banking. But the dialectical dimension is lost in the neo-Weberian current embodied by Huntington and Landes (or at least in the way they are read), in which cultures are defined as a set of permanent and objective patterns that determine the collective behaviour of actors. Cultures are defined as objects.[5]

I intend to address here the hermeneutic value of these concepts to explain current events. A general view is that religious fundamentalism is the expression of an increasing rigidity of traditional identities. The (non-Muslim) conservative view is that radical Islam is embedded in the Koran and in the history of the first Muslim society under the Prophet and his successors. The liberal perspective is that radical Islam is a reaction against Western political and cultural encroachments. But both views link religious fundamentalism with the permanence of identity.

Nevertheless, if one looks at the different forms of fundamentalism in the West and the Middle East, they are all, as we have seen, linked with deculturation and not with the permanence of a pristine culture. Fundamentalism may even struggle against culture, and it never reaffirms a cultural identity. US evangelical Protestantism and Islamic fundamentalism share, *mutatis mutandis*, many common patterns. Faith is the fault-line between the good people and the wicked. Religious norms should be at the core of human life and are not linked to any culture. Life should be reconstructed upon these norms, because wider society is secular-minded, even if it pays lip-service to religion. Culture (novels, films, music) may bring about the dereliction of mores. Religious norms and creeds can apply to anybody anywhere: hence there is no need for 'cultural sensitivity'. The divide is between believers and non-believers within so-called cultures and not between different cultures. In this sense there is no Catholic or Christian Orthodox fundamentalism because both churches acknowledge that they are embedded in a culture that can be shared by non-believers. When Pope John Paul II campaigned for the inclusion in the European constitution

5.   David Landes, *Wealth and Poverty of Nations: Why Some Are So Rich and Some are So Poor*, London: Abacus, 1999.

specific mention of the Christian roots of Europe, he saw Europeans not as being true Christians, but as sharing a common Christian culture, and as a consequence common values, even in their secularised forms (which accords with St Thomas Aquinas's concept of natural moral law).Values are beyond norms, while for any fundamentalist they are simply God's law. For Catholics religion is effectively embedded in a culture that may persist even when people cease to believe. (This is part of the evolution of Western Christian democracy, which no longer appeals solely to believers but to those who share the same values, irrespective of their faith or lack of it.) For fundamentalist Protestants it is faith that creates the divide between 'us' and 'them'.There is no concept of a shared civilisation or culture.

Fundamentalism is a factor in the disjunction between culture and norms. By placing any form of behaviour within a set of specific and explicit norms, it ignores or destroys all that is transmitted, implicit and subject to various interpretations. This works in any monotheistic religion. As we have seen in the case of halal fast food, religious norms are not so much culture-compatible as culture-blind, because they bypass the very concept of culture, in the same way as the US army dreams of an 'any-religion-compatible' combat ration. Mecca-Cola is neither a cultural answer to Coca-Cola nor the expression of an ethnic culture; it is merely a 'halal' Coca-Cola (at least according to the marketing blurb, but its success shows that it works). It is interesting to note how the negative response of many Europeans towards the Islamic presence is often linked not with a traditional Muslim way of life (ethnic restaurants or the traditional veiling of older migrant women) but with a modern assertion of Islamic symbols (the headscarf being worn by French-born schoolgirls, for instance). In Evry, near Paris, the socialist mayor supported the building of a huge mosque in the town centre, but opposed the transformation of a franchised supermarket (Franprix) into an all-halal store (which sold the same products as the Franprix chain store, except wine, pork and non-halal meat). It is the fading of borders between cultures that creates anxiety.

The culture-blind approach of neofundamentalists explains why, in Christianity as well in Islam, only fundamentalists are winning more converts in an era of globalisation and uprootedness. US Protestant evangelists are known for their aggressive policy on conversions. They learn the local language, wear local dress, and

may eat local food, but do not adapt to local cultures (for example, reading poetry or novels, or mastering traditional dancing).
Propaganda here is also a tool for uprooting and hence works
more effectively when people feel uprooted. Millions of Latinos
in the United States are turning from Catholicism to Protestantism.[6] This should be compared with the spread of Salafism among
second-generation European Muslims. The main battlegrounds for
conversion are Sub-Saharan Africa and Central Asia (specifically
Kyrgyzstan – when people turn to Christianity there it is never
to Orthodoxy). It also implicates the various sects (such as the Jehovah's Witnesses), all of which are also both the products and the
tools of deculturation. Hence the frequent accusations that Protestant missionaries are the vanguard of US influence (a charge that
President Bush's decision to make religious organisations eligible
for Federal development funds did nothing to dispel).

Fundamentalism is a means of re-universalising religions (whether it be Islam or Christianity) that has ended up being closely
identified with a given culture. Any expanding religion has three
ways to deal with cultural identity: 'going native' (the Jesuits in
seventeenth-century China);[7] considering one's own culture to be
the best vector (French or Spanish missionaries, but also many Arab
missionaries in Black Africa); or disentangling faith and cultural
identity by ignoring culture and turning religion into a universal
code of norms.

The paradox is that the more religions are decoupled from cultures, the more we tend to identify religion and culture. Islamic
fundamentalists and many conservative Muslims lobby for Islam to
be recognised as a culture in the West, using the common idiom of
multiculturalism. This too is a paradox, however, because religion
is the expression of a universal truth, while a culture is relative

6.   'Apostasy, the abandonment of one's religious faith, is a trend among Latinos.
     The percentage of Latino Catholics drops from 74 percent among the first
     generation to 72 and 62 percent among the second and third generations, ac-
     cording to the Hispanic Churches in American Public Life (HCAPL) study.
     Simultaneously, the percentage of Latino Protestants and other Christians
     increases from 15 percent in the first generation to 20 and 29 percent among
     the second and third generations.' Bruce Murray, 'Latino religion in the
     United States: demographic shifts and trends', <http://www.facsnet.org/is-
     sues/faith/espinosa.php>.
7.   Olivier Roy, *Leibniz et la Chine*, Paris: Vrin, 1972.

to other cultures by definition. The universal (religion) asks to be recognised as a particularity (defence of an identity). Religion becomes a sort of neo-ethnicity – many people, whatever their level of religious practice, citizenship or political activity, claim to react as Muslims against the US-led campaign in Iraq, but would not call themselves believers. At the same time Western leaders label 'Muslim' all the inhabitants of Muslim countries as if 'Islam' was their principal identity trait.

A common view about conflicts in the Middle East (Palestine and Iraq) is that they will widen the gap between 'Muslims' and the West (almost nobody says between Muslims and Christians). The Bush administration and Tony Blair took pains to show that their campaign in Iraq was not directed against the Muslims. President Chirac opposed the invasion partly because he considered that it would indeed alienate the Muslim world from the West, while Prime Minister Mahathir of Malaysia, in his farewell speech to the Islamic Conference Organisation at Kuala Lumpur (October 2003), unleashed his wrath not only upon the West and the Jews, but also upon Muslims who failed to address the challenge of the backwardness of the Muslim world. We see here that the word 'Muslim' has a deep political meaning. It refers not to a religion but to some sort of neo-ethnic group that is defined in its opposition to the 'West'. The Third World and Muslims are almost synonymous.[8] But why does such a comparison work apparently only for Islam? First, the main battlefields where the West (including Russia) is involved are in Muslim countries, even if none of them has anything to do with religion (Israel/Palestine, Kashmir, Chechnya and Iraq). Second, the Middle East is to the south of Europe, and the tensions between South and North inevitably take on the form of a debate between Islam and the West. Third, the spaces of social exclusion in Western Europe are populated by a growing Muslim population. All this is congruent with the fact that Islam, after the disappearance of the extreme Left, is one of the few discourses of political contestation available on the market. The other discourse of contestation in the West is the antiglobalisation movement. It

8.   For an in-depth analysis of Islamism and fundamentalism as a political protest, see François Burgat, *Face to Face with Political Islam*, London: I.B. Tauris, 2003. Let us remember that in the early USSR 'Muslims' was also used as an ethnic term, as shown by the brief episode of the 'Muslim Communist Party' in 1918.

is thus not by chance that some Islamic militants, such as Tariq Ramadan in Europe, are trying to find common ground with the antiglobalisation movement, which is also eager to reach beyond the 'white' middle classes to second-generation migrants. In Paris, on 13 November 2003, the Economic Social Forum, a coalition of antiglobalisation movements, invited Tariq Ramadan to speak, even after he had come under heavy attack for denouncing the 'communitarianist' approach (see page 20) of some French Jewish intellectuals.

Authenticity is, incidentally, a motto of authoritarian Third World rgimes (not necessarily Muslim), which also use it to oppose Western encroachments and to call for democratisation and human rights: Prime Minister Lee Kuan Yew of Singapore or President Mugabe of Zimbabwe often referred to 'authenticity' and to the need to find one's own way. The opposition 'Islam versus the West' appears less relevant if one refers to the other Third World 'cultural areas', which tend to agree with the Muslim countries in their critiques of Western cultural and political encroachments. By identifying democracy with Western culture and reproducing the clash-of-civilisations paradigm, many non-Western regimes of course want to delegitimise democracy as a universal concept. They love Huntington's statement that 'claims that Western values are universally relevant are false, immoral and dangerous'.[9] By contrast, many US 'universalists' firmly believe that democracy is a universal value, as Paul Wolfowitz stated in a speech in Singapore:

To win the war against terrorism and help shape a more peaceful world, we must speak to the hundreds of millions of moderate and tolerant people in the Muslim world, regardless of where they live, who aspire to enjoy the blessings of freedom and democracy and free enterprise. These values are sometimes described as 'Western values,' but, in fact, we see them in Asia and elsewhere because they are universal values borne of a common human aspiration.[10]

9. 'The West, Civilizations, and Civilization', Chapter 12 in Samuel Huntington, *The Clash of Civilizations and the Remaking of World Order*, New York: Simon and Schuster, 1996.
10. International Institute for Strategic Studies (IISS), 'The Gathering Storm: The Threat of Global Terror and Asia/Pacific Security', Remarks as Prepared for Delivery by U.S. Deputy Secretary of Defense Paul Wolfowitz, Asia Security Conference: The Shangri-La Dialogue, Singapore, 1 June 2002. See <http://usinfo.state.gov/topical/pol/terror/02060619.htm>.

If we extend the scope of the debate we see that it is not between Islam and the West, but between the West and many non-Western leaders. The rejection of US-style democracy, either for selfish reasons or because many people do not trust the United States, is expressed by using any available term from the toolbox of symbolic meanings. Huntington provides such a toolbox, hence his immense popularity as the man 'you love to hate' if you are a Third Worldist multiculturalist or an Islamic fundamentalist. The assimilation of Islam with a culture is a means of expressing a worldly collective political protest, and logically has nothing to do with religion (that is, with personal salvation).

Religion is used as a marker, often quite a hollow one, to recast identities in a time of deculturation and social protest. Old tools are given new tasks. Nevertheless, the fact that even conservative and fundamentalist Muslims advocate promoting a Muslim identity on the basis of multiculturalism shows how the agenda is fixed by the Western debate. The dominant discourses promoting either universalism or multiculturalism are Western inventions, as indicated by the two mirror-image quotations of Huntington and Wolfowitz.

Finally, in international relations and in domestic politics the politicisation of Islam goes hand in hand with a reluctant secularisation. Precisely because neofundamentalists are unable to throw off the concept of culture (even when they burn books and destroy Buddhas, or would like to ban novels, music and dancing), they contribute to the isolation of religion from culture, and thus the promotion of secularisation. When one refuses to give any but a negative religious meaning to a field one cannot suppress, one explicitly acknowledges that there are two separate spheres. Neofundamentalists expel culture from the scope of human activities; they ignore existing societies and political systems. Their concern for purity pushes them to ignore real life. By fighting to purify religion, fundamentalists tend to objectify religion, to define it as a closed and explicit set of norms and values, separated from a surrounding culture systematically seen as corrupting. Secularisation does not mean the end of religion, but the separation of religion from the other spheres of social life. Thus a religious revival can be perfectly compatible with growing secularisation. The Islamic revolution in Iran has been, in my opinion, one of the key factors in secularisation: who in Iran, apart a cabal of conservatives (or fanatical secularists), can speak of the growing influence of religion in society? The same is true in the United States, one of the last religious nations in the Western world. Despite a legislative backlash, the growing affirmation of people's religiosity did not really affect secularisation. The United States is still far more liberal than was the case in the 1950s (who today advocates banning homosexuality?). The more God returns, the more Satan is a frequent visitor too.

When cultural content is disappearing, differences are expressed in terms of codes and/or values. Fundamentalists of both the Muslim and the Protestant ilk speak in terms of orders from God. More liberal (or simply conservative) branches prefer to speak in terms of values (which is relevant for the Catholic Church, moderate Protestants and many mainstream Muslim organisations). As I have said previously, mainstream Muslims in the West (but increasingly also in the Middle East) tend to recast religious norms in terms of values: chastity for women, defence of the family, and opposition to legalising homosexuality, pornography and sexual freedom. These values are almost identical in all religions, along the same spectrum from strictly conservative to liberal views. In the ongoing debates in the West on ethics and values (abortion, homosexuality, genetic engineering), alignments have little to do with belonging to a given religion. Muslims increasingly align with conservative Christians and Jews, to the extent that they adopt some positions that till recently had no equivalent in Islam (for example, defining abortion as a mortal sin, or adopting the category 'homosexual' instead of speaking of 'acts of depravity').

The issue is not Western versus Muslim values. When Pim Fortuyn entered the political fray in the Netherlands on an anti-Islamic platform, it was not to defend traditional European values, but to protect the homosexual rights that had been won in the 1970s in the face of conservative Christian traditionalists. Interestingly, the Dutch-speaking Moroccan Imam el-Moumni, who triggered Fortuyn's ire by saying in a radio broadcast that homosexuality is a disease and has to do with bestiality, was not in line with traditional *ulama*, for whom homosexuality is a sin and thus punishable by death. By calling it a disease he took the same line as the Catholic Church in modern times: exonerating the homosexual of sin as long as he does not practise, but refusing to give him any legal rights as a homosexual; in the eyes of the church this is a modern and benevolent position.[11] Incidentally, Fortuyn was assassinated not by a Muslim, but by an animal rights activist who was also, in his own way, defending the freedom movement of the post-1980s.

In many instances conservative Muslims and the Christian Right are on the same side: calling for an end to compulsory coeducation, fighting the teaching of Darwinism, rejecting anything that could even come close to being a 'homosexual marriage'.[12] In France the Catholic Church and the Chief Rabbinate opposed a law forbidding the Islamic headscarf in schools, because they agreed that religion ought to be present in the public sphere. A poll taken among Arabs and Westerners showed that the opposition between them over values is not about democracy (a value in itself for 86 per cent of Westerners and 87 per cent of Arabs), but is about divorce (60 per cent of Westerners and only 35 per cent of Arabs approve), abortion (48 and 25 per cent) and homosexuality (53 and 12 per cent). This is not a conflict between 'Western' and 'Muslim' values (according to the *sharia*, divorce is easy for a male Muslim), but between religious conservatives and non-religious people. Muslims tend to align with Christian conservatives.[13]

Of course there may be some requests by fundamentalist Muslims that seem (and are) unacceptable, all of them revolving around women's rights. But once again conservative Catholics, Protestants and Jews are discomfited by sharing the anti-Islamic feminist viewpoint because they can be (and have been) targeted too: why should women be excluded from the priesthood? In any case, as we have seen, it is the West that defines the space of the debate. Often debates on Islam are no more than debates on the meaning

11. The Catholic Church at present accepts the concept of sexual orientation, so could accept the concept of a 'chaste homosexual', while for traditional canon law, as well as *sharia*, it is the performance of a sexual act that makes somebody a 'deviant' and hence a sinner because one is responsible for one's actions. For traditional believers one can be homosexual only by choice, not by nature.
12. See Harun Yahya, 'The Bloody Alliance: Darwinism and Communism' in *Islam Denounces Terrorism*, Bristol: Amal Press, 2002. See, by the same author, <http://www.darwinism-watch.com>.
13. World Values Survey, pooled sample 1995–2001; see *Freedom in the World: The Annual Survey of Political Rights and Civil Liberties*, New York: Freedom House, 1981–98. See also Ronald Inglehart and Pippa Norris, 'The True Clash of Civilizations', *Foreign Policy*, March–April 2003.

of the West. A good example is the 'headscarf affair' in France, arising from some hundred individual cases of girls wanting to wear headscarves, or veils, at school. It became a national debate, with the creation of a commission, a vote in parliament, weekly debates on television, and headlines and hundreds of passionate opinion pieces in the press. By contrast, the headscarf is not an issue in Britain, where even policewomen are allowed to wear it. This shows that the issue is not about the West and Islam; instead it is a form of French soul-searching debate about the meaning of *laïcité* (laicism) in the creation of national identity, and about the relationship between state, church and civil society. The French model of the nation-state is in crisis, due to European integration, globalisation, the crisis of the welfare state, and so on, but the debate on Islam is a way to externalise and intellectualise the issue.

The debate occurs within a single 'cultural' framework: that of the West. Many neofundamentalists are aware of this and try to prevent any debate and interaction, putting the *sharia* forward as the real dividing line, with the consequence that they can live not in the West but in a ghetto. The quest for a strict application of the *sharia* aims to re-create an absolute otherness that has no possible concrete application. Even if strict neofundamentalists reject integration into Western societies, the bulk of the conservative Muslims are eager to integrate but want to push for conservative moral values that they can share with other citizens, whatever their faith.

MILITARY STRATEGY ON ABSTRACT TERRITORIES

International Islamic terrorism is a pathological consequence of the globalisation of the Muslim world rather than a spillover of the Middle Eastern conflicts. Nevertheless, the real wars are in the Middle East.

Globalisation means that Islam has less and less to do with a given territory. The historical Muslim space of the Middle East is now reshaped by nationalisms, and too often authoritarian states appear to offer a better defence than democracy against Western encroachments. In this context radical Islamic movements have little choice but to join the national agenda. Democracy is also too often seen as an alien import, and the US military campaign in Iraq will not help to allay that view. The discrepancy between a holistic view of what a Muslim nation should be (embodied in all the failed models of Baathism and Islamism) and a world of migrations, Muslim settlement in non-Muslim countries and the decoupling of religion from given cultures and lands – all this has culminated in a general deterritorialisation of Islam.

But the fight against terrorism is still understood in terms of territory and states, as embodied in the expression 'war on terror'. An army fights to occupy a territory or to destroy a state, but international terrorist groups need no territory. The campaign in Afghanistan made sense to the extent that Bin Laden had a territorial sanctuary that had to be destroyed. Once he became deterritorialised too, what was the use of occupying the territory? Iraq has never been an asylum or training ground for Islamic radical groups (the Ansar al-Islam pocket in Kurdistan could have been dealt with without a ground invasion). The only coherent rationale is the building of democracy. By turning Muslim countries into democratic ones, through a mixture of military action, destabilising 'rogue states' and the hoped-for domino effect, we might expect to undermine support for terrorism and build peace in the Middle East. But we may also attain the reverse: an alliance or even a merger between nationalist and fundamentalist radical movements (the merger of nationalism and Islamism has already happened), which is apparently the dominant trend.

Most Al Qaeda operatives who have been arrested were caught through classical police and intelligence means, not as a consequence of a military campaign (which missed Bin Laden, Mullah Omar and Saddam Hussein, who was finally also caught through intelligence work). A military campaign can only hope at best to reshape states and societies. This presupposes some sort of long-term process of social engineering, which is exactly what Washington's neoconservatives had in mind when invading Iraq. However, such a project is based on an ideological view of human beings, societies and cultures, which ignores sociology, history and nationalism.

After 9/11, quite logically, Washington tried to target states because a state can be punished, toppled and replaced through military action. The problem is that deterritorialisation accompanies a decrease in state influence. International terrorism has triggered a debate on the role of states. 'Failed states' and 'rogue states' have been targeted as potential sources of terrorism. The problem is that the state factor is negligible among contemporary terrorist movements. Efforts to implicate Iraq in 9/11 have even been contradicted by Bush himself. The support of Syria and, to a lesser extent, Iran for Hezbollah is undeniable, but Hezbollah is not an international terrorist organisation. In Washington since 9/11 a macabre game has been played out, entitled 'Which is the real rogue state?' The official view was, of course, that Saddam's Iraq was the rogue state by definition, involved in every kind of threat (terrorism, weapons of mass destruction). Some dissident views (for example, Michael Ledeen) point to Iran.[14] Others point to Saudi Arabia,[15] while a small minority still think that Syria could be an easier target. The issue of the proliferation of weapons of mass destruction goes far beyond that of rogue states. It involves many non-state actors and some 'friendly' states (Pakistan and Russia), or states which are beyond the range of a military attack (China). The campaign against Iraq reminds me of the story of a Baghdad caliph's tailor. The caliph wanted to punish a tailor who had overcharged him. He ordered a henchman to hang the tailor at the gate of his house. The henchman came back saying that the tailor was too tall for the gate, to which the Caliph answered: 'Find a smaller tailor and hang him.' It is the defence apparatus that tailors the enemy. But failed states and poverty are not the real issue as far as terrorism is concerned.

The passage of Islam to the West and the globalisation of Islam make most of the representations that founded policies towards the Middle East, Islam and terrorism irrelevant. The culturalist approach misses the point of the westernisation of Islam, and specifically that fundamentalism is also a modern phenomenon. The strategy of the war against terror misses the deterritorialisation element. The concept of a world Muslim *ummah* as a geostrategic actor is nonsense. If the Arab neighbours of Israel have never been able genuinely to threaten its existence, where is the threat embodied by the elusive world *ummah*? Terrorism is, of course, a real security threat,

14. See, among others, Michael Ledeen, 'Time to Focus on Iran – The Mother of Modern Terrorism', address to the Policy Forum of the Jewish Institute for National Security Affairs (JINSA), Washington, DC, 30 April 2003.
15. Stephen Schwartz, *The Two Faces of Islam: The House of Sa'ud from Tradition to Terror*, New York: Doubleday, 2002. See also Laurent Murawiec who, as a Rand analyst, presented a controversial lecture to the Pentagon's Defense Policy Board on 10 July 2002, entitled 'Taking Saudi out of Arabia'. See, for example, Jack Shafer, 'The PowerPoint that Rocked the Pentagon: The LaRouchie Defector Who's Advising the Defense Establishment on Saudi Arabia', *Slate*, 7 August 2002, <http://slate.msn.com/id/2069119/>.

but it can be dealt with more effectively by using intelligence and police tools than by waging military campaigns. The terrorists do not have a long-term strategy; they are unable to change regimes in the West (the change in government in Spain following the April 2004 terrorist attack there was not a regime change), and even in the East except in the short term. Their avowed strategy is to oblige the United States to invade Muslim countries in the hope that it will become overstretched and bogged down there. Terrorists know that they cannot stir up the religious feelings of the Muslim masses in the absence of a direct occupation. Terrorism is a strategic factor only to the extent that it changes the perceptions and policies of its targets, or, more accurately, offers an opportunity to find a reason to put existing ideologies and virtual strategies into practice. The will to attack Iraq was at the core of the neoconservatives' strategy long before 9/11.

There is no geostrategy of Islam because Islam is not a territorial factor. Instead of a land of Islam or of an Islamic community, there is simply a religion that disembodies itself painfully from the ghosts of the past; there are simply Muslims who are negotiating new identities by conflicting means, usually peacefully, sometimes violently. The globalisation of Islam should be dealt with while remembering that terrorism is a marginal symptom that tells a lot, as does any symptom, and obliges everybody (above all Muslims) to go beyond wishful thinking, misgivings and passivity. I may have spent too much time dealing with terrorism in this regard, but radical violence must be placed within the larger framework of the relationship between all modern religions with secularisation, individualisation, culture and politics.

INDEX

341

The CERI Series in Comparative Politics and International Studies

Series editor CHRISTOPHE JAFFRELOT

This series consists of translations of noteworthy publications in the social sciences emanating from the foremost French research centre in international studies, the Paris-based Centre d'Etudes et de Recherches Internationales (CERI), part of Sciences Po and associated with the CNRS (Centre National de la Recherche Scientifique).

The focus of the series is the transformation of politics and society by transnational and domestic factors – globalisation, migration, and the post-bipolar balance of power on the one hand, and ethnicity and religion on the other. States are more permeable to external influence than ever before and this phenomenon is accelerating processes of social and political change the world over. In seeking to understand and interpret these transformations, this series give priority to social trends from below as much as the interventions of state and non-state actors.

Founded in 1952, CERI has forty full-time fellows drawn from different disciplines conducting research on comparative political analysis, international relations, regionalism, transnational flows, political sociology, political economy and on individual states.